Miami & the Keys

The
Everglades
p129

Miami
p53

Florida Keys &
Key West
p159

Regis St Louis, Anthony Ham, Adam Karlin

PLAN YOUR TRIP

ON THE ROAD

LUCKY-PHOTOGRAPHER/SHUTTERSTOCK ©

CAPE FLORIDA LIGHTHOUSE P77

INSPIRED BY MAPS/SHUTTERSTOCK ©

10,000 ISLANDS P146

BYVALET/SHUTTERSTOCK ©

Contents

COVID-19

We have re-checked every business in this book before publication to ensure that it is still open after 2020's COVID-19 outbreak. However, the economic and social impacts of COVID-19 will continue to be felt long after the outbreak has been contained, and many businesses, services and events referenced in this guide may experience ongoing restrictions. Some businesses may be temporarily closed, have changed their opening hours and services, or require bookings; some unfortunately could have closed permanently. We suggest you check with venues before visiting for the latest information.

MANGO'S TROPICAL CAFE,
OCEAN DRIVE P114

WELCOME TO

Miami &
the Keys

South Florida has three world-class attractions – Miami, the Everglades and the Keys. I never tire of wandering the streets of Miami Beach, taking in art-deco masterpieces followed by late-afternoon strolls along the sands, when the golden light is mesmerizing. The Everglades provides that heady dose of nature, of quiet paddles over mirror-like lakes and nighttime walks peering at gators gliding gracefully through the water. The Keys has a little of everything – peaceful mangroves for kayaking and wildlife watching, kaleidoscopic coral reefs and one wild conch capital (aka Key West) where anything goes.

By Regis St Louis, Writer
🐦 @regisstlouis 📷 regisstlouis

For more about our writers, see p256

Right: Art-deco lifeguard station, South Beach, Miami (p58)

MARIAKRAY/SHUTTERSTOCK ©

Miami & the Keys

Everglades City
Stone crabs fresh from
the source (p143)

Everglades National Park
Alligator-spotting and
bird-watching (p138)

Hell's Bay
Kayak into the
Everglades' heart (p133)

Bahia Honda State Park
Kayaking, camping and
gorgeous beaches (p176)

Overseas Highway
Tropical road trip
of a lifetime (p30)

Key West
Hemingway drank here;
shouldn't you? (p179)

North Beach
Sun-worship in pretty parks
and secluded coves (p63)

Wynwood
Dazzling street art and
vibrant nightlife (p71)

Miami Beach
Pick from an intense variety
of bars (p113)

South Beach
See titans of deco design
(p227)

Key Biscayne
Island adventures near
Downtown Miami (p76)

Calle Ocho
Explore Little Havana's
pulsing Latin heart (p73)

Coral Gables
Marvel at mansions
and villas (p75)

Biltmore Hotel
Hunt ghosts in the opulent
Biltmore (p76)

Boca Raton
Deerfield Beach

Andytown

Fort Lauderdale

Hollywood

North Miami Beach

Hialeah

Miami Beach

Miami   Key
Biscayne

Biscayne
National
Park

*Florida Keys
National Marine
Sanctuary*

Florida
City

*Biscayne
Bay*

Elliott
Key

*Key Largo
National
Marine
Sanctuary*

Key Largo

John Pennekamp
Coral Reef State Park

lantation
ey

Tavernier

Plantation

Islamorada

Upper Keys

*ATLANTIC
OCEAN*

ELEVATION
500ft
0

Dry Tortugas National Park & Key West National Wildlife Refuge

Hospital   Middle   Dry Tortugas
Key   Key   National Park

Loggerhead
Key   East Key

Bush Key

Garden Key   Long
Key

*Florida Keys
National Marine
Sanctuary*

Marquesas
Keys

*Key West National
Wildlife Refuge*

Note: Same scale as main map

Miami & the Keys' Top Experiences

Above: Zaha Hadid's One Thousand Museum

FELIX MIZIOZNIKOV/SHUTTERSTOCK © / ARCHITECT: ZAHA HADID

1 ARCHITECTURAL TREASURES

Art deco is Miami Beach's architectural eye candy, with a kaleidoscope of colors, tropical references and whimsical motifs dotting the streets of South Beach. Miami also has some fantastical century-old Mediterranean-inspired designs and jaw-dropping contemporary architecture, including works by Frank Gehry and Zaha Hadid. Key West boasts a Bahamian aesthetic, with an old town full of brightly painted, 19th-century conch houses (wooden cottages with shutters, ornate latticework, gabled roofs and wraparound verandas).

Art Deco Museum

Before wandering the Art Deco Historic District in South Beach, learn about the style, its unique design elements and very near destruction (save for the efforts of two visionary individuals who fought hard to preserve the neighborhood in the 1970s). p58

Right: Art Deco Historic District (p58)

Vizcaya Museum & Gardens

This fairy-tale estate is the most opulent, over-the-top confection in Greater Miami, complete with a lavish Renaissance Hall adorned with old-world oil paintings, and manicured greenery inspired by 18th-century Italian gardens. p74

Above: Vizcaya Museum

Hemingway House

While living in Key West, the famed American writer lived and wrote in this Spanish Colonial mansion, an 1851 beauty set with original furnishings owned by the author. Guided tours provide architectural insight, though the six-toed cats (descendants of Hemingway's own unusual felines) have the run of the place. p183

Above: Hemingway House

GABRIELE MALTINTI/SHUTTERSTOCK ©

Above: Crandon Park (p77), Key Biscayne

2 ISLAND GETAWAYS

Eye-catching barrier islands and verdant mangrove-fringed keys dot the South Florida seascape. Many are accessible by causeways and bridges, making it easy to escape for a tropical-infused getaway. Other spots can be reached only by boat, adding to the sense of resplendent isolation. Wherever you roam, you won't be far from sparkling beaches, with palms rustling in the breeze, and gorgeous views over lapping seas.

Key Biscayne

An easy hop from Downtown Miami (you can even cycle there), Key Biscayne has pretty beaches, a hands-on nature center, leafy trails, an idyllic waterfront restaurant and a photogenic lighthouse anchoring its southern tip. p76

Indian Key Historic State Park

Off Islamorada, you can kayak to an abandoned island containing the overgrown ruins of a 19th-century settlement. It's a fun DIY outing (30 minutes' paddling on calm days). Afterwards you can feed the massive tarpons at Robbie's Marina. p170

Above top: Indian Key Historic State Park

Dry Tortugas National Park

Far off Key West and surrounded by azure seas, the Dry Tortugas is a memorable outing for those making the 70-mile journey out (by ferry or seaplane). You can snorkel coral reefs, tour a massive 19th-century fort and even camp on the island. p195

Above: Fort Jefferson, Dry Tortugas National Park

3 TROPICAL MOSAIC

From camo-wearing fishermen in the Everglades to retirees sitting side by side with arrivals from every Spanish-speaking nation in the world, South Florida boasts incredible diversity. Exploring the region's rich cultural history is one of the unsung rewards of travel here: whether catching Cuban bands on Miami's Calle Ocho, attending a colorful Bahamian festival in the Keys or learning about Seminole and Miccosukee communities in the Everglades.

Miccosukee Indian Village

In the Everglades, learn about the folkways of Florida's indigenous inhabitants on guided visits of traditional homes, boat rides, and music and dance performances. p140

Below: Totem, Miccosukee Indian Village

ALEXANDER TAMARGO/GETTY IMAGES FOR A24 ©

Cubaocho

For insight into Cuban culture, visit this long-standing icon in Little Havana. Best known for its concerts, Cubaocho also has changing art exhibitions, film screenings and other events. p121

Above: Cubaocho bar

Little Haiti Cultural Complex

Browse original artwork by young Haitian Americans, pick up a beaded purse from Port-au-Prince, or catch a monthly music and food party at this colorfully painted space in Miami. p73

Right: Mural, Little Haiti Cultural Complex

JEFFREY GREENBERG/UNIVERSAL IMAGES GROUP VIA GETTY IMAGES ©

4 BEACH DAYS

Above: Bahia Honda State Park

There's no mystery to what makes South Florida so appealing. Beaches as fine and sweet as powdered sugar, warm waters, rustling mangroves: all conspire to make our workaday selves dream of the Florida sunshine. Some desire a beachside getaway of swimming, seafood and sunsets. Others seek the seaside revelry of Miami's South Beach, or music and mischief in Key West. No matter your vision of tropical paradise, South Florida has you covered.

Bahia Honda State Park

The finest beach in the Keys invites long leisurely walks and frolicking in the aquamarine seas. Book early and you can camp or stay in a cabin here – pure magic after the day-trippers depart. p176

South Beach

Reason enough to make the trip to Miami, South Beach offers prime people-watching and memorable sunrise strolls past those iconic colorfully painted lifeguard stations. p58

Crandon Park

A gorgeous palm-fringed shoreline that mixes nature and fun on Key Biscayne, just a short drive from Downtown Miami. p77

5 AQUATIC ADVENTURES

Some of South Florida's most breathtaking scenery is underwater. The impressive coral reefs south of Miami form the backdrop to fabulous snorkeling and diving, with countless wreck dives within easy access of the mainland. On the surface, there are wonderful destinations for kayakers and boaters — whether exploring islands of the Keys or taking dolphin-spotting trips off the Gulf. There are also plenty of seaside adventures just a short hop from Miami.

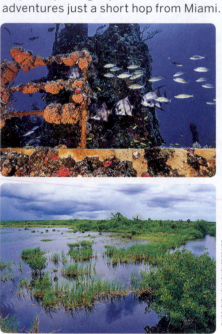

John Pennekamp Coral Reef State Park

This mostly underwater park has outstanding snorkeling and diving amid coral reefs and wrecks. You can also arrange glass-bottom boat tours, or go kayaking among a maze of mangroves. p166

Above top: Spadefish, John Pennekamp Coral Reef State Park

10,000 Islands

The Everglades meet the ocean in this fabulous aquatic wilderness. Take boat tours to spy marine life, or head off on your own to canoe the isolated islands. p146

Above bottom: 10,000 Islands

Big Pine Kayak Adventures

Paddle off into the back-country in search of Key deer, osprey and graceful stingrays. Guided tours are run by some of Florida's most knowledgeable kayakers. p177

Above right: Kayaking in the Everglades

6 THE ART SCENE

HELEN89/SHUTTERSTOCK ©

Studios of Key West

The recently revamped three-story space has over a dozen studios where talented locals showcase their works. You can catch changing exhibitions or sign up for one of many art and design workshops on offer. p183

Left: Studios of Key West

ARTIST: TRISTAN EATON, WYNWOOD WALLS, IMAGE: TORRESIGNER/GETTY IMAGES ©

Margulies Collection at the Warehouse

At this Wynwood icon, you'll find cutting-edge works by some of the top living artists. Afterwards, take in the boldly painted murals of the ever-changing Wynwood Walls nearby. p71

Rubell Museum

Blazing new trails in Allapattah, this sprawling museum features renowned works spread among some 40 different galleries. Kara Walker, Ai Weiwei, Jeff Koons and Cindy Sherman are among the regularly featured luminaries. p78

Miami has few rivals when it comes to the contemporary art scene, hosting monthly art events around town, as well as the renowned Art Basel Miami Beach (pictured above) each December. The former industrial neighborhood of Wynwood and the neighboring Design District are a must for art mavens. Elsewhere, the arts are alive and well: Key West has long been an artists' enclave, and the Keys also have a long-running arts and crafts tradition.

7 SEAFOOD FEASTS

All across South Florida, you'll have the opportunity to dine on some of the best ingredients plucked straight from the ocean. For seafood lovers, the range of offerings is truly astounding. You can slurp fresh-shucked oysters at a Miami raw bar, chow down on conch fritters in Key West and gorge on fried grouper sandwiches from one end of the Keys to the other. The setting adds to the allure, with plenty of spots right over the water.

Boater's Grill

Delicious old-fashioned seafood that's served in an unbeatable setting: an open-sided wood deck overlooking a marina out on easygoing Key Biscayne. p112

Below: Boater's Grill

INSPIRED BY MAPS/SHUTTERSTOCK ©

JEFFREY GREENBERG/UNIVERSAL IMAGES GROUP VIA GETTY IMAGES ©

Little Pearl

In Key West, mouth-watering seafood isn't hard to find, but candlelit Little Pearl is the new local favorite for its exquisitely prepared dishes with inventive global accents. p190

Above: Fresh oysters

Camellia Street Grill

Out in Everglades City, you can grab a rustic table by the waterside and nibble on blackened mahimahi, shrimp po'boys or even gator tacos. But in season (mid-October to mid-May), it's the delectable stone crabs that warrant a visit. p144

Right: Camellia Street Grill

8 LIVE MUSIC

Miami is home to a mesmerizing mix of brassy Latin jazz,

Above: Adrienne Arsht Center for the Performing Arts

Cuban *trova* and hands-in-the-air indie rock, its infectious beats spilling out of drinking dens and music halls across town. Key West is also a sonic playground, with bands performing all along Duval St. Across the region, you'll find wide-ranging offerings from top-notch orchestras playing in state-of-the-art concert halls to barefoot cover bands jamming at open-air bars in the Keys.

Adrienne Arsht Center for the Performing Arts

Downtown Miami is home to this celebrated concert hall with its high-tech acoustics and packed music calendar. p120

Cafe La Trova

One of the most reliably good times can be had over at this vintage bar and dance spot in Little Havana, with classic Cuban dance music, a fun crowd, and great food and cocktails. p121

Green Parrot

Excellent bands from Miami, New Orleans and beyond rock the scene at Key West's oldest, funkiest bar. p190

Need to Know

For more information, see Survival Guide (p235)

Currency
US dollar ($)

Languages
English, Spanish, Haitian Kreyol in Miami

Visas
Required for most foreign visitors unless eligible for the Visa Waiver Program.

Money
Twenty-four-hour ATMs widely available across Miami, the Keys and the towns that border the Everglades. Credit cards accepted at most businesses.

Cell Phones
Local SIM cards can be used in European or Australian phones. Europe and Asia's GSM 900/1800 standard is incompatible with the USA's cell-phone systems.

Time
Eastern Time (GMT/UTC minus five hours)

When to Go

Miami Beach
GO Jan–Apr

Miami
GO Oct–Dec

The Everglades
GO Jan–Apr

The Keys
GO Jan–Apr

Key West
GO Oct–Dec

Tropical, wet & dry seasons
Tropical climate, rain year-round
Warm to hot summers, mild winters
Mild to hot summers, mild winters

High Season
(Jan–Mar)

➡ South Florida winters are dry, sunny and practically perfect.

➡ You'll need to book well in advance to reserve rooms at this time.

➡ A preponderance of festivals equals lots of fun – and crowds.

Shoulder
(Apr–May & Oct–Nov)

➡ The early end of spring resembles late winter; by May the weather gets humid.

➡ October is still hurricane season, but things dry off later in the month.

➡ Festival season gears up in late fall.

Low Season
(Jun–Sep)

➡ It's hot as hell, but sea breezes are cooling.

➡ Mosquitoes are at their worst, especially in the Everglades.

➡ Hurricanes? Fortunately there are good early-warning systems in place.

Useful Websites

Everglades National Park
(www.nps.gov/ever) Handy maps and loads of info on the park.

Visit Florida (www.visitflorida.com) Official state tourism website.

Florida State Parks (www.floridastateparks.org) Primary resource for state parks.

Miami Herald (www.herald.com) News of Miami and beyond.

Florida Keys & Key West (www.fla-keys.com) Keys visitor info.

Lonely Planet (www.lonelyplanet.com/usa/florida/south-florida-the-keys) Destinations, hotel bookings, traveler forums and more.

Important Numbers

You need to dial the area code for all calls, including domestic. The only exception is the emergency number (which is also a free call).

Miami & the Keys/Everglades area codes	305, 786/239
Emergency (police/fire/ambulance)	911
Miami Beach Patrol	305-673-7714
Florida Emergency Hotline (hurricanes)	800-342-3557
Everglades National Park	305-242-7700

Exchange Rates

Australia	A$1	$0.61
Canada	C$1	$0.71
Europe	€1	$1.09
Japan	¥100	$0.93
New Zealand	NZ$1	$0.60
UK	£1	$1.24

For current exchange rates, see www.xe.com.

Daily Costs

Budget: Less than $140

➡ Hostel dorms: $30–50

➡ Budget hotel room for two: $80–140

➡ Sandwich at a deli: $7–10

➡ Bicycle rentals: from around $15 per day

➡ Ranger-led tours in the Everglades: free

Midrange: $140–280

➡ Three-star lodging in a hotel room: $140–200

➡ Dinner at a midrange restaurant: around $30–45 per person

➡ Kayak hire for the day: from $45

Top end: More than $280

➡ Double room in a boutique hotel: from $300

➡ Dinner at a top restaurant: $40–100 per person

➡ Cocktails: $9–16

➡ Day trip to Dry Tortugas: from $180

Opening Hours

Banks 8:30am–4:30pm Monday to Thursday, to 5:30pm Friday

Bars 5pm–3am

Cafes 7am or 8am–7pm

Post offices 9am–5pm Monday to Friday

Restaurants 11:30am–2:30pm and 5pm–10pm

Shops 10am–6pm Monday to Saturday, noon–5pm Sunday

Arriving in Miami

Miami International Airport
Taxis charge a flat rate for the 40-minute drive to South Beach ($35). The Miami Beach Airport Express (bus 150) costs $2.25 and makes stops all along Miami Beach, from 41st St to the southern tip.

Key West International Airport
A taxi into Old Town costs $9 per person and takes about 15 minutes. City Transit buses run every 80 minutes or so from the airport to Old Town from 5:30am to 9pm (one way $2).

Getting Around

Car Most travelers in South Florida rent cars. Traffic is always an issue in Miami and its surrounding suburbs. Rental cars generally come equipped with SunPass transponders. These devices carry credit to get you through the region's many tolls. This charge is usually added to your rental fee.

Bus Miami and Miami Beach have reliable bus systems, but getting around can be time-consuming; see www.miamidade.gov/transportation-publicworks/routes.asp for route information.

Walking & Cycling If you're staying in South Beach you can walk most of the time, or use the Citi Bike (p246) bike-sharing program. However, many parts of Miami are not bike-friendly. Key West is very walkable and bike-friendly.

For much more on **getting around**, see p246

What's New

South Florida's art scene is blazing new trails, with new galleries emerging in Miami (including in Little Haiti and Little River) and new art walks in the Keys (particularly Islamorada). Meanwhile, the downtown renaissance in Miami continues with the arrival of new cultural spaces, hotels and nightspots.

Rubell Museum

A dazzling addition to Miami's gallery scene, this new contemporary museum (p78) has a staggering 100,000 sq ft campus comprising 40 galleries, a library and a Basque restaurant in a converted industrial space in Allapattah.

Studios of Key West

Long one of the best places in Key West for getting a handle on the local art scene, the iconic Studios of Key West (p183) has recently added a rooftop bar and expanded its lineup of cultural offerings.

Art Alley

Proof that South Beach isn't frozen in its art-deco past – new sculptures tucked down a lane continue to push architectural boundaries. The Betsy Orb (p62) features a changing projection/exhibition, while the nearby Poetry Rail pays homage to the great city of Miami.

Morada Art Walk

While heading down the Keys, it's worth trying to time your visit with Islamorada's monthly **art walk** (http://moradaway.org). On the third Thursday of the month, you can browse open studios, purchase art (and crafts) and sip local microbrews. The action happens near the Florida Keys Brewing Company (p172).

Bunking in the Glades

The Everglades National Park at long last is offering lodging inside the reserve. In the south end of the park, Flamingo Adventures rents houseboats, safari-style tents and sleek new cabins.

LOCAL KNOWLEDGE

WHAT'S HAPPENING IN SOUTH FLORIDA

Regis St Louis, Lonely Planet writer

Climate change remains the hot topic of the day in a state with one of America's most threatened coastlines. With sea levels expected to rise 10in to 20in by 2040, Floridians face a daunting future. Increasingly frequent flooding from everyday storms, more devastating hurricanes and a deeply eroded coastline are among the grave threats – not to mention damage to the state's fragile ecosystems (including die-offs in the vast reef system off the Keys and irreparable harm to the Everglades).

Some policy makers still believe it's not too late to prevent the most dire scenarios (such as one in eight Floridian homes being underwater by 2100). Preparing for the future, however, will require an estimated $76 billion to mitigate the effects of climate change in the form of sea walls and other infrastructure investments. The big challenge is getting everyone on board — no easy prospect in a state where 30% oppose government spending on climate change.

Culinary Exploration

Some of Miami's best new restaurants lie well off the beaten path. At 24-seat Boia De (p108) in the Buena Vista district, young renegade chefs craft some of the best Italian cooking in South Florida. The small plates allow you to sample a wide range of culinary pyrotechnics.

Cuban Sounds

One of the best new openings in Little Havana is Cafe La Trova (p121), a live-music venue that also serves up excellent light fare and imaginative cocktails. The vibe evokes pre-Castro Havana with a vintage Cuba interior and snappily attired wait staff.

Stock Island

The once overlooked island just across a narrow channel from Key West makes a great escape from the crowds. You'll find new spaces here: art studios, a waterfront hotel and seafood restaurant, as well as a few classic Keys eateries.

Tennessee Williams Museum

Fans of the great American playwright can explore his work and learn about his deep connection to Key West at a small new museum (p184) just off Duval St.

Palihouse Miami Beach

Overlooking the Indian Creek waterway, this new boutique hotel (p91) quickly garnered a following after its 2019 opening. Expect vintage-inspired design with an art-deco exterior and well-equipped rooms (some with kitchenettes), just a two-block walk to the beach.

Pigeon Key Connection

Restoration work continues on a long stretch of the Old Seven Mile Bridge that connects Marathon with the tiny history-laden island of Pigeon Key (p173). When complete, visitors will be able to walk or bike out to the site, enjoying fabulous views along the way.

LISTEN, WATCH AND FOLLOW

For inspiration and travel tips, visit www.lonelyplanet.com/usa/florida/south-florida-the-keys/articles.

New Times (www.miaminewtimes.com) Alternative weekly listing Miami's latest news, restaurant and bar openings, and upcoming events.

Art Circuits (www.artcircuits.com) The best insider info on Miami's art events; includes rundowns on top exhibitions around town.

Flamingo (www.flamingomag.com) Magazine that delves into Florida culture in all its variety.

Miami Bites (www.miabites.com) A community of food bloggers share the latest culinary hits (and misses).

Insta @FatGirlHedonist Exploring Miami's best dishes through decadent food photography.

FAST FACTS

Food trend Creative Latin fusion

Number of alligators in the Everglades 200,000

Language Nearly 60% of Miami residents speak Spanish at home

Pop 890,000

≈ 30 people

Returning to the Keys

Some of the Keys took a heavy hit from Hurricane Irma in 2017. It took some places, like the charming Deer Run on the Atlantic (p178), several years to rebuild and reopen. Now is a great time to visit and help support these communities on the mend.

Accommodations

Find more accommodations reviews throughout the On the Road chapters (from p51)

PRICE RANGES

Accommodations rates fluctuate daily based on demand, with prices soaring during the high season (January to March). Tax isn't always included in quoted prices; some places (particularly in South Beach) also tack an extra 'resort fee' onto rates, so always ask when booking.

The following price ranges refer to a standard double room in high season (unless otherwise stated). Miami and Key West prices could be upwards of $50 higher at each budget level.

$ less than $120

$$ $120–200

$$$ more than $200

Accommodations Types

Hotels You'll find simple but well-equipped accommodations as well as high-end oceanfront digs with amenities galore. There are plenty of boutique and specialty hotels in places like South Beach and Key West.

Motels There are still a number of these one-story, drive-up options around South Florida, particularly in the Keys. Some offer simple, budget-friendly accommodations with a side of Florida kitsch, others have been renovated with pools and beach access.

B&Bs & Inns Vary from small, comfy houses with shared bathrooms to romantic, antique-filled historic homes and opulent mansions with private baths.

Hostels Basic dorm-style lodging, but some have bars and courtyards – great spots to meet other travelers. In most hostels, group dorms are mixed, though there's usually a females-only dorm room as well; occasionally alcohol is banned.

Camping & Cabins There are some lovely spots to pitch a tent or bunk in a simple cabin in the Everglades and in the Keys, though you'll have to reserve many months in advance.

Best Places to Stay

Best on a Budget

The best bet for budget lodging is a hostel, with a wealth of options in Miami, particularly in South Beach. These generally cater to young partiers; some have on-site bars. Elsewhere, you'll find more limited but appealing options, including an excellent budget base in Florida City (ideal for the southern Everglades) and several hostels in Key West. You'll also find a handful of basic budget-friendly hotels in the region.

➡ SoBe Hostel (p88) South Beach, Miami

➡ New Yorker (p95) MiMo district, Miami

➡ Extended Stay (p95) Coral Gables, Miami

➡ Seashell Motel & Key West Hostel (p186) Key West

➡ Hoosville Hostel (p146) Florida City

Best for Families

Anywhere near the beach makes a good base for families. If you want to escape the rowdiest parts of Miami Beach, look at hotels south of 6th St and north of 16th St. Resort-style hotels are also plentiful (both in Miami and the Keys), and typically offer pools and other amenities (bikes, kayaks, games), plus on-site eating and snacking options.

➡ Silver Sands Beach Resort (p97) Key Biscayne

➡ 1 Hotel (p89) South Beach, Miami

➡ MB at Key Largo (p167) Key Largo

→ Seascape Motel & Marina (p175) Marathon

→ Tranquility Bay (p175) Marathon

→ Bay Harbor Lodge (p167) Key Largo

Best for Solo Travelers

Single rooms are a rarity in Miami and the Keys, and solo travelers are typically charged the same nightly rate as a couple. To save money, you can book a bunk in a hostel (some also have small private rooms that are good value for singles). Many hotels in South Beach have a strong social component – with on-site lounges and bars that are good places to meet other travelers.

→ Freehand Miami (p91) North Beach, Miami

→ Washington Park Hotel (p89) South Beach, Miami

→ Betsy Hotel (p89) South Beach, Miami

→ Gardens Hotel (p187) Key West

→ Saint Hotel (p186) Key West

Best Historic Accommodations

You can get your fill of art-deco grandeur by booking in at one of the grand dames in Miami Beach (p58), or bask in Jazz Age swank at the Biltmore in Coral Gables. For something completely different, check out Miami's vintage 1950s motels reborn as stylish boutique stays in the MiMo (Miami Modern) district. The Keys also have some gems, including haunted Victorian mansions and early 1900s beauties backed by lush tropical gardens.

→ Biltmore Hotel (p96) Coral Gables, Miami

→ Winter Haven Hotel (p65) South Beach, Miami

→ Vagabond Hotel (p95) MiMo District, Miami

→ Artist House (p187) Key West

→ Mermaid & the Alligator (p186) Key West

Booking

It's essential to book ahead during the high season (December through March). The best-value places get snapped up quickly (particularly in the Keys), meaning you'll be limited to the most expensive options if you wait until the last minute. Shoulder season (April and May, and October and

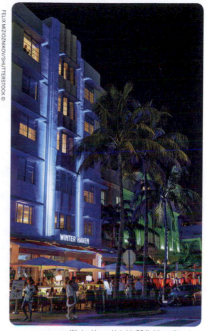

FELIX MIZIOZNIKOV/SHUTTERSTOCK ©

Winter Haven Hotel (p234), Miami Beach

PLAN YOUR TRIP ACCOMMODATIONS

November) can net decent savings. You'll generally find the best prices from June to October — when hurricanes and high temperatures deter many visitors.

Lonely Planet (lonelyplanet.com/hotels) Find independent reviews, as well as recommendations on the best places to stay – and then book them online.

Bed and Breakfast (www.bedandbreakfast.com/florida.html) Has a well-curated list of unique stays in Miami and the Keys.

Greater Miami & the Beaches (www.miamiand beaches.com/hotels) Lowdown on great stays in Miami, whether you're after luxury, architectural beauty or ocean views.

Key West (www.keywest.com) Excellent site for all things Key West, including finding charming B&Bs, pet-friendly accommodations, LGBTQI+ hot spots and vacation rentals.

Reserve America (www.reserveamerica.com) Essential for booking campsites and cabins in state parks and in the Everglades National Park. Plan to book up to 11 months in advance for the most popular campsites (like Bahia Honda State Park).

Month by Month

January

The beginning of the new year is also the height of the tourist season. Expect fair weather, crowds, higher prices than usual and a slew of special events.

◉ Martin Luther King Jr Day Parade

This Miami parade, held on the third Monday of January, celebrates the legacy of the USA's most iconic civil rights hero. It runs along NW 54th from NW 12th Ave to Martin Luther King Jr Memorial Park. A Caribbean twist gives it a distinctly Miami imprimatur.

☆ Key West Literary Seminar

(www.kwls.org) Key West has long been a haven for writers escaping the real world, and its expat authors have turned the annual Key West Literary Seminar into one of the premier festivals of letters in the USA.)

◉ Art-Deco Weekend

(www.artdecoweekend.com) Art deco is Miami's signature style and this weekend fair features guided tours of the city's many clusters of deco structures, concerts, classic-auto shows, sidewalk cafes, and vendors of arts and antiques.

🏃 Miami Marathon

(www.themiamimarathon.com) The big running event in South Florida is the Miami Marathon, which brings over 25,000 runners racing through the streets along a very scenic course. There's also a half marathon.

February

The last hurrah for northerners escaping the harsh winter, February brings arts festivals, street parties and excellent wildlife-viewing in the Everglades.

✕ South Beach Wine & Food Festival

(www.sobewff.org) A festival of fine dining and sipping that has become a fixture of South Florida's social calendar. Expect star-studded brunches, dinners and barbecues. This is the best time of year to brush shoulders with a celebrity chef.

✕ Everglades Seafood Festival

(www.evergladesseafood festival.org) Over three days in mid-February, Everglades City draws seafood lovers who come to feast on stone crabs and other delicacies. There's also live music, craft booths and carnival rides for kids.

◉ Coconut Grove Arts Festival

(www.coconutgroveartsfest. com) This late-February fair features more than 350 artists from across the globe. It's one of the most prestigious festivals of its kind in a city that doesn't lack for an artistic calendar.

March

Spring arrives, bringing warmer weather, world-class golf and tennis festivals, and St Patrick's Day. Expect to see some spring breakers behaving badly on the beach.

✯✯ Carnaval Miami

(www.carnavalmiami.com)
Miami's premier Latin
festival takes over in early
March: there's a Latin
drag-queen show, in-line-
skate competition, domino
tournament, the immense
Calle Ocho Festival, Miss
Carnaval Miami and more.

✩ Miami International Film Festival

(www.miamifilmfestival.com)
This film festival, sponsored
by Miami-Dade College, is
a two-week festival show-
casing documentaries and
features from all over the
world. Spanish-language
films are an important component of the event.

✯✯ Ultra Music Festival

(www.ultramusicfestival.com)
Miami's big electronic
music fest draws over
170,000 who pack Bayfront
Park for three days of
revelry fueled by top DJs
from across the globe.

✩ Winter Music Conference

(www.wintermusicconference.
com) Party promoters,
DJs, producers and
revelers come from around
the globe to hear new
electronic-music artists,
catch up on technology,
and party the nights away.

April

Welcome to shoulder
season with lower prices
and balmier temperatures.
This is Miami's best transition period between
winter crowds and summer
swelter.

✯✯ Miami Beach Pride

(www.miamibeachpride.com) In
April, Miami Beach proudly
flies the rainbow flag high
in this weekend festival that
culminates in a colorful
street parade along Ocean
Dr. Break out the boas,
glitter and body paint!

✯✯ Conch Republic Independence Celebration

(www.conchrepublic.com) Ten
days of fun and whimsy
in Key West, featuring a
nautically themed parade,
drag-queen races, a drunken
spelling bee, and a craft fair.

May

Spring in South Florida
can either mean pleasantly
subdued heat or sweaty
soup. This is when mosquito
season begins in earnest in
the Everglades.

✩ Miami Fashion Week

Models are like fish in the
ocean in Miami during
most of the year, but they're
simply ubiquitous during
Miami Fashion Week,
when designers descend
on the city and catwalks
become disconcertingly
commonplace.

✯✯ Goombay Festival Coconut Grove

(www.coconutgrovebahamian
goombayfestival.com) One of
a few Goombay festivals
held in South Florida, this
massive fest, held in May or
June, celebrates Bahamian
culture in Coconut Grove.
Expect music, street food
and *lots* of dancing.

June

In June the real baking
heat and wet humidity
begins in Miami, and the
events calendar tones
down a little as a result.

July

OK – not only is it hot,
but it's also hurricane
season. Yay! But seriously,
this is a good time to visit.
There are less crowds
and locals are friendlier
and more accessible to
tourists.

✩ Independence Day

July 4 features an excellent
fireworks and laser show
with live music that draws
more than 100,000 people
to breezy Bayfront Park.
The pyrotechnics light
up the sky above Biscayne
Bay in an oddly romantic
way.

◉ Hemingway Days

One of Key West's more
(in)famous annual rituals
is Hemingway Days, a
party that celebrates all
things Hemingway (our
way of saying: expect
drinking, if not game
hunting). The highlight
is the annual Ernest-
lookalike contest.

✩ International Ballet Festival

(www.internationalballet
festival.org) Some of the
most important dance
talent in the world
perform over various
weekends in late July/
early August.

September

The weather is still steamy, and autumn brings back college students – expect lots of revelry in the university 'hoods such as Coconut Grove and Coral Gables.

🎎 Womenfest

(www.gaykeywestfl.com/womenfest) Womenfest gives ladies the chance to seize the large LGBTQI+ spotlight in Key West. This is the premier event for the island's lesbian population, attracting thousands of visitors from around the world.

October

As hurricane season winds down and the weather gets properly pleasant again, Key West takes over the events calendar with raucous street celebrations.

🎎 Fantasy Fest

(www.fantasyfest.com) Held in late October, Fantasy Fest is by far the highlight of the Keys social calendar. The body paint, glitter, feathers and crazy floats come out, inhibitions are left at home, and a seriously decadent time is had by all.

🎎 Goombay Festival Key West

In the heart of Bahama Village, one of the most vibrant Caribbean neighborhoods in the country, the Bahamian Goombay Festival serves up music, food, singing and dancing in late October, during the same insane week as Fantasy Fest.

November

Tourist season kicks off at the end of the month, bringing more crowds and cooler days. Prices are still generally a bit lower than in the months ahead.

☆ Miami Book Fair International

(www.miamibookfair.com) Occurring in mid- to late-November, the Miami Book Fair International is among the most important and well-attended book fairs in the USA. The week-long event features author readings, book signings, tutorials, activities for kids and performances, including music, comedy and improv.

December

Tourist season is in full swing. Northerners book rooms well in advance so they can bask in sunshine and be here for holiday festivities.

👁 Art Basel Miami Beach

(www.artbasel.com/miami-beach) One of the world's seminal international art shows, Art Basel can reasonably claim responsibility for putting Miami Beach on the map of the international jet-setter crowd. Gallery showcases, public installations and parties appear throughout Miami and Miami Beach.

🎎 King Mango Strut

(www.kingmangostrut.org) Held annually just after Christmas since 1982, this quirky Coconut Grove parade is a politically charged, fun freak that began as a spoof on current events and the now-defunct Orange Bowl Parade.

Itineraries

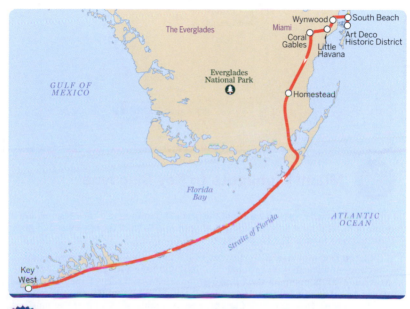

Essential South Florida

10 DAYS

On this trip you'll have a chance to explore Miami's beaches and back alleys, from white sand to classical architecture; a diverse range of neighborhoods that encapsulate the nationalities of Latin American and the Caribbean; and the unique wetland and mangrove ecosystems of the Everglades and the Florida Keys.

Start your trip in Miami's **South Beach**, which encapsulates the best of what South Florida has to offer. Exclusive hotels such as the Delano, Tides and the Shore Club capture the sheer aesthetic innovation of the South Beach experience. Enjoy people-watching on Lincoln Rd and a tour of the **Art Deco Historic District**.

Using South Beach as a base, spend the next four or five days exploring the neighborhoods of **Miami**, including the Latin flavor of **Little Havana**, the Euro-style cafes and mansions of **Coral Gables**, and the art galleries, excellent food and pumping nightlife around **Wynwood** and the **Design District**. Next, basing yourself in **Homestead**, head to the Everglades for a couple of days of wildlife watching, kayaking and stargazing. On the final leg of the journey, hop on the Overseas Highway and go down to **Key West** for two days of living large in America's prettiest bohemian enclave.

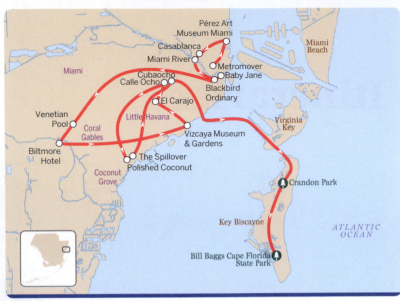

5 DAYS — Miami Highlights to Key Biscayne

On this trip you'll experience some of the best of Miami's ethnic enclaves, hobnob in some of its wealthiest neighborhoods and witness firsthand the opulence that gives Miami the nickname 'The Magic City.'

Start in Downtown, a glittering fist of steel and glass that shadows rough alleyways and cheap international flea markets. Take a long ride on the free **Metromover**, hopping on and off to see downtown sites such as the outstanding **Pérez Art Museum Miami**. Have a stroll along the **Miami River** and stop for lunch at a waterfront spot like **Casablanca**. At night, catch a bit of live music at **Blackbird Ordinary** or enjoy Caribbean cocktails at **Baby Jane**.

The next day, head to Coral Gables, making sure not to miss the **Venetian Pool** (possibly the loveliest public pool in the USA), the **Biltmore Hotel** and a shopping stroll down Miracle Mile. If that isn't opulent enough, see what happens when Mediterranean Revival, Baroque stylings and money get mashed together at the **Vizcaya Museum & Gardens**. Afterward, top off a visit to these elegant manses with dinner at one of the best restaurants in Miami in – no kidding – a gas station at **El Carajo**.

On the third day, head to Little Havana and have a stroll down **Calle Ocho**, making sure to watch the domino games at Máximo Gómez Park. Have a Cuban lunch, browse the local cigar and souvenir shops, then pop over to Coconut Grove, which retains its village-like charm amid the banyan trees. Stop in stores like **Polished Coconut**, and grab a bite and a craft brew at **The Spillover**. End the night with a live concert back in Little Havana at **Cubaocho**.

Spend your last day exploring Key Biscayne, enjoying beaches and sunbathing in areas such as **Bill Baggs Cape Florida State Park**. Before you leave, head to **Crandon Park** and stroll along the sand, or have an afternoon siesta. Is there a quiet, serene beach in manic Miami? You just found it.

4 DAYS Miami Beach and North Miami

See some of Miami's glitziest addresses, then immerse yourself in the city's most fascinating ethnic enclaves, and hipster gentrification zones.

Start your trip in **South Beach** and use this region and its excellent hotels as your base. Begin with an overview of all things deco, by taking a walking tour with the **Art Deco Welcome Center**. Afterwards, visit the **Wolfsonian-FIU** for its excellent exhibitions on decorative arts, industrial design and architecture. Next, head for **Lincoln Rd** to people-watch and browse the trendy shops. For outstanding Peruvian-Japanese food, have dinner at **Chotto Matte**, then visit friendly **Sweet Liberty** to cap the night with cocktails.

The next day, check out **Little Haiti**. This is one of the most colorful, recognizably 'foreign' neighborhoods in Miami. It can be edgy at night, but by day you're fine to explore. Feast on oxtail and other Haitian treats at **Chef Creole**. Afterwards head to the Upper East Side for poolside drinks at the **Vagabond**.

The next day visit the galleries and shops of **Wynwood** and the **Design District**. Start off with a visit to the **Wynwood Walls**, an ever-changing art installation of vibrant wall-sized murals. Next explore the **Margulies Collection at the Warehouse** where the beautifully executed artwork is always thought-provoking. Stop for an espresso at **Panther Coffee** and tacos at **Coyo Taco**, then head up to the Design District. Visit public installations like the Fly's Eye Dome, then stop by the **De La Cruz Collection**, one of Miami's best private collections. At night, grab a bite and drinks at **1 800 Lucky** or the weekend-only **Wynwood Marketplace**.

On your last day in town, head north along Collins Ave to **Mid-Beach** and **North Beach**. To get here you'll pass through the Condo Canyons – rows and rows of glittering residential skyscrapers, all testament to the power of real estate in Miami. In Mid-Beach, near the north end of South Beach, you'll find an excellent boardwalk where you can stroll near the sand.

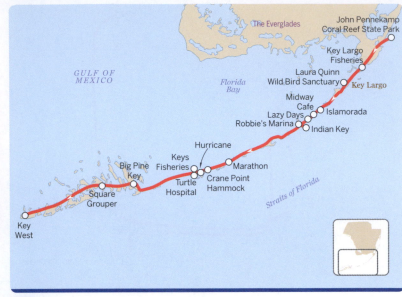

3 DAYS # Overseas Highway Road Trip

The Overseas Highway (Hwy 1) runs from the tip of the Florida mainland all the way to the famed Mile 0: Key West, the end of the road and the end of America. As you tick the mile markers down, you'll be treated to some of Florida's oddest attractions, plus the ever-inspiring view of Florida Bay on one side and the Gulf of Mexico on the other.

Well, OK, you'll get to that view, but first you have to go through the Upper Keys: larger islands that block the view of the water via big fields of scrub pine and mangroves. On northerly Key Largo, check out the diving options at **John Pennekamp Coral Reef State Park**, then have lunch at a classic waterfront spot like **Key Largo Fisheries**. Afterwards visit the injured birds at the **Laura Quinn Wild Bird Sanctuary**. End the day with a seafood feast and ocean views at **Lazy Days** in Islamorada.

Sleep in **Islamorada** on your first day in the Keys. Wake up the next morning and feed the enormous tarpon at **Robbie's Marina**. If you're feeling fit, hire a kayak for a paddle through mangroves or out to **Indian Key**. Afterward, recharge over coffee at the excellent **Midway Cafe**.

The next stop is **Marathon**, geographic center of the Keys. If you're curious about the unique ecological background of the Keys and fancy a walk in the woods, head to the **Crane Point Hammock**. Then learn about the Keys' best-loved endangered species at the **Turtle Hospital**. Eat dinner over the water at **Keys Fisheries**, then grab a beer at **Hurricane**.

Wake up and cross the Seven-Mile Bridge onto **Big Pine Key**, where tiny Key deer prance alongside the road. Stop for a meal at **Square Grouper**, one of the best restaurants south of Miami.

Another hour's drive south and you're in **Key West**. Truly, this island deserves its own itinerary – just make sure you don't miss the sunset show in Mallory Sq, the six-toed cats at the Hemingway House and a night out at the infamous Green Parrot, the mother of all Keys bars.

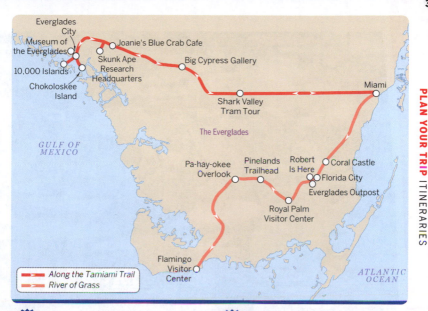

Everglades
City
Museum of
the Everglades
10,000 Islands
Chokoloskee
Island
Joanie's Blue Crab Cafe
Skunk Ape
Research
Headquarters
Big Cypress Gallery
Shark Valley
Tram Tour
Miami
The Everglades
GULF OF
MEXICO
Pa-hay-okee
Overlook
Pinelands
Trailhead
Robert
Is Here
Coral Castle
Florida City
Everglades Outpost
Royal Palm
Visitor Center
Flamingo
Visitor
Center
ATLANTIC
OCEAN

Along the Tamiami Trail
River of Grass

3 DAYS Along the Tamiami Trail

This route takes you into the heart of the Everglades, through waterlogged wetlands and cypress swamps crawling with gators, with a stay in a fishing village.

From **Miami**, go west on Tamiami Trail (US 41) to the Shark Valley entrance. Take the **Shark Valley Tram Tour** or rent a bicycle and ride back on an asphalt path (the same one used by the tram) that curves into the swamp. You're almost sure to see alligators and wading birds.

Push on to **Everglades City**, a warm hamlet that makes a fine spot for an overnight, especially after dining on stone crabs at the waterfront. Take a morning boat tour into the **10,000 Islands**, then go out to **Chokoloskee Island** for a glimpse of early 20th-century life at the Smallwood Store. Heading back north, visit the **Museum of the Everglades**.

The next day head back toward Miami. Stop at the delightfully weird **Skunk Ape Research Headquarters**, have lunch at **Joanie's Blue Crab Cafe** and visit the **Big Cypress Gallery**, which contains some of the finest photos of the Glades.

2 DAYS River of Grass

This route into the Everglades takes in vistas of long prairies and cypress domes.

Drive south from **Miami** toward Homestead and pull over by the **Coral Castle**, a maudlin monument to unrequited love. Just outside Everglades National Park, you'll find **Robert Is Here**, a fantastic farmers market and petting zoo. Continue to the **Everglades Outpost**, an animal hospital for exotic critters.

Push west to see the most impressive points in the park, including the **Royal Palm Visitor Center**, where walkways lead over dark waterways prowled by enormous alligators; the **Pinelands Trailhead**, which takes you through a grove of skeleton-thin swamp pine; and **Pa-hay-okee Overlook**, with views over the Zen quiet of the greater Glades.

Spend the night back in **Florida City** at the fantastic Hoosville Hostel. The next morning head back into the Glades for a canoeing adventure or a slough slog – a wet walk into a Cypress dome led by park rangers. End the day with sunset views (and perhaps glimpses of manatees) at the **Flamingo Visitor Center**.

Alligator, Anhinga Trail (p134), Everglades National Park

Activities

South Florida is an aquatic wonderland with ocean, bays, rivers, marsh, swamp and mangrove coastlines, plus countless islands and glorious beaches. Getting the most out of the outdoors means navigating both the land and the water, and the delicate balance they exist in.

Best Outdoor Adventures

Paddling in the Everglades

Gliding along still waters past mangroves and over glassy lakes amid abundant birdlife.

Biking Shark Valley

Spotting sunbaked gators and other Glades residents on an easygoing 15-mile pedal in the Everglades.

Manatee Spotting Off Virginia Key

Looking for grazing giants on a kayaking or stand-up paddleboarding glide around a mangrove-lined bay.

Walking in the Everglades

Taking a sunlit stroll along the wildlife-packed Anhinga Trail, then returning by night to see gators at their liveliest.

Snorkeling and Diving Off Key Largo

Taking in the coral reefs and colorful fish life found in John Pennekamp Coral Reef State Park.

Kayaking the Keys

Spotting sting rays, tiny deer and other wildlife on a back-country paddling tour off Big Pine Key.

The Lay of the Land

There's a lot to do on and off South Florida's pretty beaches: swimming, kayaking, boating, snorkeling, diving – and several different brands of boarding. This is also a great place to get under the water. Key Largo is the gateway to the largest coral reef system in North America. There you'll find the John Pennekamp Coral Reef State Park (p166), the nation's first park dedicated to underwater exploration.

On land, South Florida's most distinguishing feature is its hammock – a term for a copse or grove of hardwood trees. Hammocks grow in wetland areas that are too sodden to support them. A few extra inches of elevation gives the trees the dryness they need to grow larger and more densely; the Pineland Trail in Everglades National Park (p138) is an excellent example of a coniferous hammock. Hammocks in the Everglades typically have a distinctive teardrop shape, formed by the flow of water around the tree 'islands.'

While there are many versions of hammocks through the American southeast, the one you will most likely encounter in South Florida is the tropical hardwood hammock. Even within this category there are numerous subdivisions, including rockland hammocks in the Big Cypress National Preserve (p138), tree island hammocks in the Everglades and coastal berm hammocks in the Florida Keys. Also in the Keys: shell mound hammocks, which grew on top of the midden shell heaps left behind by the indigenous Calusa and Tequesta Indians. The Crane Point Hammock (p173) in Marathon is an excellent introduction to the many variations of hammock in South Florida in general, and the Keys in particular.

Nature Trails & Hiking

Boardwalk paths run by still-water swamps, noodle-thin tracks lace into boonies studded with lakes and rivers, and mangrove walkways encircle white beaches. Lace up your boots (or don some sandals; there are some very gentle trails here) and hit the great outdoors.

One thing Florida hikers never have to worry about is elevation gain. But if topography is easy, the weather presents greater challenges. From November through March rain, temperature, humidity and mosquitoes decrease to tolerable levels. In summer (June to September), make sure to hike first thing in the morning, or at least before noon, to avoid the midday heat and almost daily afternoon thundershowers.

South Florida swamps tend to favor 1- to 2-mile boardwalk trails; these are excellent for even out-of-shape walkers, and almost always wheelchair accessible. You'll also find lovely short trails in many state parks. The best trails in South Florida can be found in Everglades National Park and surrounds.

Miami

Most of Miami's green spaces can be found either in far north Miami and Miami Beach, on the island of Key Biscayne, which has large protected areas, and sprinkled amid the miles of tract suburbia that stretch to the south of the city.

Oleta River State Park (p64) is Florida's largest urban park, and home to a decent number of trails. Nearby Arch Creek Park (p78) offers family-friendly nature trails. These North Miami parks are a nice example of the subtropical forest and stream environment that once existed across interior South Florida.

Drive over the Rickenbacker Causeway to Key Biscayne and you'll find sandy trails leading past beaches and mangroves in Bill Baggs Cape Florida State Park (p77). Nature trails also abound in a lovely coastal ecosystem at nearby Crandon Park (p77). These Key Biscayne parks give visitors a glimpse into the shrub and low-lying hammock ecosystems common to the offshore islands that ring the southern portion of the Florida peninsula.

If you just need a good walk outdoors, we'd recommend heading to the Fairchild Tropical Garden (p75). While not hiking trails, per se, the park is so large you can have a good walk traversing its length and breadth, and you'll get a primer on tropical flora while you're out there.

The Everglades

The Everglades may largely consist of wetlands, or prairie that is liable to become waterlogged during the wet season, but it's still a magical place to walk as long as you follow the right trails. In some areas, like near the southernmost **Flamingo** (☑239-695-3101; ⊙store 7am-5:30pm Mon-Fri, from 6am Sat & Sun) portion of the park, you'll be confronted with sandy, scrubby trails that traverse stretches of dried-out mud flats and run by the lonely, windswept coast. In other areas, the vast horizons of the Everglades prairie, especially when contrasted with scattered pine hammock and cypress domes, are as humbling as any mountain range.

The **Florida National Scenic Trail** (☑877-445-3352; www.floridatrail.org) is one of America's 11 national scenic trails and takes in much of the geography of the Glades. The trail runs north from the swamps of Big Cypress National Preserve, starting at the Oasis Visitor Center (p142), and you can feasibly trek from here to Lake Okeechobee. Just be prepared for plenty of mosquitoes.

The Royal Palm Visitor Center (p141) and Fakahatchee Strand Preserve (p139) are great spots for more leisurely walks. These areas are both overlaid with long boardwalks that extend deep into the heart of genuine blackwater swamps and alligator wallows. On either of these walks, you'll come face to face with some local wildlife, usually of the avian, reptilian and amphibian kind. The same can be said for the asphalt path that runs through Shark Valley (p139), which also offers a tram tour.

The Keys

Hikes in the Keys are more like short walks along nature trails that provide insight into the unique ecosystem that has developed amid these mangrove islands. These trails are never very physically demanding, and given the plethora of teaching displays that tend to accompany them, they are usually fun (or at least, educational) if you have kids in tow. Some of our favorite nature walks in the Keys:

John Pennekamp Coral Reef State Park (p166) While this park is primarily known for its water activities, there are some small, friendly trails here for when you're finished kayaking or snorkeling.

Windley Key Fossil Reef Geological State Park (p170) Part of this Key has been carved out, which gives you a glimpse into the complex geology of the archipelago.

Indian Key State Historic Site (p170) Rotting buildings and groves of shady trees add an almost eerie touch to trekking across this island.

Lignumvitae Key State Botanical Site (p170) Genuine jungle has reclaimed this small, isolated island.

Curry Hammock State Park (p173) Narrow trails finger through the local mangrove and beachside biomes.

Crane Point Hammock (p173) The interpretative trails at this fascinating nature reserve museum are a great introductory lesson on the ecology of the Keys.

Bahia Honda State Park (p176) A great setting for a walk, with nature, beach and boardwalk trails.

Camping, Bahia Honda State Park (p178)

Camping

You'll find some fantastic sites to pitch a tent both in the Everglades and along the Keys. Plan well ahead: prime spots (like Bahia Honda State Park) book up many months in advance.

The Everglades

The National Park Service manages both primitive and developed campgrounds and can help travelers who want to pitch in the backcountry. 'Primitive' sites lack running water and electricity, while developed sites will at least possess running water and sometimes have power hookups.

Our favorite camping option in the area is finding *chickees* (wooden platforms built above the water line) and isolated beaches and mangrove strands amid the 10,000 Islands (p146). When you're out here surrounded by the stars, dolphins, birdlife, the breeze and little else, it's backcountry bliss. Offshore islands in Biscayne National Park (p148) offer a similar experience to camping in the 10,000 Islands.

The Keys

John Pennekamp Coral Reef State Park (p167) and Bahia Honda State Park (p178) both offer excellent campgrounds with a good mix of hookup sites and tent areas, but these parks are very popular, so reserve far in advance. If you really want to feel like you're sleeping at the end of the earth, reserve a spot at Dry Tortugas National Park (p195). It's self-service camping, and you'll have to bring everything with you, including water. As with other popular spots, it's essential to reserve nearly a year in advance.

Canoeing & Kayaking

To really experience South Florida's swamps and rivers, its estuaries and inlets, and its lagoons and barrier islands, you need watercraft, preferably the kind you paddle. The intimate quiet of dipping among mangroves – startling alligators and ibis – stirs wonder in the soul. It's not only the Everglades that are great for paddling. Don't forget the coasts: there are some choice options for coastal kayaking and canoeing in Miami and all along the Keys.

TREAD LIGHTLY, EXPLORE SAFELY

It goes without saying that any wilderness, even a swamp, is a fragile place. Whether hiking, biking, paddling or snorkeling, *always* practice 'Leave No Trace' ethics (see www.lnt.org for comprehensive advice). In short, stay on the trail, clean up your own mess, and observe nature rather than plucking or feeding it.

Take care of yourself too. In particular, carry lots of water, up to a gallon per person per day, and always be prepared for rain. Line backpacks with plastic bags, and carry rain gear and extra clothes for when (not if) you get soaked.

As with hiking, the winter 'dry' season is best for paddling. If it's summer, canoe near cool freshwater springs and swimming beaches, as you'll be dreaming about them in the heat.

Miami

You'll find open waters to paddle around and mangrove tunnels to paddle through in Oleta River State Park (p64), which sits next to the Haulover inlet. The other hot spot for kayaking and canoeing is Key Biscayne (p76). There's a good boat launch and seawall at Bill Baggs Cape Florida State Park (p77) that fronts No Name Harbor, while offshore paddling is a popular day-tripping activity at Crandon Park (p77).

The Everglades

You'll likely tell your grandchildren about kayaking in Everglades National Park (p138). At times, you'll feel as if there was nothing in the world but the two mirror-flat reflections of water and sky; at other moments, that soaring sense of space is compressed into claustrophobic, capillary-esque mangrove tunnels courtesy of Hell's Bay – which, by the way, is one of the most beautiful parts of the park. Don't miss it.

If you want a true ultimate adventure, consider boating the 99-mile-long Wilderness Waterway along and amid the margins of the 10,000 Islands (p146).

The Keys

Paddling is popular in the Keys, where the water is more teal than the sky and the sun is almost always bright overhead.

Near Key Largo there's excellent paddling near clumps of mangrove forest at John Pennekamp Coral Reef State Park (p166), while Curry Hammock State Park (p173) and Bahia Honda State Park (p176) also offer fine backdrops for paddling. All three of these parks offer kayaks for rent (many hotels and guesthouses up and down the Keys also provide free use of kayaks for guests).

Further south, you'll find outstanding back-country paddling off Big Pine Key – a guided tour by Big Pine Kayak Adventures (p177) is highly recommended – though you can also arrange DIY adventures here.

Two other fine kayaking destinations are Indian Key Historic State Park (p170) and Lignumvitae Key Botanical State Park (p170). Both sites are only accessible by boat. They're not too difficult to reach by paddle, but this added layer of inaccessibility, plus the combination of wilderness and the rotted ruins on Indian Key, makes a trip out here pretty magical. You can hire kayaks from Robbie's Marina (p171) nearby.

Diving & Snorkeling

South Florida has some of the best reef and wreck diving in the continental USA, and the snorkeling is just as memorable. North America's largest coral-reef system is at your fingertips. At times the clarity of the water is disconcerting, as if you were floating on air; every creature and rainbow school of fish all the way to the bottom feels just out of reach.

Biscayne National Park (p#) has developed a wreck-centric maritime trail, for avid divers. Other attractions include **Dry Tortugas National Park** (p#), which was named for its abundant sea turtles. In the Upper Keys, John Pennekamp Coral Reef State Park (p166) offers the best diving in the lower 48 states.

Snorkeling, Fort Jefferson, Dry Tortugas National Park (p195)

Sailing

If you prefer the wind in your sails, Florida is your place. Miami is a sailing sweet spot, with plenty of marinas for renting or berthing your own boat – Key Biscayne is a particular gem, and marinas in swish Coconut Grove and Brickell cater to the sailing crowd. In Key West, you can sail on a schooner with real cannons. Tour operators are plentiful throughout the Keys.

Get On Board

South Florida is no surfing hot spot; if you want to ride waves in this state it's generally best to head north to at least Jupiter Beach. But surfing isn't the only means of using a board to access the water. Kiteboarding is quite popular, and it's accessible to first-timers looking to try something new. The flat, shallow waters around Key Biscayne is kiteboarding central. Check out the following:

Miami Kiteboarding (p83) Offers a range of private and semi-private lessons from $240 for two hours of instruction. Couples get discounted rates.

Miami Watersports Complex (MWCC; ☎305-476-9253; www.miamiwatersportscomplex.com; Amelia Earhart Park, 401 E 65th St, Hialeah; ⊙10am-dusk Jun-Sep, from 11am Oct-May) Offers lessons in cableboarding, where the rider is pulled along by an overhead cable system. That means no boat, less pollution and less noise. A $59 package includes a beginner lesson, rental gear and four-hour cable pass. Call ahead to reserve a spot.

Cycling

Florida is generally too flat for mountain biking (though there are exceptions), but there are plenty of off-road opportunities, along with hundreds of miles of paved trails for those who prefer to keep their ride clean. As with hiking, avoid cycling in summer unless you like getting hot and sweaty.

Miami Beach operates a bike-share program and bicycles are easy to rent in Key West, so there's really no excuse not to get on two wheels. In Miami, the Promenade (p63), which fronts Ocean Dr, is an excellent ride for those who want to take in Miami Beach and get a little exercise in while they're at it. Unfortunately the Promenade does not extend all the way up the beach. Be careful riding on Collins Ave as it extends further north; that road is the only major artery running north–south, and people tend to speed on it. Oleta River State Park (p64)

ALTERNATIVE ACTIVITIES

So you've walked the beaches, gone kayaking amid the mangroves and snorkeled the coral reefs. What next? How about heading well off the beaten path on one of South Florida's quirky adventures?

Slough slog Don your cheapest pants and lace up those (unwanted) shoes for a walk into the muck. Free ranger-led tours (p#) take you into a cypress dome in search of plant and animal life and verdant tranquility.

Moonlight paddles Virginia Key Outdoor Center (p83) leads memorable full-moon (and new moon) paddles several times a month. You'll see a sunset and with luck bioluminescent plankton in the water.

Alligator spotting by night Maybe you've seen the big piles of crocodilians by day; come back at night to the Anhinga Trail (p134) to see these primordial creatures gliding beautifully through the water. Bring a flashlight!

Eating pizza under the sea At Jules' Undersea Lodge (p168) in Key Largo, you can pay a visit – or overnight – in a former research station under the water. You'll have to scuba dive to get there; hot (and amazingly dry!) pizza delivered to your undersea abode is part of the deal.

Sunbathing without tan lines Join the clothing-optional crowd at Haulover Beach Park (p64) in North Beach, Miami. For ocean frolicking in the buff, this is the place to be.

Feeding tremendous tarpons At Robbie's Marina (p171) down in Islamorada, you can feed some massive fish. The water sloshes like it's boiling when these giants are hungry.

offers 4 miles of novice, 3 miles of paved and 10 miles of mountain-biking trails.

Cycling is a very popular means of seeing the Everglades; just make sure you wear bright clothing and measure your distances so you don't accidentally find yourself on a lonely park road after the sun sets (it wouldn't be dangerous, but it'd probably be pretty unnerving). An easy ride along Shark Valley's paved asphalt track (p139) takes in plenty of wildlife.

In the Keys, cycling is perhaps the most logical way of exploring Key West. Those seeking a challenging, rewarding ride should consider the Florida Keys Overseas Heritage Trail (p169), which goes from Key Largo to Key West. While not complete, new sections continue to be added, and currently 90 out of 106 miles are open for cycling.

Fishing

Fishing in Florida is among the best the US offers, and for variety and abundance nowhere else can claim better. The peninsula's position offers an ideal placement for Atlantic Ocean sport fishing, but also has the calmer waters for line casting in the Gulf. There is excellent fishing infrastructure in place across the

state that caters to all skill levels, from total beginners to experienced anglers.

Still, water pollution has shrunk Florida's recreational fisheries, and the quality of the angling in the state will rise and fall based on Florida's environmental conditions.

The Keys are the best place for fishing in a state that is fantastic for fishing. In the islands, Bahia Honda and Old Seven Mile Bridge offer shore-fishing par excellence. Other good sites:

Oleta River State Park (p64) The shores of the park front the Intracoastal Waterway; plus, there's a popular local fishing pier.

Bill Baggs Cape Florida State Park (p77) Offshore fishers here pull in some truly huge hauls.

As 'Papa' Hemingway would tell you, the real fishing is offshore, where majestic sailfish leap and thrash. That's part of the reason the man moved to Key West, after all. Bluefish, marlin and mahimahi (known locally as dolphin fish, although it is not, in any way, the marine mammal) are other popular deep-water fish. The best strategy is to walk the harbor, talking with captains until you find one who speaks to your experience and interests. Don't be surprised if the cost of a charter-boat hire for a day runs into four digits, depending on the size of the boat. Smaller craft should cost less.

Conch fritters

Eat & Drink Like a Local

When South Florida sits at the table, who knows what language the menu will be written in? This region has a rich culinary identity, which is an extension of an already rich demographic identity. As a result the local culinary scene is paradoxical yet delicious: on the one hand a free-floating gastronomy for people unmoored from their homeland and detached from tradition, and on the other an attempt to connect to deeply felt roots and folkways via the immediacy of taste.

Top Food Experiences

South Beach Indulging in creative Southern comfort fare at Yardbird (p100) after a stroll on nearby Lincoln Road.

Wynwood Taste-testing your way through Miami's most creative restaurants, beginning with Kyu (p105).

Little Havana Joining Cuban expats over mouthwatering Latin fare at the iconic Versailles (p108).

Downtown Miami Enjoying the bay views at Verde (p103) after strolling the galleries at the Pérez Art Museum Miami.

Little Haiti Sitting at a picnic table listening to *kompa* while feasting on oxtail and beans at Chef Creole (p107), a much-loved Haitian takeout stand.

The Everglades Feasting on stone crab claws fresh off the boat at waterside spots like the Camellia Street Grill (p144).

Homestead Sipping magnificent smoothies and loading up on exotic fruits from around the globe, at Robert Is Here (p147), one of Florida's best farm stands.

The Keys Sampling great seafood up and down the Keys, starting with the dockside Key Largo Fisheries (p168) in the Upper Keys.

Key West Tucking into the world's best key lime pie while listening to backyard jams and watching roosters roam freely at Blue Heaven (p190).

A Global Palate

South Florida is a region defined not by any one, but a hemisphere's-worth of cultures: Southern, Creole, Cuban, Caribbean, and Central and South American, but also Jewish, Japanese, Vietnamese, Nigerian, Thai, Chinese, Spanish and more.

Few places can boast Florida's sublime fresh bounty from land and sea, and menus playfully nick influences. Gourmets can genuflect before celebrity chefs, while gourmands hunt Florida's bizarre delicacies, such as boiled peanuts, frog's legs, snake and gator. Strip malls can contain gastronomic gems, while five-star hotel restaurants can be total duds. Smell, taste, enjoy and indulge – our advice to you, and a fitting motto for Floridians and food.

Riches of the Sea

Florida has always fed itself from the sea, which lies within arm's reach from nearly every point. If it swims or crawls in the ocean, you can bet some enterprising local has shelled or scaled it, battered it, dropped it in a fryer and put it on a menu.

Grouper is far and away the most popular fish. Grouper sandwiches are to Florida what the cheese-steak is to Philadelphia or pizza to Manhattan – a defining, iconic dish, and the standard by which many places are measured. Hunting the perfect grilled or fried grouper sandwich is an obsessive Floridian quest, as is finding the creamiest bowl of chowder.

Of course, a huge range of other fish is offered. Other popular species include snapper (with dozens of varieties), mahimahi and yellowfin tuna.

Florida really shines when it comes to crustaceans: try pink shrimp and rock shrimp, and don't miss soft-shell blue crab – Florida is the only place with blue-crab hatcheries, making them available fresh year-round. Winter (October to April) is the season for Florida spiny lobster and stone crab (out of season, both will be frozen). Florida lobster is all tail, without the large claws of its Maine cousin, and stone crab is heavenly sweet, served steamed with butter or the ubiquitous mustard sauce.

Finally, the Keys popularized conch (a giant sea snail); now fished out, most conch is from the Bahamas. For information on sustainable seafood, check out www.seafoodwatch.org.

Cuban & Latin American Cuisine

Cuban food, once considered 'exotic,' is itself a mix of Caribbean, African and Latin American influences, and in Tampa and Miami it's a staple of everyday life. Sidle up to a Cuban *lonchería* (snack bar) and order a *pan cubano:* a buttered, grilled baguette stuffed with ham, roast pork, cheese, mustard and pickles.

Cuban sandwich (p43)

Integral to many Cuban dishes are *mojo* (a garlicky vinaigrette, sprinkled on sandwiches), *adobo* (a meat marinade of garlic, salt, cumin, oregano and sour orange juice) and *sofrito* (a stew-starter mix of garlic, onion and chili peppers). Main-course meats are typically accompanied by rice and beans, and fried plantains.

With its large number of Central and Latin American immigrants, the Miami area offers plenty of authentic ethnic eateries. Seek out Haitian *griots* (marinated fried pork), Jamaican jerk chicken, Brazilian barbecue, Central American *gallo pinto* (red beans and rice) and Nicaraguan *tres leches* ('three milks' cake).

In the morning, try a Cuban coffee, also known as *café cubano* or *cortadito*. This hot shot of liquid gold is essentially sweetened espresso, while *café con leche* is just *café au lait* with a different accent: equal parts coffee and hot milk.

Another Cuban treat is *guarapo* (fresh-squeezed sugarcane juice). Cuban snack bars serve the greenish liquid straight or poured over crushed ice, and it's essential

to an authentic mojito (rum, sugar, mint, lemon and club soda). It also sometimes finds its way into *batidos,* a milky, refreshing Latin American fruit smoothie.

Southern Cooking

You are technically in the South down here, but much of South Florida is so south it's *sud* as opposed to Southern if you catch our drift. Basically we're saying Miami is too international to be classified as the American South. And as such, Southern cooking basically skips Miami as a city. The Southern influence is much more keenly felt in the Everglades and the Keys.

Southern makes up in fat and pure tastiness what it may lack in refinement. Standard Southern fare is a main meat – such as fried chicken, catfish, barbecued ribs, chicken-fried steak or even chitlins (hog's intestines) – and three sides: perhaps some combination of hushpuppies (cornbread balls), cheese grits, cornbread, coleslaw, mashed potatoes, black-eyed peas, collard greens or buttery corn. End with pecan pie, and that's living.

In the Keys, Southern-style cooking melds with Caribbean gastronomy. In

SUNSHINE STATE FOOD FESTIVALS

Many of Florida's food festivals have the tumultuous air of county fairs, with carnival rides, music, parades, beauty pageants and any number of wacky, only-in-Florida happenings.

Key West Food & Wine Festival (www.keywestfoodandwinefestival.com) A week-long party and celebration of the finest in Key West gastronomy, in late January.

Everglades Seafood Festival (www.evergladesseafoodfestival.org) Not just seafood, but gator, frog's legs and, most importantly, stone crabs. Held over three days in Everglades City, early February.

South Beach Food & Wine Festival (www.sobefest.com) This Food Network–sponsored party in Miami is one of the largest food festivals in the country, held over four days in late February.

Swamp Cabbage Festival (www.swampcabbagefestival.org) In La Belle, over three days in late February. Armadillo races and crowning of the Miss Swamp Cabbage Queen.

Florida Strawberry Festival (www.flstrawberryfestival.com) In Plant City for 11 days, late February to early March. Since 1930 over half a million folks come annually to pluck, eat and honor the mighty berry.

Carnaval Miami (www.carnavalmiami.com) Negotiate drag queens and in-line skaters to reach the Cuban Calle Ocho food booths at this huge Miami fest. A fortnight in early March.

Grant Seafood Festival (www.grantsseafoodfestival.com) This small Space Coast town throws one of Florida's biggest weekend seafood parties, in early March.

Island Fest (www.islamoradachamber.com) Essentially a county fair for all things Keys-related, in Islamorada for two days late March or early April.

Taste of Key West (www.facebook.com/TasteofKeyWest) Dozens of local restaurants turn their kitchens into food carts along the Truman waterfront for one day, mid-April.

Isle of Eight Flags Shrimp Festival (www.shrimpfestival.com) Avast, you scurvy dog! Pirates invade for shrimp and a juried art show. On Amelia Island for three days, late April or early May.

Palatka Blue Crab Festival (www.bluecrabfestivalpalatka.com) Four-day Memorial Day weekend (weekend before last Monday in May). Hosts the state championship for chowder and gumbo. Yes, it's that good.

Key West Lobsterfest (www.keywestlobsterfest.com) Celebrates the opening of spiny lobster season with seafood feasting and live music over an August weekend.

Florida Seafood Festival (www.floridaseafoodfestival.com) Held in Apalachicola over two days, early November. Stand way, way back at its signature oyster shucking and eating contests.

truth, there's a lot of room for overlap, as enslaved peoples developed many of the same recipes in the USA and the Caribbean. Plus, Southern and Caribbean cooking are both unapologetically rich and heavy, and the latter may apply to you too if you're not careful when you eat in the Keys.

Cracker (pioneer or rural Floridian) cooking is Florida's rough-and-tumble variation on Southern cuisine, but with more reptiles and amphibians. And you'll find a good deal of Cajun and Creole as well, which mix in spicy gumbos and bisques from Louisiana's neighboring swamps. Southern Floridian cooking is epitomized by writer Marjorie Kinnan Rawlings' famous cookbook *Cross Creek Cookery*.

Ice tea is ubiquitous in the Everglades and the Keys, but watch out for 'sweet tea,' which is an almost entirely different Southern drink – tea so sugary your eyes will cross.

Local Specialties

While South Florida has an international palate, some dishes have been here long enough to constitute something like a local cuisine.

Cuban Sandwich

The traditional Cuban sandwich is a thing of some beauty, and a possible genuine native Florida dish. That Cubans invented the thing is agreed upon, but where they did so – here or Tampa or Havana – is a subject of debate. Cuban bread is buttered or oiled and hit with mustard. Layer on thin pickles, ham, roast pork or salami, and Swiss cheese. Press the thing in a *plancha* (a smooth panino grill) and ta-da: yumminess on warm bread.

Stone Crabs

The first reusable crustacean: only one claw is taken from a stone crab – the rest is tossed back in the sea (the claw regrows in 12 to 18 months, and crabs plucked again are called 'retreads'). The claws are so perishable that they're always cooked before selling. Mid-October through mid-May is less a 'season' than a stone-crab frenzy. Joe Weiss of Miami Beach is credited with starting it all. For straight-from-the-sea freshness, try them in Everglades City.

Colombian Hot Dog

The Colombian *perro caliente* is a work of mad genius. Colombians have...a different take on hot dogs; toppings we've seen include quail eggs, plum sauce, potato chips, pineapple and 'pink sauce' (we didn't ask). These crazy creations may not be native to South Florida, but this is about the only place you'll find them in the USA, apart from a few neighborhoods in New York.

Alligator

Alligator tastes like a cross between fish and pork. The meat comes from the tail and is usually served as deep-fried nuggets, which overwhelms the delicate flavor and can make it chewy. Try it grilled. Alligator is healthier than chicken, with as much protein but half the fat, fewer calories and less cholesterol. Most alligator is legally harvested on farms and is often sold in grocery stores. Alligator farms have their critics, but it's worth noting said farms have no worse or better a reputation than most factory farms or slaughterhouses.

Conch

The shellfish Keys natives are named for (a 'conch' is a shellfish, while a capitalized 'Conch' is a Keys native) happen to be delicious, and are difficult to find outside of South Florida (in the US). Conch meat is pleasantly springy and usually prepared according to Caribbean recipes: most of the time it's either curried or 'cracked' (fried). Either way it is seriously tasty.

Arepas

The greatness of a city can be measured by many yardsticks. The arts. Civic involvement. Infrastructure. What you eat when you're plowed at 3am. In Miami the answer is often enough *arepas* – delicious South American corn cakes that can be stuffed (Venezuelan-style) or topped (Colombian-style) with any manner of deliciousness; generally you can't go wrong with cheese.

Key Lime Pie

Key limes are yellow, and that's the color of an authentic Key lime pie, which is a custard of Key lime juice, sweetened condensed milk and egg yolks in a cracker crust, then topped with meringue. Avoid any slice that is green or stands ramrod straight. The combination of extra-tart Key lime with oversweet milk nicely captures the personality of Key West Conchs.

From Farm (& Grove) to Table

Florida has worked long and hard to become an agricultural powerhouse, and is renowned for its citrus products. The state is the nation's largest producer of oranges, grapefruits, tangerines and limes, not to mention mangoes and sugarcane. Scads of bananas,

Above: Key lime pie (p43)

Left: Key West Lobsterfest (p42)

STONE CRAB CLAWS

Enormous stone crab claws are a staple of Floridian seafood menus, but some may have concerns with the way they are harvested. The crabs are legal to harvest from October 15 through May 15, although fishermen must toss back any ovigerous (egg-laying) female crabs.

The male crabs have a different fate. Their claws are broken off and the crab, now a limb down, is tossed back into the water. After roughly three molts (a period when a crab regrows its shell, which usually takes a year) the claw will have grown back, only for the process to repeat itself.

Defenders of the harvest say that the act of tossing the crabs back, even with one arm, makes for a more sustainable fishery considering the alternative is simply keeping the whole crab. But the Department of Fish and Wildlife estimates some 28% of crabs die from the amputation; that number climbs to 47% for a double amputation. Those casualty numbers can be significantly reduced if a fisherman knows how to make a clean cut of the limb.

strawberries, coconuts, avocados (once called 'alligator pears') and the gamut of tropical fruits and vegetables are also grown in Florida. Homestead is a major agricultural region, with citrus groves and fields of crops extending all the way to the edge of the Everglades.

However, only relatively recently – with the advent of the USA's locavore, farm-to-table movement – has Florida started featuring vegetables in its cooking and promoting its freshness on the plate. Florida's regional highlights – its Southern and Latin American cuisines – do not usually emphasize greens or vegetarianism. But today, most restaurants with upscale or gourmet pretensions promote the local sources of their produce and offer appealing choices for vegetarians.

Inside Miami you'll find a delightful variety of vegetarian options, including a few vegan-friendly places. Outside Miami, dedicated vegetarian restaurants are few, and in many Keys and Everglades restaurants vegetarians can be forced to choose between iceberg-lettuce salads and pastas. Key West, on the other hand, has several excellent vegetarian eateries.

One indigenous local delicacy is heart of palm ('swamp cabbage'), which has a delicate, sweet crunch. The heart of the sabal palm, Florida's state tree, it was a mainstay for Florida pioneers. Try it if you can find it served fresh (don't bother if it's canned; it's not from Florida).

Floribbean Cuisine

OK, somebody worked hard to come up with 'Floribbean' – a term for Florida's tantalizing gourmet mélange of just-caught seafood, tropical fruits and eye-watering peppers, all dressed up with some combination of Nicaraguan, Salvadoran, Caribbean, Haitian, Cajun, Cuban and even Southern influences. Some call it 'Fusion,' 'Nuevo Latino,' 'New World,' 'Nouvelle Floridian' or 'Palm Tree Cuisine,' and it could refer to anything from a ceviche of lime, conch, sweet peppers and scotch bonnets to grilled grouper with mango, *adobo* and fried plantains.

Where to Eat

South Florida has a dazzling range of eating options. Aside from casual places, it's wise to book tables ahead of time – especially on weekends. For top-end restaurants, reserve two weeks or more in advance.

Restaurants South Florida's restaurants range from easygoing waterfront shacks to glittering, award-winning dining rooms, and cover every cuisine you can imagine.

Cafes Open from morning to early evening, cafes are good for a simple breakfast or lunch, plus coffee and snacks.

Food stands When you want a meal in a hurry, hit a taco stand, a pizza counter or a food truck.

SELF-CATERING IN MIAMI

For the freshest picnic items around, hit one of the following farmers' markets:

Adrienne Arsht Center for the Performing Arts, Downtown (1300 Biscayne Blvd; ◷4-8pm Mon)

Aventura Mall, Aventura (19501 Biscayne Blvd; ◷10am-9pm Sat & noon-8pm Sun mid-Feb–Oct)

Brickell Center, Downtown (btwn 7th & 8th Sts under the Metromover tracks; ◷10am-4pm Sun)

Grande Ave, Coconut Grove (3300 Grand Ave at Margaret St; ◷10am-7pm Sat)

Lincoln Road, South Beach (btwn Washington and Meridian Aves; ◷9am-5pm Sun)

Legion Park, Upper East Side (Biscayne Blvd at 66th St, ◷9am-2pm Sat)

Merrick Park, Coral Gables (405 Biltmore Way; ◷8am-2pm Sat mid-Jan–Mar)

Normandy Village Fountain, North Beach (7892 Rue Vendome; ◷9am-4pm Sat)

Drinks

Be it a lime stuffed into a Corona on a dock in the Keys, or rum served in countless permutations, South Florida really likes a drink. There's a phrase you'll hear in the Keys that describes the islands as 'Drinking towns with a fishing problem,' which more or less nails it. Miami loves its booze too, but the focus is often on whatever is the trendy drink of the moment.

Beer

The beer market in South Florida offers astonishing variety. A demand for quality brew means you can find a gallery of international beers at some bars; on the other hand, you can go from being very international to totally local by trying a brew pub. There are also countless microbreweries in the region. If you're a beer fan, it's worth adding the following spots to your itinerary:

Wynwood Brewing Company (Map p96; ☏305-982-8732; www.wynwoodbrewing.com; 565 NW 24th St; ◷noon-10pm Sun-Tue, to midnight Wed-Sat) The first (and arguably still the best) craft brewer in Wynwood.

Boxelder (p116) A Wynwood-based craft beer bar that showcases the great things happening in the local beer scene.

Abbey Brewery (p114) Buzzing brewpub in South Beach, Miami.

Miami Brewing Company (p147) In Homestead, this brewery makes a fine detour before heading into the Everglades.

Florida Keys Brewing Co (p172) Much-loved local brewery in Islamorada.

Craft Cocktails

Unique cocktails created by professional mixologists are all the drinking rage. You can find some incredible concoctions, too – as well as poorly mixed drinks that cost a rich man's price tag.

Funnily enough, Miami's obsession with mixology represents a bit of a cocktail renaissance down here. Cuban bartenders became celebrities in the 1920s for what they did with all that sugarcane and citrus: the two classics are the Cuba libre (rum, lime and cola) and the mojito, traditionally served with *chicharrónes* (deep-fried pork rinds).

Miami is known for its celebrity nightlife scene, but one of the first famous drinkers here was down in Key West. Old Ernest Hemingway, it was said, favored piña coladas, and lots of them. In the same neighborhood, Jimmy Buffett memorialized the margarita – so that now every sweaty beach bar along the peninsula claims to make the 'best.'

Plan Your Trip
Family Travel

Aside from frolicking on palm-fringed beaches, South Florida offers countless attractions for young travelers. Boardwalks that wind past prehistoric creatures, dolphin-spotting boat rides and eye-opening museums are just a few ways to spend a sun-drenched afternoon. There are also loads of family-friendly hotels and restaurants, plus plenty of green space for unscheduled free time.

Children Will Love...

Beaches, Pools & Waterparks

South Pointe Park, South Beach, Miami (p63) Ice-cream stands, soft grass, a beach and mini waterpark.

Mid-Beach Boardwalk, North Beach, Miami (p64) A vast stretch of family-friendly beach, backed by boardwalk.

Venetian Pool, Coral Gables, Miami (p82) A breathtaking pool that makes for an unforgettable day's outing.

Bahia Honda State Park, Lower Keys (p176) Spend the day playing in the water off the prettiest beach in the Keys.

Bill Baggs Cape Florida State Park, Key Biscayne (p77) A quick escape from Miami into tropical beauty, with a lighthouse and an attractive sweep of beach.

Fort Zachary Taylor State Park, Key West (p183) A small but enticing beach, plus snorkeling and a 19th-century fort to explore.

Boat Trips

John Pennekamp Coral Reef State Park, Key Largo (p166) Colorful coral reefs you can visit by snorkel or glass-bottom boat tour.

Biscayne National Park Institute, Biscayne National Park (p149) Offers a range of boat cruises, paddling trips and snorkeling tours in a spectacular setting.

Keeping Costs Down

Accommodation

Reserve well ahead to find the best deals, especially in high season (December through March). There are some excellent camping options in the area, including in North Miami Beach and Key Biscayne, as well as in the Everglades and the Keys (reserve many months ahead).

Transport

If you're sticking to Miami Beach, you'll save money (in exorbitant parking fees) by getting around on foot, by bus (where small children travel free) and taxi or car share. If you're hiring a car, bring your own car seat rather than hiring one if you can.

Eating Out

Most midrange Florida restaurants have a dedicated kids' menu. Cheap ethnic eateries – a delicious, ubiquitous constant in the South Florida dining scene – are also good at accommodating children.

Activities

Nature walks, picnics and beach outings are great ways to spend a day without breaking the bank. The Everglades National Park also offers excellent free activities (guided walks, night outings, canoeing), and many state parks also have free hands-on activities for kids.

Everglades Adventures, Everglades City (p144) Take a kayaking or canoeing tour amid the wildlife-filled mangroves (good for kids age seven and up).

Smallwood Store Boat Tour, Chokoloskee (p146) Look for dolphins on an action-filled boat tour amid the 10,000 Islands.

Jolly Rover, Key West (p185) Board a pirate ship (80ft schooner) for a scenic sunset sail past the island's iconic sites.

Animal Encounters

Royal Palm Visitor Center, Everglades (p141) Spy alligators, turtles and long-legged birds on a boardwalk trail over some of the most beautiful wetland landscapes.

National Key Deer Refuge, Big Pine Key (p177) Kids love spotting these endangered cute-as-Bambi mini deer.

Laura Quinn Wild Bird Sanctuary, Tavernier (p166) Injured birdlife is sheltered along several windy paths at this refuge.

Turtle Hospital, Marathon (p174) Turtles get tender loving care from a staff of dedicated volunteers. Visitors welcome (and appreciated).

Robbie's Marina, Islamorada (p171) A sort of 'working' harbor and aquatic petting zoo.

Robert Is Here, Everglades (p147) This favorite farmers market has a petting zoo and fresh juice.

Interactive Museums

Miami Children's Museum, Miami (p71) Extensive role-playing environments where kids can learn while having a blast.

Patricia and Phillip Frost Museum of Science, Miami (p69) A new museum with lots of fun and stimulating exhibits.

Florida Keys Eco-Discovery Center, Key West (p183) Fantastic and entertaining displays pull together Florida Keys ecology.

Crane Point Hammock, Marathon (p173) Excellent introduction to the ecology of the Keys with intriguing exhibits, nature trails and a small bird sanctuary.

Miccosukee Indian Village, Everglades (p140) On Tamiami Trail, this Native American village is something of an open-air museum with culture shows and alligator wrestling.

Region by Region
Miami

Miami has loads of attractions for young travelers. You'll find lovely beaches, grassy parks, nature trails, megamalls, zoos and other animal-centric attractions. Plus, there's plenty of great snacks, from Italian-style gelato to Venezuelan *arepas* (corn cakes). There are also loads of family-friendly hotels and restaurants to keep your young ones happy on holiday. Good places to add to the top of your list for the family trip include the magnificent Fairchild Tropical Garden (p75) and the Oleta River State Park (p64) with its waterfront access and canoe rental.

Miami is also within easy reach of Key Biscayne (p76), with its enormous, central park devoted to kids and surrounded by child-friendly nature trails and public beaches.

The Everglades

What child isn't deeply impressed and/or utterly terrified by the sight of an 8ft-long alligator gliding silently through murky waters? There's other wildlife-watching opportunities too, from spying manatees (and perhaps the endangered American crocodile) at Flamingo Marina (p140), to seeing dolphins leap in the spray on a boat ride (p135) through the 10,000 Islands, and watching herons on the hunt along the Anhinga Trail (p134).

In addition to the natural wonders of the Everglades, kids (and grown-ups) can discover Native American culture. Ah-Tah-Thi-Ki Seminole Indian Museum (p140) shows how Seminoles thrived in the Everglades, while Miccosukee Indian Village (p140) features performances, crafts and guided tours of traditional homes. And there are plenty of other surprises, like the strange Coral Castle (p145).

Florida Keys & Key West

Active families with older kids will adore the snorkeling, diving, fishing, boating and all-around no-worries vibe found throughout the Keys (especially in Key West). The world's third-largest coral reef lies just off the Keys, and you can go snorkeling or take a glass-bottom boat tour from John Pennekamp Coral Reef State

Park (p166; there's also a visitor center with aquarium, a beach area and kayak rental).

The Keys have only a few small beaches, despite being islands. However, Bahia Honda State Park (p176) is safe, reasonably nature-focused while still fun in a beachy way, and has a small, kid-oriented science center. Sombrero Beach (p174) on Marathon is another obligatory beach stop.

Good to Know

Look out for the 👪 icon for family-friendly suggestions throughout this guide.

Accommodations Motels and hotels typically have two double beds, which are ideal for families. Some also have roll-away beds or cribs that can be brought into the room for an extra charge. Note that some B&Bs don't allow children.

Dining Out Many restaurants have high chairs and booster seats, crayons for coloring and changing tables in restrooms. Go right at opening time (usually 5pm for dinner) to avoid the crowds.

Playgrounds You can find playgrounds in Miami Beach (particularly along the waterfront) and around the Keys. They're less common in the Everglades.

Car Travel Children under age three must be in a car seat, and children under five in a booster seat. Every car-rental agency should be able to provide an appropriate seat (with charges around $13 or more per day). Order it in advance.

Changing Facilities Many public toilets have a baby-changing table (sometimes in men's toilets, too).

Stuff for Babies Supermarkets and pharmacies sell baby formula, diapers and other essentials.

Useful Resources

Lonely Planet Kids (www.lonelyplanetkids.com) Loads of activities and great family travel blog content.

Miami & Beaches (www.miamiandbeaches.com) Extensive info on many family-friendly attractions in Miami and beyond.

Florida State Parks (www.floridastateparks.org) Great site to explore the many opportunities to enjoy nature in South Florida.

Everglades National Park (www.nps.gov/ever) A handy resource for trip planning in Florida's 1.5 million-acre national park.

Kids' Corner

Did You Know? ℹ️

- Miami is one of the only US cities founded by a woman (Julia Tuttle).

- The six-toed cats that roam the Hemingway House and grounds are descended from the writer's own cats.

Say What?

Slang for 'kid'	*Jit*
Slang for chillin' out	*Vibin*
Cleaning yourself in a pool rather than a shower	Florida bath
Flip flops	*chancleta* or *chanclas*

Have You Tried?

Arepa
A corncake stuffed with meat, cheese or other goodies.

Regions at a Glance

Miami

Food
Nightlife
Architecture

Edible Exploration

Be it delectable Haitian *griot* (fried pork) or Peruvian-Japanese fusion, the shabbiest Central American shack or Italian *osterias* prepping truffles and pasta, this city has a taste for both low-key ethnic eateries and high-end, four-star dining rooms.

Party People

With a large Latin population, warm tropical evenings and money to burn, Miami doesn't like to stay at home. Bump shoulders with students in Coconut Grove or dance to EDM and trip-hop in the clubs that adjoin Wynwood and Downtown.

Deco Decor

In North Beach, the Miami Modern movement is felt in the shadows of enormous condos. In South Beach, art deco rules the day. Take a few hours to wander the Art Deco Historic District, one of the most distinctive pockets of architectural preservation in the USA.

p53

The Everglades

Wildlife
Quirkiness
Outdoor Adventures

Gator-Gawking

Wildlife-viewing is good in the Glades any time of year, but if you visit in the winter dry season you'll see a *Jurassic Park*–style landscape of prehistoric reptiles, plus an avian rainbow of wading birds.

Only in Florida

From a blue-crab shack across from the USA's smallest post office, to a giant Coral Castle next to a sanctuary housing hyenas and tigers, the Everglades attracts America's eccentrics.

Early-Morning Kayaking

There is something magical about paddling a kayak or canoe over sheets of sunrise-dappled water, be it a slow marsh trickle or the wide teal expanses of Florida Bay. This is how mornings were made to be spent.

p129

Florida Keys & Key West

Scenery
Arts
Food

Mangroves & Hammocks

The Keys are an ecological anomaly in the USA – a series of mangrove islands that conceal hammocks or groves of palm, pine and tropical hardwoods found nowhere else in the country.

Authors & Artists

Thanks mainly to its historical toleration of the gay community, the Keys (especially Key West) have long been an artist colony. Authors, from Hemingway to Judy Blume, have also been attracted to the island and its piratical, creative cast.

Fish & Mango Salsa

Folks here are mad for fishing and the natural culinary accompaniment to said hobby. Find it topped by tropical garnishes; follow it with the famous Key lime pie.

p159

On the
Road

The Everglades
p129

Miami
p53

Florida Keys &
Key West
p159

AT A GLANCE

POPULATION
470,000

NATIVE SPANISH SPEAKERS
60%

BEST FOOD MARKET
1 800 Lucky (p104)

BEST RECORD STORE
Sweat Records (p123)

BEST CUBAN COCKTAILS
Cafe La Trova (p121)

WHEN TO GO

Dec–Mar
Warm, dry weather and festivals draw in tourists; Miami's liveliest season.

Apr–Jun
Not as muggy as summer, but lusher and greener than winter.

Jul–Oct
Prices plummet. When it's not as hot as an oven, there are storms: it's hurricane season.

Futura 2000 Entrance Mural, The Wynwood Walls (p71)
DENNIZN/SHUTTERSTOCK ©

Miami

Miami is the ultimate synthesis of the United States, the Caribbean and Latin America, a place possessed of brash ambition, endless hustle and a ceaseless appreciation for beauty, good food, fun times and more beauty. This is a city of bewildering diversity, as measured by both citizens and neighborhoods. You can admire graffiti murals in Wynwood, sip a sugarcane and guava milkshake in Little Havana, rub shoulders with art mavens at a contemporary exhibition Downtown, then cross the bridge to the models and deco playgrounds of Miami Beach.

Nature lies just beyond the city fringes, encompassing verdant botanical gardens (Coral Gables), peaceful mangroves for kayaking (Virginia Key) and a vast estuarine park (Oleta River State Park). Miami will wear you out, but that's the price for exploring a city relentlessly dedicated to squeezing the juice out of life (and while we're at it, another sugarcane and guava smoothie, *por favor*).

INCLUDES

Miami Highlights

1 Art Deco Historic District (p58) Seeing South Beach's art-deco beauties at their most alluring.

2 Pérez Art Museum Miami (p64) Checking out the latest show and wandering the waterfront sculpture garden.

3 Wynwood Walls (p71) Being bowled over by the stunning murals at the epicenter of Wynwood.

4 South Beach (p58) Sitting on the sands with glamor-seekers from around the world.

5 Vizcaya Museum & Gardens (p74) Marveling at the eclectic collection of art and antiquities.

ATLANTIC OCEAN

Haulover Beach Park
Collins Ave
Golden Beach
Aventura
Oleta River State Park
Indian Creek
Ancient Spanish Monastery
NORTH MIAMI BEACH
Biscayne Blvd
Arch Creek Park
Southern Memorial Park
Museum of Contemporary Art North Miami
Intracoastal Waterway
See North Beach Map (p92)
Collins Ave
Dade Blvd
Alton Rd
Julia Tuttle Cswy

Ives Dairy Rd
NE 163rd St
NE 6th Ave
Griffing Blvd
NW 2nd Ave
N Miami Ave
NW 7th Ave
W Dixie Hwy
909

Little Haiti & the Upper East Side Map (p106)
UPPER EAST SIDE
Little Haiti Cultural Complex 7
See Wynwood & the Design District Map (p96)
WYNWOOD

441
OPA-LOCKA
NW 119th St
NW 27th Ave
Little River Canal
NW 79th St
NW 62nd St
NW 54th St
NW 36th St
LIBERTY CITY
MIAMI
9
821
NW 37th Ave
CAROL CITY
Palmetto Expwy
N Le Jeune Rd
E 4th Ave
W 4th Ave
924
Gratigny Pkwy
NW 57th Ave
HIALEAH
826
75
Palmetto Expwy
112

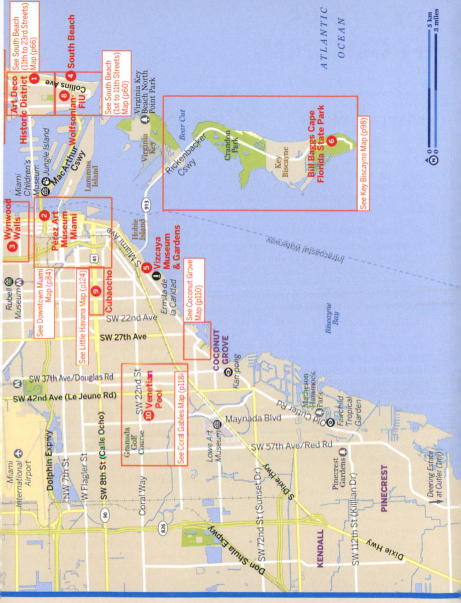

ATLANTIC OCEAN

See South Beach (11th to 23rd Streets) Map (p66)

Art Deco Historic District ①

See South Beach (1st to 11th Streets) Map (p60)

④ South Beach

⑧ **FIU**

Collins Ave

Virginia Key Beach North Point Park

MacArthur Cswy

Bear Cut

Miami Children's Museum

Jungle Island

Lummus Island

Virginia Key

Rickenbacker Cswy

Crandon Park

Key Biscayne

Bill Baggs Cape Florida State Park ⑥

See Key Biscayne Map (p98)

Wynwood Walls ②

③ Little Haiti

② Pérez Art Museum Miami

See Downtown Miami Map (p84)

Rubell Museum

See Little Havana Map (p124)

⑨ **Cubaocho**

41

N Miami Ave

Hobie Island

Vizcaya Museum & Gardens ⑤

① **Cubaocho**

Intracoastal Waterway

Ermita de la Caridad

See Coconut Grove Map (p110)

SW 22nd Ave

SW 27th Ave

COCONUT GROVE

Biscayne Bay

Kampong

Matheson Hammock Park

SW 37th Ave/Douglas Rd

SW 42nd Ave (Le Jeune Rd)

SW 22nd St

⑩ **Venetian Pool**

Old Cutler Rd

Maynada Blvd

Fairchild Tropical Garden

Granada Golf Course

See Coral Gables Map (p118)

Lowe Art Museum

SW 57th Ave/Red Rd

Miami International Airport

Dolphin Expwy

NW 7th St

W Flagler St

SW 8th St (Calle Ocho)

Coral Way

SW 72nd St (Sunset Dr)

Pinecrest Gardens

SW 112th St (Killian Dr)

PINECREST

S Dixie Hwy

Deering Estate at Cutler (4mi)

90

826

Don Shula Expwy

Dixie Hwy

KENDALL

5 km
3 miles

N

DAY TRIPS FROM MIAMI

FORT LAUDERDALE

Miami's northerly neighbor is upscale and elegant, but it can also be as show off-y as the yachts that frequently dock at her canals. It's an attractive place inhabited by fairly attractive people, with a noticeable LGBTQI+ scene and a very Floridian commitment to enjoying the heck out of life.

☆ Best Things to See/Do/Eat

◉ Riverwalk The easiest way to soak up a good chunk of what Fort Lauderdale has to offer is a stroll along this pathway, which takes in much of the city's Latin-meets-Anglo opulence, Mediterranean-esque architecture, and some nice waterfront views besides.)

✈ Las Olas Gondola They call this city the American Venice, so let's just lean into the cliché, alright? There are more than 300 miles of canals here; get poled out among them on an actual Venetian gondola, complete with Italian music, and check out the homes of the rich and even more rich.

✘ Lester's Diner Fort Lauderdale can be overwhelmingly fancy. Offset the posh with a visit to this greasiest of spoon diners. Have some pancakes, hash browns, eggs, and wash it down with coffee and a good taste of pure Americana.)

☆ How to Get There

Car I-95 and Florida's Turnpike can both get you to Fort Lauderdale, which is about 30 miles north of Downtown Miami.

Tri-Rail This commuter train runs between Miami Airport and Fort Lauderdale (one way $5, 45 minutes), among other locations. A feeder system of buses has connections at no charge. Free parking is provided at most stations. Provide ample cushion for delays. Amtrak also uses Tri-Rail tracks.

THE KEYS

It's a bit far to day-trip all the way out to Key West, which sits at the (imagine that) western end of this offshore archipelago. But a jaunt to the Upper Keys is quite doable, and will give you a good taste of the odd allure of Florida's own island chain.

☆ Best Things to See/Do/Eat

◉ Anne's Beach Contrary to popular perceptions, there aren't a ton of beaches in the Keys. But Anne's, on the island of Islamorada (Eye-luh-moe-raw-duh), is a very fine stretch of blue green water and squidgy tidal flats. (p170)

◉ John Pennekamp Coral Reef State Park Explore the first underwater park in the USA, which includes some 75 sq miles of watery environs. The snorkeling here (which can be arranged with the park) is some of the best in the Lower 48 states. (p166)

✘ Lazy Days Rock up and order some fresh bread, the catch of the day and a bowl of delicious conch chowder at this wonderful Islamorada restaurant, which captures the tropical laid-back elegance of fine Keys dining. (p80)

☆ How to Get There

Car The Keys are connected to the mainland by US Rte 1, known in these parts as the Overseas Hwy. It's a beautiful 90-mile drive from Miami to Islamorada over multiple causeways and bridges. Beware of weekend traffic, which can cause bumper-to-bumper gridlock.

THE EVERGLADES

One of the most unique ecosystems in North America sits mere miles from Miami: the 'River of Grass,' a flooded prairie and forest that contains within its green depths a collage of prehistoric wildlife and vistas of vast, gentle, tide-lapped beauty.

☆ Best Things to See/Do/Eat

◉ **Anhinga Trail** One of the most accessible trails in the Everglades is happily also one of the best, a series of walkways and boardwalks where you can almost always catch sight of a wild alligator, plus scores of wetland birds. (p134)

🐟 **Garls Coastal Kayaking** Head to this outfitter in Homestead to get set up with paddling excursions and 'hikes' that are like wet-wading into the heart of the watery Glades – very fun and highly recommended! (p133)

✗ **Robert Is Here** Part fruit stand, part farmers market, part petting zoo, all enjoyable, Robert's is an old Florida institution that happens to sell some of the best orange juice on the planet. (p147)

☆ How to Get There

Car It's a roughly 50- to 60-mile drive from Miami to the entrance to the eastern edge of Everglades National Park, but keep in mind the park spans 1.5 million acres. You need your own set of wheels to properly explore it.

Miami sits at the center of South Florida's weird and wonderful buffet of attractions, which happens to include alligator swamps, mangrove-fringed offshore islands and the USA's own version of Venice.

◉ Sights

◉ South Beach

South Beach (SoBe) is everything Miami is known for – the sparkling beach, beautiful art-deco architecture, top-end boutiques, and buzzing bars and restaurants. Still, there's more to this district than velvet ropes and high-priced lodging (though there's a lot of this too). You'll find some great down-to-earth bars, good eating and cool museums, all set against a backdrop of relentlessly attractive pastel deco architecture.

★ Wolfsonian-FIU   MUSEUM
(Map p60; ☑ 305-531-1001; www.wolfsonian.org; 1001 Washington Ave; adult/child $12/8, 6-9pm Fri free; ☺ 10am-6pm Mon, Tue, Thu & Sat, to 9pm Fri, noon-6pm Sun) Visit this excellent design museum early in your stay to put the aesthetics of Miami Beach into context. It's one thing to see how wealth, leisure and the pursuit of beauty manifest, but it's another to understand the roots and shadings of local artistic movements. By chronicling the interior evolution of everyday life, the Wolfsonian reveals how these trends manifested architecturally in SoBe's exterior deco.

Take a look at the Wolfsonian's own noteworthy architectural features with its Gothic-futurist angles and lion-head-studded grand elevator.

Art Deco Historic District   AREA
(Map p66; Ocean Dr) The world-famous art deco district of Miami Beach is pure exuberance: an architecture of bold lines, whimsical tropical motifs and a color palette that evokes all the beauty of the Miami landscape. Among the 800 deco buildings listed on the National Register of Historic Buildings, each design is different and strolling among these restored beauties from a bygone era is utterly enthralling. Classic art-deco structures are positioned beautifully between 11th and 14th Sts – each bursting with individuality.

Close to 11th St, the Congress Hotel (p63) shows perfect symmetry in its three-story facade. About a block north, the **Tides** is one of the finest of the nautical-themed hotels, with porthole windows over the entryway, a reception desk of Key limestone (itself imprinted with fossilized sea creatures) and curious arrows on the floor, meant to denote the ebb and flow of the tide. Near 13th St, the **Cavalier** (Map p66; ☑ 305-673-1199; www.cavalier

southbeach.com; 1320 Ocean Dr; r $145-255, ste $285; P ❋ ☎) plays with the seahorse theme, in stylized depictions of the sea creature, and also has palm-tree-like iconography.

Note that it's best to go early in the day when the crowds are thinnest and the light is best for picture-taking. For deeper insight into the architecture, take a guided walking tour of the area offered daily by the Miami Design Preservation League (p83).

SoundScape Park   PARK
(Map p66; www.nws.edu; 500 17th St) Outside of the New World Center, this park is one of the best places for open-air screenings in Miami Beach. During some New World Symphony performances, the outside wall of the Frank Gehry–designed concert hall features a 7000-sq-ft projection of the concert within. Bring a picnic and enjoy the free WALLCAST show. In addition, there are free once-monthly yoga sessions on the lawns. Check the website for dates.

Art Deco Museum   MUSEUM
(Map p60; ☑ 305-672-2014; www.mdpl.org; 1001 Ocean Dr; ☺ 10am-5pm Tue-Sun) **FREE** This small museum is one of the best places in town for an enlightening overview of the art-deco district. Through videos, photography, models and other displays, you'll learn about the pioneering work of Barbara Baer Capitman, who helped save these buildings from certain destruction back in the 1970s, and her collaboration with Leonard Horowitz, the talented artist who designed the pastel color palette that became an integral part of the design visible today.

The museum also touches on other key architectural styles in Miami, including Mediterranean Revival (typefied by the **Villa Casa Casuarina** (Map p66; ☑ 786-485-2200; www.vmmiamibeach.com; 1116 Ocean Dr; r $700-1400; P ❋ ☎ ✉)) and the post-deco boom of MiMo (Miami Modern), which emerged after WWII, and is particularly prevalent in North Miami Beach. The guided art-deco tour is $30 per person and takes around two hours (10:30am daily, plus 6:30pm Thursday) touching on art deco, MiMo and Mediterranean Revival movements.

South Beach   BEACH
(Map p66; Ocean Dr; ☺ 5am-midnight) When most people think of Miami Beach, they envision South Beach, a label that applies to both the beach itself and the neighborhood that adjoins it. The latter includes clubs, bars, restaurants and a distinctive veneer

of art-deco architecture. The beach is a sweep of golden sands, dotted with colorful deco-style lifeguard stations and countless souls uploading panorama shots to their social media platforms. The shore gets crowded in high season (December to March) and most weekends.

You can escape the masses by avoiding the densest parts of the beach (5th to 15th Sts) – heading south of 5th street, to the area known as SoFi, is a good means of eluding the crowds. Keep in mind that there's no alcohol (or pets) allowed on the sand.

New World Center
NOTABLE BUILDING

(Map p66; ☑ 305-680-5866, tours 305-428-6776; www.nws.edu/new-world-center; 500 17th St; tours $5; ⊙ tours 4pm Tue & Thu, 1pm Fri, 3pm Sat) Designed by Frank Gehry, this performance hall rises majestically out of a manicured lawn just above Lincoln Rd. Not unlike the ethereal power of the music within, the glass-and-steel facade encases characteristically Gehry-esque sail-like shapes that help create the magnificent acoustics and add to the futuristic quality of the concert hall. The grounds form a 2.5-acre public park aptly known as SoundScape Park.

Some performances inside the center are projected outside via a 7000-sq-ft projection wall (the so-called WALLCAST), which might make you feel like you're in the classiest (and free!) open-air theater on the planet. Reserve ahead for a 45-minute guided tour.

Holocaust Memorial
MEMORIAL

(Map p66; www.holocaustmmb.org; cnr Meridian Ave & Dade Blvd; ⊙ 9:30am-10pm) Even for a Holocaust piece, this memorial is particularly powerful. With more than 100 sculptures, its centerpiece is the *Sculpture of Love and Anguish*, an enormous, oxidized bronze arm that bears an Auschwitz tattoo number – chosen because it was never issued at the camp. Terrified camp prisoners scale the sides of the arm, trying to pass their loved ones, including children, to safety only to see them later massacred, while below lie figures of all ages in various poses of suffering.

Around the perimeter of the memorial are dozens of panels, which detail the grim history that led to the greatest genocide of the 20th century. This is followed by names of many who perished. The memorial doesn't gloss over the past. The light from a Star of David is blotted by the racist label of *Jude* (the German word for 'Jew') representative of the yellow star that Jews in ghettos were forced to wear. Two menorah sculptures, flanking the Dome of Contemplation descent to the center, show the transformation from life to death in a rather lurid fashion. It's impossible to spend time here and not be moved.

The memorial was completed in 1990 through the efforts of Miami Beach Holocaust survivors, local business leaders and sculptor Kenneth Treister. Download the excellent free app (Holocaust Memorial Miami Beach) for iPhone or Android to learn more about the sculpture as well as hear testimonials from survivors, peruse slideshows, view interactive maps and additional audio and video.

The Bass
MUSEUM

(Map p66; ☑ 305-673-7530; www.thebass.org; 2100 Collins Ave; adult/child $15/8; ⊙ 10am-5pm Wed-Sun) The best art museum in Miami Beach has a playfully futuristic facade, a crisp interplay of lines and a bright, white-walled space – like an Orthodox church on a space-age Greek isle. All designed, by the way, in 1930 by Russell Pancoast (grandson of John A Collins, who lent his name to Collins Ave). The collection isn't shabby either: there is a focus on cutting-edge contemporary art, although some temporary exhibitions showcase older work. The museum forms one point of the Collins Park Cultural Center triangle, which also includes the three-story Miami City Ballet (p120) and the lovingly inviting Miami Beach Regional Library, which is a great place for free wi-fi.

Jewish Museum of Florida-FIU
MUSEUM

(Map p60; ☑ 305-672-5044; www.jmof.fiu.edu; 301 Washington Ave; adult/student & senior $12/8, Sat free; ⊙ 10am-5pm Tue-Sun, closed Mon & Jewish holidays) Housed in a 1936 Orthodox synagogue that served Miami's first congregation, this small museum chronicles the large contribution Jews have made to the state of Florida. After all, it could be said that while Cubans made Miami, Jews made Miami Beach, both physically and culturally. Yet there were times when Jews were barred from the American Riviera they carved out of the sand, and this museum tells that story, along with some amusing anecdotes (like seashell Purim dresses).

There are also walking tours of the area that take in famous local Jewish landmarks and businesses, as well as foodie tours of local Jewish restaurants (three-hour tour including food $48; two-hour tour without food $20).

MIAMI SIGHTS

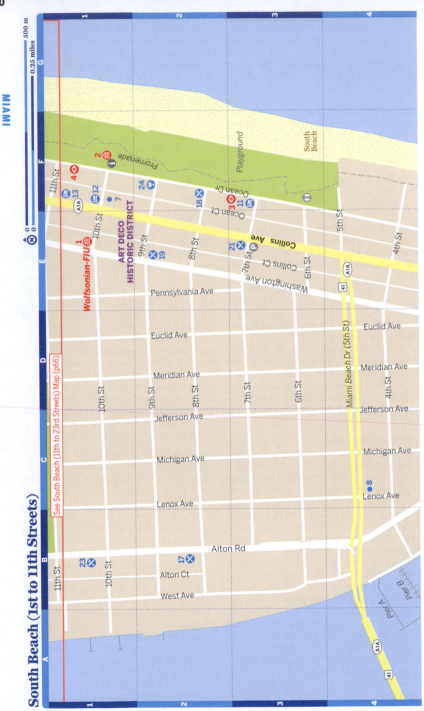

MIAMI

South Beach (1st to 11th Streets)

ART DECO
HISTORIC DISTRICT

Wolfsonian-FIU

See South Beach (11th to 23rd Streets) Map (p66)

South Beach

Promenade

Playground

Ocean Dr

Ocean Ct

Collins Ave

Collins Ct

Washington Ave

Miami Beach Dr (5th St)

Pennsylvania Ave

Euclid Ave

Euclid Ave

Meridian Ave

Meridian Ave

Jefferson Ave

Jefferson Ave

Michigan Ave

Michigan Ave

Lenox Ave

Lenox Ave

Alton Rd

Alton Ct

West Ave

Pier A

Pier B

11th St

10th St

9th St

8th St

7th St

6th St

5th St

4th St

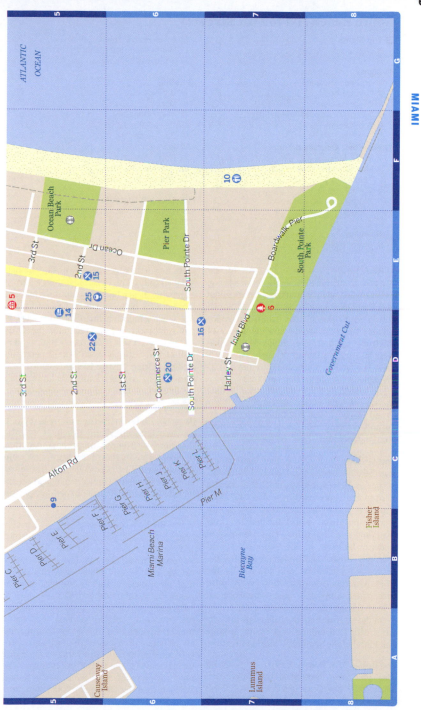

ATLANTIC OCEAN

Ocean Beach Park

3rd St

2nd St

Ocean Dr

Pier Park

South Pointe Dr

5

25

14

22

20

16

South Pointe Dr

Commerce St

1st St

2nd St

3rd St

Alton Rd

9

Pier C

Pier D

Pier E

Pier F

Pier G

Pier H

Pier J

Pier K

Pier L

Pier M

Miami Beach Marina

Causeway Island

Lummus Island

Biscayne Bay

Harley St

Inlet Blvd

Boardwalk Pier

South Pointe Park

10

Government Cut

Fisher Island

South Beach (1st to 11th Streets)

Oolite Arts   GALLERY

(Map p66; ☎305-674-8278; https://oolitearts.org;
924 Lincoln Rd, 2nd fl; ⊗noon-6pm Mon-Fri, 1-6pm
Sat & Sun) Once known as ArtCenter/South
Florida South Beach, this exhibition space
includes some 52 artists' studios, many of
which are open to the public. Oolite also
offers an exciting lineup of classes and lectures. The facility is scheduled to move to 75
NW 72nd St (in Little Haiti) in 2022.

The residences are reserved for artists
who do not have major exposure, so this is
a good place to spot up-and-coming talent.
Monthly rotating exhibitions keep the pres-
entation fresh and pretty avant-garde.

Post Office   ARCHITECTURE

(Map p66; ☎305-672-2447; 1300 Washington Ave;
⊗8am-5pm Mon-Fri, 8:30am-2pm Sat) Make it a
point to mail a postcard from this 1937 deco
gem of a post office, the very first South
Beach renovation project tackled by preservationists in the 1970s. This Depression
moderne building in the 'stripped classic'
style was constructed under President Roosevelt's administration and funded by the
Works Progress Administration (WPA) initi-
ative, which supported artists who were out
of work during the Great Depression.

On the exterior note the bald eagle and the
turret with iron railings and, inside, a large
wall mural of the Seminole's Florida invasion.

The Betsy Orb/Poetry Rail   PUBLIC ART

(Map p66; www.thebetsyhotel.com/explore/arts-
culture; 14th Pl btwn Ocean Dr & Collins Ave; ⊗24hr)
FREE Two excellent examples of public art

grace Española Way where it runs by the Betsy Hotel (p89). The Orb is just that: a sort of
giant white beach ball-ish sculpture squashed
into an alley between Ocean Dr and Collins
Ave. Once a month a video and/or photography exhibition is projected onto the Orb's
surface. Steps away is the Poetry Rail, a metal
wall etched with the words of 13 poets, including Adrian Castro, Richard Blanco, and
Gerald Stern, paying tribute to Miami's multicultural population and unique geography.

Colony Hotel   ARCHITECTURE

(Map p60; 736 Ocean Dr) The Colony is the oldest deco hotel in Miami Beach. It was the
first hotel in Miami, and perhaps America,
to incorporate its sign (a zigzaggy neon wonder) as part of its overall design. Inside the
lobby are excellent examples of space-age interiors, including Saturn-shaped lamps and
Flash Gordon elevators.

World Erotic Art Museum   MUSEUM

(Map p66; ☎305-532-9336; www.weam.com;
1205 Washington Ave; over 18yr $15; ⊗11am-10pm
Mon-Thu, to midnight Fri-Sun) The World Erotic
Art Museum has a frankly staggering collection of erotica, including sexually charged
pieces by Rembrandt and Picasso, ancient
sex manuals, Victorian peep-show photos,
the oversized sculpted genitals used as a
murder weapon in *A Clockwork Orange*, and
an elaborate four-poster (four-phallus rather) Kama Sutra bed, with carvings depicting
various ways (138 in fact) to get intimate. The
museum dates back to 2005, when Naomi
Wilzig turned her 5000-piece collection into a
South Beach mainstay.

South Pointe Park · PARK

(Map p60; ☎305-673-7779; 1 Washington Ave; ☺sunrise-10pm; 🚻🚼) The very southern tip of Miami Beach has been converted into a lovely park, replete with manicured grass for lounging and warm, scrubbed-stone walkways, as well as a tiny water park for the kids. There's also a restaurant and refreshment stand for all the folks who want to enjoy the great weather and teal ocean views minus the South Beach strutting.

Promenade · WATERFRONT

(Map p66; Ocean Dr) This beach promenade, a wavy ribbon sandwiched between the beach and Ocean Dr, extends from 5th St to 15th St. A popular location for photo shoots, especially during crowd-free early mornings, it's also a breezy, palm-tree-lined conduit for inline skaters, cyclists, volleyball players (there's a net at 11th St), dog walkers, yahoos, locals and tourists.

The beach that it edges, called Lummus Park, sports six floridly colored lifeguard stands.

1111 Lincoln Rd · ARCHITECTURE

(Map p66; www.1111lincolnroad.com; Ⓟ) The west side of Lincoln Rd is anchored by a most impressive parking garage: a geometric pastiche of sharp angles, winding corridors and incongruous corners that looks like a lucid fantasy dreamed up by Pythagoras after a long night out.

In fact, the building was designed by Swiss architecture firm Herzog & de Meuron, who describe the structure as 'all muscle without cloth.' Besides parking, 1111 Lincoln Rd is filled with retail shops and residential units.

A1A · BRIDGE

The A1A causeway, coupled with the Rickenbacker Causeway in Key Biscayne, is one of the great bridges in America, linking Miami and Miami Beach via the glittering turquoise of Biscayne Bay.

To drive this road in a convertible or with the windows down, with a setting sun behind you, enormous cruise ships to the side, the palms swaying in the ocean breeze, and a synthwave playlist blasting, is like starring in your own music video.

Miami Beach Community Church · CHURCH

(Map p66; ☎305-538-4511; www.miamibeach communitychurch.com; 1620 Drexel Ave; ☺service 10:30am Sun) In rather sharp and refreshing contrast to all the uber-modern structures muscling their way into the art-deco design

of South Beach, this community church puts one in mind of an old Spanish mission – humble, modest and elegantly understated in an area where overstatement is the general philosophy.

Fourteen stained-glass windows line the relatively simple interior, while the exterior is built to resemble coral stone in a Spanish Revival style. The congregation is LGBTQI+-friendly and welcomes outside visitors.

Temple Emanu-El · SYNAGOGUE

(Map p66; www.tesobe.org; Washington Ave at 17th St) An art-deco temple? Not exactly, but the smooth, bubbly dome and sleek, almost aerodynamic profile of this Conservative synagogue, established in 1938, fits right in on SoBe's deco parade of moderne this and streamline that. Shabbat services are on Friday at 7pm and on Saturday at 10am.

Cardozo Hotel · ARCHITECTURE

(Map p66; 1300 Ocean Dr; Ⓟ) The Cardozo and its neighbor, the **Carlyle** (Map p66; 1250 Ocean Dr), were the first deco hotels saved by the Miami Design Preservation League (p83), and in the case of the Cardozo, we think it saved the best first. Its beautiful lines and curves evoke a classic automobile from the 1930s.

Congress Hotel · ARCHITECTURE

(Map p60; 1052 Ocean Dr) Close to 11th St, the Congress Hotel is an art-deco classic, with a perfectly symmetrical three-story facade. It has window-shading eyebrows and a long marquee down the middle that's reminiscent of the grand movie palaces of the 1930s.

Miami Beach Botanical Garden · GARDENS

(Map p66; ☎305-673-7256; www.mbgarden.org; 2000 Convention Center Dr; suggested donation $2; ☺9am-5pm Tue-Sun) FREE This lush but little-known 2.6 acres of plantings is operated by the Miami Beach Garden Conservancy, and is a veritable green haven in the midst of the urban jungle – an oasis of palm trees, flowering hibiscus trees and glassy ponds. It's a great spot for a picnic. While touring the garden, you can dial 305-423-1525 for a free self-guided tour.

⊙ North Beach

Aside from the beach, many of the sights in North Beach require some effort to access. You'll need a car for a day's exploring here.

Faena Forum
CULTURAL CENTER

(Map p92; 305-534-8800; www.faena.com; Collins Ave & 33rd St) This cultural center has been turning heads since its opening in late 2016. The circular Rem Koolhaas–designed building features rooms for performances, exhibitions, lectures and other events. Check the website to see what's coming up.

Oleta River State Park
STATE PARK

(305-919-1844; www.floridastateparks.org/oleta river; 3400 NE 163rd St; vehicle/pedestrian & bicycle $6/2; 8am-sunset; P) Tequesta people were boating the Oleta River estuary as early as 500 BCE, so you're following a long tradition if you canoe or kayak in this park. At almost 1000 acres, this is the largest urban park in the state and one of the best places in Miami to escape the madding crowd. Boat out to the local mangrove island, watch the eagles fly by, or just chill on the pretension-free beach.

On-site ROAM Oleta River Outdoor Center (p82) rents out kayaks, canoes, stand-up paddleboards and mountain bikes. It also offers paddling tours, yoga classes on stand-up paddleboards and other activities. The park is off 163rd St NE/FL 826 in Sunny Isles, about 8 miles north of North Miami Beach.

Fontainebleau
HISTORIC BUILDING

(Map p92; www.fontainebleau.com; 4441 Collins Ave) As you proceed north on Collins, the condos and apartment buildings grow in grandeur and embellishment until you enter an area nicknamed Millionaire's Row. The most fantastic jewel in this glittering crown is the Fontainebleau hotel (p93). The hotel – mainly the pool, which has since been renovated – features in Brian de Palma's classic *Scarface.*

This iconic 1954 leviathan is a brainchild of the great Miami Beach architect Morris Lapidus and has undergone many renovations; in some ways, it is utterly different from its original form, but it retains that early glamour.

Boardwalk
BEACH

(Map p92; www.miamibeachboardwalk.com; 21st -46th Sts) Posing is what many people do best in Miami, and there are plenty of skimpily dressed hotties on the Mid-Beach boardwalk, but there are also middle-class Latinos and Orthodox Jews, who walk their dogs and play with their kids here, giving the entire place a laid-back, real-world vibe that contrasts with the nonstop glamour of South Beach.

Haulover Beach Park
PARK

(305-947-3525; www.miamidade.gov/parks/ haulover.asp; 10800 Collins Ave; per car Mon-Fri $5, Sat & Sun $7; sunrise-sunset; P) Swimsuits are optional in at least part of this 40-acre beach park hidden behind vegetation from the sight of condos, highways and prying passersby. You don't have to get into your birthday suit if you don't fancy it – in fact, most of the beach is clothed and there's even a **dog park**. It is one of the nicer spots for sand in the area and is located about 4.5 miles north of 71st St on Collins Ave..

Downtown Miami

Downtown Miami, the city's international financial and banking center, is split between tatty indoor shopping arcades, and new condos and high-rise luxury hotels in the area known as Brickell – said high-rises stretch all the way down Brickell Ave. At night, the towers are illuminated in hot pinks and cool blues, and the entire effect is unmistakably magical.

Even though construction is a near constant in this area, there are still pockets of small-scale, creative, authentic spaces, and the city's best museum.

★Pérez Art Museum Miami
MUSEUM

(PAMM; Map p84; 305-375-3000; www.pamm. org; 1103 Biscayne Blvd; adult/senior & student $16/12, 1st Thu & 2nd Sat of month free; 10am-6pm Fri-Tue, to 9pm Thu; P) One of Miami's most impressive spaces, designed by Swiss architects Herzog & de Meuron, this museum integrates tropical foliage, glass, concrete and wood – a melding of tropical vitality and fresh modernism that fits perfectly in Miami. PAMM stages some of the best contemporary exhibitions in the city, with established artists and impressive newcomers.

The permanent collection rotates through unique pieces every few months – drawing from a treasure trove of work spanning the past 80 years. Don't miss it. The temporary shows and retrospectives bring major crowds. The outdoor space has hanging gardens that took an entire two months to install.

If you need a little breather amid all this contemporary culture, PAMM has a first-rate cafe, or you can simply hang out in the grassy park or lounge on a deck chair enjoying the views over the water.

This art institution inaugurated Museum Park, a patch of land that oversees the broad blue swath of Biscayne Bay.

City Walk
Art-Deco Miami Beach

START ART DECO MUSEUM
END 960 OCEAN DR
LENGTH 1.2 MILES; 2-3 HOURS

Start at the ❶ **Art Deco Museum** (p58), at the corner of Ocean Dr and 10th St (named Barbara Capitman Way here, after the Miami Design Preservation League's founder). Step in for an exhibit on art-deco style, then head out and north along Ocean Dr. Between 12th and 14th Sts you'll see three examples of deco hotels: the ❷ **Leslie**, a boxy shape with eyebrows (cantilevered sunshades) wrapped around the side of the building; the ❸ **Carlyle** (p63), featured in the film *The Birdcage* and boasting modernistic styling; and the graceful ❹ **Cardozo Hotel** (p63), built by Henry Hohauser, owned by Gloria Estefan and featuring sleek, rounded edges.

At 14th St take a peek inside the sun-drenched ❺ **Winter Haven Hotel** (p234) to see its fabulous terrazzo floors, made of stone chips set in mortar that's polished when dry. Turn left and down 14th St to Washington Ave and the ❻ **US Post Office** (p62), at 13th St. It's a curvy block of white deco in the stripped classical style. Step inside to admire the wall mural, domed ceiling and marble stamp tables. Lunch at the ❼ **11th Street Diner** (p100), a gleaming aluminum Pullman car that was imported in 1992 from Wilkes-Barre, PA. Get a window seat and gaze across the avenue to the corner of 10th St and the stunningly restored ❽ **Hotel Astor**, designed in 1936 by T Hunter Henderson.

After your meal, walk half a block east from the Astor to the imposing ❾ **Wolfsonian-FIU** (p58), an excellent design museum, formerly the Washington Storage Company. Wealthy snowbirds of the '30s stashed their pricey belongings here before heading back up north. Continue walking on Washington Ave, turn left on 8th St and then continue north along Collins Ave to the ❿ **Hotel of South Beach**, featuring an interior and roof deck by Todd Oldham. L Murray Dixon designed the hotel as the Tiffany Hotel, with a deco spire, in 1939. Go two blocks to Ocean Dr, where you'll spy nonstop deco beauties; at b 960 Ocean Dr you'll see an exterior designed in 1935 by deco legend Henry Hohauser.

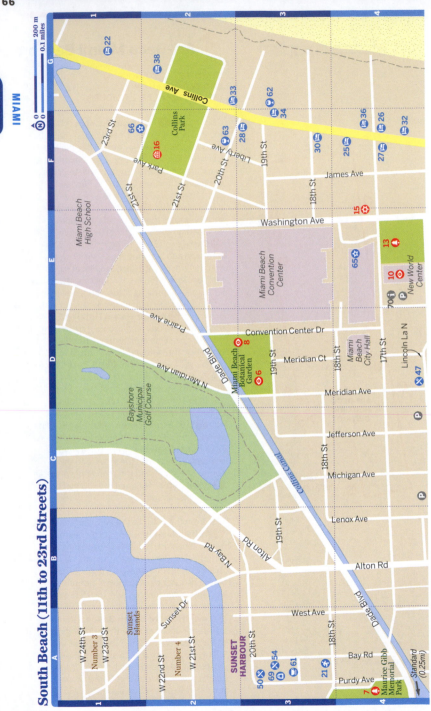

South Beach (11th to 23rd Streets)

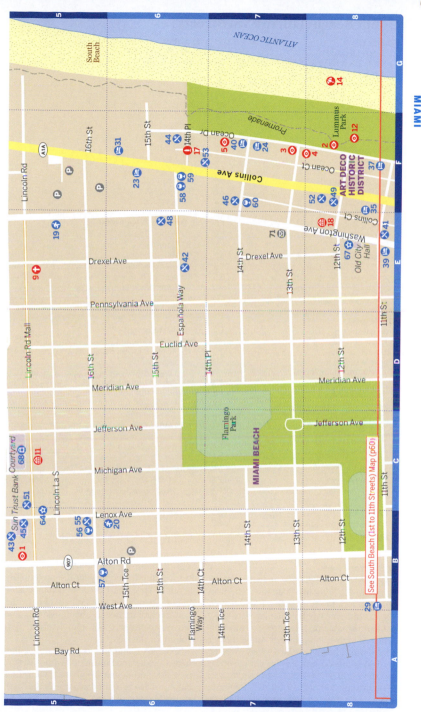

South Beach (11th to 23rd Streets)

★ **Bayfront Park**   PARK
(Map p84; ☏ 305-358-7550; www.bayfrontpark
miami.com; 301 N Biscayne Blvd) Few American
parks can claim to front such a lovely stretch
of sea as Biscayne Bay, but Miamians are lucky
like that. Notable park features are two performance venues: the Klipsch Amphitheater
(p120), which boasts excellent views over the
bay and is a good spot for live-music shows,
and the smaller 200-seat (lawn seating can
accommodate 800 more) **Tina Hills Pavilion**,
which hosts free springtime performances.

Look north for the **JFK Torch of Friend-ship**,
and a fountain recognizing the accomplish-
ments of longtime US congressman Claude
Pepper. There are a huge variety of activities
here, including flying trapeze classes and
free yoga classes (p82), plus a great playground for the kids.

Noted artist and landscape architect Isamu
Noguchi redesigned much of Bayfront Park in
the 1980s and dotted the grounds with three
sculptures. In the southwest corner is the **Chal-
lenger Memorial**, a monument designed for

the astronauts killed in the 1986 space-shuttle explosion, built to resemble both the twisting helix of a human DNA chain and the shuttle itself. The **Light Tower** is a 40ft, somewhat abstract allusion to Japanese lanterns and moonlight over Miami. Our favorite is the **Slide Mantra**, a twisting spiral of marble that doubles as a playground piece for the kids.

HistoryMiami
MUSEUM

(Map p84; ☎ 305-375-1492; www.historymiami. org; 101 W Flagler St; adult/child 6-12yr $10/5; ☺ 10am-5pm Tue-Sat, from noon Sun; ⊛) South Florida – a land of escaped slaves, guerrilla Native Americans, gangsters, land grabbers, pirates, tourists, drug dealers and alligators – has a special history, and it takes a special kind of museum to capture that narrative. This highly recommended place, located in the **Miami-Dade Cultural Center**, does just that, weaving together the stories of the region's successive waves of population, from Native Americans to Nicaraguans.

The collection is spread between two buildings. Start off in the permanent collection, which has interactive exhibits showing life among the Seminoles, early Florida industries such as sponge diving, and wealth made from 'wreckers' (those who salvaged treasure lost on the reefs). More recent-era exhibits touch on the history of Jewish and African American communities in South Beach, Cuban refugees and cultural expression in public spaces (highlighting traditions such as street art, parades, protests, vehicle customizing and religious practices). Get off the Metromover at the Government Center stop.

Patricia & Phillip Frost Museum of Science
MUSEUM

(Map p84; ☎ 305-434-9600; www.frostscience. org; 1101 Biscayne Blvd; adult/child $25/22; ☺ 9:30am-6pm; ⓟ⊛) This sprawling new Downtown museum spreads across 250,000 sq ft that includes a three-level aquarium, a 250-seat state-of-the-art planetarium, and two distinct wings that delve into the wonders of science and nature. Exhibitions range from weather phenomena to creepy-crawlies, feathered dinosaurs and vital microbe displays, while Florida's fascinating Everglades and biologically rich coral reefs play starring roles.

Miami Riverwalk
WATERFRONT

(Map p84) This pedestrian walkway follows along the northern edge of the river as it bisects Downtown, and offers some peaceful vantage points of bridges and skyscrapers dotting the urban landscape. You can start the walk at the south end of Bayfront Park, and follow it under bridges and along the waterline till it ends just west of the SW 2nd Ave Bridge. The Riverwalk is one small section of the ambitious Miami River Greenway project, which aims to extend a green path along both banks of the river all the way to the river's intersection with the Dolphin Expwy.

Brickell City Centre
AREA

(Map p84; ☎ 786-475-5536; www.brickellcity centre.com; 701 S Miami Ave; ☺ 10am-9:30pm Mon-Sat, noon-7pm Sun) One of Miami's favorite shopping centers, this massive billion-dollar complex spreads across three city blocks, encompassing glittering residential towers, modernist office blocks and a soaring five-star hotel (the EAST, Miami; p94). There's much to entice both Miami residents and visitors to the center, with restaurants, bars, a cinema and loads of high-end retailers (Ted Baker, All Saints, Kendra Scott). You'll find shops scattered across both sides of S Miami Ave between 7th and 8th Sts, including a massive Saks Fifth Ave. There is a three-story Italian food emporium, with restaurants, cafes, a bakery, an enoteca and a culinary school.

MiamiCentral
NOTABLE BUILDING

(Virgin MiamiCentral; Map p84; https://virgin miamicentral.com; NW 1st Ave btwn NW 3rd St & NW 8th St; ⬚ Government Center) **FREE** This train station has been converted into a 9-acre mixed-use complex that houses a food hall, shopping arcades, plus office and residential space. Architecturally, it's like the space age has landed in South Florida, an unmissable jumble of odd angles, enormous windows and twisted steel, designed by Skidmore, Owings & Merrill, the firm responsible for Dubai's Burj Khalifa. The station will be the Miami home of Brightline trains.

KEEPING IT KOSHER IN MIAMI BEACH

They are no shtetls, but Arthur Godfrey Rd (41st St) and Harding Ave between 91st and 96th Sts in Surfside are popular thoroughfares for the Jewish population of Miami Beach. Just as Jewish people have shaped Miami Beach, so has the beach shaped them: you can eat lox *y arroz con moros* (salmon with rice and beans) and while the Orthodox men don yarmulkes and the women wear headscarves, many have nice tans and drive flashy SUVs.

Freedom Tower
HISTORIC BUILDING

(Map p84; 600 Biscayne Blvd; ⊘10am-5pm) An iconic slice of Miami's old skyline, the richly ornamented Freedom Tower is one of two surviving towers modeled after the Giralda bell tower in Spain's Cathedral of Seville. As the 'Ellis Island of the South,' it served as an immigration processing center for almost half a million Cuban refugees in the 1960s. Placed on the National Register of Historic Places in 1979, it was also home to the *Miami Daily News* for 32 years.

In the beautifully restored lobby, above the elevators and stretching toward the coffered ceiling, you can see reliefs of men at work on the printing presses. The tower also houses the MDC Museum of Art & Design.

Black Archives
Historic Lyric Theater
HISTORIC BUILDING

(Map p84; ☑786-708-4610; www.bahlt.org; 819 NW 2nd Ave; ⊘archives 9:30am-4:30pm Tue-Fri) Duke Ellington and Ella Fitzgerald once walked across the stage of the Lyric, a major stop on the 'Chitlin' Circuit – the black live-entertainment trail of pre-integration USA. As years passed both the theater and the neighborhood it served, Overtown, fell into disuse. Then the **Black Archives History & Research Foundation of South Florida** took over the building. Today the theater hosts occasional shows, while the Archives hosts exhibitions exploring African American heritage, both in Miami and beyond.

Brickell Avenue
Bridge & Brickell Key
ISLAND

(Map p84) Crossing the Miami River, the lovely Brickell Avenue Bridge, between SE 4th St and SE 5th St, was made wider and higher several years ago, which was convenient for the speedboat-driving drug runners being chased by Drug Enforcement Administration agents on the day of the bridge's grand reopening! Note the 17ft bronze statue by Cuban-born sculptor Manuel Carbonell of a Tequesta warrior and his family, which sits atop the towering Pillar of History column. Walking here is the best way to get a sense of the sculptures and will allow you to avoid one of the most confusing traffic patterns in Miami. Brickell Key looks more like a floating porcupine, with glass towers for quills, than an island. To live the life of Miami glitterati, come here, pretend you belong, and head into a patrician hangout like the Mandarin Oriental Miami (p94) hotel, where the lobby and intimate lounges afford sweeping views of Biscayne Bay.

MDC Museum of Art & Design
MUSEUM

(Freedom Tower; Map p84; ☑305-237-7700; www.mdcmoad.org; 600 Biscayne Blvd; adult/student $12/5; ⊘1-6pm Wed & Fri-Sun, to 8pm Thu) Miami-Dade College operates a small but well-curated art museum in Downtown; the permanent collection includes works by Matisse, Picasso and Chagall, and focuses on minimalism, pop art and contemporary Latin American art. The museum's home building is art itself: it's set in the soaring 255ft (78m) Freedom Tower, a masterpiece of Mediterranean Revival, built in 1925.

Miami City Cemetery
CEMETERY

(Map p96; 1800 NE 2nd Ave; ⊘7am-3:30pm Mon-Fri, 8am-4:30pm Sat & Sun) This quiet graveyard, the final resting place of some of Miami-Dade's most important citizens, is a sort of narrative of the history of the city cast in bone, dirt and stone. The dichotomy of the past and modernity gets a nice visual representation in the form of looming condos shadowing the last abode of the Magic City's late, great ones. More than 9000 graves are divided into separate white, black and Jewish sections. Buried here are mayors, veterans (including about 90 Confederate soldiers) and the godmother of South Florida, Julia Tuttle, who purchased the first orange groves that attracted settlers to the area.

Miami Center for
Architecture & Design
MUSEUM

(Old US Post Office; Map p84; ☑305-448-7488; www.miamicad.org; 310 SE 1st St; ⊘10am-5pm Mon-Fri) **FREE** The Miami branch of the American Institute of Architects shares a building with the Downtown Miami Welcome Center. MCAD houses lectures and events related to architecture, design and urban planning, and hosts temporary exhibitions on all of the above subjects. Two-hour walking tours on alternate Saturdays depart from here (at 10am), and take in some of the historic buildings of Downtown. Visit the website for upcoming times and reservations.

Miami River
RIVER

(Map p84) For a taste of old Florida, take a stroll along the Miami River. A shoreline promenade (p69) leads past a mix of glittering high-rise condos and battered warehouses tinged with graffiti, with a few small tugboats pulling along the glassy surface. Fisherfolk float in with their daily catch – en route to places such as Casablanca (p103) – while fancy yachts make their way in and out of the bay.

There are some photogenic vantage points over the river from the bridges – particularly the Brickell Ave bridge at dusk, when the city lights glow against the darkening night sky.

Miami Children's Museum   MUSEUM
(☎305-373-5437; www.miamichildrensmuseum. org; 980 MacArthur Causeway; $22; ☺10am-6pm; P♿) This museum, located between South Beach and Downtown Miami, is a bit like an uber-playhouse, with areas for kids to practice all sorts of adult activities – banking and food shopping, caring for pets, and acting as a local cop or firefighter. Adults must go accompanied by children, and vice versa.

Other imaginative areas let kids make music, go on undersea adventures, make wall sketches, explore little castles made of colored glass, or simply play on outdoor playgrounds.

Jungle Island   ZOO
(☎305-400-7000; www.jungleisland.com; 1111 Parrot Jungle Trail, off MacArthur Causeway; adult/ child $40/25; ☺10am-5pm; P♿) Jungle Island, packed with tropical birds, alligators, orangutans, chimps, lemurs and a Noah's Ark of other animals, is a ton of fun. It's one of those places kids (justifiably) beg to go, so just give up and prepare for some bright-feathered, bird-poop-scented fun in this artificial, self-contained jungle. Also on offer: rope bridges among the trees ($35), a flight-generating wind tunnel ($60), an escape room ($60) and Adventure Bay, an area with rock-climbing walls and kid-friendly bungee jumping ($60).

Miami-Dade Public Library   LIBRARY
(Map p84; ☎305-375-2665; www.mdpls.org; 101 W Flagler St; ☺9:30am-6pm Mon-Sat) To learn more about Florida (especially South Florida), take a browse through the extensive Florida Collection, or ask about the Romer Photograph Collection, an archive of some 17,500 photos and prints that chronicles the history of the city from its early years to 1945.

◉ Wynwood & the Design District

Wynwood is Miami's hippest neighborhood, and it knows it. This is an adult playground of graffiti, murals, restaurants, bars, shops and galleries. Whatever is cool and on trend in the world is emulated, if not started, on these streets, in the shadow of some excellent public art. The Design District is a high-end shopping area, where the line between neighborhood and mall is tough to draw.

★ Wynwood Walls   PUBLIC ART
(Map p96; www.thewynwoodwalls.com; NW 2nd Ave btwn 25th & 26th Sts) **FREE** One of the most photographed locations in Miami (if social media hashtags are anything to go by), Wynwood Walls is a collection of murals and paintings laid out over an open courtyard that invariably bowls people over with its sheer exuberant colors and commanding presence. What's on offer tends to change with the coming and going of major arts events, such as Art Basel (p26), but it's always interesting stuff.

★ Margulies Collection at the Warehouse   GALLERY
(Map p96; ☎305-576-1051; www.margulies warehouse.com; 591 NW 27th St; adult/student $10/5; ☺11am-4pm Tue-Sat mid-Oct–Apr) Encompassing 45,000 sq ft, this vast not-for-profit exhibition space houses one of the best art collections in Wynwood – Martin Margulies' awe-inspiring 4000-piece collection includes sculptures by Isamu Noguchi, George Segal, Richard Serra and Olafur Eliasson, among many others, plus sound installations by Susan Philipsz and jaw-dropping room-sized works by Anselm Kiefer. Thought-provoking, large-format installations are the focus at the Warehouse, and you'll see works by some leading 21st-century artists here.

Bakehouse Art Complex   GALLERY
(BAC; Map p96; ☎305-576-2828; www.bacfl.org; 561 NW 32nd St; ☺noon-5pm; P) **FREE** One of the pivotal art destinations in Wynwood, the Bakehouse has been an arts incubator since well before the creation of the Wynwood Walls. Today this former bakery houses galleries and some 60 studios, and the range of works is quite impressive. Check the schedule for upcoming artist talks and other events.

De La Cruz Collection   GALLERY
(Map p96; ☎305-576-6112; www.delacruz collection.org; 23 NE 41st St; ☺10am-4pm Tue-Sat) **FREE** Housing one of Miami's finest private collections, this 30,000-sq-ft gallery has a treasure trove of contemporary works scattered across three floors, which you can roam freely. Rosa and Carlos de la Cruz, who originally hail from Cuba, have particularly strong holdings in postwar German paintings, as well as fascinating works by Jim Hodges, Ana Mendieta and Felix González-Torres. You have to ring the bell to gain admittance.

WYNWOOD & THE DESIGN DISTRICT

Hangouts The Wynwood Marketplace (p72) embodies the spirit of this diverse 'hood, with food trucks, a bar (front and center), outdoor dining at picnic tables, and a changing lineup of music.

Beer lore Boxelder (p116) is the go-to spot for brew lovers, and showcases local beers in a friendly, unpretentious setting.

Art revelry On the second Saturday of the month, Wynwood and the Design District hold an Art Walk (p87), where galleries host special exhibitions, plus there's live music, a craft market and more.

Wynwood Marketplace   MARKET

(Map p96; ☎305-461-2700; www.wynwood-marketplace.com; 2250 NW 2nd Ave; ☺1pm-2am Fri & Sat, noon-9pm Sun) An enormous open-air marketplace takes over several blocks of Wynwood real estate on weekend evenings, and plays hosts to artisan shops, food trucks, a performance stage, live music, art exhibitions, etc. The Marketplace is more or less a weekly carnival, and given Miami's consistently good weather, it's a pleasant one to stroll. While booze is sold, the vibe is family friendly.

Museum of Graffiti   MUSEUM

(Map p96; ☎786-580-4678; https://museumof graffiti.com; 299 NW 25th St; adult/child $16/free; ☺11am-7pm Wed-Mon; ♿) The Museum of Graffiti gives visitors a quick dive into the history of this particular art form, which is so obviously and brilliantly in evidence on the urban blocks of surrounding Wynwood. It's a bit small, but passionate: there are kids' art classes on Sundays (11am, free with parent admission), photos from graffiti's earliest days, temporary exhibitions from graffiti masters, and beginners' graffiti workshops ($100, 2pm Saturday). The gift shop alone is a must for anyone who likes graffiti or pop art.

Palm Court   COURTYARD

(Map p96; 140 NE 39th St) At the epicenter of the Design District is this lavish courtyard, which opened just before Art Basel back in 2014. It's set with tall palm trees, reflecting mirrors along the sides, two floors of high-end retailers and one eye-catching sculpture, namely the Fly's Eye Dome.

Fly's Eye Dome   SCULPTURE

(Map p96; 140 NE 39th St, Palm Court) Installed during Art Basel (p26) in 2014, Buckminster Fuller's striking geodesic dome looks otherworldly as it appears to float in a small reflecting pool surrounded by slender, gently swaying palm trees. The 24ft-tall sculpture was dubbed an 'autonomous dwelling machine' by Fuller when he conceived it back in 1965.

There are some fantastic vantage points for photographers both inside and outside the dome – which also serves as the covered entry/exit point connecting the below-ground parking lot with the plaza.

Locust Projects   GALLERY

(Map p96; ☎305-576-8570; www.locust projects.org; 3852 N Miami Ave; ☺11am-5pm Tue-Sat) FREE Locust Projects has become a major name for emerging artists in the contemporary art scene. Run by artists as a nonprofit collective since 1998, LP has exhibited work by more than 250 local, national and international artists over the years. The gallery often hosts site-specific installations by artists willing to take a few more risks than those in more commercial venues.

Bacardi Building   ARCHITECTURE

(National YoungArts Foundation Headquarters; Map p96; ☎800-970-2787; www.youngarts.org/ national-headquarters; 2100 Biscayne Blvd; ☺tours 10am 2nd & 4th Tue of month, gallery 9am-5pm Mon-Fri) FREE The former Miami headquarters of Bacardi is a masterpiece of tropical architecture, and holds a spot on the National Register of Historic Places. The main event is a beautifully decorated jewel-box-like building built in 1973 that seems to hover over the ground from a central pillar supporting the entire structure. The building currently serves as the headquarters of the nonprofit YoungArts, which offers one-hour tours of the complex and also manages an on-site art gallery. Register for tours online.

One-inch-thick pieces of hammered glass cover the exterior in a wild Mesoamerican-style pattern modeled after a mosaic designed by German artist Johannes M Dietz. Also on-site is the older 1963 building, a tower covered with blue-and-white handmade tiles – some 28,000 in fact – in a striking ceramic pattern designed by Brazilian artist Francisco Brennand.

◉ Little Haiti & the Upper East Side

These two neighborhoods are at the northern edge of mainland Miami gentrification with restaurants, hotels and galleries increasingly setting up shop every year. Little Haiti is the largest Haitian community in North America, and while it feels as Caribbean as the rest of Miami, it is also undeniably distinct: the Kreyol language dominates, as do Haitian businesses and community institutions. Further east, the Upper East Side is best known for its striking modernist buildings lining Biscayne Blvd.

Little Haiti Cultural Complex   GALLERY

(Map p106; ☑ 305-960-2969; www.littlehaiticultural center.com; 212 NE 59th Tce; ◷ 10am-9pm Mon-Fri, 10am-4pm Sat) **FREE** This cultural center hosts an art gallery with often thought-provoking exhibitions from Haitian painters, sculptors and multimedia artists. You can also find dance classes, drama productions and a Caribbean-themed market during special events. The building itself is quite a confection of bold tropical colors, steep A-framed roofs and lacy decorative elements. Don't miss the mural in the palm-filled courtyard.

Miami Ironside   ARTS CENTER

(Map p106; ☑ 305-438-9002; www.miami ironside.com; 7610 NE 4th Ct; 🖐🎨) 🅿 Ironside is a pleasant hub of creativity in Miami in an otherwise industrial corner of the city. Here you'll find art and design studios, showrooms and galleries, as well as a few eating and drinking spaces. It's a lushly landscaped property, with some intriguing public art.

Opening hours vary between the on-site businesses; see the website for more details.

Morningside Park   PARK

(Map p106; 750 NE 55 Tce) On the waterfront, this aptly named park is a great spot to be in the morning, when the golden light is just right for getting a bit of fresh air. There's lots going on in the park, with walking paths, basketball courts, tennis courts, sports fields, a playground for kids and a swimming pool (admission $3).

If you come on Saturday, you can rent kayaks (from $12 per hour) and stand-up paddleboards (from $20 per hour).

PanAmerican Art Projects   GALLERY

(PAAP; Map p106; ☑ 305-751-2550; www.pan americanart.com; 274 NE 67th St; ◷ 10am-5pm Tue-Fri, from 11am Sat) Despite the name, PanAmerican also showcases work from the occasional European artist. But much of what is on display comes from artists representing Latin America, the Caribbean and the USA.

Formerly located in Wynwood, PAAP made the move up to Little Haiti in 2016 – a growing trend as gallerists get priced out of the neighborhood they helped popularize.

◉ Little Havana

The Cuba-ness of Little Havana is slightly exaggerated for visitors, though it's still an atmospheric area to explore, with the crack of dominoes, the scent of wafting cigars and the sound of salsa spilling into the street. Keep an eye out for murals; older art often references the Cuban revolution, while newer pieces contain contemporary references to hip-hop and the Miami Heat.

Little Havana's main thoroughfare, Calle Ocho (SW 8th St), is the heart of the neighborhood. In many ways, this is every immigrant enclave in the USA – full of restaurants, mom-and-pop convenience shops and phone-card kiosks, except here you get intermittent tourists posing and taking selfies.

★ Máximo Gómez Park   PARK

(Map p124; cnr SW 8th St & SW 15th Ave; ◷ 9am-6pm) Little Havana's most evocative reminder of Cuba is Máximo Gómez Park ('Domino Park'), where the sound of elderly men trash-talking over games of dominoes is harmonized with the quick clack-clack of slapping tiles – though the tourists taking photos all the while does take away from the experience. The heavy cigar smell and a sunrise-bright mural of the 1994 Summit of the Americas add to the atmosphere.

Cuban Memorial Boulevard Park   MONUMENT

(Map p124; SW 13th Ave btwn 8th & 11th Sts) Stretching along SW 13th Ave just south of Calle Ocho (SW 8th St), Cuban Memorial Boulevard Park contains a series of monuments to Cuban and Cuban American icons. The memorials include the **Eternal Torch in Honor of the 2506th Brigade**, for the exiles who died during the Bay of Pigs Invasion; a **José Martí memorial**; and a **Madonna statue**, supposedly illuminated by a shaft of holy light every afternoon.

There's also a map of Cuba, with a quote by José Martí. At the center of the map is a massive ceiba tree, still revered by followers of Santería (a syncretic religion that evolved in Cuba among African slaves in the 18th century).

MIAMI SIGHTS

LOCAL KNOWLEDGE

LITTLE HAVANA

Cuban style Pick up a new outfit at the Havana Collection (p124). *Guayaberas* are the unofficial dress shirts of the neighborhood and you'll fit right in.

Friday fun On the third Friday of the month, Little Havana lets her hair down in a spirited night of live music and special art exhibitions during Viernes Culturales (p88).

Supermarket dining Hidden in the grocery store of the same name, El Nuevo Siglo (p108) is a well-loved local haunt known for its delicious and reasonably priced cooking.

Bay of Pigs Museum & Library   LIBRARY
(Map p124; ☑305-649-4719; http://bayofpigs 2506.com; 1821 SW 9th St; ⊙9am-4pm Mon-Fri) This small museum is more of a memorial to the 2506th Brigade, otherwise known as the crew of the ill-fated Bay of Pigs invasion. Whatever your thoughts on the late Fidel Castro and Cuban Americans, pay a visit here to flesh out one side of this contentious story. You may meet a few survivors of the Bay of Pigs, who like to hang out here surrounded by pictures of comrades who never made it back to the USA.

At the time of research, the museum's collection was slated to move to a new building way out in Hialeah Gardens, so call before visiting to check where things are at.

◉ Coconut Grove

Coconut Grove was once a hippie colony, but these days its demographic is upper-middle-class, mall-going Miamians and college students. It's a pleasant place to explore, with intriguing shops and cafes, and a walkable village-like vibe. It's particularly appealing in the evenings, when residents fill the outdoor tables of its bars and restaurants. Coconut Grove backs onto the waterfront, with a pretty marina and some pleasant green spaces.

★Vizcaya
Museum & Gardens   HISTORIC BUILDING
(☑305-250-9133; www.vizcaya.org; 3251 S Miami Ave; adult/child/6-12yr/student & senior $22/ 10/15; ⊙9:30am-4:30pm Thu-Mon; 🅿) If you want to see something that is 'very Miami,' this is it – lush, big and over the top,

a patchwork of all that a rich US businessman might want to show off to his friends. Which is essentially what industrialist James Deering did in 1916, starting a Miami tradition of making a ton of money and building ridiculously grandiose digs. He employed 1000 people (then 10% of the local population) and stuffed his home with Renaissance furniture, tapestries, paintings and decorative arts.

The mansion is a classic of Miami's Mediterranean Revival stye. The largest room in the house is the informal living room, sometimes dubbed 'the Renaissance Hall' for its works dating from the 14th to the 17th centuries. The music room is intriguing for its beautiful wall canvases, which come from Northern Italy, while the banquet hall evokes all the grandeur of imperial dining rooms of Europe, with its regal furnishings.

On the south side of the house stretch a series of lovely gardens that are just as impressive as the interior of Vizcaya. Modeled on formal Italian gardens of the 17th and 18th centuries, these manicured spaces form a counterpoint to the wild mangroves beyond. Sculptures, fountains and vine-draped surfaces give an antiquarian look to the grounds, and an elevated terrace (the Garden Mound) provides a fine vantage point over the greenery. The on-site Vizcaya Cafe has light snacks and coffee to keep energy levels up while perusing the lavish collections.

Kampong   GARDENS
(☑305-442-7169; https://ntbg.org/gardens/ kampong; 4013 Douglas Rd; adult/child/senior & student $20/5/15; ⊙tours by appointment only 9:30am-3pm Tue-Fri, from 10:15am Sat) David Fairchild, the Indiana Jones of the botanical world and founder of Fairchild Tropical Garden, would rest at the Kampong (Malay/ Indonesian for 'village') in between journeys in search of beautiful and profitable plant life. Today this lush garden is listed on the National Register of Historic Places and the lovely grounds serve as a classroom for the National Tropical Botanical Garden. Self-guided tours (allow at least an hour) are available by appointment, as are $25 one-hour guided tours.

Peacock Park   PARK
(Map p110; 2820 McFarlane Rd) Extending down to the edge of the waterfront, Peacock Park serves as the great open backyard of Coconut Grove. Young families stop by the

playground and join the action on the ball fields, while power-walkers take in the view on a scenic stroll along the bayfront.

Plymouth Congregational Church   CHURCH
(Map p110; ☎305-444-6521; www.plymouth miami.org; 3400 Devon Rd; ☺services 10am Sun; P) This 1917 coral church is striking, from its solid masonry to a hand-carved door from a Pyrenees monastery, which looks like it should be kicked in by Antonio Banderas carrying a guitar case full of explosives and Salma Hayek on his arm. Architecturally this is one of the finest Spanish Mission–style churches in a city that does not lack for examples of the genre.

The church opens rarely, though all are welcome at the organ- and choir-led 10am Sunday service.

Ermita de la Caridad   MONUMENT
(☎305-854-2404; https://ermita.org; 3609 S Miami Ave; ☺7am-5:30pm, mass noon Mon-Sat, 11am & 3pm Sun) The Catholic diocese purchased some of the bayfront land from Deering's Villa Vizcaya estate and built a shrine here for its displaced Cuban parishioners. Symbolizing a beacon, it faces the homeland, exactly 290 miles due south. There is also a mural that depicts Cuban history. Just outside the church is a grassy stretch of waterfront that makes a fine spot for a picnic.

Barnacle Historic State Park   STATE PARK
(Map p110; ☎305-442-6866; www.florida stateparks.org/thebarnacle; 3485 Main Hwy; admission $2, house tours adult/child $3/1; ☺9am-5pm Wed-Mon;) In the center of Coconut Grove village is the residence of pioneer Ralph Munroe, Miami's first honorable snowbird. The house, which was built in 1891, is open for guided tours (every 90 minutes between 10am and 2:30pm), and the 5-acre park it's located in is a shady oasis for strolling. Barnacle hosts frequent (and lovely) moonlight concerts, from jazz to classical.

Eva Munroe's Grave   HISTORIC SITE
(Map p110; 2875 McFarlane Rd) Tucked into a small gated area near the Coconut Grove Library, you'll find the humble headstone of one Ms Eva Amelia Hewitt Munroe, Ralph Munroe's first wife. Eva, who was born in New Jersey in 1856 and died in Miami in 1882, lies in the oldest American grave in Miami-Dade County (a sad addendum: local African American settlers died before Eva, but their deaths were never officially recorded).

◉ Coral Gables

The lovely city of Coral Gables, filled with a pastel rainbow of Mediterranean-style buildings, feels a world removed from the rest of Miami. Here you'll find pretty banyan-lined streets and a walkable village-like center, dotted with shops, cafes and restaurants. The big draws are the striking Biltmore Hotel, a lush tropical garden and one of America's loveliest swimming pools.

★Fairchild Tropical Garden   GARDENS
(☎305-667-1651; www.fairchildgarden.org; 10901 Old Cutler Rd; adult/child/senior $25/12/18; ☺10am-4pm; P) If you need to escape Miami's madness, consider a green day in one of the country's largest tropical botanical gardens. A butterfly grove, tropical plant conservatory and gentle vistas of marsh and keys habitats, plus frequent art installations from artists like Roy Lichtenstein, are all stunning. In addition to easy-to-follow, self-guided walking tours, a free 45-minute tram tour takes in the entire park, departing hourly on the hour from 10am to 3pm (till 4pm weekends).

A favorite among the garden's youngest visitors is the **Wings of the Tropics** exhibition. Inside an indoor gallery, hundreds of butterflies flutter freely through the air, the sheen of their wings glinting in the light. There are some 40 different species represented, including exotics from Central and South America, like blue morphos and owl butterflies. Visitors can also watch in real time as chrysalises emerge as butterflies at **Vollmer Metamorphosis Lab**.

CORAL GABLES

Theater Gables residents have a small but vibrant theater scene, with performances at GableStage (p122) in the Biltmore.

Markets In front of City Hall (p76), the Coral Gables Farmers Market is the spot to load up on seasonal fruits, fresh breads and other goodies. It happens Saturdays from 8am to 2pm mid-January through March.

Hangouts Threefold (p111) is a neighborhood institution, and a great place to start the day.

The lushly lined pathways of the **Tropical Plant Conservatory** and the **Rare Plant House** contain rare philodendrons, orchids, begonias, rare palms, rhododendrons, ferns and moss, while the **Richard H Simons Rainforest**, though small in size, provides a splendid taste of the tropics, with a little stream and waterfalls amid orchids, plus towering trees with lianas (long woody vines) and epiphytes up in the rainforest canopy. There are a couple of on-site cafes serving simple light fare or you can bring your own picnic and eat on the grounds.

Fairchild Tropical Garden lies about 6 miles south of Coral Gables downtown. It's easiest to get here by car or taxi. Another option is to take Metrorail to South Miami, then transfer to bus 57.

★ Biltmore Hotel HISTORIC BUILDING

(Map p118; ☑855-311-6903; www.biltmore hotel.com; 1200 Anastasia Ave; P) In the most opulent neighborhood of one of the showiest cities in the world, the Biltmore still manages to stand out. This was the greatest of the grand hotels of the American Jazz Age and if it were a fictional character from a novel it would be, without question, Jay Gatsby. Al Capone had a speakeasy on-site and the Capone Suite is said to be haunted by the spirit of Fats Walsh, who was murdered here.

Back in the day, imported gondolas transported celebrity guests like Judy Garland and the Vanderbilts around because, of course, there was a private canal system out the back. It's gone now, but the largest hotel pool in the continental USA, which resembles a sultan's water garden from *One Thousand & One Nights,* is still here.

Lowe Art Museum MUSEUM

(☑305-284-3535; www.lowe.miami.edu; 1301 Stanford Dr; adult/student/child $12.50/8/free; ☺10am-4pm Tue-Sat, from noon Sun) The Lowe, located on the campus of the University of Miami, has a solid collection of modern art, a lovely permanent collection of Renaissance and baroque paintings, Western sculpture from the 18th to 20th centuries, and archaeological artifacts, art, and crafts from Asia, Africa, the South Pacific and pre-Columbian America.

Coral Gables City Hall HISTORIC BUILDING

(Map p118; 405 Biltmore Way; ☺8am-5pm Mon-Fri) It's a little funny to think of the often tedious grind of city council business being conducted in this grand building, which opened in 1928 and, architecturally, suggests romance and power, as opposed to parking ordinances. Check out Denman Fink's *Four Seasons* ceiling painting in the tower, as well as his framed, untitled painting of the underwater world on the 2nd-floor landing.

There's a small farmers market on site from 8am to 2pm on Saturdays from mid-January to March.

Granada Entrance LANDMARK

(Map p118; cnr Alhambra Circle & Granada Blvd) Coral Gables–designer George Merrick planned a series of elaborate entry gates to the city. The Granada Entrance is among the completed gates worth seeing.

Coral Gables Congregational Church CHURCH

(Map p118; ☑305-448-7421; www.gablesucc.org; 3010 De Soto Blvd; ☺hours vary) Developer George Merrick's father was a New England Congregational minister, so perhaps that accounts for him donating the land for the city's first church. Built in 1924 as a replica of a church in Costa Rica, the yellow-walled, red-roofed exterior is as far removed from New England as…well, Miami. The interior is graced with a beautiful sanctuary and the grounds are landscaped with stately palms.

It isn't open much, though you can stop in for a look during Sunday services at 9am and 11am.

Matheson Hammock Park PARK

(☑305-665-5475; www.miamidade.gov/parks/ matheson-hammock.asp; 9610 Old Cutler Rd; per car weekday/weekend $5/7; ☺sunrise-sunset; P ♿) This 630-acre county park is the city's oldest, and one of its most scenic. It offers good swimming for children in an enclosed tidal pool, lots of hungry raccoons, dense mangrove swamps and (pretty rare) alligator-spotting. It's just south of Coral Gables.

◉ Key Biscayne

Key Biscayne and neighboring Virginia Key are a quick and easy getaway from Downtown Miami. Once you pass those scenic causeways you'll feel like you've left Miami for a floating suburb with magnificent beaches, lush nature trails in state parks and aquatic adventures aplenty. The stunning skyline views of Miami alone are worth the trip out.

★ Bill Baggs Cape Florida State Park
STATE PARK

(Map p98; ☎786-582-2673; www.floridastate parks.org/capeflorida; 1200 S Crandon Blvd; per car/person $8/2; ⊙8am-sunset, lighthouse 9am-5pm; Ⓟ🅿️♿) 🅿️ If you don't make it to the Florida Keys, come to this park for a taste of their unique island ecosystems. The 494-acre space is a tangled clot of tropical fauna and dark mangroves – look for the 'snorkel' roots that provide air for half-submerged mangrove trees – all interconnected by sandy trails and wooden boardwalks, and surrounded by miles of pale ocean. A concession shack rents out kayaks, bikes, in-line skates, beach chairs and umbrellas.

At the state recreation area's southernmost tip, the 1845 brick **Cape Florida Lighthouse** is the oldest structure in Florida (it replaced another lighthouse that was severely damaged in 1836 during the Second Seminole War). Free tours run at 10am and 1pm Thursday to Monday. If you're not packing a picnic, there are several good places to dine in the park, including Boater's Grill (p112) and **Lighthouse Cafe** (Map p98; ☎305-361-8487; www.lighthousecafekb.com; 1200 Crandon Blvd; mains $12-36; ⊙9am-7pm).

Virginia Key Beach North Point Park
STATE PARK

(off 3861 Rickenbacker Causeway, Virginia Key; per car weekday/weekend $6/8; ⊙8:15am-5pm Nov-Mar, 9:15am-6pm Apr-Oct) This lovely green space has several small but pleasing beaches, and some short nature trails. Pretty waterfront views aside, there are two big reasons to come here. The first is to get out on the water by hiring kayaks or stand-up paddleboards at Virginia Key Outdoor Center (p83). The second is to go mountain biking in a gated-off section known as the Virginia Key North Point Trails (p83), with a series of trails ranging from beginner to advanced.

The mountain bike trails, which are tucked away at the northern tip of the park, are free to use, but you'll need your own bike (and helmet), which you can rent from the nearby Virginia Key Outdoor Center. Coming from Miami, this is the first park entrance (the second leads to the smaller Historic Virginia Key Beach Park).

Historic Virginia Key Park
STATE PARK

(Map p98; www.virginiakeybeachpark.net; 4020 Virginia Beach Dr, Virginia Key; per car weekday/weekend $5/8, bike & pedestrian free; ⊙9am-5pm Mon-Thu, 7am-5pm Fri-Sun; ♿) A short drive (or bike ride) from Downtown Miami, the Historic Virginia Key Park is a fine place for a dose of nature, with a small but pretty beachfront and playgrounds for the kids (as well as a carousel). From time to time there are concerts, ecology-minded family picnics and other events. Coming from Downtown Miami, this is the second park entrance on the left (just past the entrance to the Virginia Key Beach North Point Park).

In the dark days of segregation, this beachfront, initially accessible only by boat, was an official 'colored only' recreation site (African Americans were not allowed on other beaches). Opened in 1945, it remained a major destination for African American communities (as well as Cubans, Haitians and many others from Latin America) seeking to enjoy a bit of the Miami coastline. It was popular until the early 1960s when the city's beaches were finally desegregated.

Marjory Stoneman Douglas Biscayne Nature Center
MUSEUM

(Map p98; ☎305-361-6767; www.biscayne naturecenter.org; 6767 Crandon Blvd, Crandon Park; ⊙10am-4pm; Ⓟ♿) 🅿️ FREE Marjory Stoneman Douglas was a beloved environmental crusader and worthy namesake of this child-friendly nature center. It's a great introduction to South Florida's unique ecosystems, with hands-on exhibits as well as aquariums in the back full of parrot fish, conch, urchins, tulip snails and a fearsome-looking green moray eel. You can also stroll a nature trail through coastal hammock (hardwood forest) or enjoy the pretty beach in front.

Once a month, the center hosts naturalist-led walks ($14 per person) through sea-grass in search of marine life. It's always a big hit with families. Reserve ahead.

Crandon Park
PARK

(Map p98; ☎305-365-2320; www.miamidade. gov/parks/crandon.asp; 6747 Crandon Blvd; per car weekday/weekend $5/7; ⊙sunrise-sunset; Ⓟ♿🅿️) This 1200-acre park boasts **Crandon Park Beach**, a glorious stretch of sand that spreads for 2 miles. Much of the park consists of a dense coastal hammock and mangrove swamps. The beach here is clean and uncluttered by tourists, faces a lovely sweep of teal goodness, and is regularly named one of the best beaches in the USA. Pretty cabanas at the south end of the park can be rented by the day ($40).

◉ Greater Miami

★ Rubell Museum GALLERY

(☎305-573-6090; www.rubellmuseum.org; 1100 NW 23rd St; ☺10:30am-5:30pm Wed-Sun; Ⓟ) The Rubell family's private art collection made Miami synonymous with the contemporary art scene, and their Wynwood museum helped set the stage for that neighborhood's gentrification. The family museum has relocated to Allapattah, where an enormous campus has been converted into one of the largest private contemporary art institutions in North America. The sleek museum consists of some 100,000 sq ft of soaring exhibition space divided into 40 galleries. Artists on display include Kehinde Wiley, Jeff Koons, Cindy Sherman and Cady Noland.

Zoo Miami ZOO

(Metrozoo; ☎305-251-0400; www.zoomiami.org; 12400 SW 152nd St; adult/child $23/19; ☺10am-5pm; Ⓟ★) Miami's tropical weather makes strolling around the Metrozoo almost feel like a day in the wild. Look for Asian and African elephants, rare and regal Bengal tigers prowling an evocative Hindu temple, pygmy hippos, Andean condors, a pack of hyenas, cute koalas, colobus monkeys, black rhinoceroses and a pair of Komodo dragons from Indonesia. For a quick overview (and because the zoo is so big), hop on the Safari Monorail; it departs every 20 minutes.

Deering Estate at Cutler LANDMARK

(☎305-235-1668; www.deeringestate.org; 16701 SW 72nd Ave; adult/child under 14yr $15/7; ☺10am-5pm; Ⓟ★) The Deering estate is sort of 'Vizcaya lite,' which makes sense as it was built by Charles, brother of James Deering (of Vizcaya mansion fame; p72). The 150-acre grounds are awash with tropical growth, an animal-fossil pit of bones dating back 50,000 years and the remains of Native Americans who lived here 2000 years ago. There's a free tour of the grounds at 3pm included in admission, and the estate often hosts jazz evenings under the stars.

Arch Creek Park PARK

(☎305-944-6111; www.miamidade.gov/parks/arch-creek.asp; 1855 NE 135th St; ☺9am-5pm Wed-Sun; Ⓟ★) This compact and cute park, located near Oleta River, encompasses a cozy habitat of tropical hardwood species that surrounds a pretty, natural limestone bridge. Naturalists can lead you on kid-friendly ecotours of the area, which include a lovely butterfly garden, or visitors can peruse a small but well-stocked museum of Native American and pioneer artifacts. The excellent Miami EcoAdventures (p87) is based here. The park is just off North Biscayne Blvd, 7 miles north of the Design District.

Ancient Spanish Monastery CHURCH

(☎305-945-1461; www.spanishmonastery.com; 16711 W Dixie Hwy; adult/child $10/5; ☺10am-4:30pm Mon-Sat, from 11am Sun; Ⓟ) Finding a fully intact medieval monastery in North Miami Beach is yet another reason why the moniker 'Magic City' seems so fitting. Constructed in 1141 in Segovia, Spain, the Monastery of St Bernard de Clairvaux is a striking early-Gothic and Romanesque building that rather improbably found its way to South Florida. The property – today a church that's part of the Episcopal diocese – gets busy for weddings, so call before making the long trip out here. It's roughly 15 miles north of Downtown Miami.

Pinecrest Gardens PARK

(☎305-669-6990; www.pinecrest-fl.gov/gardens; 11000 SW 57th Ave; adult/child/senior $5/5/3; ☺9am-6pm; Ⓟ★) When Parrot Jungle – now Jungle Island (p71) – flew the coop for the big city, the village of Pinecrest purchased the property in order to keep it as a municipal park. It's now a quiet oasis with some of the best tropical gardens this side of the Gulf of Mexico, topped off by a gorgeous centerpiece banyan tree. Outdoor movies and jazz concerts are held here, and all in all this is a total gem that is utterly off the tourism trail.

Monkey Jungle ZOO

(☎305-235-1611; www.monkeyjungle.com; 14805 SW 216th St; adult/child/senior $30/24/28; ☺9:30am-5pm, last entry 4pm; Ⓟ★) Step into the cage while monkeys run around, wild and free! Indeed, you'll be walking through screened-in trails, with primates swinging, screeching and chattering all around you. It's incredibly fun, and just a bit odorous. The big show of the day takes place at feeding time, when crab-eating monkeys and Southeast Asian macaques dive into the pool for fruit and other treats.

Museum of Contemporary Art North Miami MUSEUM

(MOCA; ☎305-893-6211; www.mocanomi.org; 770 NE 125th St; adult/student/child under 12yr $10/3/free; ☺11am-5pm Tue-Fri & Sun, 1-9pm Sat; Ⓟ) The Museum of Contemporary Art has long been a reason to hike up to North Miami – its galleries feature excellent rotating exhibitions of contemporary art by local, national and international artists, usually themed along socially engaged lines of interest. There is a 'pay what you wish' gallery policy during Jazz@MOCA from 7pm to 10pm on the last Friday of every month, when live outdoor jazz concerts are held.

🏃 Activities

Miami doesn't lack for ways to keep yourself busy. From sailing the teal waters to hiking through tropical undergrowth, yoga in the parks and (why not?) trapeze artistry above the city's head, the Magic City rewards those who want an active holiday.

🏃 South Beach

Fritz's Skate, Bike & Surf　　　SKATING
(Map p66; ☑305-532-1954; www.fritzsmiami beach.com; 1620 Washington Ave; bike & skate rental per hour/day/5 days/7 days $10/24/69/89; ⊙11am-9pm) Rent your wheels from Fritz's, which offers skateboards, longboards, in-line skates, roller skates, scooters and bicycles (cruisers, mountain bikes, kids' bikes). Protective gear is included with skate rentals, and bikes come with locks. Be mindful that there's a deposit for each rental – skates $100, longboards $150 and bicycles $200.

Spa at the Setai　　　SPA
(Map p66; ☑855-923-7908; www.thesetaihotels. com; 101 20th St, Setai Hotel; treatments $190-750; ⊙9am-9pm) Pamper yourself with a day in this silky Balinese haven, itself located in one of South Beach's most beautiful hotels (p89). Services include Balinese massages, rose petal and Himalayan salt baths, and full-body kneading.

Green Monkey Yoga　　　YOGA
(Map p66; ☑305-397-8566; www.greenmonkey. net; 1800 Bay Rd; drop-in class/1-week pass $25/89) This yoga studio has a beautiful setting with

huge windows on the top floor of a building in Sunset Harbour. There's a wide range of classes throughout the day, including Vinyasa, power yoga, hip-hop flow and meditation. If you're around for a while ask about the new student special ($69 for one month of unlimited classes).

SoBe Surf　　　SURFING
(☑321-926-6571; www.sobesurf.com; group/private lessons from $70/120) This outfit offers surf lessons both in Miami Beach and in Cocoa Beach, where there tends to be better waves. Instruction on Miami Beach usually happens around South Point. All bookings are done by phone or email.

Glow Hot Yoga　　　YOGA
(Map p66; ☑305-534-2727; www.glowhotyoga miami.com; 1560 Lenox Ave; drop-in class/weekly unlimited rate $27/59) This company offers excellent hot yoga classes in a big, inviting studio that's kept sparkling clean. There's also an outdoor patio where you can unwind after an intense Bikram class. Located just south of Lincoln Rd.

🏃 North Beach

Russian & Turkish Baths　　　MASSAGE
(Map p92; ☑305-867-8315; www.russianand turkishbaths.com; 5445 Collins Ave; treatments from $40; ⊙noon-midnight) This is an excellent spot for getting reasonably priced wellness treatments in a local – very local – environment. Go for a *platza*: a treatment where you're beaten by oak-leaf brooms called *venik* in a lava-hot spa (for $40). The Russians swear by it. There's Dead Sea salt and mud exfoliation ($55), plus the on-site cafe serves delicious borscht, blintzes and dark bread with smoked fish. The crowd is interesting too: hipsters, older Jews, model types, Europeans and tons of Russian expats.

CYCLING IN MIAMI

The Miami-Dade County Parks and Recreation Department maintain a list of traffic-free cycling paths as well as downloadable maps on its website (www.miamidade.gov/parks masterplan/bike-trails-map.asp). For less strenuous rides, try the side roads of South Beach or the shady streets of Coral Gables and Coconut Grove. Some good trails include the **Old Cutler Trail**, which starts at the traffic circle at Ingraham Terrace Park and continues south for 4 miles on to Pinecrest Gardens, passing Fairchild Tropical Garden and Matheson Hammock Park on the way. The **Rickenbacker Causeway** takes you up and over the bridge to Key Biscayne for an excellent workout combined with gorgeous water views (from the mainland to Bill Baggs State Park is about 7 miles). A bit further out, the **Oleta River State Park** has a challenging dirt trail with hills for off-road adventures. Need to rent a trail bike? Try Bike & Roll (p87).

LAZY DAYS IN MIAMI

There are many ways to spend an easygoing day in Miami, from basking on an island beach to taking a meandering stroll through some of the world's best public art.

A DAY AT THE POOL

When the surf is too rough or you need a break from the beach, make your way to one of Miami's lovely swimming pools. Coral Gables' **Venetian Pool** (p82) is an aquatic wonderland, complete with tiny waterfalls and a mini island. You can also spend the day at the **Biltmore Hotel** (p96), with its enormous pool, plus various on-site restaurants.

SHOPPING SOUTH BEACH

The pedestrian-only strip of **Lincoln Road** is a great spot for a relaxing amble. Dotted with palm trees and fountains, the promenade is packed with eye candy of all sorts: colorful stores, outdoor eateries and a wide cross section of Miami society.

ISLAND ESCAPE

Just a short drive from Miami, **Key Biscayne** (p76) has fine beaches, a hands-on nature center for kids, and an excellent park at the southern tip. It's hard to match **Bill Baggs Cape Florida State Park** (p77), where you can stroll scenic nature trails, check out a lighthouse, and then unwind on a lovely beach.

WANDERING WYNWOOD

Head to **Wynwood** (p71) for a leisurely afternoon stroll, checking out Miami's most creative side. You'll find art galleries, indie shops and plenty of cafes and restaurants around the neighborhood, particularly along NW 2nd Ave near the **Wynwood Walls** (p71).

FOTOLUMINATE LLC/SHUTTERSTOCK ©

1. Lincoln Road, South Beach (p58)
2. Biltmore Hotel (p96), Coral Gables
3. Crandon Park, Key Biscayne (p77)

Carillon Miami Wellness Resort
SPA

(Map p92; 866-800-3858; www.carillonhotel. com; 6801 Collins Ave, Carillon Hotel; treatments $179-345; 8am-9pm) For pure pampering the Carillon's 70,000-sq-ft spa and wellness center is hard to knock. It has an excellent range of treatments and fitness classes (spinning, power yoga, meditation, core workouts) plus pretty views of the crashing waves.

ROAM Oleta River Outdoor Center
WATER SPORTS

(786-274-7945; https://oletariveroutdoors.com; 3400 NE 163rd St; kayak/canoe rental per 90min $30/45; 9am-6pm Mon-Fri, 8am-7pm Sat & Sun;) Located in the Oleta River State Park, this outfitter rents loads of watersports gear; two-hour rental options include single/ tandem kayaks ($35/45), canoes ($50), stand-up paddleboards ($40) and bikes (from $30).

It also organizes group tours: sunset paddles (on Fridays, from $35), once-a-month full-moon paddles ($50), stand-up paddleboard classes ($40), and stand-up paddleboard yoga classes (Sundays at 10:30am, $30).

Normandy Isle Park & Pool
SWIMMING

(Map p92; 305-673-7750; 7030 Trouville Esplanade; adult/child $10/6; 6:30am-8:30pm;) For a fun day out, head to this family-friendly four-lane pool. It's lap swimming only at various times of day (before 9am and after 7pm), but otherwise it's open to all. There's also an outdoor splash-play area for the kids, with cascades to keep things interesting.

DON'T MISS

YOGA WITH A SIDE OF SALT BREEZE

The beach is definitely not the only place to salute the sun in Miami. There are **Yoga by the Sea** (Map p110; 305-442-6866; www.thebarnacle.org; 3485 Main Hwy, Coconut Grove; class $15; 6:30-7:45pm Mon & Wed) lessons offered at the Barnacle Historic State Park (p75) in Coconut Grove. If you don't feel like breaking out your wallet, try the free yoga classes at Bayfront Park (p68), held outdoors at Tina Hills Pavilion, at the south end of the park.

Studios offer a large range of classes; bring your own mat (though some places rent out mats as well for around $2 a class).

Downtown Miami

Yoga at Tina Hills Pavilion
YOGA

(Map p84; www.bayfrontparkmiami.com/Yoga Classes.html; Biscayne Blvd, Bayfront Park; 6pm Mon-Thu, 9am Sat) **FREE** Tina Hills is a small open-air pavilion in Bayfront Park (p68) that frequently hosts free events, including free 75-minute yoga sessions, suitable for all levels.

Spa at Mandarin Oriental Miami
SPA

(Map p84; 305-913-8332; www.mandarin oriental.com/miami/brickell-key/luxury-spa; 500 Brickell Key Dr, Mandarin Oriental Miami; manicures $55-95, spa treatments $165-555; 9:30am-8:30pm Mon-Thu, 8:30am-9:30pm Fri-Sun) Calling this spa over the top is an understatement. Treatments utilize materials like bamboo and rice paper, and services include Ayurvedic herbal baths, aromatherapy, oiled massages and lots more self-care.

Little Haiti & the Upper East Side

★ Venetian Pool
SWIMMING

(Map p118; 305-460-5306; www.coralgables. com/venetian-pool; 2701 De Soto Blvd; adult/child Sep-May $15/10, Jun-Aug $20/15; 11am-6:30pm Mon-Fri, 10am-4:30pm Sat & Sun Jun-Aug, closed Dec-Feb, reduced hours Mar-Apr & Oct-Nov;) One of the few pools listed on the National Register of Historic Places, this is a wonderland of rock caves, cascading waterfalls, a palm-fringed island and Venetian-style moorings. Back in 1923 rock was quarried for one of the most beautiful Miami neighborhoods, leaving an ugly gash – cleverly, it was laden with mosaic and tiles, and filled up with water.

It looks like a Roman emperor's aquatic playground, an absolute delight. Take a swim and follow in the footsteps of stars like Esther Williams and Johnny 'Tarzan' Weissmuller.

KOTR Konpa Dance Studio
DANCING

(Map p106; www.wikotr.com; 5706 NE 2nd Ave) We can't imagine a more appropriate activity in Little Haiti than learning *konpa* dancing. *Konpa* (also called *compas*) is a sort of merengue, and widely considered Haiti's national genre of music. KOTR offers several different *konpa* classes that are open to the public; check the website for times, but classes usually run for an hour in the evening and cost $10. Some courses are for women only.

MIAMI CRITICAL MASS

If you're in Miami at the beginning of the weekend late in any given month, you may spot hordes of cyclists and, less frequently, some skateboarders, roller-skaters and other self-propelled individuals. So what's it all about?

It's Miami Critical Mass. The event is meant to raise awareness of cycling and indirectly advocate for increased bicycle infrastructure in the city. Anyone is welcome to join; the mass ride gathers at Government Center by HistoryMiami (p69) on the last Friday of each month.

The event is loosely organized, but you can usually find information on it at www. themiamibikescene.com. Generally, the riders gather around 6:30pm, before departing on the 12-to-18-mile trek at 7:15pm. The average speed of the ride is a not-too-taxing 12mph, and you will be expected to keep up (at the same time, you're not to go faster than the pacesetters). All in all it's a fun experience, and a good way to meet members of the local cycling community.

🏃 Key Biscayne

⭐ **Virginia Key Outdoor Center** OUTDOORS
(VKOC; ☎786-224-4777; www.vkoc.net; 3801 Ricken-backer Causeway, Virginia Key; 2hr kayak or 4hr bike rental from $35, 2hr paddleboard $40; ⊗9am-6pm Mon-Fri, 8am-7pm Sat & Sun Mar-Aug, reduced hour Sep-Feb) This highly recommended outfitter will get you out on the water in a hurry with kayaks and stand-up paddleboards, which you can put in the water just across from its office. The small mangrove-lined bay (known as Lamar Lake) has manatees, and makes for a great start to the paddle before you venture further out.

One of the highlights is partaking in one of VKOC's guided sunset and full moon paddles, which happen several times a month. You can also rent mountain bikes for the nearby Virginia Key North Point Trails.

Virginia Key
North Point Trails MOUNTAIN BIKING
(☎786-224-4777; 3801 Rickenbacker Causeway, Virginia Key Beach North Point Park; ⊗10am-5pm Mon-Fri, 8am-6pm Sat & Sun) FREE In a wooded section at the north end of the Virginia Key Beach North Point Park, you'll find a series of short mountain-bike trails, color coded for beginner, intermediate and advanced. It's free to use the trails, though you'll have to pay for parking at the Virginia Key Beach North Point Park to get here. If you are not traveling with a bike, rent one from the nearby Virginia Key Outdoor Center.

Crandon Golf Course GOLF
(Map p98; ☎305-361-9129; www.golfcrandon.com; 6700 Crandon Blvd; 18 holes $176; ⊗6:30am-7:45 pm) On Key Biscayne, this course has great views over the water. Avid golfers consider it to be one of the loveliest and most challenging par-72 courses in Florida.

Miami Kiteboarding WATER SPORTS
(Map p98; ☎305-345-9974; www.miamikite boarding.com; 6747 Crandon Blvd, Crandon Park; private/semiprivate classes from $360/240; ⊗10am-6pm Apr-Sep, 9am-5pm Oct-Mar) This outfit offers a range of private lessons on how to kiteboard – basically sail over the water while attached to a parachute. Semi-private classes never have more than two students per instructor.

🎓 Courses & Tours

👉 South Beach

Miami Design
Preservation League WALKING
(MDPL; Map p60; ☎305-672-2014; www.mdpl.org; 1001 Ocean Dr; guided tours adult/student $30/25) The Miami Design Preservation League tells the stories and history behind the art-deco buildings in South Beach. The lively regular guided tours last 90 minutes. It also offers tours of Jewish Miami Beach, Gay & Lesbian Miami Beach, and tours of Mediterranean architecture and the MiMo district by request. Check the website for details and for tour days and times.

Miami Food Tours FOOD & DRINK
(Map p60; ☎786-361-0991; www.miamifood tours.com; 429 Lenox Ave; South Beach tour adult/child $58/35, Wynwood tour $75/55, Swooped with Forks $129/109; ⊗tours South Beach 11am & 4:30pm daily, Wynwood 10:30am Mon-Sat) This highly rated tour explores various facets of the city – culture, history, art and, of course,

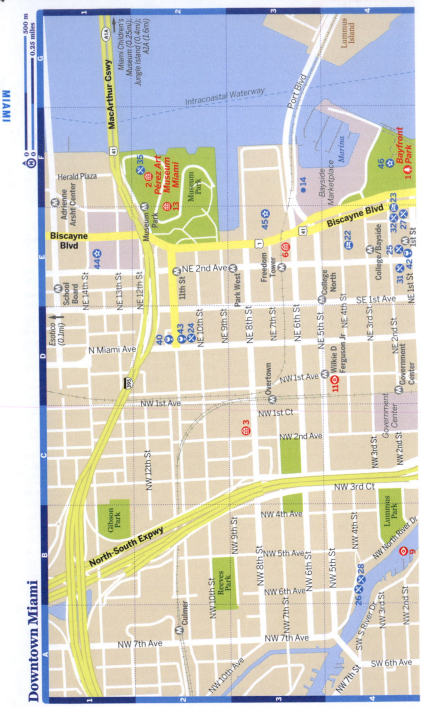

Downtown Miami

500 m
0.25 miles

MacArthur Cswy

Miami Children's
Museum (0.25mi);
Jungle Island (0.4mi);
A1A (1.6ml)

Intracoastal Waterway

Port Blvd

Lummus
Island

Herald Plaza

Perez Art Museum Miami

2 35

13

Adrienne
Arsht Center

Museum Park

Museum
Park

Bayside
Marketplace

14

46

Bayfront Park

1

Biscayne Blvd

45

Biscayne Blvd

23

School Board

NE 14th St

NE 13th St

NE 12th St

11th St

NE 2nd Ave

Park West

Freedom Tower

6

College North

College/Bayside

22

25

32

27

Esotico (0.1mi)

N Miami Ave

40

43 24

NE 10th St

NE 9th St

NE 8th St

NE 7th St

NE 6th St

NE 5th St

NE 4th Ave

NE 3rd Ave

NE 2nd Ave

SE 1st Ave

31

42

NE 1st St

1st St

395

NW 1st Ave

Overtown

NW 1st Ct

Wilkie D Ferguson Jr

11

Government Center

Government Center

NW 2nd Ave

3

NW 2nd Ave

NW 3rd St

NW 2nd St

NW 12th St

NW 3rd Ct

Gibson Park

North-South Expwy

NW 4th Ave

Lummus Park

NW 9th St

NW 8th St

NW 5th Ave

NW 6th St

NW 5th St

NW 4th St

NW North River Dr

9

NW 10th St

Reeves Park

NW 6th Ave

NW 7th St

SW S River Dr

26

28

NW 3rd St

NW 2nd St

Culmer

NW 7th Ave

NW 7th Ave

NW 10th Ave

SW 7th St

SW 6th Ave

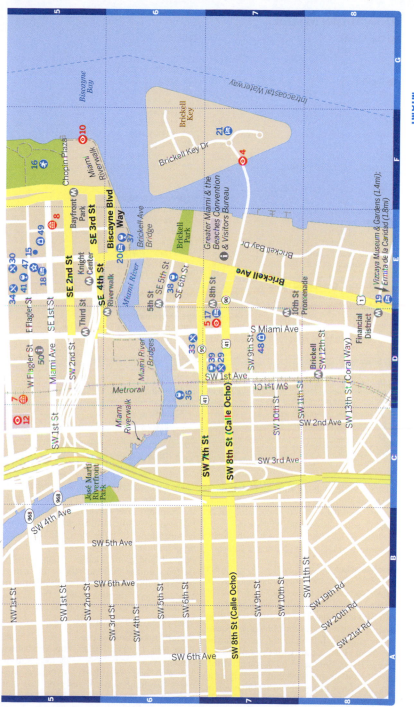

Downtown Miami

cuisine – while making stops at restaurants and cafes along the way. It's a walking tour, though distances aren't great, and takes place in South Beach and Wynwood.

There is also the Swooped with Forks food tour that takes you places in a golf cart.

Rumbachiva   BUS
(☎305-925-7571; www.rumbachiva.com; single/group pass per person $50/35; ⊙Fri & Sat 8:30am-11:30pm) How do you want to spend your nights in Miami? If the answer is, 'Ride around in an open-top bus blasting reggaeton music while hitting up the clubs,' maybe you should book a tour with this outfit? You have to BYOB, but there's a DJ, you get drink specials and/or free cover at participating bars, and for a little bit, you feel like you're in a Pitbull video.

Group rates are available for a crowd of 15 or more. You work out pickup locations with the company after booking. The bus doesn't follow a set route, but instead sort of slowly meanders (15 miles per hour) through neighborhoods like Wynwood, South Beach, Brickell and Coral Gables. Mainly you're partying on the bus; bar stops are for buying more drinks or going to the bathroom. You can book the bus Sunday through to Thursday, but you have to book the whole bus ($525 for two hours).

Ocean Force Adventures   BOATING
(Map p60; ☎305-372-3388; https://oceanforce adventures.com; tours $150; ⊙2hr tours 9:30am, 11:45am & 3pm) Ocean Force Adventures conducts two-hour tours of Biscayne Bay that take in seaside mosaics, celebrity homes,

inter-coastal islands, and Stiltsville, the remains of a village built on the water once inhabited by smugglers, gamblers and those who just couldn't fit in on dry land.

Island Queen, also offers infrequent trips to Stiltsville (approximately once a month), on three-hour tours narrated by Dr Paul George. Check www.historymiami.org/city-tour for the latest schedule.

Bike & Roll
CYCLING

(Map p60; ☎ 305-604-0001; www.bikemiami.com; 210 10th St; rental per 2/4hr from $15/20, per day from $25, tours $49; ☺9am-7pm) This well-run outfit offers a good selection of bikes, including single-speed cruisers, geared hybrids and speedy road bikes; all rentals include helmets, lights, locks and maps. Staff move things along quickly, so you won't have to waste time waiting to get out and riding. Bike tours are also available (daily at 10am).

☞ Downtown Miami

History Miami Tours
TOURS

(☎305-375-1492; www.historymiami.org/city-tour; tours $30-60) Historian extraordinaire Dr Paul George leads fascinating walking tours, including culturally rich strolls through Little Haiti, Little Havana, Downtown and Coral Gables at twilight, plus the occasional boat trip to Stiltsville and Key Biscayne. Tours happen once a week or so. Get the full menu and sign up online.

Urban Tour Host
WALKING

(Map p84; ☎305-416-6868; www.miamicultural tours.com; 25 SE 2nd Ave, Suite 1048; tours from $20) Urban Tour Host runs a program of custom tours that provide face-to-face interaction in all of Miami's neighborhoods. For something different, sign up for a Miami cultural community tour that includes Little Haiti and Little Havana, with opportunities to visit Overtown, Liberty City and Allapattah. Other tours take in South Beach, Downtown and Coral Gables; Wynwood and the Design District; and the Everglades, among other places.

Island Queen
BOATING

(Map p84; ☎844-292-2610; www.islandqueen cruises.com; 401 Biscayne Blvd; adult/child from $28/20; ☺11am-6pm, boats leave hourly) This outfit, based out of the Bayside Marketplace, runs 90-minute boat tours that take in Millionaire's Row, the Miami River and Fisher Island.

DON'T MISS

MIAMI ECOADVENTURES

The Dade County parks system leads a variety of **Miami EcoAdventures** (☎305-666-5885; www.miamidade.gov/ecoadventures; bike tours $5, kayaking & canoeing $30-45) tours, including excellent bike tours on Key Biscayne and out in the Everglades. You can also go on one of six different canoe trips, out on the Oleta River, on the Matheson Mangrove trek or paddling to Indian Key down in the Keys. There's also kayaking, snorkeling trips, walking tours and birdwatching. Trips depart from different locations; call or go online for details.

☞ Wynwood & the Design District

Art Classes in Wynwood
ARTS & CRAFTS

(Map p96; https://artclasseswynwood.com; 151 NW 36 St; 2/3hr classes $35/45) If you're going to explore the ostensibly artsiest neighborhood in Florida, you might as well take an art class while you're here, right? Check the website or call for a full schedule; classes run for two or three hours, and cover topics such as clay sculpture, painting and drawing.

Wynwood Art Walk
WALKING

(☎305-814-9290; www.wynwoodartwalk.com; tours from $29) Not to be confused with the monthly art celebration of the same name, this Wynwood Art Walk is actually a 90-minute guided tour taking you to some of the best gallery shows of the day, plus a look at some of the top street art around the 'hood. It also offers other tours like a golf cart trip around the area's best graffiti ($39).

☞ Coral Gables

Coral Gables Tours
OUTDOORS

(Map p118; ☎305-603-8067; www.coralgables museum.org/tours; 285 Aragon Ave; tours $10) The Coral Gables Museum runs various tours throughout the month, including downtown walking tours (Saturdays at 11am, $10), exhibition tours at the museum (Sundays at 1pm, free with admission) and bike tours (third Sunday of the month at 10am, $10).

Best of all are the two-hour paddling tours on the Coral Gables Waterway (last Sunday of the month at 9:30am, $40)

Call ahead to reserve a spot on a tour.

MIAMI'S TOP EVENTS

➡ Art-Deco Weekend (p24), January

➡ Coconut Grove Arts Festival (p24), February

➡ Carnaval Miami (p24, March

➡ Ultra Music Festival (p25), March

➡ Art Basel Miami Beach (p26), December

🎊 Festivals & Events

Viernes Culturales
CULTURAL

(Cultural Fridays; www.viernesculturales.org; ⊘7-11pm 3rd Fri of month) No wine-sipping art walk this; Cultural Fridays in Little Havana are like little carnival seasons, with music, old men in *guayaberas* (Cuban dress shirts) crooning to the stars, and Little Havana galleries throwing open their doors for special exhibitions.

The Little Havana Arts District has an energetic strip of galleries and studios (concentrated on 8th St between SW 15th and SW 17th Aves), and there's no better time to visit it all than on the third Friday of each month for Viernes Culturales.

Wynwood Art Walk Block Party
ART

(📞 305-461-2700; www.wynwoodartwalkblockparty.com; ⊘1pm-midnight 2nd Sat of month) The Wynwood Art Walk Block Party has become an incredibly popular (free) nightlife option where a big party of people wander around murals and galleries with food trucks, ever-flowing drinks (not always free), live music and special markets. The party is centered on the Wynwood Marketplace (p72), which is a good spot to get things started.

Sounds of Little Haiti
CULTURAL

(https://littlehaiticulturalcenter.com/sounds-of-little-haiti; 212 NE 59 Terrace, Little Haiti Cultural Center; ⊘6-10pm 3rd Fri of month; 🚌) FREE This family-friendly fest, held on the third Friday of every month, is an easy introduction to Haitian culture. The celebration is rife with music, Caribbean food and kids' activities.

🛏 Sleeping

Miami has some of the finest hotels in the world, bar none, boasting lodging options that balance cutting-edge design with amenity breakthroughs. Indeed, both Miami Beach's initial heyday in the 1920s and its revitalization in the 1980s, was fueled by a blossoming of art-deco hotel architecture.

You are spoiled for choice, from boutique beauties in South Beach to Downtown high-rises with sweeping views and endless amenities to historic charmers in Coral Gables to mid-century modern – MiMo – 'motels' along Biscayne Blvd.

🛏 South Beach

Note that rates in South Beach can swing wildly week by week depending on events, festivals and concerts.

SoBe Hostel
HOSTEL $

(Map p60; 📞 305-534-6669; www.sobe-hostel.com; 235 Washington Ave; dm $15-22, r $100; ❄@🅰) On a quiet end of SoFi (the area south of 5th St, South Beach), this massive multilingual hostel has a happening common area and spartan rooms. The staff are friendly and the on-site bar (open 24/7) is a good spot to meet other travelers. Free breakfasts are included in the rates. There are loads of activities on offer – from volleyball games to mojito-making nights, screenings of big games and bar crawls.

Aqua Hotel
BOUTIQUE HOTEL $

(Map p66; 📞 305-538-4361; www.dot-hotels.com/aqua-hotel-miami-beach; 1530 Collins Ave; r $100-200; 🅿❄🅰) On the outside this hotel stays true to name and embraces marine-like hues, while the rooms within have a crisp white paint job, with wood floors and a few touches of artwork. Although there's no pool, you can escape the noise of Collins Ave in the small backyard. Rates include breakfast.

Standard
BOUTIQUE HOTEL $$

(📞 305-673-1717; www.standardhotels.com/miami; 40 Island Ave; r $160-285; 🅿❄🅰🛎) Look for the upside-down 'Standard' sign on the old Lido building on Belle Island (between South Beach and Downtown Miami) and you'll find the Standard – which is anything but. This boutique hotel blends a bevy of spa services, hipster funk and South Beach sexiness, and the result is a '50s motel gone glam.

There are raised white beds, spa rain showers and gossamer curtains that open onto a courtyard of earthly delights, including a heated *hammam* (Turkish bath).

Miami Beach International Hostel
HOSTEL $$

(Map p60; 📞 305-534-0268; www.hostelmiamibeach.com; 1051 Collins Ave; dm $22-34, r $130-150; ❄@🅰) An extensive makeover has turned this reliable old hostel into something like a boutique club with dorm rooms. Bright plaster, marble accents, deco-and-neon decor and hip, clean rooms all make for a good base in South Beach. Wallflowers need not apply: there's a party-friendly social vibe throughout.

Greystone Miami Beach
HOTEL $$

(Map p66; ☏ 305-847-4000, reservations 833-895-1918; www.greystonemiamibeach.com; 1920 Collins Ave; r $140-280; ☎☒) With rounded walls, half-circle 'eyebrows' providing shade, and porthole windows, the Greystone is a deco gem. It's also a 21 and over hotel with bright white rooms offset by little Aegean swatches of blue. Cocktail bar and restaurants are on-site, and if you want some sand, the beach is just mere steps away.

Catalina Hotel
BOUTIQUE HOTEL $$

(Map p66; ☏ 305-674-1160; www.catalinahotel.com; 1732 Collins Ave; r $128-248; P☀☎☒) The Catalina is a lovely example of midrange deco style. Most appealing, besides the playfully minimalist rooms, is the vibe – the Catalina doesn't take itself too seriously, and staff and guests all seem to be having fun as a result. The back pool, concealed behind the main building's crisp white facade, is particularly attractive and fringed by a whispery grove of bamboo trees. It was renovated to incorporate the Dorset, next door, which means that it now has two pools, a roof terrace and a reasonable Mexican restaurant.

★1 Hotel
HOTEL $$$

(Map p66; ☏ hotel 305-604-1000, reservations 833-625-3111; www.1hotels.com/south-beach; 2341 Collins Ave; r $430-1155, ste $909-2829; ☀☎☒) ⌀ One of the top hotels in the USA, the 1 Hotel has 400-plus gorgeous rooms that embrace both luxurious and ecofriendly features – including tree-trunk coffee tables/desks, custom hemp-blend mattresses and salvaged driftwood feature walls, plus in-room water filtration (no need for plastic bottles). The common areas are impressive, with four pools, including an adults-only rooftop infinity pool.

The list of amenities is long, with a lavish spa, a 14,000-sq-ft gym (with many classes), water-sports activities, a kids' club and, of course, direct access to the fine sands of South Beach. The Seedlings program provides daily 'adventures' and low-key excursions for kids.

★Betsy Hotel
BOUTIQUE HOTEL $$$

(Map p66; ☏ hotel 305-531-6100, reservations 844-539-2840; www.thebetsyhotel.com; 1440 Ocean Dr; r $340-670, ste $1300-1800; P☀☎☒☒) One of South Beach's finest hotels, the Betsy is a historic gem with two wings and rooms set in either a tropical Colonial style or an art-deco aesthetic. The owners are committed to the local literary scene; the Betsy frequently hosts writers and public readings, and has heavily curated photography exhibitions on-site. Thoughtful touches include orchids in the rooms, a 24-hour fitness center, two swimming pools and rather curious bathroom mirrors with inbuilt LCD TVs. The property is pet friendly, to the point that you can get a couples massage with your dog.

★Washington Park Hotel
BOUTIQUE HOTEL $$$

(Map p66; ☏ 305-421-6265; www.wphsouthbeach.com; 1050 Washington Ave; r $200-500; ☀☎☒) In a great location two blocks from the beach, the Washington Park is spread among five beautifully restored art-deco buildings fronted by a pool and a palm-fringed courtyard. The rooms are all class, with muted color schemes, distressed laminate wood flooring and elegant design touches like bedside globe lamps and wood and cast-iron work desks. The vibe is welcoming and fun, with bocce in the courtyard, complimentary yoga classes, and stylish green Martone bikes for zipping about town.

★Surfcomber
HOTEL $$$

(Map p66; ☏ 305-532-7715; www.surfcomber.com; 1717 Collins Ave; r $200-480; P☀☎☒☒) The Surfcomber has a classic art-deco exterior with strong lines and shade-providing 'eyebrows' that zigzag across the facade. But the interior is the really impressive part – rooms have undeniable appeal, with elegant lines in-keeping with the art-deco aesthetic, while bursts of color keep things contemporary.

The lobby and adjoining restaurant are awash with bold colors, decorative wood elements, playful tropical themes and skylights, while a terrace overlooking Collins Ave connects indoor and outdoor spaces. Head around the back for a dazzling view: a massive sun-drenched pool, fringed by palm trees and backed by lovely oceanfront, with the beach just steps away.

★Setai
BOUTIQUE HOTEL $$$

(Map p66; ☏ 305-600-3099; www.thesetaihotel.com; 2001 Collins Ave; ste $725-2650; P☀☎☒) Inside a deco building, the Setai has a stunning interior that mixes elements of Southeast Asian temple architecture and contemporary luxury. The spacious rooms are decked out in chocolate teak wood, with clean lines and Chinese and Khmer embellishments. The amenities are exquisite, with a heavenly spa, three palm-fringed swimming pools, a top restaurant and a great beach location.

Gale South Beach
HOTEL $$$

(Map p66; ☑ 305-673-0199; www.galehotel.com; 1690 Collins Ave; r $185-410; P ❄ 🛜 🌊) The Gale's exterior is an admirable recreation of classic boxy deco aesthetic expanded to the grand dimensions of a modern SoBe super-resort. This blend of classic and haute South Beach carries on indoors, where you'll find bright rooms with a handsome color scheme, sharp lines and a retro chic vibe inspired by the mid-century modern movement. The elegant rooftop pool is rather narrow but gets sun all day, plus a crowd of pretty people.

Royal Palm
HOTEL $$$

(Map p66; ☑ 305-604-5700; www.royalpalm southbeach.com; 1545 Collins Ave; r from $120, ste $529-1310; P ❄ 🛜 🌊) Even the tropical fish tank with its elegant curves and chrome accents has a touch of deco flair, to say nothing of the streamlined bar with mint-green accents – all of which adds up to South Beach's most striking example of building-as-cruise-liner deco theme. The shipboard style carries into the plush rooms, which are also offset by bright whites and minty subtle marine-like hues.

As with other big properties anchored between the beach and Collins Ave, the Royal Palm has extensive amenities, including two pools and good drinking and dining spaces, including Byblos, a recommended Greek restaurant.

Stiles Hotel
BOUTIQUE HOTEL $$$

(Map p66; ☑ 305-674-7800; www.thestileshotel. com; 1120 Collins Ave; r $209-409; P ❄ 🛜 🌊) Bring the beach to your room at the Stiles; guest chambers balance pale sandy hues and crisp, sunny whites with natural fiber carpeting, modular bedside lamps and blackout curtains. The courtyard, with three small spa pools, is a fine spot to unwind.

Shore Club
BOUTIQUE HOTEL $$$

(Map p66; ☑ 305-695-3100; www.shoreclub.com; 1901 Collins Ave; r $250-1000; P ❄ @ 🌊) In a highly coveted location in South Beach (backing onto lovely beachfront), the Shore Club has airy but rather simply furnished rooms with a few color splashes amid the otherwise white design scheme. There are some appealing areas for amusement, including the **Skybar** (🕐4pm-2am Mon-Wed, to 3am Thu-Sat), which is a fine garden-like spot for a drink (though located rather surprisingly at ground level).

Redbury South Beach
BOUTIQUE HOTEL $$$

(Map p66; ☑ 305-604-1776; www.theredbury.com/ southbeach; 1776 Collins Ave; r $180-370; ❄ 🛜 🌊) What sets the Redbury apart is its refusal to toe the line of identikit South Beach minimalist rooms. Rather, the interior here references art across the 20th century, with fun but easygoing comfort in mind (striped carpets, Italian linens, and in-room record players – and albums! – available upon request). A rooftop pool makes for some chilled-out lounging, while the lobby channels East Asian exoticism, plus there's a giant ornamental cage just outside the entrance.

W Hotel
RESORT $$$

(Map p66; ☑ 305-938-3000; www.wsouthbeach. com; 2201 Collins Ave; r $440-720, ste $1160-2800; P ❄ 🛜 🌊) There's an astounding variety of rooms available at the South Beach outpost of the W chain, which touts the whole W-brand mix of luxury and style in a big way. The 'spectacular studios' balance long panels of reflective glass with cool tablets of Cipollino marble, while the Oasis suite lets in so much light you'd think the sun had risen in your room. The attendant bars, restaurants, clubs and pool built into this complex are some of the best-regarded on the beach.

Sagamore
BOUTIQUE HOTEL $$$

(Map p66; ☑ 305-535-8088; www.sagamore hotel.com; 1671 Collins Ave; r $220-455, ste $770-830; P ❄ 🛜 🌊) This hotel-cum-exhibition-hall likes to blur the boundaries between interior decor, art and conventional hotel aesthetics. Almost every space here, from the lobbies to the rooms, doubles as an art gallery thanks to a talented curator and an impressive roster of contributing artists. Rooms? Soft whites and rich tones, accented by artsy photography and sleek designer touches.

Delano
BOUTIQUE HOTEL $$$

(Map p66; ☑ 305-672-2000; www.delano-hotel. com; 1685 Collins Ave; r $314-389; P ❄ 🛜 🌊) The Delano opened in the 1990s and immediately started ruling the South Beach roost. If there's a quintessential 'I'm-too-sexy-for-this...' South Beach moment, it's when you walk into the Delano's lobby, which has all the excess of an overbudgeted theater set. Rooms are almost painfully white and bright: all long, smooth lines, reflective surfaces and modern, luxurious amenities. The pool area resembles the courtyard of a Disney princess's palace.

Mondrian South Beach
RESORT $$$

(Map p66; ☎305-514-1500; www.mondrian-miami.com; 1100 West Ave; r $235-505; P❄️🛜🛗) Morgan Hotel Group hired Dutch designer Marcel Wanders to crank it up to 11 at the Mondrian. The theme's inspired by Sleeping Beauty's castle – columns carved like giant table legs, a 'floating' staircase and spectacular bay views from the floor-to-ceiling windows. Upstairs the design whimsy continues with plush rooms sporting Delft tiles with beach scenes instead of windmills, and chandelier-like rainfall showers.

🏖 North Beach

⭐ Freehand Miami
BOUTIQUE HOTEL $$

(Map p92; ☎305-531-2727; www.thefreehand.com; 2727 Indian Creek Dr; dm $28-55, r $120-340; ❄️🛜🛗) The Freehand is the brilliant re-imagining of the old Indian Creek Hotel, a classic of the Miami Beach scene. Rooms are sunny and attractively designed, with local artwork and wooden details. The vintage-filled common areas are the reason to stay here though – especially the lovely pool area and backyard that transforms into one of the best bars in town. Dorms serve the hostel crowd, while private rooms are airy and decorated with pop art. There are also bungalows for self-catering groups.

Palihouse Miami Beach
BOUTIQUE HOTEL $$

(Map p92; ☎305-763-8006; www.palisociety.com/hotels/miami-beach; 3101 Indian Creek Dr; r $185-215, ste $255-295; 🛜🛗🐾) From the sunset-toned rooms with bohemian vintage decor accented by Mediterranean tiles, to an airy, deco-inspired lobby, the Palihouse evokes Miami Beach's early-20th-century heyday, while providing guests with a 21st-century hotel experience. The property gets bonus points for maximum utilization of natural light, and for allowing four-legged friends (up to 30 pounds, and charges a $150 registration fee).

Croydon Hotel
BOUTIQUE HOTEL $$

(Map p92; ☎305-938-1145; www.hotelcroydonmiamibeach.com; 3720 Collins Ave; r $128-435; ❄️🛜🛗) The Croydon earns high marks for its bright, classically appointed rooms with dark-wood floors, luxurious beds and modern bathrooms with CO Bigelow products. Head to the ground-floor restaurant with its elaborately patterned ceramic floors for good meals. Fringed by palms, the terrace around the pool has a crisp modern design.

There's also beach service – though the hotel is a block away from the sands.

HOTEL POOLS

Miami has some of the most beautiful hotel pools around, and they're more about seeing and being seen than swimming. Most of these pools double as bars, lounges or even clubs. Some hotels have a guests-only policy when it comes to hanging out at the pool, but if you buy a drink at the poolside bar you should be fine.

➡ Delano (p90)

➡ Shore Club (p90)

➡ Kimpton EPIC Hotel (p94)

➡ Biltmore Hotel (p96)

➡ Fontainebleau (p93)

Landon Hotel
BOUTIQUE HOTEL $$

(☎305-868-4141; www.thelandon.com; 9660 E Bay Harbor Dr; r $129-289; P❄️🛜) The Landon is a cheerful, hip place about 3 miles north of Miami Beach. It looks, from the outside, like a large B&B that's been fashioned for MTV and Apple employees. This vibe continues in the lobby and the rooms: cool, clean lines offset by bright, bouncy colors, plus a nice list of amenities such as flat-screen TVs, in-room Keurig coffeemakers, gym access and the rest.

Circa 39
BOUTIQUE HOTEL $$

(Map p92; ☎305-538-4900; www.circa39.com; 3900 Collins Ave; r $120-300; P❄️🛜🛗) If you love South Beach style but loathe South Beach attitude, Circa has got your back. The lobby has molded furniture and wacky embellishments, and staff go out of their way to make guests feel welcome. Chic (if small) rooms, bursting with lime green and subtle earth tones, are attractive enough for the most design-minded visitors.

Red South Beach
BOUTIQUE HOTEL $$

(Map p92; ☎305-531-7742; www.redsouthbeach.com; 3010 Collins Ave; r $165-400; ❄️🛜🛗) Red is indeed the name of the game, from the cushions on the sleek chairs in the lobby to the flashes dancing around the marble pool to deep, blood-crimson headboards and walls wrapping you in warm sexiness in the small but beautiful guest rooms. Come evening, the pool-bar complex is a great place to unwind and meet fellow guests. If you score an online deal, Red can be good value for money. Friendly, down-to-earth staff add to the appeal.

North Beach

Normandy Isle
N Shore Dr
Normandy Shores Golf Course
S Shore Dr
Normandy Dr
Trouville Esplanade
5

77th St
Josh's Deli (1.6mi);
Mendel's Backyard BBQ (1.6 mi);
Landon Hotel (2.3mi);
Chayhana Oasis (5 mi);
Jelly & Burger (7.5 mi)
Harding Ave
Collins Ave
23
22
71st St
71st St Bridge
21
18
4

JFK/79th St Cswy
20
NORTH BAY VILLAGE

W 63rd St
6
A1A

Biscayne Bay

La Gorce Country Club

La Gorce Dr
Pine Tree Dr
Alton Rd
Collins Ave

Enlargement
Indian Creek
Indian Creek Dr
Collins Ave
Miami Beach Boardwalk
8
9
7
2
14 16
11
South Beach
MID-BEACH
15
13
1
12
17
0   200 m
0   0.1 miles

Dade Blvd
907
10
3
A1A

41st St/Arthur Godfrey Rd
19

See Enlargement
Indian Creek Dr
Collins Ave
South Beach

195 Julia Tuttle Cswy

Sunset Islands
N Chase Ave
N Bay Rd
Alton Rd
N Chase Ave
Bayshore Municipal Golf Course
Sheridan Ave
Pine Tree Dr
W 28th St

North Beach

⭐ **Faena Hotel Miami Beach**   HOTEL **$$$**
(Map p92; ☎844-798-9712; www.faena.com/miami-beach; 3201 Collins Ave; r $780-970, ste $1065-2425; ❄🖥🛜🏊🏊) The Faena has lavish, artfully designed spaces inside and out. The rooms, set with a royal red and teal color scheme, are full of beauty and whimsy: animal-print fabrics, coral and seashell decorative touches, and window seats (or terraces) for taking in the views. Each room has butler service, because this is Miami, damn it. Gilded columns and exquisite tropical murals line the lobby, with a pretty pool in back – a few paces away from a fully intact gold-covered woolly mammoth skeleton created by British artist Damien Hirst. The hotel boasts a massive spa that takes up one whole floor of the hotel, plus lavish drinking dens and a 150-seat theater inspired by Europe's grand old auditoriums.

Miami Beach Edition   HOTEL **$$$**
(Map p92; ☎786-257-4500; www.editionhotels.com/miami-beach; 2901 Collins Ave; r $489-1400, ste $1499-6859; ❄🛜🏊) Design guru Ian Schrager spearheaded the gorgeous retooling of this 1950s Mid-Beach classic. Luxurious rooms are kitted out in warm-ish neutral tones meant to evoke the presence of the beach in your bedchambers, while the artfully designed lobby and common spaces stay true to mid-century style, showcasing minimalist geometric design and flashes of tropical color.

The best features are the pool with its hanging gardens, the plush spa, a top restaurant (Matador by Jean-Georges), a Studio 54–esque nightclub (called Basement Miami) and an indoor skating rink.

Fontainebleau   RESORT **$$$**
(Map p92; ☎800-548-8886; www.fontainebleau.com; 4441 Collins Ave; r $409-569, ste $619-2070; 🅿❄🛜🏊🏊) The grand Fontainebleau opened in 1954, when it became a celeb-sunning spot. Numerous renovations have added beachside cabanas, a shopping mall, a fabulous swimming pool and a nightclub. The rooms are bright and cheerful, with an unpretentious elegance.

Eden Roc Miami Beach   RESORT **$$$**
(Map p92; ☎786-801-6886; www.nobueden-roc.com; 4525 Collins Ave; r $330-579, ste $619-799; 🅿❄🛜🏊🏊) The Roc's immense inner lobby draws inspiration from the Rat Pack glory days of Miami Beach cool, and rooms in the Ocean Tower boast lovely views over the Intracoastal Waterway. All the digs here have smooth, modern embellishments and a beautiful ethereal design – we prefer the lofts, two-level rooms that efficiently maximize your space.

The amenities are staggering: three swimming pools, two Jacuzzis, an extensive spa, 24-hour fitness center and on-site restaurants, cafes and bars

Casa Faena   HOTEL **$$$**
(Map p92; ☎305-604-8485; www.faena.com/casa-faena; 3500 Collins Ave; r $325-400; ❄) Part of the growing Faena empire in Mid-Beach, this 1928 Mediterranean-style palace feels like an (Americanized) Tuscan villa, with a honey-stone courtyard, frescoed walls and gleaming stone floors. The sunny rooms have abundant old-world charm, and some have private terraces.

Palms Hotel
HOTEL $$$

(Map p92; 305-534-0505; www.thepalmshotel.com; 3025 Collins Ave; r $200-470; P❄@🛜🏊) The Palms' lobby manages to be imposing and comfortable all at once; the soaring ceiling, cooled by giant, slow-spinning rattan fans, makes for a Colonial-villa-on-convention-center-steroids vibe. Upstairs the rooms are perfectly fine, though a touch on the masculine side. Thoughtful touches include comfy high-end mattresses, iPod docking stations, in-room coffeemakers and Aveda bath products.

🛏 Downtown Miami

Eurostars Langford
HERITAGE HOTEL $$

(Map p84; 305-420-2200; www.eurostarshotels.co.uk/eurostars-langford.html; 121 SE 1st St; r $180, ste $240-530; ❄🛜) Set in a beautifully restored 1925 beaux-arts high-rise, the Langford's 126 rooms blend comfort and nostalgia, with elegant fixtures and vintage details, including oak flooring and lush furniture. Thoughtful design touches abound, and there's a rooftop bar and an excellent ground-floor restaurant on-site.

YVE
HOTEL $$

(Map p84; 305-358-4555; www.yvehotelmiami.com; 146 Biscayne Blvd; r $120-200; ❄🛜🏊) The YVE is a simple but trendy choice for those who want to be close to the pulsing neon heart of the Downtown experience at a competitive rate. Rooms mix dark carpets with minimalist white bedding. A fitness center is on-site, and pets can stay for $50 extra.

EAST, Miami
HOTEL $$$

(Map p84; 305-712-7000; www.east-miami.com; 788 Brickell Plaza; r $279-549; ❄🛜🏊) Part of the burgeoning Brickell City Centre development, this cosmopolitan hotel has loads of style in its 352 spacious, attractively furnished rooms and suites. Apart from the beach (a 20-minute drive away), you've got everything at your fingertips, with swimming pools, a state-of-the-art fitness center, an excellent Uruguayan-style grillhouse, and a tropically inspired rooftop bar.

Kimpton EPIC Hotel
HOTEL $$$

(Map p84; 305-424-5226; www.epichotel.com; 270 Biscayne Blvd Way; r $265-550, ste from $605; P❄🛜🏊) Epic indeed! This massive Kimpton hotel is one of the more attractive Downtown options and it possesses a coolness

cred and youthful energy that could match any spot on Miami Beach. Of particular note is the outdoor pool and sun deck, which overlook a gorgeous sweep of Brickell and the surrounding condo canyons. The rooms are outfitted in designer-chic furnishings and some have similarly beautiful views of greater Miami-Dade.

Mandarin Oriental Miami
HOTEL $$$

(Map p84; 305-913-8288; www.mandarinoriental.com/miami; 500 Brickell Key Dr; r $299-419, ste $799-1589; P❄🛜🏊) The Mandarin shimmers on Brickell Key, which is actually annoying – you're a little isolated from the city out here. Not that it matters; there's a luxurious world within a world inside this exclusive compound, from swanky restaurants to a private beach and skyline views that look back at Miami from the far side of Biscayne Bay.

The Guild Downtown Miami
APARTMENT $$$

(Map p84; 512-623-7480; https://theguild.co; 230 NE 4th St; apt $200-550; P❄🛜🏊) If you're staying downtown and want some privacy to complement the Miami skyline, consider these one-, two- and three-bedroom apartments, which feature furniture that has a contemporary, design-forward vibe, and cool, light-filled common spaces. Guests will have access to a patio, pool, parking and gym, and kids are more than welcome.

Four Seasons Miami
HOTEL $$$

(Map p84; 305-358-3535; www.fourseasons.com/miami; 1435 Brickell Ave; r/ste from $435/640; P❄🛜🏊) The marble common areas double as art galleries, a massive spa caters to corporate types, and there are sweeping, could-have-been-a-panning-shot-from-*Miami-Vice* views over Biscayne Bay in some rooms. The 7th-floor terrace bar, Edge, is pure mojito-laced swankiness.

🛏 Wynwood & the Design District

Krymwood Flats
APARTMENT $

(Map p96; 954-763-2000; www.krymwoodflats.com; 145 NW 29th St; apt $67-108; ❄🛜) These fully furnished apartments, ranging from studios to one-bedroom flats, make an attempt at Wynwood-y bohemian funkiness with mixed results – some rentals have graffiti and contemporary art aplenty, others look pretty plain. Still, they're clean and comfortable, and the cheaper ones are really a steal given their proximity to the heart of the action.

Fortuna House
APARTMENT $

(Map p96; ☑954-232-4705; www.fortunahouse.com; 432 NE 26th St; apt $90-190; ☀🛜) The Fortuna House is an affordable base for exploring the neighborhood's galleries and bars – though it's still a good 20-minute (1-mile) walk to Wynwood's epicenter. It's set in an attractive but aging three-story building on a quiet street. The accommodations are small and minimally furnished, but not a bad option for short stays.

Real Living Residence
APARTMENT $$

(Map p96; ☑877-707-0461; www.rlmiami.com; 2700 N Miami Ave, entrance on N 28th St; apt $150-350; P☀🛜⛵) A short stroll to the galleries and restaurants of Wynwood, this modern place has studio apartments with a minimal design of polished-concrete floors, tall ceilings and high-end furnishings. The best (and priciest) studios are rather spacious with a living room and dining area (though still within the one-room space). All have small kitchen units, washer-dryer, satellite TV and free parking.

🛏 Little Haiti & the Upper East Side

New Yorker
HOTEL $

(Map p106; ☑305-759-5823; wwww.hotelnewyorkermiami.com; 6500 Biscayne Blvd; r $100-180; P☀🛜⛵) Dating back to the 1950s, the New Yorker has an eye-catching design that's right at home in the architecturally rich MiMo district. The New Yorker has comfortable rooms done up with pop art, geometric designs and solid colors.

Catch a drink at the excellent outside Patio Bar (☑305-759-0357; 589 Northeast 65th St; ☺5pm-1am Tue-Thu, to 3am Fri & Sat, to 11pm Sun).

★Vagabond Hotel
BOUTIQUE HOTEL $$

(Map p106; ☑305-400-8420; www.thevagabondhotelmiami.com; 7301 Biscayne Blvd; r $170-340; P☀🛜⛵) An icon in the MiMo district, the Vagabond is a 1953 motel and restaurant where Frank Sinatra and other Rat Packers used to hang out. Today it's a boutique hotel, though it's lost none of its allure, with plush retro-inspired rooms that stepped out of a mid-century modern design catalogue, and a lushly landscaped pool complete with gurgling fountain. There's also a great bar (p117) fronting the pool – well worth visiting even if you're not lodging here.

🛏 Coconut Grove

Mutiny Hotel
HOTEL $$

(Map p110; ☑305-441-2100; www.providentresorts.com/mutiny-hotel; 2951 S Bayshore Dr; 1-bedroom ste $170-320, 2-bedroom ste $400-600; P☀🛜⛵) This small, luxury bayfront hotel, with one- and two-bedroom suites featuring balconies, boasts indulgent staff, high-end bedding, gracious appointments, fine amenities and a small heated pool and Jacuzzi. Although it's on a busy street, you won't hear the traffic once inside. The property has fine views over the water.

Mr C
BOUTIQUE HOTEL $$$

(Map p110; ☑305-800-6672; www.mrchotels.com/mrccoconutgrove; 2988 McFarlane Rd; r/ste from $167/434; P🛜⛵) It was only a matter of time before the hip Mr C boutique hotel brand came to Miami. Many thought the Magic City's outpost would be in South Beach, but instead it occupies this gorgeous, unique, art-deco-meets-the-space-age structure. A stylized wall of futuristic portholes adjoins a five-story building filled with rooms decked out in neutral colors and cool pastels.

A lush back courtyard adjoins an elegant lobby that is far more vintage chic than the ultramodern exterior.

Life House Little Havana
BOUTIQUE HOTEL $$$

(Map p124; ☑866-466-7534; www.lifehousehotels.com/hotels/miami/little-havana; 528 SW 9th Ave; r $215-290; 🛜) Life House is a design-conscious hotel brand, and its Little Havana outpost is a fabulous blend of minimalist decor and old Havana vibe: elegant dark wooden touches and vintage photos enliven crisp minimalist rooms. The roof terrace is a jungly escape from the street, and offers wonderful views of the Downtown skyline. If you're in a group, consider a bunk bed quad room ($270).

🛏 Coral Gables

Extended Stay
HOTEL $$

(Map p118; ☑305-443-7444; www.extendedstayamerica.com; 3640 22nd St; r $120-180; P☀🛜⛵) Sure it's a chain hotel, but this place has spacious, modern rooms that are decent value for the price, and the good location puts you within walking distance of Coral Gables' attractions and eateries.

Rooms get plenty of light and are well equipped with small kitchens.

Wynwood & the Design District

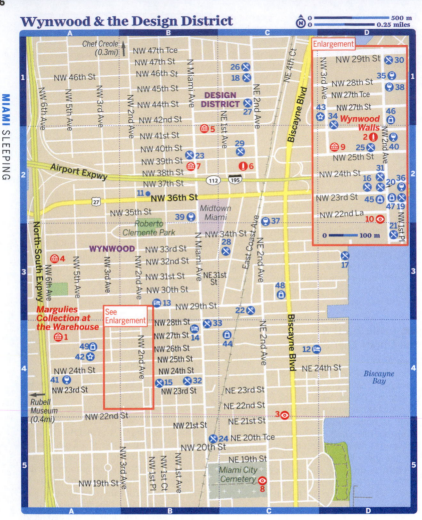

Hotel St Michel

HOTEL $$

(Map p118; ☎305-444-1666; www.hotelstmichel.
com; 162 Alcazar Ave; r $180-282; P❋⬆️) Built
in 1926, this building exudes class, with an
elegant sense of style that feels more Old Eu-
rope than South Florida. Renovations have
added more light and a refined look to the
rooms, while still maintaining the histori-
cal charm beneath. You won't have to go far
for a meal. An excellent Italian restaurant
opened on the property in 2017 – though the
hotel's location puts you within walking dis-
tance of other appealing spots in downtown
Coral Gables.

★ Biltmore Hotel

HISTORIC HOTEL $$$

(Map p118; ☎855-311-6903, 305-445-1926; www.
biltmorehotel.com; 1200 Anastasia Ave; r $329-
699, ste from $730; P❋⬆️🏊) A stay here is a
chance to sleep in one of the great laps of US
luxury. The grounds are so palatial it would
take a week to explore everything the Biltmore has to offer – sunbathe underneath
enormous columns and take a dip in the
largest hotel pool in continental USA. Rooms
themselves are surprisingly business-like,
with some baroque furniture flashes.

Wynwood & the Design District

🛏 Key Biscayne

Silver Sands Beach Resort   RESORT $$
(Map p98; ☎305-361-5441; www.silversandskey
biscayne.net; 301 Ocean Dr; r $169-189, cottages
$329-349; ⓟ❄🐾🏊) Silver Sands: aren't you
cute, with your one-story, stucco tropical
tweeness? How this little, Old Florida–style
independent resort has survived amid the
corporate competition is beyond us, but
it's definitely a warm, homey spot for those
seeking some intimate, individual attention
– to say nothing of the sunny courtyard, gar-
den area and outdoor pool.

Ritz-Carlton Key Biscayne   RESORT $$$
(Map p98; ☎305-365-4500; www.ritzcarlton.com;
455 Grand Bay Dr; r $424-770, ste $820-1400;
ⓟ❄🐾🏊) Many Ritz-Carlton outposts feel
a little cookie-cutter, but the Key Biscayne
outpost of the empire is pretty impressive.
There's the magnificent lobby, vaulted by
four giant columns lifted from a Cecil B

DeMille set. Tinkling fountains, the view
of the bay and the marble grandeur speak
less of a chain hotel and more of early-20th-
century glamour. Rooms and amenities are
predictably excellent.

✖ Eating

Miami has tons of immigrants from every inhabited continent, and it's a sucker for food
trends. Thus you get a good mix of cheap
ethnic places to eat and high-quality top-end
cuisine, alongside some poor-value dross in
touristy zones. You can eat well anywhere
here, from cutting-edge trendsetters Downtown to tiny Cuban cafes in Little Havana.

✖ South Beach

Panther Coffee   CAFE $
(Map p66; ☎305-677-3952; www.panthercoffee.
com; 1875 Purdy Ave, Sunset Harbour; coffees $3-
6; ⏰7am-7pm) Panther has the best coffee
in Miami Beach, though the location is not

Key Biscayne

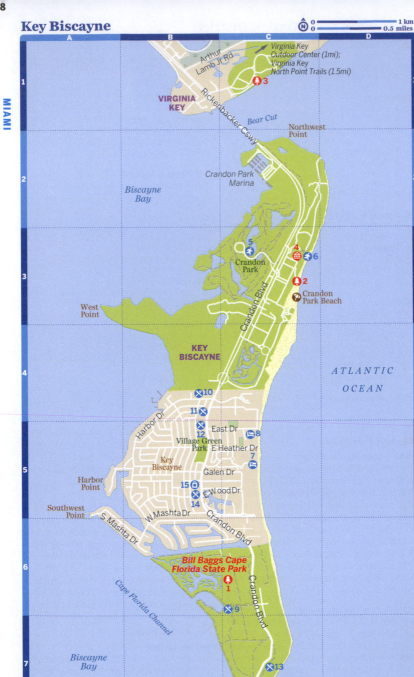

MIAMI

0 ——— 1 km
0 ——— 0.5 miles

Arthur Lamb Jr Rd

Virginia Key Outdoor Center (1mi); Virginia Key North Point Trails (1.5mi)

⚲3

VIRGINIA KEY

Rickenbacker Cswy

Bear Cut

Northwest Point

Biscayne Bay

Crandon Park Marina

5

Crandon Park

4 **⚑6**

⚲2

Crandon Park Beach

West Point

KEY BISCAYNE

ATLANTIC

OCEAN

⊗10

11 ⊗

Harbor Dr

12

East Dr

Village Green Park

E Heather Dr

8

7

Key Biscayne

Galen Dr

15

14

W ood Dr

Harbor Point

Southwest Point

S Mashta Dr

W Mashta Dr

Crandon Blvd

Bill Baggs Cape Florida State Park

⚲1

Crandon Blvd

⊗9

Cape Florida Channel

Biscayne Bay

⊗13

Cape Florida

Cape Florida Lighthouse

Key Biscayne

all that convenient if you're on the beach. It has the same elegant vintage-chic vibe as its Wynwood branch, plenty of pastries, and outdoor seating to boot.

Taquiza   MEXICAN $

(Map p66; ☎ 305-203-2197; www.taquizatacos. com; 1351 Collins Ave; tacos $3.50-5; ⊗ noon-midnight) Taquiza has acquired a stellar reputation among Miami's street-food lovers. The takeout stand with a few outdoor tables serves delicious perfection in its steak, pork, shrimp or veggie tacos (but no fish options) served on handmade blue-corn tortillas. They're small, so order a few. It also serves craft beers.

True Loaf   BAKERY $

(Map p66; ☎ 786-216-7207; 1894 Bay Rd, Sunset Harbour; pastries $3-5; ⊗ 7am-5pm Mon-Sat, from 8am Sun) The best bakery in South Beach is True Loaf, a small space where you can pick up heavenly croissants and berry tarts. With nowhere to eat these goodies, you'll have to take them around the corner to the waterfront **Maurice Gibb Memorial Park** (Map p66; 18th St & Purdy Ave, Sunset Harbour; 🚻) – stopping for Panther Coffee (p97) on the way of course. Fair warning: True Loaf may run out of its best baked goods by lunchtime

Lincoln Eatery   FOOD HALL $

(Map p66; ☎ 305-695-8700; www.thelincoln eatery.com; 723 N Lincoln Ln; mains $8-17; ⊗ 8am-10pm Mon-Thu, to 11pm Fri-Sun) It's easy to feel overwhelmed with food choice in South Beach, which is why we love the Lincoln Eatery. OK, to be fair, this is a food hall, so there are still a lot of choices: taco spots, sushi counters, even a kosher barbecue stand. But at least all of these options are concentrated in one easy-to-navigate arcade.

Moshi Moshi   JAPANESE $

(Map p66; ☎ 305-531-4674; www.moshimoshi.us; 1448 Washington Ave; mains $10-15; ⊗ noon-5am; 🛜) The best-known name in South Beach when it comes to sushi, Moshi Moshi serves up mouthwatering perfection in its tender rolls, daikon salads and steaming noodle soups. Prices are fair and it's open late, meaning you can join the party crowd when sushi cravings strike at 3am.

Puerto Sagua   CUBAN $

(Map p60; ☎ 305-673-1115; 700 Collins Ave; mains $8-18; ⊗ 7:30am-2am) Puerto Sagua challenges the US diner with this reminder: Cubans can greasy-spoon with the best of them. If you're never leaving South Beach, at least get a taste of authentic Cuban cuisine at this beloved institution, which has been slinging hash since 1962. Portions of favorites such as *picadillo* (spiced ground beef) are enormous.

La Sandwicherie   SANDWICHES $

(Map p66; ☎ 305-532-8934; www.lasandwicherie. com; 229 14th St; mains $6-11; ⊗ 7am-5am; 🚻) Closed for just a few hours each day, this boxcar-long eatery does a roaring trade in filling baguette sandwiches sold at rock-bottom prices. Ingredients are fairly classic: roast beef, smoked salmon, avocado or combos like prosciutto with mozzarella, though you can load up with toppings for a deliciously satisfying meal. Seating is limited to stools lining the restaurant's outside counter, but you can always get it to go and head to the beach.

Segafredo L'Originale   CAFE $

(Map p66; ☎ 305-673-0047; www.sze-originale. com; 1040 Lincoln Rd; mains $8-16; ⊗ 10am-1am Sun-Thu, to 2am Fri & Sat; 🚻) Immensely popular with Europeans and South Americans, this chic cafe serves up tasty snacks – pizzas, sandwiches, antipasti plates – and, of course, excellent Segafredo coffee. Credited with being the first Lincoln Rd business to open its trade to the outside street.

11th Street Diner
DINER $

(Map p66; ☑305-534-6373; www.eleventhstreet diner.com; 1065 Washington Ave; mains $10-20; ⏰7am-midnight Mon & Tue, 24hr Wed-Sun) A gorgeous slice of Americana, this Pullman-car diner trucked down from Wilkes-Barre, PA, is where you can replicate Edward Hopper's *Nighthawks* – if that's something you've always wanted to do. The food is as classic as the architecture, with oven-roasted turkey, baby back ribs and mac 'n' cheese among the hits, plus breakfast at all hours.

A La Folie
FRENCH $

(Map p66; ☑305-538-4484; www.alafoliecafe. com; 516 Española Way; mains $10-20; ⏰9am-midnight; 🍴) It's easy to fall for this charming French cafe on the edge of picturesque Española Way. You can enjoy duck confit salad, a decadent onion soup and savory galettes (buckwheat crepes) before satisfying your sweet tooth with dessert crepes – try the Normande (with caramelized apples and Calvados cream sauce). Vine-trimmed outdoor seating makes for a peaceful setting – and a fine break from the mayhem of Ocean Dr.

Pizza Rustica
PIZZA $

(Map p60; ☑305-674-8244; www.pizza-rustica. com; 863 Washington Ave; slices $5-7, pizzas $9-27; ⏰11am-6am) One of South Beach's favorite pizzerias has several locations to satisfy the demand for crusty Roman-style slices topped with an array of exotic offerings. A slice is a meal unto itself and sure hits the spot after a night of drinking (hence the late hours).

★ Yardbird
SOUTHERN US $$

(Map p66; ☑305-538-5220; www.runchicken run.com; 1600 Lenox Ave; mains $18-38; ⏰11am-midnight Mon-Fri, from 9am Sat & Sun; 🍴) Yardbird has earned a die-hard following for its haute Southern comfort food. The kitchen churns out some nice shrimp and grits, St Louis–style pork ribs, and biscuits with smoked brisket, but it's most famous for its supremely good plate of fried chicken, spiced watermelon and waffles with bourbon maple syrup. The setting is a shabby-chic interior of distressed wood, painted white brick columns, wicker basket-type lamps and big windows for taking in the passing street scene.

★ Pubbelly
FUSION $$

(Map p66; ☑305-532-7555; http://pubbelly global.com; 1424 20th St; plates $9-24; ⏰noon-11pm Sun-Thu, to midnight Fri & Sat; 🍴) A mix of Asian and Latin flavors, Pubbelly serves hip fusion takes on small plates, and sushi such

as grilled miso black cod with spring onions, beef tartare rolls with mustard and truffle poached egg, and Japanese fried chicken with kimchi. Super-popular and decently priced, it's a South Beach foodie spot that delivers.

Macchialina
ITALIAN $$

(Map p60; ☑305-534-2124; www.macchialina. com; 820 Alton Rd; mains $21-40) This buzzing Italian trattoria has all the right ingredients for a terrific night out; namely great service and beautifully turned-out cooking, served in a warm rustic-chic interior of exposed brick and chunky wood tables (plus outdoor tables in front).

Lilikoi
CAFE $$

(Map p60; ☑305-763-8692; www.lilikoiorganic living.com; 500 S Pointe Dr; mains $12-21; ⏰8am-7pm Mon-Wed, to 8:30pm Thu-Sun; 🍴) Head to the quieter, southern end of South Beach for healthy, mostly organic and veg-friendly dishes at this laid-back, indoor-outdoor spot. Start the morning off with big bowls of açai and granola or bagels with lox (and eggs Benedict on weekends); or linger over kale Caesar salads, mushroom risotto and falafel wraps at lunch.

Rossella's Kitchen
ITALIAN $$

(Map p60; ☑305-397-8852; www.rossellas sobe.com; 110 Washington Ave; mains lunch $12-18, dinner $16-29; ⏰8:30am-11pm; 🍴) Rossella's well-executed Italian fare served in SoFi ('south of Fifth St') makes this a favorite haunt morning, noon and night. The outdoor tables on the sidewalk feel like the perfect spot for good Italian cooking made with care.

Big Pink
DINER $$

(Map p60; ☑305-532-4700; https://myles restaurantgroup.com/big-pink; 157 Collins Ave; mains $13-26; ⏰8am-midnight Mon-Wed, to 2am Thu, to 5am Fri & Sat) Big Pink does American comfort food with joie de vivre and a dash of whimsy. The Americana menu is consistently good throughout the day; pulled Carolina pork holds the table next to a nicely done Reuben. The interior is somewhere between a '50s sock hop and a South Beach club; expect to be seated at a long communal table.

Spiga
ITALIAN $$

(Map p66; ☑305-534-0079; www.spigarestaurant. com; 1228 Collins Ave; mains $16-32; ⏰6pm-midnight) This romantic nook is a perfect place to bring your partner and gaze longingly at one another over candlelight, before you both snap out of it and start digging into excellent traditional Italian such as baby

SELF-CATERING

If you can tear yourself away from the Cuban sandwiches, celebrity hot spots and farm-to-table gems, Miami has a decent selection of options for self-caterers offering fresh produce and obscure ingredients aplenty.

Many of the more than two dozen **Publix** supermarkets throughout Miami are quite upscale, and the **Whole Foods Market** (Map p60; ☑305-938-2800; www.wholefoods market.com; 1020 Alton Rd; ☉8am-9pm) is the biggest high-end grocery store around, with an excellent produce department, a pretty good deli and a so-so salad bar; its biggest draw is for vegetarians or health nuts who are seeking a particular brand of soy milk or wheat-free pasta.

There are six **Milam's** markets around town that offer high-end ingredients, from stone-crab claws to filet mignon. Out on Key Biscayne, Golden Hog (p112) is a brilliant spot for fine meats and cheeses, while the iconic Marky's (p108) offers excellent ingredients beloved by any number of South Florida ethnic communities: Spanish deli meats and tinned fish, Italian truffles, kosher smoked salmon, and, most famously, genuine Russian caviar.

clams over linguine or red snapper with kalamata olives, tomatoes and capers.

Planta
VEGETARIAN **$$**

(Map p60; ☑305-397-8513; www.plantarestaurants. com/location/planta-miami; 850 Commerce St; mains $18-25; ☉noon-3pm Mon-Fri, from 11am Sat & Sun, 5:30-10pm Sun-Thu, to 11pm Fri & Sat; ☑) Planta brings South Beach diners a garden-to-table vegetarian and vegan experience. Mushroom and squash pizza is made with almond parmesan, udon noodles come with truffle cream, and a long list of small plates includes cauliflower tots and split-pea fritters. The setting is open and airy, located in the quieter corner of SoFi.

Front Porch Cafe
AMERICAN **$$**

(Map p66; ☑305-531-8300; www.frontporchocean drive.com; 1458 Ocean Dr; mains $12-29; ☉7am-11pm; ☑) An open-sided perch just above the madness of the cruising scene, the Porch has been serving salads, sandwiches and the like since 1990 (eons by South Beach standards). Breakfast is justifiably popular; the challah French toast is delicious, as are fluffy omelets, eggs Benedict and strong coffees.

Osteria del Teatro
ITALIAN **$$**

(Map p66; ☑305-538-7850; www.osteriadel teatro.miami; 1200 Collins Ave; mains $18-40; ☉6-11pm Sun-Thu, to midnight Fri & Sat) A mainstay of the fine Italian dining scene in these parts, Osteria remains a gem. When you get here, let the gracious Italian waiters seat you, coddle you, and guide you along the first-rate menu, with temptations such as polenta with wild mushrooms, black squid-ink linguine and locally caught red snapper.

News Cafe
AMERICAN **$$**

(Map p60; ☑305-538-6397; www.newscafe.com; 800 Ocean Dr; mains $11-32; ☉7am-1am Sun-Thu, 24hr Fri & Sat; ☎) News Cafe is an Ocean Dr landmark that attracts thousands of travelers. We find the food to be pretty uninspiring, but the people-watching is good, so take a perch, eat some over-the-average but not-too-special food and enjoy the anthropological study that is South Beach as it skates, salsas and otherwise shambles by.

Chotto Matte
PERUVIAN **$$$**

(Map p66; ☑305-690-0743; https://chotto-matte.com/miami; 1664 Lenox Ave; small plates $13-29, mains $18-55; ☉4pm-midnight Mon-Fri, noon-1am Sat & Sun; ☑) Chotto Matte is a strong contender for most physically beautiful restaurant in Miami, and that's saying something in this city of impressive design. Peruvian-Japanese cuisine – such as avocado doused with a truffle ponzu or beef in a spicy teriyaki sauce – is served in a roofless space that encloses a tropical garden. Even if you're not hungry, pop by for a drink and to gawk at the layout.

Juvia
FUSION **$$$**

(Map p66; ☑305-763-8272; www.juviamiami.com; 1111 Lincoln Rd, access via Lenox Ave elevator; mains $27-46; ☉6-11pm daily, noon-3pm Sat & Sun) Juvia blends the trendsetters that have staying power in Miami's culinary world: France, Latin America and Japan. Chilean sea bass comes with maple-glazed eggplant, while sea scallops are dressed with okra and oyster mushrooms. The big, bold, beautiful dining room and open-air terrace, which sit on the high floors of 1111 Lincoln Rd (p63), are quintessential South Beach glam.

On top of the regular menu are dishes cooked on a Binchotan charcoal grill (ie fancy Japanese charcoal); shrimps, steaks and the like cooked on the grill will run you $40 to $160.

✗ North Beach

Josh's Deli
DELI $

(☎ 305-397-8494; 9517 Harding Ave; sandwiches $14-18; ⊙ 8:30am-3:30pm) Josh's is simplicity itself. Here in the heart of Jewish Miami, you can nosh on thick cuts of house-cured pastrami sandwiches and matzo-ball soup for lunch or challah French toast, eggs and house-cured salmon for breakfast. It's a deliciously authentic slice of Mid-Beach culture.

Roasters 'n Toasters
DELI $

(Map p92; ☎ 305-531-7691; www.roastersn toasters.com; 525 Arthur Godfrey Rd; mains $10-18; ⊙ 6am-3:30pm) Given the crowds and the satisfied smiles of customers, Roasters 'n Toasters meets the demanding standards of Miami Beach's large Jewish demographic, thanks to juicy deli meat, fresh bread, crispy bagels and warm latkes. Sliders (mini-sandwiches) are served on challah bread, an innovation that's as charming as it is tasty.

★ 27 Restaurant
FUSION $$

(Map p92; ☎ 786-476-7020; www.freehandhotels. com; 2727 Indian Creek Dr, Freehand Miami Hotel; mains $17-30; ⊙ 6-11:30pm Mon-Sat, 11am-3pm Sat & Sun; ✎) Part of Freehand Miami and the very popular bar Broken Shaker (p114), 27 has a lovely setting – akin to dining in an old tropical cottage, with worn floorboards, candlelit tables, and various rooms slung with artwork and curious knickknacks, plus a lovely terrace. Try the braised octopus, crispy pork shoulder, kimchi fried rice and yogurt-tahini-massaged kale. Book ahead. Brunch is also quite popular.

Cafe Prima Pasta
ITALIAN $$

(Map p92; ☎ 305-867-0106; www.cafeprimapasta. com; 414 71st St; mains $17-29; ⊙ 5-11pm Mon-Thu, to 11:30pm Fri & Sat, 4-10:30pm Sun) We're not sure what's better at this Argentine-Italian place: the much-touted pasta, which deserves every one of the accolades heaped on it, or the atmosphere, which captures the dignified sultriness of Buenos Aires. You can't go wrong with the small, well-curated menu, with standouts including gnocchi formaggi, baked branzino, and squid-ink linguine with seafood in a lobster sauce.

Chayhana Oasis
UZBEK $$

(☎ 305-917-1133; http://chayhanaoasis.com; 250 Sunny Isles Blvd; mains $13-34; ⊙ noon-11pm) Chayhana claims to be an oasis, but with its elaborate tile work and light fixtures, it feels more like a Samarkand palace. A flush and flash Central Asian, Russian and American crowd dine here on steamed dumplings filled with spiced lamb meat, pea soup served with yogurt, *samsa* (traditional savory baked Uzbek pastries) and other Silk Road delights.

Shuckers
AMERICAN $$

(Map p92; ☎ 305-866-1570; www.shuckers barandgrill.com; 1819 79th St Causeway; mains $12-26; ⊙ 11am-1am; 🐾) With excellent views overlooking the waters from the 79th St Causeway, Shuckers has to be one of the best-positioned restaurants around. The food is pub grub: burgers, fried fish and the like. The chicken wings, basted in several mouthwatering sauces, deep-fried and grilled again, are famous.

Mendel's Backyard BBQ & Brew
BARBECUE $$

(☎ 305-763-8818; www.backyardbbqmiami.com; 9472 Harding Ave; mains $13-42; ⊙ noon-11pm Sun-Thu, to 3pm Fri, 8-11pm Sat; 🐾) If you didn't think 'kosher barbecue' was a restaurant genre, come to Mendel's Backyard. Chicken, fish, and beef (but not pork, obviously) are slow-smoked to perfection, yielding a tasty if oddly hybridized menu of Southern American and Ashkenazi Jewish gastronomy: schnitzel on the one hand, burgers and ribs on the other. Speaking of ribs, give the lamb ribs a go. Popular with families, not least because of its kids' menu.

✗ Downtown Miami

★ All Day
CAFE $

(Map p84; ☎ 305-699-3447; www.alldaymia.com; 1035 N Miami Ave; coffee from $3.50, breakfast $10-19; ⊙ 7am-5pm Mon-Fri, from 9am Sat & Sun; 🐾) All Day is positively Miami's best cafe – with locally sourced ingredients forming the basis of its simple menu, as well as excellent coffees, teas, beer and wine, and an airy, light Scandinavian-style decor, this is a winner all-around. Stylish chairs, wood-and-marble tables, friendly staff and an always enticing soundtrack lend it an easygoing vibe. Featuring ingredients sourced from small Florida farms, the cooking is first rate.

Manna Life Food
VEGAN $

(Map p84; ☑ 786-717-5060; www.mannalifefood. com; 80 NE 2nd Ave; mains $8-12; ☺10am-6pm Mon-Fri, 11am-4pm Sat; 🍴) This airy, stylish eatery has wowed diners with its plant-based menu loaded with superfoods. Filling 'life bowls,' *arepas* (corn cakes) and *noritos* (like a burrito but wrapped with seaweed rather than a tortilla) are packed with flavorful ingredients. There's also healthy smoothies, delicious soups and a decadent guacamole. It's all plant based and entirely vegan save for a few dishes with raw honey.

Bali Cafe
INDONESIAN $

(Map p84; ☑ 305-358-5751; 109 NE 2nd Ave; mains $10-15; ☺11am-4pm daily, 6-10pm Mon-Fri; 🍴) It's odd to think of the clean flavors of sushi and the bright richness of Indonesian cuisine coming together in harmony, but they're happily married in this tropical hole-in-the-wall. Have some spicy tuna rolls followed by *soto betawi* – beef soup cooked with coconut milk, ginger and shallots.

La Moon
COLOMBIAN $

(Map p84; ☑ 305-860-6209; www.lamoon restaurant.com; 97 SW 8th St; mains $7-17; ☺11am-midnight Sun & Tue-Thu, to 6am Fri & Sat) Nothing hits the spot after a late night of partying quite like red beans, rice, sausage, pork belly and plantains, or sweetcorn cakes stuffed with steak. These street-food delicacies are available well into the wee hours on weekend nights, plus La Moon is conveniently located within stumbling distance of bars including Blackbird Ordinary (p115).

⭐ NIU Kitchen
SPANISH $$

(Map p84; ☑ 786-542-5070; www.niukitchen. com; 134 NE 2nd Ave; sharing plates $14-26; ☺noon-3:30pm & 6-10pm Mon-Thu, to 11pm Fri, 1-4pm & 6-11pm Sat, 6-10pm Sun; 🍴) NIU is a stylish living-room-sized restaurant serving delectable contemporary Catalan cuisine. It's a showcase of culinary pyrotechnics, featuring imaginative sharing plates like Ous (poached eggs, truffled potato foam, *jamón ibérico* and black truffle) or Toninya (smoked tuna, green *guindillas* and pine nuts). The wine list is excellent.

Verde
AMERICAN $$

(Map p84; ☑ 786-345-5697; www.pamm.org/ dining; 1103 Biscayne Blvd; mains $15-25; ☺11am-4pm Mon, Tue & Fri, to 9pm Thu, to 5pm Sat & Sun; 🍴) Inside the Pérez Art Museum Miami (p64), Verde is a local favorite for its tasty market-fresh dishes and great setting – with outdoor seating on a terrace overlooking the bay. Crispy mahimahi (dorado fish) tacos, pizza with squash blossoms and goat cheese, and grilled endive salads are among the temptations.

River Oyster Bar
SEAFOOD $$

(Map p84; ☑ 305-530-1915; www.therivermiami. com; 650 S Miami Ave; mains $12-40; ☺noon-10:30pm Sun-Thu, to midnight Fri & Sat) A few paces from the Miami River, this buzzing little spot with a classy vibe whips up excellent plates of seafood. Start off with their fresh showcase oysters and ceviche before moving on to grilled red snapper or yellowfin tuna. For a decadent meal, go for a grand seafood platter ($125), piled high with Neptune's culinary treasures.

Garcia's Seafood Grille & Fish Market
SEAFOOD $$

(Map p84; ☑ 305-375-0765; www.garciasmiami. com; 398 NW N River Dr; mains $10-28; ☺11am-10pm Mon-Fri, to 11pm Sat & Sun) Crowds of office workers lunch at Garcia's, which feels more like you're in a smugglers' seafood shack than the financial district. Expect freshly caught and cooked fish and pleasant views of the Miami River.

Casablanca
SEAFOOD $$

(Map p84; ☑ 305-371-4107; www.casablanca seafood.com; 400 N River Dr; mains $14-40; ☺11am-10pm Mon-Thu, to 11pm Fri, 7am-10pm Sat & Sun) Perched over the Miami River, Casablanca serves excellent seafood. The setting is a big draw – with tables on a long wooden deck just above the water, and the odd seagull winging past. But the fresh fish is the real star here.

CVI.CHE 105
PERUVIAN $$

(Map p84; ☑ 305-577-3454; www.ceviche105. com; 105 NE 3rd Ave; mains $12-30; ☺noon-10pm Sun-Thu, to 11pm Fri & Sat) White is the design element of choice in Juan Chipoco's ever-popular Peruvian Downtown eatery. Beautifully presented ceviches, *lomo saltado* (marinated steak) and *arroz con mariscos* (seafood rice) are ideal for sharing and go down nicely with a round of Pisco Fuegos (made with jalapeño-infused pisco) and other specialty Peruvian cocktails.

Soya e Pomodoro
ITALIAN $$

(Map p84; ☑ 305-381-9511; www.soyaepomodoro. com; 120 NE 1st St; lunch $10-19, dinner $13-29; ☺11:30am-4:30pm Mon-Fri, 7-11:30pm Wed-Sat) Soya e Pomodoro feels like a bohemian retreat for Italian artists and filmmakers, who can dine on bowls of fresh pasta under vintage posters, rainbow paintings and curious wall hangings. Adding to the vibe is live Latin jazz (on Thursday nights from 9pm to midnight), plus readings and other arts events that take place here on select evenings.

Pollos & Jarras
PERUVIAN $$

(Map p84; ☑786-567-4940; www.pollosyjarras. com; 115 NE 3rd Ave; $9-26; ◷11:30am-10pm Mon-Thu, to 11pm Fri & Sat, noon-10pm Sun) The same celebrated team behind CVI.CHE 105 (p103) next door also operate this festive spot with an outdoor patio. The focus is less on seafood and more on meat: namely outstanding barbecued chicken (and chicken crackling – ie deep-fried skin – oh yes!), though of course signature dishes (including ceviche) are also available.

✖ Wynwood & the Design District

★ Enriqueta's
LATIN AMERICAN $

(Map p96; ☑305-573-4681; 186 NE 29th St; mains $6-14; ◷6am-4pm Mon-Fri, to 2pm Sat) Enriqueta's is an outpost of pre-gentrification Miami in the heart of that city's most gentrified neighborhood, a roadhouse diner where local Spanish speakers, as opposed to international installation artists, rule the roost. Notable for its excellent coffee, *pan con bistec* (steak sandwiches), *croquetas* (croquettes), Cuban sandwiches, and daily specials such as *picadillo* and *lechón asado* (roast pork).

1 800 Lucky
FOOD HALL $

(Map p96; ☑305-768-9826; www.1800lucky.com; 143 NW 23rd St; mains $7-16; ◷noon-2am Mon-Thu, to 3am Fri-Sun) Another example of Wynwood becoming a sort of adult playground for cosmopolitan world wanderers, 1 800 Lucky tries to recreate an Asian food hall in the midst of South Florida. The atmosphere is excellent: red lanterns, booming lounge and hip-hop, a slick bar, beautiful people.

The food is pretty good too, ranging from sashimi bowls to Thai-style chicken wings to Chinese pork belly buns. The food hall becomes an outdoor bar as the night wears on, as popular as any packed Miami club.

Coyo Taco
MEXICAN $

(Map p96; ☑305-573-8228; www.coyo-taco.com; 2300 NW 2nd Ave; mains $7.50-13; ◷11am-3am Mon-Sat, to 11pm Sun; ☑) If you're in Wynwood and craving tacos, this is the place to be. You'll have to contend with lines day or night, but those beautifully turned-out tacos

are well worth the wait – and come in creative varieties such as chargrilled octopus, marinated mushrooms or crispy duck, along with the usual array of steak, grilled fish and roasted pork.

Kush
AMERICAN $

(Map p96; ☑305-576-4500; www.kushwynwood. com; 2003 N Miami Ave; mains $12-16; ◷noon-11pm Sun-Tue, to midnight Wed & Thu, to 1am Fri & Sat; ☑) Gourmet burgers plus craft brews is the simple but winning formula at this lively eatery and drinking den on the southern fringe of Wynwood. Juicy burgers topped with hot pastrami, Florida avocados and other decadent options go down nicely with drafts from Sixpoint and Funky Buddha.

There are great vegetarian options too, including a house-made black-bean burger and vegan jambalaya.

Panther Coffee
CAFE $

(Map p96; ☑305-677-3952; www.panthercoffee. com; 2390 NW 2nd Ave; coffees $3-6; ◷7am-9pm Sun-Thu, to 11pm Fri & Sat; ☎) Miami's best independent coffee shop specializes in single-origin, small-batch roasts, fired up to perfection. Aside from sipping on a zesty brewed-to-order Chemex-made coffee (or a creamy latte), you can enjoy microbrews, wines and sweet treats. The front patio is a great spot for people-watching.

SuViche
FUSION $

(Map p96; ☑305-501-5010; www.suviche. com; 2751 N Miami Ave; sushi $7-12, ceviche $8-15; ◷11:30am-11pm Mon-Thu, to midnight Fri, noon-midnight Sat, noon-11pm Sun) SuViche is just fun: an open-sided setting of garrulous couples chatting over swinging chairs, graffiti-esque murals and good beats. The menu – and you may have guessed this based off the name – is a blend of Peruvian dishes and sushi, which goes down nicely with the creative *macerados* (pisco-infused cocktails). Visit the website for other locations, including South Beach and Brickell.

Zak the Baker
DELI $

(Map p96; ☑786-294-0876; www.zakthebaker.com; 295 NW 26th St; sandwiches $8-17; ◷7am-7pm Sun-Fri) This kosher bakery is admired by all for its delicious breads, bagels and sandwiches. Lines will often stretch around the block for all of the above, but the wait is worth it.

Salty Donut
DONUTS $

(Map p96; ☑305-639-8501; www.saltydonut.com; 50 NW 23rd St; doughnuts $3-6; ◷7:30am-6pm

Tue-Fri, from 8am Sat & Sun; ☎) Although 'artisanal doughnuts' sounds pretentious, no one can deny the merits of these artfully designed creations featuring seasonal ingredients. Maple and bacon, guava and cheese, and brown butter and salt are a few classics, joined by changing hits such as pistachio and white chocolate or strawberry and lemon cream.

Buena Vista Deli   CAFE $
(Map p96; ☑ 305-576-3945; www.buenavista deli.com; 4590 NE 2nd Ave; mains $8-15; ⊙ 7am-11pm) Never mind the uninspiring name; French-owned Buena Vista Deli is a charming Parisian-style cafe that warrants a visit no matter the time of day. Come in the morning for fresh croissants and other bakery temptations, and later in the day for thick slices of quiche, big salads and hearty sandwiches – plus there's wine, beer and good coffees.

Lemoni Café   CAFE $
(Map p96; ☑ 305-571-5080; www.mylemoni cafe.com; 4600 NE 2nd Ave; mains $10-18; ⊙ 11am-10:30pm Mon-Sat, to 6pm Sun; 🖉) Lemoni is a small, dimly lit cafe with a creative Mediterranean-inspired menu in its panini, salads and appetizers (including hummus, bruschetta and spicy Moroccan eggplant). Weekend brunch (till 2pm Saturday, till 5pm Sunday) features beautifully turned-out French toast and blueberry pancakes. Located in the pretty Buena Vista neighborhood, this is a fine place to grab a sidewalk alfresco lunch or dinner.

Dasher & Crank   ICE CREAM $
(Map p96; ☑ 305-213-1569; www.dasherand crank.com; 2211 NW 2nd Ave; ice cream $5-10; ⊙ 11am-11pm Sun-Thu, to noon Fri & Sat; 🖉) Escape the heat of the concrete jungle at Dasher & Crank, which (literally) churns out ice cream in delectable flavors, ranging from Salty Beach (coconut, salt and graham cracker) to lemon and speculoos cookie cream. Many varieties are vegan friendly.

★ Kyu   FUSION $$
(Map p96; ☑ 786-577-0150; www.kyumiami.com; 251 NW 25th St; sharing plates $17-44; ⊙ noon-11:30pm Mon-Sat, 11am-10:30pm Sun, bar till 1am Fri & Sat; 🖉) 🍃 Kyu has been dazzling locals and food critics alike with its creative Asian-inspired dishes, most of which are cooked over the open flames of a wood-fired grill. Try the Florida red snapper, beef tenderloin and a magnificent head of cauliflower. There's also grilled octopus,

soft-shell-crab steamed buns and smoked beef brisket. Book ahead, or turn up and wait (usually around an hour).

Michael's Genuine   MODERN AMERICAN $$
(Map p96; ☑ 305-573-5550; www.michaels genuine.com; 130 NE 40th St; mains lunch $16-29, dinner $17-48; ⊙ 11:30am-11pm Mon-Sat, to 10pm Sun) This upscale tavern combines excellent service with a well-executed menu of wood-fired dishes, bountiful salads and raw bar temptations (including oysters and stone crabs). Michael's tends to draw a well-dressed crowd, and the place gets packed most days. There's also outdoor dining on the plant-lined pedestrian strip out front.

Butcher Shop   AMERICAN $$
(Map p96; ☑ 305-846-9120; www.butchershop miami.com/tbs; 165 NW 23rd St; mains $12-39; ⊙ 11am-midnight Sun-Thu, to 2am Fri & Sat) It's called the Butcher Shop for a reason, and that reason is it is unashamedly aimed at carnivores. From bone-in rib eyes to smoked sausages to full charcuterie, meat lovers have reason to rejoice. Beer lovers too: this butcher doubles as a beer garden, which gets lively as the sun goes down.

Mandolin   GREEK $$
(Map p96; ☑ 305-749-9140; www.mandolinmiami. com; 4312 NE 2nd Ave; mains $16-44; ⊙ noon-11pm; 🖉) It's all Mediterranean whites and blues at this Greek restaurant in the midst of the Buena Vista neighborhood. The back courtyard is beautifully lit in the evenings and the Greek cooking is good – try grilled sea bass marinated in lemon and olive oil, lamb kabobs with spicy yogurt or satisfying mezes, such as smoked eggplant and grilled octopus.

Palmar   CHINESE $$
(Map p96; ☑ 305-573-5682; www.palmar miami.com; 180 NW 29 St; mains $15-27; ⊙ 6-11pm Tue-Fri, from noon Sat & Sun) Palmar is putting the hipster Wynwood spin on Chinese classics in a sweet space bedecked with rattan lamps. Discerning diners pack in for Mongolian chicken with fermented chili, kimchi fried rice, *char siu* (pork) ribs, and a whole slew of dim sum, ranging from duck confit dumplings to crispy prawns with passion-fruit chili sauce.

Harry's Pizzeria   PIZZA $$
(Map p96; ☑ 786-275-4963; www.harryspizzeria. com; 3918 N Miami Ave; pizzas $13-17, mains $12-24; ⊙ 11:30am-10pm Sun-Thu, to midnight Fri & Sat; 🖉) A stripped-down yet sumptuous dining

Little Haiti & the Upper East Side

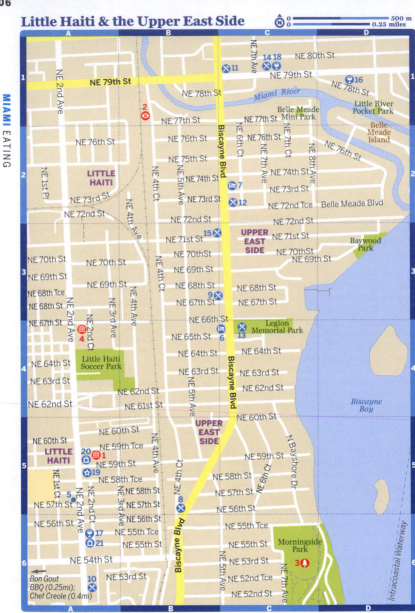

experience awaits pizza lovers in the Design District. Harry's tiny kitchen and dining room dishes out deceptively simple wood-fired pizzas topped with creative ingredients (shrimp, lemon and manchego, or spicy pepperoni). Add in some not-to-be missed appetizers like polenta fries and you have a great, haute-cuisine meal served for a very reasonable rate.

Maska

INDIAN $$

(Map p96; ☑ 786-971-9100; www.maskamiami.com; 3252 NE 1st Ave; mains $16-32, lunch thali $22-

Little Haiti & the Upper East Side

28; ⊙noon-3pm & 6-11pm Tue-Thu, to midnight Fri & Sat, noon-3:30pm & 6-10pm Sun) Maska is at the forefront of high-end Indian dining in Miami. The dining room, awash in subcontinental art and contemporary-design flourishes, accommodates diners feasting on crunchy soft-shell buns, tandoori lamb chops, and Kashmiri short ribs. Come at lunch for solid *thalis* (an all-you-can-eat plate of curries, chutneys, vegetables and starches).

★ **Alter** MODERN AMERICAN **$$$**
(Map p96; ☑305-573-5996; www.altermiami.com; 223 NW 23rd St; set menu 5/7 courses $90/110; ⊙7-11pm Tue-Sun) Alter's changing menu showcases high-quality Florida ingredients from sea and land in seasonally inspired dishes with Asian- and European-flavored haute cuisine. Expect dishes such as eggs with sea-scallop foam, truffle pearls and Siberian caviar, or 'Pelin' duck with dashi, turnip, and Jamaican ginger beer. Reserve soon, preferably yesterday.

Amara at Paraiso AMERICAN **$$$**
(Map p96; ☑305-702-5528; https://amaraat paraiso.com; 3101 NE 7th Ave; mains $24-150; ⊙11:30am-3pm & 5:30-11pm Mon-Thu, to midnight Fri & Sat, to 10pm Sun) You pay for the privilege at this gorgeous waterfront restaurant, but the rewards are delicious: new American/Latin American hybrid cuisine like a bone-in rib eye the size of a small child, a banana-wrapped mixed seafood grill, vegetarian cilantro rice, and grilled sweetbreads with chimichurri.

✗ **Little Haiti & the Upper East Side**

Chef Creole HAITIAN **$**
(☑305-754-2223; www.chefcreole.com; 200 NW 54th St; mains $10-22; ⊙11am-10pm Mon-Wed, to 11pm Thu-Sat) When you need Caribbean food on the cheap, head to the edge of Little Haiti and this excellent takeout shack. Order up fried conch, oxtail or fish, ladle rice and beans on the side, and you'll be full for a week. Enjoy the food on nearby picnic benches while Haitian music blasts out of tiny speakers – as island an experience as the food.

Jimmy's East Side Diner DINER **$**
(Map p106; ☑305-754-3692; 7201 Biscayne Blvd; mains $7-13; ⊙6:30am-4pm) Come to Jimmy's, a classic greasy spoon (that happens to be very LGBTQI+-friendly; note the rainbow flag out front), for big cheap breakfasts of omelets, French toast or pancakes, and turkey clubs and burgers later in the day. As an aside, the diner played a starring role in the final scene of Barry Jenkins' powerful film *Moonlight,* which won the Oscar for Best Picture in 2017.

Legion Park Farmers Market MARKET **$**
(Map p106; cnr Biscayne Blvd & 66th St, Legion Park; ⊙9am-2pm Sat) For a taste of local culture, stop by this small farmers market held each Saturday in the Upper East Side's Legion Park. It's got all the produce (especially tropical fruits), cheese and breads you'd need for a good picnic, and as with most markets of this ilk, it's a nice place to wander and soak up the community vibe. It's open year-round.

★ Blue Collar
AMERICAN $$

(Map p106; ☑ 305-756-0366; www.bluecollar miami.com; 6730 Biscayne Blvd; mains $17-27; ⊙ 11:30am-3:30pm daily, 6-10pm Sun-Thu, to 11pm Fri & Sat; P ☑ ⊕) ⊘ True to name, Blue Collar tosses pretension aside and fires up American comfort food done to perfection in a classic 1960s coffee-shop-style interior. Start off with shrimp and grits or the four-cheese Mac(aroni) before moving on to seared rainbow trout, a smoky plate of ribs or lip-smacking jambalaya.

A well-curated veg board keeps non-carnivores happy.

Phuc Yea
VIETNAMESE $$

(Map p106; ☑ 305-602-3710; www.phucyea.com; 7100 Biscayne Blvd; mains $16-27; ⊙ 6-10pm Mon-Thu, to 11pm Fri & Sat, 11:30am-3:30pm & 6-9pm Sun) Phuc Yea started as a pop-up and went wildly popular with its delicious Cajun-Vietnamese cooking (the name got about as much attention). Get yourself some lobster summer rolls, the excellent fish curry, spicy chicken wings, and other great sharing plates.

The venue is industrial with graffiti, soft lighting and loud hip-hop. The raw bar in front doles out sushi, fresh oysters and creative cocktails (happy hour from 5pm to 7pm). There's also outdoor dining in a paper-lantern-filled garden.

Bon Gout BBQ
BARBECUE $$

(☑ 305-381-5464; www.bongoutbbq.com; 99 NW 54th st; mains $10-25; ⊙ noon-10pm Tue-Sat, to 6pm Sun) A small dining room conceals a kitchen turning out enormous platters of meat that should get any proper carnivore salivating. Yes, you are in Little Haiti, and there is a tropical edge to the flavors, but the primary palette here is fantastically executed smokiness, which infuses all of the barbecue, from ribs to brisket to chicken wings.

Fried fish and *griot* (fried pork) add more Haitian color to the menu.

Andiamo
PIZZA $$

(Map p106; ☑ 305-762-5751; www.facebook.com/andiamopizzamiami; 5600 Biscayne Blvd; pizzas $12-21; ⊙ 11am-11pm Sun-Thu, to midnight Fri & Sat; ☑) Miami's best thin-crust pizzas come from the brick oven at this converted industrial space (once a tire shop). With more than 30 varieties, it's a lively setting to start off the night, with flickering tiki torches scattered around the outdoor tables and large screens showing sports on big-game nights.

Cake Thai
THAI $$

(Map p106; ☑ 786-534-7906; www.cakethaikitchen. com; 7919 Biscayne Blvd; mains $12-24; ⊙ noon-9:30pm Mon-Thu, to 11pm Fri & Sat, to 10:30pm Sun; ☑) Chef Phuket Thongsodchaveondee (who goes by the name 'Cake') is a Godfather of Thai cuisine in Miami, whipping up roasted duck salad, Panang pork belly, baby back ribs with garlic and black pepper, and pad thai with prawns – plus several variations of fried rice for good measure.

★ Boia De
ITALIAN $$$

(Map p106; ☑ 305-967-8866; www.boiade restaurant.com; 5205 NE 2nd Ave; small plates $8-24; ⊙ 5:30-10:30pm Sun-Thu, to 11:30pm Fri & Sat) Tucked into a faceless strip mall, Boia De is not your average Miami Italian eatery. The kitchen crew of punk rock-y chefs have an uncompromising commitment to their food, and no see-and-be-seen vibe has crept in (yet). The menu has a small plates approach, and you'll likely need more than one dish to fill up. Reservations are recommended.

Marky's Gourmet
RUSSIAN $$$

(Map p106; ☑ 305-758-9288; www.markys.com; 687 NE 79th St; ⊙ 9am-7pm Mon-Wed, to 9pm Thu-Sat, 10am-5pm Sun) A Miami institution among Russians, Russophiles and those that simply love to explore global cuisine, Marky's has been going strong since 1983. In-the-know foodies from afar flock here to load up on gourmet cheeses, olives, European-style sausages, wines, teas, jams, caviar and much more. As in the good old days of the Soviet Union, service does not come with a smile.

✗ Little Havana

★ Versailles
CUBAN $

(☑ 305-444-0240; www.versaillesrestaurant.com; 3555 SW 8th St; mains $6-21; ⊙ 8am-1am Mon-Thu, to 2:30am Fri & Sat, 9am-1am Sun) Versailles is an institution – one of the mainstays of Miami's Cuban gastronomic scene, and perhaps the most iconic Cuban restaurant in the nation. Try the excellent black bean soup or the fried yucca before moving onto heartier meat and seafood plates. Generations of Cuban Americans, along with Miami's Latin political elite, all rub elbows here.

★ El Nuevo Siglo
LATIN AMERICAN $

(Map p124; ☑ 305-854-1916; 1305 SW 8th St; mains $7-13; ⊙ 7am-9pm) Clouds of locals come to El Nuevo Siglo supermarket and rock up at the shiny black countertop counter for delicious cooking at excellent prices, plus unfussy ambience. Everything is good: nibble on roast meats, fried yucca, tangy Cuban sandwiches, grilled snapper with rice, beans and plantains, and other daily specials.

Lung Yai Thai Tapas
THAI **$**

(Map p124; 786-334-6262; www.lung-yai-thai-tapas.com; 1731 SW 8th St; mains $10-15; ⊙noon-3pm & 5pm-midnight Tue-Thu, to 1am Fri & Sat, 5pm-midnight Sun) This tiny gem in Little Havana has some excellent Thai cooking – and provides a nice change of palate in the area. Chef and owner Bas Trisransi produces a menu ideal for sharing, hence the 'tapas' in the name. Try the perfectly spiced fried chicken wings, tender duck salad or a much-revered *kaho soi gai* (a rich noodle curry).

Taqueria Viva Mexico
MEXICAN **$**

(Map p124; 786-350-6360; 502 SW 12th Ave; tacos $2.50-3; ⊙11am-9pm Tue-Thu, to 11pm Fri & Sat, to 6pm Sun) Head up busy 12th Ave for some of the best tacos in Little Havana. From a takeout window, smiling Latin ladies dole out heavenly tacos topped with steak, tripe, sausage and other meats. You can also grab a quesadilla ($6 to $12), if that's your thing. There are a few outdoor tables – or get it to go.

Yambo
LATIN AMERICAN **$**

(1643 SW 1st St; mains $5-12; ⊙24hr) If you're a bit drunk in the middle of the night and can find a cab or a friend willing to drive to Little Havana, direct them to Yambo. At night Yambo does a roaring trade selling trays and takeout boxes about to burst with juicy slices of *carne asada* (grilled beef), piles of rice and beans, and sweet fried plantains.

San Pocho
COLOMBIAN **$**

(Map p124; 305-854-5954; www.sanpocho.com; 901 SW 8th St; mains $6.50-17; ⊙7am-8pm Mon-Thu, to 9pm Fri-Sun) For a quick journey to Colombia, head to friendly, always hopping San Pocho. The meat-centric menu features hearty platters such as *bandeja paisa* (with grilled steak, rice, beans, an egg, an *arepa* and fried pork skin). There's also *mondongo* (tripe soup) as well as Colombian-style tamales and requisite sides such as *arepas*.

Azucar
ICE CREAM **$**

(Map p124; 305-381-0369; www.azucaricecream.com; 1503 SW 8th St; ice cream $4-6; ⊙11am-9pm Mon-Wed, to 11pm Thu-Sat, to 10pm Sun) One of Little Havana's oldest ice-cream parlors serves delicious ice cream just like *abuela* (grandmother) used to make. Deciding isn't easy with dozens of tempting flavors,

including rum raisin, dulce de leche, guava, mango, cinnamon, jackfruit and lemon basil.

El Exquisito Restaurant
CUBAN **$**

(Map p124; 305-643-0227; www.elexquisitomiami.com; 1510 SW 8th St; mains $9-13; ⊙7am-11pm) Great Cuban cuisine in the heart of Little Havana – the roast pork has a tangy citrus kick and the *ropa vieja* (spiced shredded beef and rice) is wonderfully rich. Even standard sides such as beans and rice and roasted plantains are executed with a little more care and are extra tasty. Prices are a steal, too.

★ El Carajo
SPANISH **$$**

(305-856-2424; www.el-carajo.com; 2465 SW 17th Ave; tapas $5-15; ⊙noon-10pm Sun-Wed, to 11pm Thu-Sat;) Walk past the motor oil inside the Citgo gas station on SW 17th Ave (yes, really!) into this Granadan wine cellar and get yourself a seat at the bar. Order the divine bacon-wrapped stuffed dates, fluffy *tortilla de patata* (thick Spanish omelets) and don't miss the sardines – cooked with a bit of salt and olive oil till they're dizzyingly delicious.

★ Doce Provisions
MODERN AMERICAN **$$**

(Map p124; 786-452-0161; www.doceprovisions.com; 541 SW 12th Ave; mains $12-25; ⊙noon-3:30pm & 5-10pm Mon-Thu, noon-3:30pm & 5-11pm Fri, noon-11pm Sat, noon-9pm Sun) For a break from old-school Latin eateries, stop in at Doce Provisions. The industrial interior is stylish and sets the stage for dining on creative American fare – rock shrimp mac 'n' cheese, fried chicken with sweet plantain waffle, short-rib burgers and truffle fries – plus local microbrews. Brunch is justifiably popular on Sunday (11am to 3pm). There's a nice leafy terrace out back.

✖ Coconut Grove

Coral Bagels
DELI **$**

(305-854-0336; www.coralbagels.com; 2750 SW 26th Ave; mains $7-11; ⊙6:30am-8pm Tue-Fri, 7am-8pm Sat, to 4pm Sun, 6:30am-3pm Mon;) Miami has a large 'Juban' (Jewish-Cuban) population, and this spot is sort of like a Juban given brick-and-mortar restaurant form. The buzzing little deli serves proper bagels, rich omelets and decadent potato pancakes with apple sauce and sour cream. You'll be hard-pressed to spend double digits, and you'll leave satisfied.

Bianco Gelato
ICE CREAM **$**

(Map p110; 786-717-5315; www.biancogelato.com; 3137 Commodore Plaza; ice cream $3.50-7;

Coconut Grove

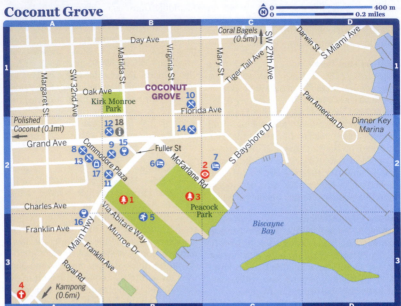

Coconut Grove

⊙ noon-11pm Mon-Thu, to 11:30pm Fri, 11am-11:30pm Sat, 11am-11pm Sun) A much-loved spot in the neighborhood, Bianco whips up amazing gelato that's all made from organic milk and natural ingredients. Flavors change regularly, but a few hits have included guava and cheese, avocado with caramelized nuts, hazelnut and vegan chocolate.

Last Carrot　　　　　　　VEGETARIAN $

(Map p110; ☑ 305-445-0805; 3133 Grand Ave; mains $5-9; ⊙ 10:30am-6pm Mon-Sat, 11am-4:30pm Sun;

✐ 🚻) Going strong since the 1970s, and set in a decidedly unglamorous corner of Coconut Grove, the Last Carrot serves fresh juices, delicious pita sandwiches, avocado melts, veggie burgers and rather-famous spinach pies. The Carrot's endurance is testament to the quality of its good-for-your-body food.

Spillover　　　　　　MODERN AMERICAN $$

(Map p110; ☑ 305-456-5723; www.spillovermiami.com; 2911 Grand Ave; mains $17-32; ⊙ noon-10pm Sun-Thu, to 11pm Fri, 11am-11pm Sat, 11am-10pm Sun; 🐾✐) Tucked down a pedestrian strip near the CocoWalk, the Spillover serves locally sourced seafood and creative bistro fare in an affected vintage setting (cast-iron stools and recycled doors around the bar, suspenders-wearing staff, brassy jazz playing overhead). Come for crab cakes, buffalo shrimp tacos, spear-caught fish and chips, or a melt-in-your-mouth lobster Reuben.

LoKal   AMERICAN $$
(Map p110; ☑ 305-442-3377; www.lokalmiami.com; 3190 Commodore Plaza; burgers $15-16; ⊙ noon-10pm Mon & Tue, to 11pm Wed-Fri, 11:30am-11pm Sat, 11:30am-10pm Sun; ✲ ✏ ⊞) ✏ This little Coconut Grove joint does two things very well: burgers and craft beer. The former come in several variations, all utilizing excellent beef (bar the oat and brown-rice version). When in doubt, go for the *frita*, which adds in guava sauce, melted Gruyère and crispy bacon.

Atchana's Homegrown Thai   THAI $$
(Map p110; ☑ 305-774-0404; https://atchanas.com; 3194 Commodore Plaza; mains $16-21; ⊙ noon-10pm Sun-Thu, to 11pm Fri & Sat; ⊞) Woodsy, airy environs are the setting at this standout Thai restaurant, which takes diners on a culinary tour of many of the regional cuisines from that nation. Yes, you can get massaman curry, but there's also *khao soi* from northern Thailand (coconut curry chicken soup) and rarer treats like a crispy fried whole red snapper. It also has a kids' menu.

Bombay Darbar   INDIAN $$
(Map p110; ☑ 305-444-7272; www.bombaydarbar.com; 2901 Florida Ave; mains $17-22; ⊙ noon-3pm Mon-Sat, 6-10pm Mon-Thu, to 11pm Fri & Sat, noon-10pm Sun; ✏) Indian food can be tough to find in Miami and all the more so in Coconut Grove, which makes Bombay Darbar even more of a culinary gem. Run by a couple from Mumbai, this upscale but friendly place hits all the right notes, with its beautifully executed tandooris and tikkas, best accompanied by piping-hot naan.

GreenStreet Cafe   AMERICAN $$
(Map p110; ☑ 305-444-0244; www.greenstreetcafe.net; 3468 Main Hwy; mains $15-31; ⊙ 7:30am-12:30am Sun-Tue, to 2am Wed-Sat) Sidewalk spots don't get more popular than GreenStreet, where the Grove's pretty and gregarious congregate at sunset. The menu of high-end pub fare ranges from roast vegetable and goat cheese lasagna to blackened *mahimahi*.

✖ Coral Gables

Threefold   CAFE $
(Map p118; ☑ 305-704-8007; www.threefoldcafe.com; 141 Giralda Ave; mains $10-16; ⊙ 7:30am-3pm Mon, to 4pm Tue-Fri, 7am-4pm Sat & Sun; ☎ ✏) One of Coral Gables' most talked-about cafes is a buzzing, Aussie-run charmer that serves perfectly pulled espressos (and a good flat white), along with creative breakfasts and lunch fare. Start the morning with waffles and berry compote, smashed avocado toast or a slow-roasted leg of lamb with fried eggs.

Frenchie's Diner   FRENCH $$
(Map p118; ☑ 305-442-4554; www.frenchiesdiner.com; 2618 Galiano St; mains lunch $12-36, dinner $21-36; ⊙ 11am-3pm & 6-10pm Tue-Fri, 6-10pm Sat) Located on a side street, Frenchie's has a tucked-away appeal that is quite, well, French. But if the location is 'French-y,' the restaurant itself is the eating out equivalent of blasting 'La Marseillaise'. There are black-and-white checkered floors, a chalkboard menu, old prints on the walls, and lots of bistro classics.

Matsuri   JAPANESE $$
(Map p118; ☑ 305-663-1615; 5759 Bird Rd; mains $7-22; ⊙ 11:30am-2:30pm Tue-Fri, 5:30-10pm Sun & Tue-Thu, 5:30-11pm Fri & Sat) There are many trendy sushi spots in Miami, but while this strip mall restaurant lacks scene, it is often packed with customers seeking real deal, delicious Japanese cuisine (including quite a few South American Japanese). Spicy *toro* (fatty tuna) and scallions, and grilled mackerel with natural salt are all *oishii* (delicious).

Bulla Gastrobar   SPANISH $$
(Map p118; ☑ 786-810-6215; www.bullagastrobar.com; 2500 Ponce de Leon Blvd; small plates $7-19; ⊙ noon-10pm Mon & Tue, to 11pm Wed & Thu, to midnight Fri & Sat, 11am-10pm Sun; ✏) With a festive crowd chattering away, this stylish spot has great ambience that evokes the lively eating and drinking dens of Madrid. *Patatas bravas* (spicy potatoes), and *huevos* 'bulla' (eggs, *serrano* ham and truffle oil) keep the crowds coming throughout the night.

Ortanique On the Mile   CARIBBEAN $$$
(Map p118; ☑ 305-446-7710; https://ortanique restaurants.com; 278 Miracle Mile; mains lunch $17-26, dinner $25-58; ⊙ 11:30am-10pm Mon-Thu, to 11pm Fri, 6-11pm Sat, 5:30-9:30pm Sun; ✏) Eating at Caribbean-derived Ortanique is like a white tablecloth version of having a Red Stripe on the beach, which totally

A LITTLE WINDOW ON VENTANITA CULTURE

What's the most common kind of restaurant in Miami? Chain fast-food joints? Hotel bars? Yet *another* Peruvian-Japanese fusion place?

Escucha, dear readers, and learn about the *ventanita*. The word means 'little window,' and these places are just that: small windows attached to storefronts, gas stations, some auntie's house etc, that typically serve small cups of rocket fuel Cuban coffee, also known as a *cafe Cubano* or *cafecito* (espresso with foam made from beating sugar and coffee).

Also on the menu – usually – is *cafe con leche* (a cup of steamed milk served alongside a shot of espresso), loaves of buttered Cuban bread, *pastelitos* (flaky, filled pastries; the most common fillings are guava, cheese, guava and cheese, and meat), sandwiches, etc – the options are fairly limitless.

Many *ventanitas* are attached to larger restaurants (there's a very good one at Versailles; p108), but they can be found almost anywhere in the city that hasn't become overly gentrified. Even if you order a *cafecito* at a *ventanita* (and you should), we recommend just watching the bustle at these coffee stands on any given morning. Customers get together, talk trash, flirt, make predictions about the Heat, etc. You might say they're a fascinating *little window* into Miami's day to day.

scans, seeing as one of the best appetizers is Red Stripe steamed clams and mussels. Other standouts are jerked Cornish hen, seared ahi tuna with mango salsa, and an ever-changing slate of vegetarian specials.

Eating House Miami   AMERICAN $$$
(☏305-448-6524; www.eatinghousemiami.com; 804 Ponce de Leon Blvd; small plates $7-16, large plates $18-34; ⊙11:30am-10pm Tue-Thu, to 11pm Fri, 11am-11pm Sat, to 3pm Sun) Eating House is one of the stars of the Gables fine dining scene, but the vibe is consciously counterculture: graffiti on the walls, and a playful menu of souped-up Miami comfort food, from chicken and waffles to pork-belly-and-arborio-rice *croquetas*. We recommend ordering lots of small plates, then going wild.

Pascal's on Ponce   FRENCH $$$
(Map p118; ☏305-444-2024; 2611 Ponce de Leon Blvd; mains lunch $22-31, dinner $31-45; ⊙11:30am-2:30pm Mon-Fri, 6-10pm Mon-Thu, to 11pm Fri & Sat) They're fighting the good fight here: sea scallops with beef short rib, crispy duck confit with wild mushroom fricasée and other French fine-dining classics set the stage for a night of high-end feasting. Pascal's is a favorite among Coral Gables foodies who appreciate time-tested standards.

The menu and the atmosphere rarely change, and frankly that's not a bad thing. After all, if it ain't broke…

Caffe Abbracci   ITALIAN $$$
(Map p118; ☏305-441-0700; www.caffeabbracci. com; 318 Aragon Ave; mains $26-47; ⊙11:30am-3:30pm Mon-Fri, 6-11pm Sun-Fri, to midnight Sat)

Perfect moments in Coral Gables come easy. Here's a simple formula: you, a loved one, a muggy Miami evening, some delicious pasta and a glass of red at a sidewalk table at Abbracci – one of the finest Italian restaurants in the Gables.

✖ Key Biscayne

La Boulangerie Boul'Mich   CAFE $
(Map p98; ☏305-365-5260; www.laboulangerie usa.com; 328 Crandon Blvd; mains $12-15, pastries $3-6; ⊙7:30am-8pm Mon-Sat, 8am-4pm Sun; ☏ 🖈) This delightful French-style bakery whips up delicious quiches, satisfying veggie- or meat-filled empanadas, heavenly pastries and, of course, perfectly buttery croissants. It's also a fine place for breakfast (fruit platters, eggs Benedict) or lunch (prosciutto and mozzarella sandwiches, four-cheese gnocchi, quinoa salads). The shop may close earlier if it runs out of stuff.

Golden Hog Gourmet   SUPERMARKET $
(Map p98; ☏305-361-1300; https://thegolden hogmarket.com; 91 Harbor Dr; mains $8-15; ⊙8am-9pm Mon-Sat, to 7pm Sun) Tucked into a small shopping complex, this is the best place in Key Biscayne to grab picnic fare before hitting the beach or state parks. Aside from good cheeses, bakery items, tasty spreads and fresh fruits, there are various counters where you can order takeout sandwiches, soups and ready-made dishes.

Boater's Grill   SEAFOOD $$
(Map p98; ☏305-361-0080; www.boatersgrill. com; 1200 S Crandon Blvd, Bill Baggs Cape Florida

State Park; mains $14-41; ◷9am-8:30pm Sun-Wed, to 10pm Thu-Sat) Located in Bill Baggs Cape Florida State Park, this waterfront restaurant (actually there's water below and all around) has a menu that is packed with South Florida maritime goodness: stone crabs, mahimahi, and seafood paella.

Kebo
SPANISH $$

(Map p98; ☑305-365-1244; www.facebook.com/keborestaurant; 200 Crandon Blvd; mains $16-39; ◷noon-10pm Sun-Thu, to 11pm Fri & Sat) This fantastic Spanish restaurant would be packed on the mainland; as it is, Kebo is very popular, but its Key Biscayne location gives it an out-of-the-way romantic atmosphere. This is all underlined by a pleasantly austere interior, and courses such as wild mushroom risotto, grilled prawns, and Galician octopus – the attention to detail, and resulting flavors, are outstanding.

Novecento
ARGENTINE $$$

(Map p98; ☑305-362-0900; www.novecento.com; 620 Crandon Blvd; mains $15-39; ◷11:30am-11pm Mon-Thu, to midnight Fri & Sat, to 10pm Sun) Need a nice night out on this little urban island? Tough to do better than this Argentine mainstay, especially if you're a fan of a nicely marbled steak. Other delights include tagliatelle with meat sauce, octopus salad, and a nice gnocchi in a four-cheese sauce.

✗ Greater Miami

★ Islas Canarias
CUBAN $

(☑305-559-6666; http://islascanariasrestaurant.com; 13695 SW 26th St; mains $6-18; ◷7am-10pm Sun-Thu, to 11pm Fri & Sat; ℗) If you ask Miami natives where the city's best Cuban food is served, an argument will probably break out. But Islas Canarias will likely as not be mentioned multiple times. Located a fair drive from the main tourism districts, this spot is particularly famous for its *ropa vieja*, Cuban coffee, and *croquetas*, but really, everything is outstanding. Don't pass up on the signature homemade chips, especially the ones cut from plantains.

★ Stephen's Deli
JEWISH $

(☑https://www.stephensdeli.com; www.stephensdeli.com; 1000 E 16th St, Hialeah; sandwiches $11-15; ◷11am-5pm) Stephen's is a Jewish deli for the 21st century. Yes, it has a '50s malt-shop vibe, and there is a literal shrine to the show *Seinfeld*. But all of the above is done with a 21st-century self-referential sense of playfulness. Also, the food is *good*. All deli

meats, especially the pastrami, corned beef, and turkey, are mouthwateringly juicy, while the bread is fresh and fragrant. Don't miss this one.

Jelly & Burger
VENEZUELAN $

(☑305-760-2149; 17010 W Dixie Hwy; mains $6-13; ◷8am-3:30pm; ℗) Odd name? A bit, but the food makes up for it at this takeout spot where you can get, yes, excellent burgers (including the *lechón* – marinated pulled pork), but also savor Venezuelan favorites like *cachapas*, a thick, soft, delicious corn cake, similar but distinct from an *arepa*.

🍷 Drinking & Nightlife

Miami has an intense variety of bars, ranging from grotty jazz and punk dives (with excellent music) to beautiful lounges, cocktail bars blended with tropical gardens, and Cuban dance halls. Miami's nightlife reputation for being all about wealth, good looks and phoniness is thankfully mostly isolated to the South Beach scene.

🍷 South Beach

★ Sweet Liberty
BAR

(Map p66; ☑305-763-8217; www.mysweetliberty.com; 237 20th St; ◷4pm-5am Mon-Sat, from noon Sun) A much-loved local haunt near Collins Park, Sweet Liberty has all the right ingredients for a fun night out: friendly, easygoing bartenders who whip up excellent cocktails (try a mint julep), great happy-hour specials (including 75¢ oysters) and a relaxed crowd. The space is huge, with flickering candles, a long wooden bar and the odd band adding to the cheer.

★ Mac's Club Deuce Bar
BAR

(Map p66; ☑305-531-6200; www.macsclubdeuce.com; 222 14th St; ◷8am-5am) The oldest bar in Miami Beach (established in 1926), the Deuce is a real neighborhood bar and hype-free zone. It's just straight-up seediness, which depending on your outlook can be quite refreshing. Plan to see everyone from tourists to drag queens to off-shift bar staff – some hooking up, some talking rough, all having a good time.

Bodega
COCKTAIL BAR

(Map p66; ☑305-704-2145; www.bodegataqueria.com; 1220 16th St; ◷noon-5am) Bodega looks like your average cool-kid Mexican joint – serving delicious tacos ($3 to $5) from a converted Airstream trailer to a party-minded

MIAMI DRINKING & NIGHTLIFE

SOUTH BEACH SIPPIN'

Greater Miami's coffee scene has improved in leaps and bounds in recent years, though Miami Beach still has limited options (we don't count stand-up Cuban coffee counters, as you can't sit there and read a book or work on your laptop, although if you speak Spanish, they're a good place for hearing local gossip). That said, there are a handful of decent options in Miami Beach.

➡ Panther Coffee (p97) The Wynwood chain has opened a great spot in Sunset Harbour.

➡ A La Folie (p100) A *très* French cafe with some excellent pastries.

➡ Segafredo L'Originale (p99) Pulls an excellent espresso on Lincoln Rd.

➡ Lilikoi (p100) The best spot in SoFi for a pick-me-up.

crowd. But there's actually a bar hidden behind that blue porta-potty door on the right. Head inside (or join the long line on weekends) to take in a bit of old-school glam in a sprawling drinking den.

Mango's Tropical Café
BAR

(Map p60; ☑305-673-4422; www.mangos.com; 900 Ocean Dr; $10, dinner & show ticket $26; ⏱11:45am-5am) Visitors from across the globe mix things up at this famous bar on Ocean Dr. Every night feels like a celebration, with a riotously fun vibe, and plenty of entertainment: namely minimally dressed salsa dancing on the bar, doing Michael Jackson impersonations, shimmying in feather headdresses or showing off some amazing salsa moves. It's a kitschy good time, which doesn't even take into consideration the small dance floor and stage in the back, where brassy Latin bands get everyone moving.

Kill Your Idol
BAR

(Map p66; ☑305-672-1852; www.facebook.com/killyouridolmiami; 222 Española Way; ⏱8pm-5am) Kill Your Idol is a lovable hipster dive, with graffiti and shelves full of retro bric-a-brac covering the walls, plus drag shows on Monday and DJs spinning danceable old-school grooves. The crowd is a mix of cool-kid locals and fashionable out-of-towners.

Story
CLUB

(Map p60; ☑305-479-4426; www.storymiami.com; 136 Collins Ave; ⏱11pm-5am Thu-Sat) For the big megaclub experience, Story is a top destination. Some of the best DJs (mostly EDM) from around the globe spin at this club, with parties lasting late into the night. It has a fairly roomy dance floor, but gets packed on weekend nights. Be good-looking and dress to impress, as getting in can be a pain.

Lost Weekend
BAR

(Map p66; ☑305-672-1707; www.sub-culture.org/lost-weekend-miami; 218 Española Way; ⏱4pm-5am) The Weekend is a grimy, sweaty dive, filled with pool tables, cheap domestics and – hell yeah – *Golden Tee* and *Big Buck Hunter* arcade games. God bless it. It is popular with local waiters, kitchen staff and bartenders.

Abbey Brewery
MICROBREWERY

(Map p66; ☑305-538-8110; www.abbeybrewinginc.com; 1115 16th St; ⏱1pm-5am) The oldest brewpub in South Beach is on the untouristed end of South Beach (near Alton Rd). It's friendly and packed with folks listening to throwback hits (grunge, '80s new wave) and slinging back some excellent homebrew: give Father Theo's stout or the Immaculate IPA a try.

🍷 North Beach

⭐ **Broken Shaker**
BAR

(Map p92; ☑305-531-2727; www.freehandhotels.com; 2727 Indian Creek Dr, Freehand Miami Hotel; ⏱5:30pm-2am Mon-Thu, 4:30pm-3am Fri, 1pm-3am Sat, to 2am Sun) A single small room with a well-equipped bar produces expert cocktails, which are mostly consumed in the beautiful, softly lit garden – all of it part of the Freehand Miami hotel (p91). There's a great soundtrack at all times, and the drinks are excellent.

The clientele is a mix of hotel guests (young and into partying) and cool locals.

Bob's Your Uncle
BAR

(Map p92; ☑786-542-5366; www.bobsyouruncle miami.com; 928 71st St; ⏱3pm-3am) Bob's Your Uncle's name doesn't just derive from the saying. 'Bob' is simple, and so is this bar:

classic cocktails, good beer, spacious seating, old games, friendly service, and the chillest vibe in Miami Beach. It's just a decently priced spot where you can grab a drink and catch up with friends, and that's something beautiful.

On The Rocks
SPORTS BAR

(Map p92; ☑305-864-2444; https://ontherocks miamibeach.com; 217 71st St; ⊕8am-5am) This convivial neighborhood dive feels pulled from another era, a feeling underlined by the multiple racks of old liquor bottles behind the bar and the nicely faded feel of the whole establishment. Grab a cold beer, watch the game with locals on either side of you, and relax.

Downtown Miami

★ Lost Boy
BAR

(Map p84; ☑305-372-7303; www.lostboydry goods.com; 157 E Flagler St; ⊕noon-2am Mon-Sat, to midnight Sun) Miami is a city full of impressive-looking bars, but few pull off vintage aesthetics like Lost Boy, which makes sense, as it is housed in one of the oldest-standing buildings in Downtown. Vintage Cuban furniture, brass knobs, exposed brick and lots of old wood come together into an enormous pub with straightforward cocktails and beers served in imperial pint glasses.

★ The Corner
BAR

(Map p84; ☑305-961-7887; www.thecorner miami.com; 1035 N Miami Ave; ⊕4pm-5am Sun-Thu, to 8am Fri & Sat) This excellent bar sits near Eleven Miami, which is ironic as the Corner couldn't have a more different vibe. The interior, all dark wood and dim lighting, looks like it could double as a fancy old British library. Many folks still choose to drink outdoors – this is Miami – sipping classic cocktails and cold beers. It attracts a non-fussy, creative professional crowd.

★ Baby Jane
BAR

(Map p84; ☑786-623-3555; www.babyjane miami.com; 500 Brickell Ave; ⊕noon-3am Sun-Thu, to 5am Fri & Sat) Small but sexy, Baby Jane is a Brickell outpost filled with tropical accents, neon, and Pacific Rim meets the Caribbean cocktails like the Big Trouble in Little Havana, which features *flor de caña* rum infused with wontons, a sentence we could only write in Miami. The crowd seems to mainly be Downtown cool kids, but the vibe is laid back.

Blackbird Ordinary
BAR

(Map p84; ☑305-671-3307; www.blackbird ordinary.com; 729 SW 1st Ave; ⊕3pm-5am Mon-Fri, from 5pm Sat & Sun) This is an excellent bar, with great cocktails and a vibe that manages to strike a good balance between laid-back and Miami hedonism. The only thing 'ordinary' about the place is the sense that all are welcome for a fun and pretension-free night out. You can often catch great live music, and on quiet nights there's always a pool table.

Mama Tried
BAR

(Map p84; http://mamatriedmia.com; 207 NE 1st St; ⊕3pm-5am Mon-Fri, from 5pm Sat & Sun) She really did. And she pulled off a very fine bar here in the heart of Downtown. Look for an orange neon sign, then walk into a dark bar with a speakeasy feel, giant metallic light fixtures, and a big square bar. It's got a laid-back, even neighborhood vibe on weekdays, but turns into an absolute Miami dance party on weekend nights.

Esotico
COCKTAIL BAR

(☑305-800-8454; www.esoticomiami.com; 1600 NE 1st Ave; ⊕5pm-1am Mon-Thu, to 2am Fri & Sat) Who knew there was a jungle in the middle of Downtown Miami? That's the sense one gets after walking into Esotico, all leafy plants, green murals and hot neon. Tiki drinks are as sultry as the setting, ranging from Zombies to new spins on the Colada. A breakfast cocktail of rum, ginger syrup, lime juice and bananas is flat-out stunning.

Eleven Miami
CLUB

(E11EVEN; Map p84; ☑786-460-4803; www.11 miami.com; 29 NE 11th St; ⊕24hr) Since its opening in 2014, Eleven Miami has remained one of the top Downtown clubs. There's much eye candy here (and not just the attractive club-goers): go-go dancers, aerialists and

LOCAL KNOWLEDGE

DOWNTOWN MIAMI

Bar-hopping Have a stumbling pub crawl from Mama Tried (p115) to Lost Boy (p115).

Yoga in the park The open-air views of the bay are a perfect backdrop to sun salutations at free classes by the Tina Hills Pavilion (p82).

Hangouts Linger over excellent coffee and breakfast served at all hours at All Day (p102).

DON'T MISS

ROOFTOP BARS

Miami's high-rises are put to fine use by the many rooftop bars you'll find scattered around the city. These are usually located in high-end hotels found in Miami Beach and in Downtown. The view is of course the big reason to come – and it can be sublime, with the sweep of Biscayne Bay or a sparkling beachfront in the background. Despite being in hotels, some spots are a draw for locals and it can be quite a scene, with DJs, a dressy crowd and a discriminating door policy at prime time on weekend nights. If you're here for the view and not the party, come early. Happy hour is fabulous – you can catch a fine sunset and getting in is usually not a problem.

racy (striptease-esque) performances, amid a state-of-the-art sound system, with top DJs working the crowd into a frenzy.

Sugar
LOUNGE

(Map p84; 786-805-4655; www.east-miami.com/en/restaurants-and-bars/sugar; 788 Brickell Plaza, EAST, Miami Hotel, 40th fl; noon-1am Sun-Wed, to 3am Thu-Sat) One of Miami's hottest bars sits on the 40th floor of the EAST, Miami hotel (p94). Calling it a rooftop bar doesn't quite do the place justice. Verdant oasis is more like it, with a spacious open-air deck full of plants and trees – and sweeping views over the city and Key Biscayne.

Area 31
ROOFTOP BAR

(Map p84; 305-424-5234; www.area31restaurant.com; 270 Biscayne Blvd Way, Klimpton Epic Hotel; 6-10pm Sun-Thu, to 11pm Fri & Sat) On the rooftop of the Kimpton Epic Hotel (p94), this open-air bar draws in the after-work happy-hour crowd, which morphs into a more party-minded gathering as the evening progresses. The view – overlooking the river and the high-rises of Downtown – is stunning.

American Social Club
SPORTS BAR

(Map p84; 305-570-4468; https://americansocialbar.com/brickell; 690 SW 1st Ct; 11:30am-1am Mon-Wed, to 2am Thu, to 3am Fri & Sat, to midnight Sun) There's a surprising lack of waterfront bars in Downtown Miami, but American Social Club fills the gap nicely. This is a big bar with a frat-y vibe that attracts a mix of conference attendees, pro athletes and locals who want a riverside drink.

🍷 Wynwood &
the Design District

Wood Tavern
BAR

(Map p96; 305-748-2828; www.facebook.com/woodtavern; 2531 NW 2nd Ave; 5pm-3am Tue-Sat, 3pm-midnight Sun, 5pm-2am Mon) The crowd here is local kids who want something stylish, but don't want South Beach. Food specials are cheap, the beer selection is excellent and the crowd is friendly. The outdoor space has picnic benches, a wooden stage complete with bleachers, a giant Jenga game, and an attached art gallery with rotating exhibits.

Boxelder
BAR

(Map p96; 305-942-7769; www.bxldr.com; 2817 NW 2nd Ave; 4pm-midnight Mon, 1pm-midnight Tue-Thu, to 2am Fri & Sat, to 10pm Sun) This long, narrow space is a beer-lover's Valhalla, with a menu of brews from near and far, though its 20 rotating beer taps give pride of place to South Florida beers. There's also more than 100 different varieties by the bottle. The down-to-earth vibe keeps the place humming.

Gramps
BAR

(Map p96; 305-699-2669; www.gramps.com; 176 NW 24th St; 11am-1am Sun-Wed, to 3am Thu-Sat) Friendly and unpretentious (just like some grandpas), Gramps always has something afoot whether it's live music and DJs, dueling synthesizers (awesome) or bingo. The big draw though is really just the sizable backyard that's perfect for alfresco drinking and socializing.

R House
BAR

(Map p96; 305-576-0201; www.rhousewynwood.com; 2727 NW 2nd Ave; 3-10pm Wed & Thu, to 3am Fri, 11:30am-3am Sat, to 9pm Sun, brunch 11:30am & 2:30pm Sat & Sun) R House specializes in a lot: cocktails, happy hours, and shareable happy-hour bites ($3 to $7).But it's best known for its immensely popular drag brunch. You need to reserve seats ($45 to $65, food included) *way* in advance for this raucous affair that has a deserved reputation as one of the best midday parties in Miami.

Coyo Taco
BAR

(Map p96; 305-573-8228; www.coyo-taco.com; 2300 NW 2nd Ave; 11am-3am Mon-Sat, to 11pm Sun) Secret bars hidden behind taco stands are all the rage in Miami. To find this one, head inside Coyo Taco, down the corridor past the bathrooms and enter the unmarked door. Inside you'll find a classy low-lit spot with a DJ booth, with brassy Latin rhythms and Afro Cuban funk filling the space.

Lagniappe
BAR

(Map p96; 305-576-0108; www.lagniappe house.com; 3425 NE 2nd Ave; 6pm-2am Sun-Thu, to 3am Fri & Sat) Lagniappe copycats a New Orleans model of outdoors drinking spaces fronted by an old-fashioned bar packed with art, faded vintage furnishings and weathered walls. There's live music (9pm to midnight, 10pm to 1am Friday and Saturday), in a sprawling back garden filled with palm trees and fairy lights. It gets *very* crowded here on weekends.

Little Haiti & the Upper East Side

★ The Anderson
BAR

(Map p106; 786-401-6330; www.theanderson miami.com; 709 NE 79th St; 5pm-2am Sun-Thu, to 4am Fri & Sat) The Anderson is a great neighborhood bar with a dimly lit interior sprinkled with red couches, animal-print fabrics, and neon wallpaper that will put you in mind of an '80s dance-music video. Head to the large outdoor back area for more of a tropical-themed setting where you can dip your toes in the sand (never mind the absent oceanfront).

Vagabond Pool Bar
BAR

(Map p106; 305-400-8420; www.thevagabond hotelmiami.com; 7301 Biscayne Blvd; 5pm-midnight Mon-Fri, from noon Sat & Sun) Tucked behind the Vagabond Hotel, this is a great spot with perfectly mixed cocktails courtesy of pro bartenders (the kind who will shake your hand and introduce themselves). The outdoor setting overlooking the palm-fringed pool and eclectic crowd pairs nicely with elixirs such as the Lost in Smoke (mezcal, amaro, amaretto and orange bitters).

Churchill's
BAR

(Map p106; 305-757-1807; www.churchillspub. com; 5501 NE 2nd Ave; 3pm-3am Sun-Thu, to 5am Fri & Sat) A Miami icon that's been around since 1979, Churchill's is a Brit-owned pub in the midst of what could be Port-au-Prince. There's a lot of live music here, mainly punk, indie, hip-hop, and more punk.

Boteco
BAR

(Map p106; 305-345-7615; www.botecomiami.com; 916 NE 79th St; noon-11pm Sun-Thu, to midnight Fri & Sat) If you're missing the *cidade maravilhosa* (aka Rio de Janeiro), come to Boteco on Friday evening to see the biggest Brazilian expat

ART WALKS: NIGHTLIFE MEETS ART

Ever-flowing (not always free) wine and beer, great art, a fun crowd and no cover charge (or velvet rope): welcome to the wondrous world where art and nightlife collide. The Wynwood and Design District Art Walks are among the best ways to experience an alternative slice of Miami culture. Just be careful, as a lot of galleries in Wynwood are separated by short drives (the Design District is more walkable). Art Walks (p88) take place on the second Saturday of each month, from 7pm to 10pm (some galleries stretch to 11pm); when it's all over, lots of folks repair to Wood Tavern (p116) or the **Sylvester** (Map p96; 305-814-4548; www.thesylvesterbar. com; 3456 N Miami Ave; 5pm-2am Tue-Thu & Sun, to 3am Fri & Sat). Visit www. artofmiami.com/maps/art-walks for information on participating galleries.

reunion in Miami. *Cariocas* (Rio natives) and their compatriots flock here to listen to samba and bossa nova, and chat each other up over the best caipirinhas in town.

Little Havana

★ Los Pinareños Frutería
JUICE BAR

(Map p124; 305-285-1135; 1334 SW 8th St; snacks & drinks $3-6; 7am-6pm Mon-Sat, to 3pm Sun) Nothing says refreshment on a sultry Miami afternoon like a cool glass of fresh juice (or *batidos* – milkshakes) at this fruit and veggie stand, beloved by generations of Miamians. Sip a *guarapa* (sugarcane extract) *batido* while roosters cluck and folks gossip and argue in Cuban-accented Spanish; this is as Miami as it gets, short of being in a Pitbull song.

Ball & Chain
BAR

(Map p124; 305-643-7820; www.ballandchain miami.com; 1513 SW 8th St; 11am-midnight Mon-Wed, to 2am Thu, to 3am Fri & Sat, to 1am Sun) The Ball & Chain has survived several incarnations over the years. Back in 1935, when 8th St was more Jewish than Latino, it was the sort of jazz joint Billie Holiday would croon in. That iteration closed in 1957, but today's Ball & Chain is still dedicated to music and good times – specifically, Latin music and tropical cocktails.

Coral Gables

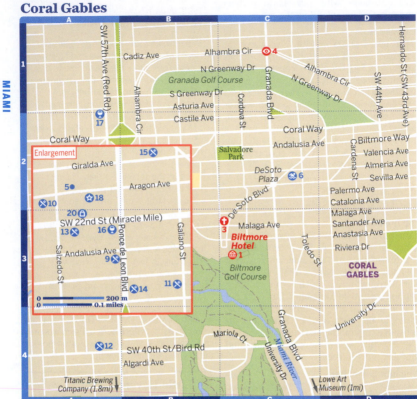

Coral Gables

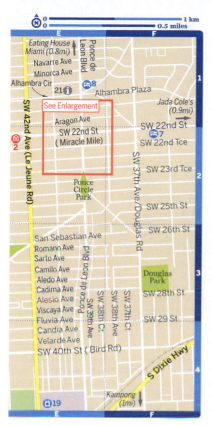

🍷 Coconut Grove

Taurus
BAR

(Map p110; 📞 305-529-6523; https://taurusbeer andwhiskey.com; 3540 Main Hwy; ⏰ 4pm-3am Mon-Fri, from noon Sat & Sun) The oldest bar in Coconut Grove is a cool mix of wood paneling, smoky-leather chairs, about 100 beers to choose from and a convivial vibe – as Miami neighborhood bars go, this is one of the best.

Barracuda
BAR

(Map p110; 📞 305-918-9013; https://barracuda-taphouse-grill.business.site; 3035 Fuller St; ⏰ noon-3am Tue-Sun, from 6pm Mon) Coconut Grove has its share of divey, pretension-free bars, and Barracuda is one of the better ones, with a fine jukebox, pool table, darts, and sports playing on the various TV screens. It's a fine retreat from the Grove's shiny shopping vibe – the inside is decorated with wood salvaged from an old Florida shrimp boat.

🍷 Coral Gables

Seven Seas
BAR

(Map p118; 📞 305-266-6071; www.facebook.com/ sevenseasbar; 2200 SW 57th Ave; ⏰ noon-1am Sun-Wed, to 2am Thu-Sat) Seven Seas is a genuine Miami neighborhood dive, decorated on the inside like a nautical theme park and filled with University of Miami students, Cuban workers, gays, straights, lesbians and folks from around the way.

Come for the best karaoke in Miami on Tuesday, Thursday and Saturday, and for trivia on Monday.

Copper 29
BAR

(Map p118; 📞 786-580-4689; http://copper29 bar.com; 206 Miracle Mile; ⏰ 5pm-1am Mon & Tue, to 2am Wed & Thu, 4pm-2am Fri, noon-2am Sat, to 1am Sun) Portraits of celebrities like Brad Pitt in a Napoleonic military uniform or the Mona Lisa in hipster glasses gaze at a crowd of Coral Gables pretty people throwing back serious cocktails like the La Vie en Rose (tequila, mezcal, blood orange and vanilla foam). There's a dark and sexy speakeasy vibe, although come the weekend the spot becomes more of a dance-y lounge.

Titanic Brewing Company
MICROBREWERY

(📞 305-668-1742; www.titanicbrewery.com; 5813 Ponce de Leon Blvd; ⏰ 11:30am-1am Sun-Thu, to 2am Fri & Sat) By day Titanic is an all-American-type brewpub, but at night it turns into a popular University of Miami watering hole. Titanic's signature brews are refreshing and there's good pub grub on hand, including sriracha wings and peel-and-eat shrimp.

⭐ Entertainment

Miami's arts scene draws from an enviable creative demographic base. Immigrants from around the world come here to create a better life, and in the process they've also created world-class art, live music and theater – all of it given a unique, sexy twist thanks to the sultry weather and sheer compressed diversity of South Florida.

⭐ South Beach

New World Symphony
CLASSICAL MUSIC

(NWS; Map p66; 📞 305-680-5866; www.nws. edu; 500 17th St) Housed in the New World Center (p59) – a funky explosion of cubist lines and geometric curves, fresh white against the blue Miami sky – the acclaimed New World Symphony (NWS) holds performances from October to May. The deservedly heralded NWS serves as a three- to four-year preparatory program for talented musicians from prestigious music schools.

Colony Theatre
PERFORMING ARTS

(Map p66; ☎ 305-674-1040, box office 800-211-1414; www.colonymb.org; 1040 Lincoln Rd) The Colony was built in 1935 and was the main cinema in upper South Beach before it fell into disrepair in the mid-20th century. It was renovated and revived in 1976 and now boasts 465 seats and great acoustics. It's an absolute art-deco gem, with a classic marquee and Inca-style crenelations, and now serves as a major venue for performing arts.

O Cinema South Beach
CINEMA

(Map p66; ☎ 786-471-3269; www.o-cinema.org/venue/o-cinema-south-beach; 1130 Washington Ave) This much-loved nonprofit cinema screens indie films, foreign films and documentaries. You'll find thought-provoking works you won't see elsewhere. The venue itself is a hybrid theater/bookstore/library that occupies the old Miami Beach city hall, built in 1927 by real-estate mogul Carl Fischer.

Miami City Ballet
DANCE

(Map p66; ☎ 305-929-7010; www.miamicityballet.org; 2200 Liberty Ave) Formed in 1985, this troupe is based out of a lovely three-story headquarters designed by famed local architectural firm Arquitectonica. The facade allows passersby to watch the dancers rehearsing through big picture windows, which makes you feel like you're in a scene from *Fame,* except the weather is better and people don't spontaneously break into song.

Fillmore Miami Beach
PERFORMING ARTS

(Map p66; ☎ 305-673-7300; www.fillmoremb.com; 1700 Washington Ave) Built in 1951, South Beach's premier showcase for touring Broadway shows, orchestras and other big musical productions has 2700 seats and excellent acoustics.

Jackie Gleason chose to make the theater his home for the long-running 1960s TV show, but now you'll find an eclectic lineup: Catalan pop or indie rock one night, the comedian Bill Maher or an over-the-top vaudeville group the next.

☆ North Beach

North Beach Bandshell
LIVE MUSIC

(Map p92; ☎ 786-453-2897; www.northbeachbandshell.com; 7275 Collins Ave) This outdoor venue features an excellent lineup of concerts, dance, theater, opera and spoken word throughout the year. Some events are free. It's run by the nonprofit Rhythm Foundation, and the wide-ranging repertoire features sounds from around the globe, with many family-friendly events. Check online to see what's on the roster.

☆ Downtown Miami

★Adrienne Arsht Center for the Performing Arts
PERFORMING ARTS

(Map p84; ☎ 305-949-6722; www.arshtcenter.org; 1300 Biscayne Blvd; ☉ box office noon-5pm Mon-Fri, plus 2hr before performances) This magnificent venue manages to both humble and enthrall visitors. Today the Arsht is where the biggest cultural acts in Miami come to perform; a show here is a must-see on any Miami trip. There's an Adrienne Arsht Center stop on the Metromover.

This performing-arts center is Miami's beautiful, beloved baby. Designed by César Pelli (the man who brought you Kuala Lumpur's Petronas Towers), the center has two main components, connected by a thin pedestrian bridge.

Inside the theaters there's a sense of ocean and land sculpted by wind; the rounded balconies rise up in spirals that resemble a sliced-open seashell. Hidden behind these impressive structures are highly engineered, state-of-the-art acoustics ensuring that no outside sounds can penetrate, creating the perfect conditions to enjoy one of the 300 performances staged at the center each year.

Klipsch Amphitheater
LIVE MUSIC

(Map p84; www.klipsch.com/klipsch-amphitheater-at-bayfront-park; 301 N Biscayne Blvd, Bayfront Park) In Bayfront Park in Downtown Miami, the Klipsch Amphitheater stages a wide range of concerts throughout the year. The open-air setting beside Biscayne Bay is hard to top.

American Airlines Arena
STADIUM

(Map p84; ☎ 786-777-1000; www.aaarena.com; 601 N Biscayne Blvd) Resembling a massive spaceship that perpetually hovers at the edge of Biscayne Bay, this arena has been the home of the city's NBA franchise, the **Miami Heat**, since 2000. The **Waterfront Theater**, Florida's largest, is housed inside; throughout the year it hosts concerts, Broadway performances and the like.

Olympia Theater
PERFORMING ARTS

(Map p84; ☑ 305-374-2444; www.olympiatheater. org; 174 E Flagler St) This elegantly renovated 1920s movie palace services a huge variety of performing arts including film festivals, symphonies, ballets and touring shows. The acoustics are excellent.

Miami loves modern, but the Olympia Theater at the Gusman Center for the Performing Arts is vintage-classic beautiful. The ceiling, which features 246 twinkling stars and clouds cast over an indigo-deep night, frosted with classical Greek sculpture and Vienna Opera House–style embellishment, will melt your heart. The theater first opened in 1925.

⭐ Wynwood & the Design District

Light Box at Goldman Warehouse
PERFORMING ARTS

(Map p96; ☑ 305-576-4350; www.miamilight project.com; 404 NW 26th St) The Miami Light Project, a nonprofit cultural foundation, stages a wide range of innovative theater, dance, music and film performances at this intimate theater. It's in Wynwood, and a great place to discover cutting-edge works by artists you might not have heard of. It is particularly supportive of troupes from South Florida.

Punch Bowl Social
KARAOKE

(Map p96; ☑ 786-796-5242; https://punchbowl social.com; 2660 NW 3rd Ave; bowling $16-18, karaoke rooms $35-45; ⊗11am-11pm Mon-Fri, from 10:30am Sat & Sun) It's hard to pin down just what Punch Bowl Social is, other than fun. Let's tick off the constituent parts: a big, industrial facility with hip lighting; a large bar that serves cocktails, both in glasses and shareable via punch bowls; a bowling alley; a place to rock out with karaoke; or play pool, or Ping-Pong...yeah. Hard to define. Fun to be at.

Note the bowling is duckpin bowling, a variation on the game with a smaller ball.

⭐ Little Haiti & the Upper East Side

Villain Theater
COMEDY

(Map p106; ☑ 786-391-2241; www.villaintheater. com; 5865 NE 2nd Ave; tickets $5-15) This laid-back theater showcases local stand-up artists, improv and sketch comedy, which makes this villain kind of a hero in our book (see what we did there?). The performance calendar is packed, and there's free improv classes on the first Saturday of the month from 4pm to 6pm – bonus.

⭐ Little Havana

★ Cafe La Trova
LIVE MUSIC

(Map p124; ☑ 786-615-4379; www.cafelatrova. com; 971 SW 8th St; ⊗noon-midnight Mon-Thu, to 2am Fri & Sat, 11am-midnight Sun) A lot of Miami places try to (re)create a romanticized old Cuba. La Trova, with its wood accents, immaculately dressed bartenders, and faded Havana-esque walls, really executes the concept. Regular live shows featuring classic Cuban dance music accompanied by a crowd decked out in their best dresses and *guayaberas* is insanely fun; if the scene here doesn't get you dancing, we're not sure what will.

You've got the Cuban trifecta of food, drink and music going here, including a menu serving Cuban sandwiches and braised pork (mains $14 to $34). The house-made cocktails have an old-school tropical theme, and a good sense of humor – we had to chuckle at a strong drink named *La Chancleta* (the term for a cheap plastic sandal Cuban and Puerto Rican moms use to enforce discipline in the house).

★ Cubaocho
LIVE PERFORMANCE

(Map p124; ☑ 305-285-5880; www.cubaocho.com; 1465 SW 8th St; ⊗11am-3am) Jewel of the Little Havana Art District, Cubaocho is renowned for its concerts, with excellent bands from across the Spanish-speaking world. It's also a community center, art gallery and research outpost for all things Cuban. The interior resembles an old Havana cigar bar, yet the walls are decked out in artwork that references both the classical past of Cuban art and its avant-garde future.

Aside from the busy concert schedule, Cubaocho also has film screenings, drama performances, readings and other events.

Tower Theater
CINEMA

(Map p124; ☎ 305-237-2463; www.towertheater miami.com; 1508 SW 8th St; tickets $11.75) This renovated 1926 landmark theater has a proud deco facade and a handsomely renovated interior, thanks to support from the Miami-Dade Community College. In its heyday it was the center of Little Havana social life and, via the films it showed, served as a bridge between immigrant society and American pop culture. Today it frequently shows independent and Spanish-language films (sometimes both).

☆ Coral Gables

Coral Gables Art Cinema
CINEMA

(Map p118; ☎ 786-385-9689; www.gablescinema. com; 260 Aragon Ave) In the epicenter of Coral Gables' downtown, you'll find one of Miami's best art-house cinemas. It shows indie and foreign films in a modern 144-seat screening room. Check out cult favorites shown in the original 35mm format at Saturday midnight screenings (part of the After Hours series).

GableStage
THEATER

(Map p118; ☎ 305-445-1119; www.gablestage.org; 1200 Anastasia Ave) Founded as the Florida Shakespeare Theatre in 1979 and now housed on the property of the Biltmore Hotel in Coral Gables, this company still performs an occasional Shakespeare play, but mostly presents contemporary and classical pieces.

☆ Greater Miami

Miami Symphony Orchestra
CLASSICAL MUSIC

(☎ 305-275-5666; www.themiso.org; tickets $20-50) Miami's well-loved hometown symphony has many fans. Its yearly series (from November to May) features world-renowned soloists performing at either the Adrienne Arsht Center for the Performing Arts (p120) or the Fillmore Miami Beach (p120).

Hard Rock Stadium
FOOTBALL

(☎ 305-943-8000; www.hardrockstadium.com; 347 Don Shula Dr, Miami Gardens; tickets from $35) The renovated (and renamed) Hard Rock Stadium (formerly known as Sun Life Stadium) is the home turf of the Miami Dolphins. 'Dol-fans' are respectably crazy about their team, even if a Super Bowl showing has evaded them since 1985. Games are wildly popular and the team is painfully successful, in that they always raise fans' hopes but never quite fulfill them.

🛍 Shopping

Miami boasts plenty of high-end fashion, designer sunglasses, vintage clothing, books, records, Latin American crafts, artwork, gourmet goodies and more. While there are plenty of malls in Miami, new shopping centers are often built in the style of outdoor arcades or bazaars, allowing shoppers to enjoy the sunny weather.

🛍 South Beach

Taschen
BOOKS

(Map p66; ☎ 305-538-6185; www.taschen.com; 1111 Lincoln Rd; ⊗ 11am-9pm Mon-Thu, to 10pm Fri & Sat, noon-9pm Sun) An incredibly well-stocked collection of art, photography, design and coffee-table books from this high-quality illustrated-books publisher. Check out David Hockney's color-rich art books, the *New Erotic Photography* (always a great conversation starter) and Annie Liebovitz's witty society portraits.

Books & Books
BOOKS

(Map p66; ☎ 305-532-3222; www.booksand books.com; 927 Lincoln Rd; ⊗ 11am-9pm) Stop in this fantastic indie bookstore for an excellent selection of new fiction, beautiful art and photography books, award-winning children's titles and more. The layout – a series of elegantly furnished rooms – invites endless browsing, and there's a good restaurant and cafe in front of the store.

Sunset Clothing Co
FASHION & ACCESSORIES

(Map p66; www.facebook.com/SunsetClothingCo; 1895 Purdy Ave; ⊗ 10am-7pm Mon-Fri, to 6pm Sat, 11am-4pm Sun) A great little men's and women's fashion boutique in Sunset Harbour for stylish gear that won't cost a fortune (though the merchandise isn't cheap either). You'll find well-made long-sleeved shirts, soft cotton T-shirts, lace-up canvas shoes, nicely fitting denim (including vintage Levi's), warm pullover sweaters and other casual gear. Helpful, friendly service too.

Alchemist
FASHION & ACCESSORIES

(Map p66; ☎ 305-531-4815; 1111 Lincoln Rd; ⊗ 11am-8pm) Inside one of Lincoln Rd's most striking buildings, this high-end boutique has a wild collection of artful objects, including Warhol-style soup-can candles, heavy gilded corkscrews, Beats headphones by Dr Dre, and mirrored circular sunglasses that are essential for the beach. The clothing here tends to be fairly avant-garde (straight from the runway, it seems).

🔒 Downtown Miami

Mary Brickell Village
SHOPPING CENTER

(Map p84; ☑ 305-381-6130; www.marybrickell
village.com; 901 S Miami Ave; ☺ 10am-9pm Mon-
Sat, noon-6pm Sun) This outdoor shopping
and dining complex has helped revitalize
the Brickell neighborhood, with a range of
boutiques, restaurants, cafes and bars. It's a
magnet for new condo residents in the area,
with a central location in the heart of the
financial district.

Supply & Advise
CLOTHING

(Map p84; ☑ 305-960-2043; www.supplyand
advise.com; 223 SE 1st St; ☺ 11am-7pm Mon-Sat)
Supply & Advise brings a heavy dose of
men's fashion to Downtown Miami, with
rugged, well-made and handsomely tailored
clothing, plus shoes and accessories, set in
a historic 1920s building. Most merchandise
here is made in the USA. There's also a bar-
bershop, complete with vintage chairs and
that impeccable look of bygone days.

🔒 Wynwood & the Design Distric

Nomad Tribe
CLOTHING

(Map p96; ☑ 305-364-5193; www.nomadtribe
shop.com; 2301 NW 2nd Ave; ☺ noon-8pm) 🌿
This boutique earns high marks for carrying only ethically and sustainably produced merchandise. You'll find cleverly
designed jewelry from Miami-based Kathe
Cuervo, Osom Brand socks (made of up-
cycled thread), ecologically produced graphic T-shirts from Thinking MU, and THX
coffee and candles (which donates 100% of
profits to nonprofit organizations), among
much else.

Art by God
GIFTS & SOUVENIRS

(Map p96; ☑ 305-573-3011; www.artbygod.com;
60 NE 27th St; ☺ 10am-5pm Mon-Fri, 11am-4pm
Sat) Purses? Jackets? *Pssht.* When we go
shopping, we like to buy fossilized dinosaur
poop, and clumps of amethysts, and stuffed
full-sized zebras. It's all on offer at Art by
God, as well as rhino heads, dinosaur bones,
and more portable things like home furnishings from all of earth's continents.

Rupees
GIFTS & SOUVENIRS

(Map p96; ☑ 305-576-4368; www.facebook.com/
rupeessareesmiami; 415 NW 27th St; ☺ 11am-
6:30pm Mon-Sat) Rupees feels like the sort
of old-school international goods store that
wouldn't hack it in ultramodern Wynwood,

but it is going strong, selling South Asian
crafts and gifts, along with a huge range of
fabrics, alongside books about the local con-
temporary-art scene.

Out of the Closet
THRIFT STORE

(Map p96; ☑ 305-764-3773; www.outofthe
closet.org; 2900 Biscayne Blvd; ☺ 10am-7pm
Mon-Sat, to 6pm Sun) You'll find all manner
of treasure-trash at this sizable thrift store
on busy Biscayne Blvd: men's and women's
clothing, accessories, books, CDs, records,
housewares and more. Friendly staff can
help guide you on the search. The store ben-
efits the AIDS Healthcare Foundation.

Harold Golen Gallery
ART

(Map p96; ☑ 305-989-3359; https://harold
golen.gallery; 2294 NW 2nd Ave; ☺ noon-7pm)
Original artwork is exhibited at this small
gallery, mainly of a very animation/anime/
tiki-influenced pop art variety, often painted in rainbow palettes set to neon levels of
bright. There is also a ton of art-adjacent
gifts – posters, books, stickers, patches and
prints – influenced by this playful aesthetic.
One of the few Wynwood galleries younger
kids will get a kick out of.

Malaquita
ARTS & CRAFTS

(Map p96; www.malaquitadesign.com; 2613 NW
2nd Ave; ☺ 11am-8pm) This artfully designed
store has merchandise you won't find elsewhere, including lovely handblown vases,
embroidered clothing, Mesoamerican tapestries, vibrantly painted bowls, handwoven
palm baskets and other fair-trade objects –
some of which are made by indigenous artisans in Mexico.

🔒 Little Haiti & the Upper East Side

Sweat Records
MUSIC

(Map p106; ☑ 786-693-9309; www.sweatrecords
miami.com; 5505 NE 2nd Ave; ☺ noon-10pm Mon-
Sat, to 5pm Sun) Sweat's almost a stereotypical
indie record store – there's funky art and
graffiti on the walls, it sells weird Japanese
toys, there are tattooed staff with thick glasses arguing over LPs and EPs you've never
heard of and, of course, there's coffee and
vegan snacks.

Libreri Mapou
BOOKS

(Map p106; ☑ 305-757-9922; http://mapoubooks.
com; 5919 NE 2nd Ave; ☺ 11am-7pm Mon-Fri, 10am-
8pm Sat, 11am-5pm Sun) The center of literary
life in Little Haiti, this bookstore specializes

Little Havana

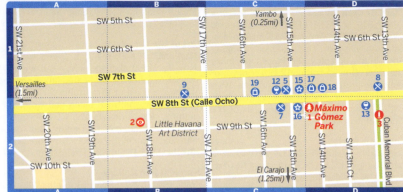

Little Havana

in English, French and Creole titles and periodicals, with thousands of great titles and live events. The owner, Jan Mapou, is a writer and political thinker, of some distinction.

🛍 **Little Havana**

Havana Collection   CLOTHING
(Map p124; ☎786-717-7474; www.facebook.com/TheHavanaCollection; 1421 SW 8th St; ⊕10am-6pm) One of the best and most striking collections of the classic traditional *guayaberas* in Miami can be found in this shop. Prices are high (plan on spending about $85 for a shirt), but so is the quality, so you can be assured of a long-lasting product.

La Isla   ART
(Map p124; ☎786-317-3051; https://laislausa.com; 1561 SW 8th St; ⊕9am-5pm) This hip outpost of the new(er) Little Havana showcases

Cuban-inspired pop art, graphic design and clever gifts (a poster of a certain *Star Wars* droid smoking a cigar titled 'Arturito' had us cracking up). La Isla promotes a Cuba more rooted in contemporary cool than black-and-white photos of cigar rollers, and is a great spot for a unique souvenir.

Guantanamera   CIGARS
(Map p124; ☎786-618-5142; www.guantanameracigars.com; 1465 SW 8th St; ⊕10:30am-8pm Sun-Wed, to 10pm Thu, to 3am Fri & Sat) In a central location in Little Havana, Guantanamera sells high-quality hand-rolled cigars, plus strong Cuban coffee. It's an atmospheric shop, where you can stop for a smoke, a drink (there's a bar here) and some friendly banter. There's also some great live music most nights of the week. The rocking chairs in front are a fine perch for people-watching.

🛍 Coconut Grove

Polished Coconut FASHION & ACCESSORIES
(☎305-443-3220; www.facebook.com/Polished Coconut; 3600 Grand Ave Village West; ⊗11am-6pm Mon-Sat, noon-5pm Sun) 🌿 Colorful textiles from Central and South America are transformed into lovely accessories and home decor at this eye-catching store in the heart of Coconut Grove. You'll find handbags, satchels, belts, sun hats, pillows, bedspreads and table runners made by artisans inspired by traditional indigenous designs.

Midori Gallery ANTIQUES
(Map p110; ☎305-443-3399; www.midorigallery.com; 3168 Commodore Plaza; ⊗11am-6pm Tue-Sat) Filled with antiques and oddities from across Asia, the Midori Gallery also surprises with a lacquer Japanese sake flash here and a standing Burmese Buddha there. It feels like the sort of shop Indiana Jones uses to decorate his study.

🛍 Coral Gables

★ **Retro City Collectibles** MUSIC
(Gables Records n Comics; Map p118; ☎786-879-4407; 277 Miracle Mile, 2nd fl; ⊗3-6pm Wed-Fri, 1-7pm Sat, to 4pm Sun) This cluttered little upstairs den of geekery is a fun place to browse, with all manner of eye-catching and collectible genre artifacts. You'll find comic books, records, baseball cards, Pez dispensers, old film posters and action figures (*Star Wars, Star Trek, Doctor Who* etc).

Books & Books BOOKS
(Map p118; ☎305-442-4408; https://booksandbooks.com; 265 Aragon Ave; ⊗9am-11pm Sun-Thu, to midnight Fri & Sat) The best indie bookstore in South Florida – with branches across town – is a wonderful place to stock up on your beach reading material and see authors in action at one of the frequent in-store events. There's a nice cafe and restaurant, with dining on a Mediterranean-like patio fronting the shop.

Boy Meets Girl CHILDREN'S CLOTHING
(Map p118; ☎305-445-9668; www.bmgkids.com; 358 San Lorenzo Ave, Village of Merrick Park; ⊗10am-8pm Mon-Sat, 11am-7pm Sun) Fantastically upscale and frankly expensive clothing for wee ones – if the kids are getting past puberty, look elsewhere, but otherwise they'll be fashionable far before they realize it.

🛍 Key Biscayne

Boheme Boutique CLOTHING
(Map p98; ☎305-361-7474; www.modaboheme.com; 650 Crandon Blvd; ⊗11am-8pm Mon-Sat) Simple-but-chic dresses, flow-y wraps, wispy tunics: there's an aesthetic to the clothes here, one that is light and linen-y, and perfect for Miami's more relaxed offshore island. Bonus points for the friendly, enthusiastic staff.

ℹ Information

MEDICAL SERVICES

Mount Sinai Medical Center (☎305-676-6496, emergency room 305-563-8026; www.msmc.com; 4300 Alton Rd; ⊗24hr) The area's best emergency room.

TOURIST INFORMATION

Art Deco Welcome Center (Map p60; ☎305-672-2014; www.mdpl.org; 1001 Ocean Dr, South Beach; ⊗9:30am-5pm Fri-Wed, to 7pm Thu) Run by the Miami Design Preservation League (MDPL), it has tons of art-deco-district information and organizes excellent walking tours. There's a museum (p58) attached to the center that provides a great overview of the art-deco district.

Greater Miami & the Beaches Convention & Visitors Bureau (Map p84; ☎305-539-3000; www.miamiandbeaches.com; 701 Brickell Ave, 27th fl; ⊗8:30am-6pm Mon-Fri) This visitors bureau offers loads of info on Miami and keeps up-to-date with the latest events and cultural offerings. It is located in an oddly intimidating high-rise building.

LGBT Visitor Center (Map p66; ☎305-397-8914; www.gogaymiami.com; 1130 Washington

Ave; ⊘9am-6pm Mon-Fri, 11am-4pm Sat & Sun) An excellent source for all LGBTQI+ info on Miami, this friendly welcome center has loads of recommendations on sights, restaurants, nightlife and cultural goings-on. It also hosts meetings and other events.

Check the website for Pink Flamingo–certified hotels, ie hotels that are most welcoming to the LGBTQI+ crowd.

🚹 Getting There & Away

The majority of travelers come to Miami by air, although it's feasible to arrive by car, bus or even train. Miami is a major international airline hub, with flights to many cities across the USA, Latin America and Europe. Most flights come into Miami International Airport (MIA), although many are also directed to Fort Lauderdale-Hollywood International Airport (FLL). Figure 3½ hours from New York City, five hours from Los Angeles, and 10 hours from London or Madrid.

Flights, tours and rail tickets can be booked online at www.lonelyplanet.com/bookings.

AIR
Miami International Airport

Located 6 miles west of Downtown, the busy **Miami International Airport** (MIA; ☑305-876-7000; www.miami-airport.com; 2100 NW 42nd Ave) has three terminals and serves more than 45 million passengers each year. Around 60 airlines fly into Miami. The airport is open 24 hours and is laid out in a horseshoe design. There are left-luggage facilities at Concourse E in the Central Terminal (call 305-869-1163 for more information).

Fort Lauderdale-Hollywood International Airport

Fort Lauderdale-Hollywood International Airport (FLL; www.fll.net), around 26 miles north of Downtown Miami, largely serves domestic passengers and is well connected to major hubs like New York and Atlanta.

BOAT

Though it's doubtful you'll be catching a steamer to make a trans-Atlantic journey, it is quite possible that you'll arrive in Miami via a cruise ship, as the **Port of Miami** (☑305-347-4800; www.miamidade.gov/portmiami), which receives around five million passengers each year, is known as the cruise capital of the world. Arriving in the port will put you on the edge of Downtown Miami; taxis and public buses to other local points are available from nearby Biscayne Blvd.

BUS

For bus trips, **Greyhound** (www.greyhound.com) is the main long-distance operator. Megabus (p127) offers a service to Tampa and Orlando.

Greyhound's main bus terminal (p245) is near the airport.

If you are traveling very long distances (say, across several states), bargain airfares can sometimes undercut buses. On shorter routes, renting a car can sometimes be cheaper. Nonetheless, discounted (even half-price) long-distance bus trips are often available by purchasing tickets online seven to 14 days in advance.

TRAIN

The main Miami terminal of **Amtrak** (☑305-835-1222; www.amtrak.com; 8303 NW 37th Ave, West Little River), about 9 miles northwest of Downtown, connects the city with several other points in Florida (including Orlando and Jacksonville) on the Silver Service line that runs up to New York City. Travel time between New York and Miami is 27 to 31 hours. The Miami Amtrak station is connected by Tri-Rail to Downtown Miami and has a left-luggage facility.

MiamiCentral (p69) station, located Downtown, will be the home of Brightline trains, which will connect to West Palm Beach and Orlando.

🚹 Getting Around

TO/FROM THE AIRPORT
Miami International Airport

Buses Metro buses leave from Miami Airport Station (connected by electric rail to the airport) and run throughout the city; fares are $2.25. The Miami Beach Airport Express (bus 150) also costs $2.25 and makes stops all along Miami Beach, from 41st to the southern tip; it runs from 6am to 11:40pm.

Shuttles Some hotels offer free shuttles.

Taxi From Miami International Airport, taxis charge a flat rate, which varies depending on where you're heading. It's $22 to Downtown, Coconut Grove or Coral Gables; $35 to South Beach; and $44 to Key Biscayne. Count on 40 minutes to South Beach in average traffic, and about 25 minutes to Downtown. Note that 'average traffic' is more of a happy exception than the rule in this town. Rush hours and/or accidents could mean you're spending an hour in the cab.

Fort Lauderdale-Hollywood International Airport

Shuttles Shared van service is available from the airport with **GO Airport Shuttle** (☑773-363-0001; https://goairportshuttle.com). Prices are around $25 to South Beach.

Taxi Count on at least 45 minutes from the airport to Downtown by taxi, and at least an hour for the ride to South Beach. Prices are metered. Expect to pay about $75 to South Beach and $65 to Downtown.

Train Take the free shuttle (with stops at the west end of terminal 1, between terminals 2 and 3, and between terminals 3 and 4) to the airport's Tri-Rail station (www.tri-rail.com). There you can hop aboard this commuter train into Miami ($3.75 to $5), which connects with Miami-Dade's Metrorail Orange Line. The schedule is infrequent though (trains run every 30 to 60 minutes), so be mindful of departure times to avoid long waits.

BICYCLE

Citi Bike (p246) is a bike-share program where you can borrow a bike from scores of kiosks spread around Miami and Miami Beach. Miami is flat, but traffic can be horrendous (abundant and fast-moving), and there isn't much of a biking culture (or respect for bikers) just yet. Free paper maps of the bike network are available at some kiosks, or you can find one online. There's also a handy app that shows you where the nearest stations are.

For longer rides, clunky Citi Bikes are not ideal (no helmet, no lock and only three gears).

Note that a variety of scooters are also available to rent via third party apps throughout Miami Beach, Downtown and Wynwood.

BUS

Miami's local bus system is called **Metrobus** (☑ 305-891-3131; www.miamidade.gov/transit/routes.asp; tickets $2.25). It can get you most places you're trying to go, but it won't get you there very quickly. Each bus route has a different schedule and routes generally run from about 5:30am to 11pm, though some are 24 hours. Rides cost $2.25 and must be paid in exact change (coins or a combination of bills and coins) or with an Easy Card (available for purchase from Metrorail stations and some shops and pharmacies). An easy-to-read route map is available online. Note that if you have to transfer buses, you'll have to pay the fare each time if paying in cash. With an Easy Card, transfers are free.

Megabus (https://us.megabus.com; Miami International Center, 3801 NW 21st St) Megabus offers a bus service to Orlando and Tampa. Buses depart from a stop near the airport.

MIAMI TROLLEYS

A free bus service serves Miami, Miami Beach, Coconut Grove, Little Havana and Coral Gables, among other locations. Called the Trolley (www.miamigov.com/trolley) it's actually a hybrid-electric bus disguised as an orange-and-green trolley. There are numerous routes, though they're made for getting around neighborhoods and not *between* them.

The most useful for travelers are the following:

Biscayne Travels along Biscayne Blvd; handy for transportation from Brickell to Downtown and up to the edge of Wynwood.

Brickell Connects Brickell area (south of the Miami River in the Downtown area) with the Vizcaya Museum & Gardens.

Coral Way Goes from Downtown (near the Freedom Tower) to downtown Coral Gables.

Wynwood Zigzags through town, from the Adrienne Arsht Center for the Performing Arts up through Wynwood along NW 2nd Ave to 29th St.

MIAMI BEACH TROLLEYS

Miami Beach has four free trolleys (www.miamibeachfl.gov/transportation) running along different routes, with arrivals every 10 to 15 minutes from 6am to midnight (from 8am on Sundays).

Alton-West Loop Runs up (north) Alton Rd and down (south) West Ave between 6th St and Lincoln Rd.

Collins Link Runs along Collins Ave from 37th St to 73rd St. Catch it southbound from Abbott Ave and Indian Creek Dr.

Middle Beach Loop Runs up Collins Ave and down Indian Creek Dr between 20th and 44th Sts (southbound it also zigzags over to Lincoln Rd).

North Beach Loop Runs 65th to 88th St.

TRAIN

The **Metromover** (☑ 305-891-3131; www.miamidade.gov/transit/metromover.asp; ⏰ 5am-midnight), which is equal parts bus, monorail and train, is helpful for getting around Downtown Miami. It offers visitors a great perspective on the city and a free orientation tour of the area.

Metrorail (www.miamidade.gov/transit/metrorail.asp; one-way ticket $2.25) is a 21-mile-long heavy-rail system that has one elevated line running from Hialeah through Downtown Miami and south to Kendall/Dadeland. Trains run every five to 15 minutes from 6am to midnight. Pay with either the reloadable Easy Card or single-use Easy Ticket, which are sold from vending machines at Metrorail stations.

The regional **Tri-Rail** (☑ 800-874-7245; www.tri-rail.com) double-decker commuter trains run the 71 miles between Dade, Broward and Palm Beach counties. Fares are calculated on a zone basis; the shortest distance traveled costs $4.40 round-trip; the most you'll ever pay is for the ride between MIA and West Palm Beach ($11.55 round trip). No tickets are sold on the train, so allow time to make your purchase before boarding. All trains and stations are accessible to riders with disabilities. For a list of stations, log on to the Tri-Rail website.

AT A GLANCE

POPULATION
95,000

BIRD SPECIES
350

BEST FRUIT STAND
Robert Is Here (p147)

BEST GUIDED WALK
Slough slog (p135)

BEST RESTAURANT
Havana Cafe (p144)

WHEN TO GO
Dec–Mar
Dry season: top wildlife viewing along watercourses, but some kayaking will be difficult.

Apr–Jun
Although the weather gets pretty hot, there's a good mix of water and wildlife.

Jul–Nov
Lots of heat, lots of bugs and chances of hurricanes.

Anhinga Trail (p134)
CHRISTIAN OUELLET/SHUTTERSTOCK ©

The Everglades & Biscayne

There is no wilderness in America quite like the Everglades. Called the 'River of Grass' by Native American inhabitants, this is not just a wetland, or a swamp, or a lake, or a river, or a prairie, or a grassland – it is all of those, twisted together into a series of soft horizons, long vistas, and sunsets that stretch across your entire field of vision, all animated by an extraordinary cast of wild creatures.

The park's quiet majesty is evident when you see anhinga flexing their wings before breaking into a corkscrew dive, or the slow, rhythmic flap of a great blue heron gliding over its domain while being watched by alligators below, or the shimmer of light on miles of untrammeled saw grass as the sun sets behind hunkering cypress domes. In a nation where natural beauty is measured by its capacity for drama, the Everglades subtly, contentedly flows on.

Florida Panther
National Wildlife
Refuge ⑩

Golden
Gate

Naples

Everglades Parkway (Alligator Alley) (toll)

Tamiami Trail

Fakahatchee Strand
Preserve Park

Big Cypress
National
Preserve

Turner River Rd

Marco
Island

Collier-
Seminole
State Park

Monroe
Station

Ochopee

Cape
Romano

Everglades City

⑨ Museum of the
Everglades

⑦
10,000
Islands

⑧
Loop Road

Chevelier
Bay

Ferry

Big
Lostmans
Bay

The Everglades

Everglades National Park Boundary

Gulf of
Mexico

Tarpon
Bay

Shark
Point

Whitewater
Bay

Cape
Sable

Christian
Point

⑤
Flamingo
Marina

③

N
0   50 km
0   25 miles

The Everglades Highlights

❶ **Anhinga Trail** (p134)
Spotting alligators by day or
night, and watching nesting
waterbirds.

❷ **Shark Valley** (p139)
Spying gators, turtles and birds
on a walk, bike ride or tram tour.

❸ **Christian Point** (p134)
Hiking one of the best walks in
the southern Everglades.

❹ **Hell's Bay Canoe Trail**
(p132) Paddling through
scenic swamps and mangrove
creeks.

❺ **Flamingo Marina** (p140)
Looking for manatees and
crocodiles in the far south.

❻ **Pa-hay-okee Overlook**
(p141) Watching the sun set
over the ingress road from the
roof of your car.

The Everglades

- 27
- 75
- Miccosukee Indian Reservation
- The Everglades
- Miami Canal
- 869
- Florida's Turnpike (toll)
- 595
- 75
- 820
- 821
- 441
- 826
- 27
- 9
- 95
- A1A
- Lauderdale-by-the-Sea
- 1
- Fort Lauderdale
- Dania Beach
- Hollywood
- North Miami Beach
- Hialeah
- Miami Beach
- Miami
- 821
- 826
- 41
- 953
- Miccosukee Village
- **Shark Valley** ❷
- Tram Tour
- 94
- **Everglades National Park**
- Key Biscayne
- **Bill Baggs Cape Florida State Park**
- ATLANTIC OCEAN
- Peters
- Goulds
- 997
- 821
- **Pa-hay-okee Overlook** ❻
- Homestead
- Black Point
- *Biscayne Bay*
- Biscayne National Park
- Boca Chita Key
- Coon Point
- *Sands Cut*
- Florida Keys National Marine Sanctuary
- Florida City
- Turkey Point
- Elliott Key
- **Anhinga Trail** ❶
- 9336
- 1
- Adams Key
- *Card Sound*
- 9336
- **Hell's Bay Canoe Trail** ❹
- *Barnes Sound*
- Key Largo
- John Pennekamp Coral Reef State Park
- Key Largo
- Key Largo National Marine Sanctuary
- *Florida Bay*
- Florida Keys National Marine Sanctuary
- Islamorada

❼ **10,000 Islands** (p146) Canoeing or kayaking through the scattered islands amid dolphins and crocs.

❽ **Loop Road** (p140) Taking a drive amid striking wetland scenery.

❾ **Museum of the Everglades** (p143) Learning about the fascinating human settlement of the Everglades.

❿ **Florida Panther National Wildlife Refuge** (p144) Walking the boardwalks in search of the Everglades' most elusive presence, the Florida panther.

EXPLORING THE EVERGLADES

KAYAKING & CANOEING

The waterways of the Everglades rank among the best kayaking destinations anywhere in the US – there are infinite trails, plenty of wildlife to keep you company, and numerous highly professional operators to get you out on the water.

☆ Northern Everglades

Paddlers have seemingly endless choice here, with countless Everglades channels to choose from and the 10,000 Islands lying just offshore.

Wilderness Waterway (99 miles) This route between Everglades City and Flamingo is the longest canoe trail in the area. Most islands are fringed by narrow beaches with sugar-white sand, but note that the water is brackish, and very shallow most of the time. It's not Tahiti, but it's fascinating. You can camp on your own island for up to a week.

Everglades Adventures (p144) This highly recommended outfitter offers a range of half-day kayak tours, from sunrise paddles to twilight trips through mangroves that return under a sky full of stars. Tours shuttle you to places like Chokoloskee Island, Collier-Seminole State Park, Rabbit Key or Tiger Key for excursions. Everglades Adventures also provides one-way shuttle services (from Flamingo back to Everglades City) for those making the seven- to 10-day trip along the Wilderness Waterway.

☆ Southern Everglades

The real joy in this part of the park is paddling into the bracken-filled heart of the swamp. There are plenty of push-off points, all with names that sound like they come from Frodo's map to Mordor, including Hell's Bay, Snake Bight and Graveyard Creek. If you plan to camp along any of the following trails, you need to pick up a backcountry permit (p142) from any park visitor center. Rent canoes and kayaks at Flamingo Everglades (p135).

A little local knowledge can take you a very long way in the Everglades. Hike along trails and boardwalks, kayak the waterways or take a tour to get the expert low-down on this spectacular wilderness.

Nine Mile Pond (3- or 5.2-mile loop) Paddle through grassy marshes and mangrove islands, following the numbered white poles; for the shorter version, take the cut-through from marker #44. Allow four hours for the full loop. It's good for spotting alligators, wading birds and turtles.

Noble Hammock (2 miles return) Short loop with some challenging tight corners; check water levels in the dry season before setting out.

Hell's Bay (5.5 miles one way) Despite the frightening name (and terrible mosquitoes), this can be a magnificent place to kayak. 'Hell to get into and hell to get out of' was how this sheltered launch was described by old Glades aficionados, but once inside you'll find a capillary network of mangrove creeks, saw-grass islands and shifting mudflats, where the brambles form a green tunnel and all you can smell is sea salt and the dark organic breath of the swamp. Three *chickee* (wooden platform above the waterline) sites are spaced along the trail. Allow six to eight hours for the return trip.

West Lake (7.7 miles one way) Cross open lakes linked by narrow creeks to Alligator Creek; good for alligators and crocodiles.

Mud Lake (7 miles return) Paddle through mangroves between Coot Bay Pond and Mud Lake.

Bear Lake (11.5 miles one way) Classic Everglades trail, but closed since 2017 due to hurricane damage; check at the Flamingo Visitor Center to see if it has reopened.

For operators, try the following:

On the property of the Robert Is Here (p147) fruit stand, **Garls Coastal Kayaking Everglades** (☏305-393-3223; www.garlscoastal kayaking.com; 19200 SW 344th St, Homestead; single/double kayak per day $40/55, half-/full-day tour $125/160) leads highly recommended excursions into the Everglades. A full-day 'Day in the Glades' outing includes hiking (more of a wet walk or slog into the lush landscape of cypress domes), followed by kayaking in both the mangroves and in Florida Bay, and, time

permitting, a night walk. For a DIY adventure, you can also hire kayaks as well as other equipment – including tents, sleeping bags and fishing gear.

The most isolated portion of the park is a squat marina where you can go on a back-country boat tour or rent boats. Due to its isolation, this area is subject to closure during bad weather. You can rent kayaks and canoes from Flamingo Everglades (p135); if you do, you're largely left to explore the channels and islands of Florida Bay on your own. During rough weather be cautious, even when on land, as storm surges can turn an attractive spread of beach into a watery stretch of danger fairly quickly.

HIKING

Getting out on the water may allow you to go deeper into the Everglades wilderness, but the numerous hiking trails are more accessible, even to those with very basic levels of fitness. Most trails are no longer than 1 mile return, although there are a couple of longer trails to really leave the world behind you.

☆ Northern Everglades

All along the Tamiami Trail, short and well-signposted boardwalk tracks take you just beyond the road. The Fakahatchee Strand Preserve (p139) is another possibility.

Kirby Storter Roadside Park (1 mile return) Probably the pick of the short walks close to the main road. Though short in terms of length, this elevated **boardwalk** (☏239-695-2000; www.nps.gov/bicy/planyourvisit/kirby-storter-roadside-park.htm; ◷24hr) [FREE] leads to a lovely overlook where you can often see a variety of birdlife (such as ibis and red-shouldered hawks) amid tall cypresses and strangler figs, plus of course alligators.

Bobcat Boardwalk Trail (0.5-mile loop) At the park entrance going into Shark Valley, this easy trail makes a loop through a thick copse of tropical hardwoods before emptying you out right back into the Shark Valley parking lot.

Otter Cave Trail (0.25 miles one-way)
In a similar area, this trail heads over a limestone shelf that has been Swiss-cheesed into a porous sponge by rainwater. Animals now live in the eroded holes (although it's not likely you'll spot any) and Native Americans used to live on top of the shelf.

Shark Valley Trail (15 miles return) This excellent trail takes you past small creeks, tropical forest and 'borrow pits' (human-made holes that are now basking spots for gators, turtles and birdlife). The pancake-flat trail is perfect for bicycles, which can be rented at the entrance for $10 per hour. Bring water.

Florida National Scenic Trail There are some 31 miles of the Florida National Scenic Trail within Big Cypress National Preserve. From the southern terminus, which can be accessed via Loop Rd, the trail runs 8.3 miles north to US 41. The way is flat, but it's hard going: you'll almost certainly be wading through water, and you'll have to pick through a series of solution holes (small sinkholes) and thick hardwood hammocks (forests). There is often no shelter from the sun, and the bugs are...plentiful. There are three primitive campsites with water wells along the trail; pick up a map and a free hiking permit (required) at the Oasis Visitor Center (p142).

☆ Southern Everglades

Anhinga Trail (0.8 mile one way) You'll get a close-up view of gators and birds on this short trail that begins at the Royal Palm Visitor Center (p141). The park also offers periodic ranger-led walks along the boardwalk at night, though you can always do this by yourself.

West Lake Trail (1.8 miles one way) This trail runs through the largest protected mangrove forest in the Northern Hemisphere.

Snake Bight (1.8 miles one way) Signposted off the main park road a few miles northeast of the Flamingo Visitor Center (p142), this walk skirts a bay and passes through tropical hardwood hammock, a real Everglades specialty; high tide brings good birdlife.

Rowdy Bend (2.6 miles one way) Follow an overgrown access road through buttonwoods and coastal prairie; the trail has an option to connect with the Snake Bight Trail.

Christian Point (2 miles one way) This dramatic walk takes you under tropical forest, past columns of white cypress and over a series of mudflats, and ends with a dramatic view of the windswept shores of Florida Bay.

Bear Lake (1.6 miles one way) Hardwood hammock and mangroves line the Homestead Canal along a trail rich in woodland birds and Caribbean tree species. You can drive to the trailhead from the main State Rd 9336; otherwise, add 2 miles to the walk one way.

Shark Valley (p139)

BEST FREE PARK ACTIVITIES

The $30 entrance fee for the Everglades National Park ends up being great value if you take advantage of the park's many free ranger-led activities. Reserve popular activities (canoeing, biking) up to one week in advance. Among the highlights:

Slough slog Escape the crowds and immerse yourself in the wilderness on a 1–2 mile guided walk/wade through muddy and watery terrain into a cypress dome. Wear long pants, socks and lace-up shoes that can get wet. Meets at Royal Palm Visitor Center (p141).

Starlight walk Evening walk along the Anhinga Trail (p134) looking for gators and other creatures by nightfall. Bring a flashlight.

Bike hike A 2½-hour bike ride exploring the Everglades on two wheels. Bikes and helmets provided. Departs from Ernest Coe Visitor Center (p140).

Canoe the wilderness A three-hour morning paddle through some of the Everglades' best scenery. Meets at Flamingo Visitor Center (p142) and at Gulf Coast Visitor Center (p142).

Early bird walk Join a morning hike looking for, and learning about, some of the Everglades' feathered species. Meets at Flamingo Visitor Center (p142).

Glades glimpse Learn about some of the wonders of the Everglades at a daily talk given by rangers at the **Royal Palm Visitor Center** (p141) and at the Shark Valley Visitor Center (p142), typically from 1:30pm to 2pm.

Coastal Prairie Trail (7.5 miles one way) Follow the traditional path of fishers across open prairies and stands of buttonwoods. It begins at the Flamingo Campground (p142); a shorter version off the main trail called **Bayshore Loop (2-mile loop)** is an alternative for those with limited time.

Eco Pond (0.5 mile return) Across the main road from the Flamingo Visitor Center, this short loop around Eco Pond is good for seeing birds and gators.

Other Short Walks All of the following are half a mile long. **Mahogany Hammock** leads into an 'island' of hardwood forest floating on the waterlogged prairie, while the **Pinelands** takes you through a copse of rare spindly swamp pine and palmetto forest. Further on, **Pa-hay-okee Overlook** (p141) is a raised platform that has some of the best views in the Everglades.

BOAT TOURS

The best selection of boat tours operate in the northern Everglades, from along the Tamiami Trail, Everglades City, and out into the 10,000 Islands. In addition to the other operators, the Gulf Coast Visitor Center (p142) rents out kayaks and canoes in Everglades City. Be sure to take a map with you (they're available in the visitor center). Boaters will want to reference NOAA Charts 11430 and 11432. Keep an eye out for manatees in the marina. In the southern Everglades, **Flamingo Everglades** (☏855-798-2207; www.flamingoeverglades.com; tours per adult/child $40/20, canoe rental 2/4/8hr $20/28/38, kayak rental half-/full-day $35/45; ⏰marina 7am-7pm Mon-Fri, from 6am Sat & Sun) also runs guided boat tours. Listed below are outfits operating boat tours:

Everglades National Park Boat Tours (☏239-695-2591; www.nps.gov/ever/planyourvisit/guidedtours.htm; 905 Copeland Ave) Tours, lasting just under two hours, go either into the mangrove wilderness (adult/child $50/25) or out among the 10,000 Islands (adult/child $40/20), where if you're lucky you may see dolphins.

Everglades Florida Adventures (☏855-793-5542; https://evergladesfloridaadventures.com; 815 Oyster Bar Lane; adult/child $40/20) Departing from the marina next to the Gulf Coast Visitor Center, this a 90-minute boat trip into the 10,000 Islands. Houseboat and kayak rentals are also available.

Everglades Adventure Tours (EAT; ☏800-504-6554; www.evergladesadventuretours.com; 40904 Tamiami Trail E; 2hr kayak/pole-boat tour per person from $99/108) The EAT guys are based out of the same headquarters as the Skunk Ape people and offersome of the best private Everglades tours. Whether you go on a swamp hike, a 'safari' or a night tour, being poled around in a canoe or skiff by some genuinely funny guys with deep local knowledge of the Grassy Waters is an absolute treat.

Smallwood Store Boat Tour (p146) Departing from a dock below the Smallwood Store (p143), this small family-run outfit offers excellent private tours taking you out among the 10,000 Islands. You'll see loads of birds, and more than likely a few bottlenose dolphins.

History

Following the European settlement of Florida, some pioneers saw the potential for economic development of the Grassy Waters.

Cattle ranchers and sugar growers, attracted by mucky waters and Florida's subtropical climate (paradise for sugarcane), successfully pressured the government to make land available to them. In 1905 Florida governor Napoleon Bonaparte Broward personally dug the first shovelful of earth for a diversion that connected the Caloosahatchee River to Lake Okeechobee. Hundreds of canals were cut through the Everglades to the coastline to 'reclaim' the land, and the flow of lake water was restricted by a series of dikes. Farmland began to claim areas previously uninhabited by humans.

In her famous book, *The Everglades: River of Grass*, Marjory Stoneman Douglas (1890–1998) revealed that Gerard de Brahm, a colonial cartographer, named the region the River Glades, which became Ever Glades on later English maps.

Native American Everglades

The Everglades were an utter wilderness for thousands of years. Even Native Americans avoided the Glades; the 'native' Seminole and Miccosukee actually settled here as exiles escaping war and displacement from other parts of the country.

When a changing climate helped to form the Everglades as we now know it around 5000 years ago, two Native American peoples, the Calusa and Tequesta, inhabited the area; the former's territory centred on Fort Myers and as far north as Tampa, while the latter lived in Florida's southeast. Both were hunter-gatherer peoples and while they fished and hunted in the Everglades, they never lived within them, save for temporary campsites. As was the case for so many indigenous groups, the arrival of Spanish explorers and settlers from the 17th century onward wrought devastation upon indigenous society, and very few survived.

The Muscogee (Creek) Nation, originally from Alabama and Georgia, incorporated the remnants of other, smaller tribes, as well as, according to some reports, a number of escaped former slaves. In the process of migrating south through Florida, some of these bands became known as the Seminoles – the name is believed to come from a Spanish word that may mean 'those who have broken away.' By the mid-19th century, the Seminole and Miccosukee, another band of descendants from the Muscogee (Creek) nation, were living in the Everglades region, as well as further north. The three Seminole Wars pitted the US army against Native Americans, and more than 4000 Native Americans were killed or displaced; many Native Americans were removed from the area and resettled in Oklahoma. Rather than surrender, more than 100 Seminole and Miccosukees sought refuge in the Everglades. There they lived in what became known as 'hammock camps,' and they survived relatively undisturbed for almost a century.

BOOKS ABOUT THE EVERGLADES

➜ *The Everglades: River of Grass* (Marjory Stoneman Douglas, 1947) This landmark book introduced the Everglades to the outside world and was a call to action to protect the Everglades ecosystem.

➜ *Death in the Everglades: The Murder of Guy Bradley, America's First Martyr to Environmentalism* (Stuart B McIver, 2003) True crime story that takes you into the murky world of the resistance faced by conservationists who would save the Everglades.

➜ *The Swamp: The Everglades, Florida, and the Politics of Paradise* (Michael Grunwald, 2007) Fascinating and highly readable journey through Everglades history, with detailed studies of the threats to the Everglades and some of the conservation efforts to save it.

➜ *Shadow Country* (Peter Matthiessen, 2008) National Book Award–winning novel set in the 10,000 Islands and surroundings during the pioneer days. There is no more beautiful evocation of the Everglades and its history.

➜ *Swamplandia* (Karen Russell, 2011) Fast-paced fictional family drama set in the Everglades and a gator-wrestling theme park.

ⓘ EVERGLADES PRACTICALITIES

Gateway Towns

Although you could visit from Naples or Miami, the main gateway towns for Everglades National Park are Everglades City (p143), northwest of the park, and Homestead and Florida City (p145), for the east and southeast.

Park Entrances

There are three main entrances and three main areas of the park:

Gulf Coast section The park's northwest region, past Everglades City.

Shark Valley section At the central-north side on the Tamiami Trail.

Ernest Coe section Along the southeast edge near Homestead and Florida City.

Admission Fee

The admission fee – $30 per vehicle, $15 per hiker and cyclist – covers the whole park, and is good for seven consecutive days. Because the Tamiami Trail is a public road, there's no admission to access national park sights along this highway, aside from Shark Valley.

Throughout the 20th century, the growing settler population in south Florida, the building of roads like the Tamiami Trail, the development of towns such as Everglades City, and increasing tourism infrastructure and visitors all contributed to the decline of traditional ways of life. Most Seminole and Miccosukee people now depend upon indigenous-owned casinos and tourism for their livelihoods. Most of those who remain in the region are descendants of those who hid out in the Everglades during and after the Seminole Wars.

For a glimpse of traditional life, visit the Miccosukee Indian Village (p140) along the Tamiami Trail or the Ah-Tah-Thi-Ki Seminole Indian Museum (p140) in the Big Cypress Preserve.

Natural History

It's tempting to think of the Everglades as a swamp, but 'flooded prairie' may be a more apt description. The Glades, at the end of the day, are grasslands that happen to be flooded for most of the year: visit during the dry season (winter) and you'd be forgiven for thinking the Everglades was the Everfields.

So where's the water coming from? Look north on a map of Florida, all the way to Lake Okeechobee and the small lakes and rivers that band together around Kissimmee. Florida dips into the Gulf of Mexico at its below-sea-level tip, which happens to be the lowest part of the state geographically

and topographically. Run-off water from central Florida flows down the peninsula via streams and rivers, over and through the Glades, and into Florida Bay. The glacial pace of the flood means this seemingly stillest of landscapes is actually in constant motion. Small wonder the Native Americans called the area Pa-hay-okee (grassy water).

So what happens when nutrient-rich water creeps over a limestone shelf? The ecological equivalent of a sweaty orgy. Beginning at the cellular level, organic material blooms in surprising ways, clumping and forming into algal beds, nutrient blooms and the ubiquitous periphyton, which are basically clusters of algae, bacteria and detritus (ie stuff).

Periphyton ain't pretty: in the water it resembles streaks of vomit, and the dried version looks like hippo turds. But you should kiss this biological soup when you see it (well, maybe not) because in the great chain of the Everglades, this slop forms the base of a very tall organic totem pole. The smallest tilt in elevation alters the flow of water and hence the content of this nutrient soup, and thus the landscape itself: all those patches of cypress and hardwood hammock (not a bed for backpackers; in this case, hammock is a fancy Floridian way of saying a forest of broadleaf trees, mainly tropical or subtropical) are areas where a few inches of altitude create a world of difference between ecosystems.

EVERGLADES NATIONAL PARK

This vast **wilderness** (📞305-242-7700; www. nps.gov/ever; 40001 State Rd 9336, Homestead; vehicle pass $30, pedestrian & cyclist $15; ⏱visitor center 9am-5pm; ♿), encompassing 1.5 million acres, is one of America's great natural treasures and certainly the best place to see wildlife in Florida. Utterly unlike anywhere else in the state, this is a place where the natural world takes over, with a vast network of islands and watery channels sheltering plenty of alligators, abundant birdlife and a real sense of being far from the world and its noise. There's much to see and do – from hiking past basking alligators as herons stalk patiently through nearby waters in search of prey, to kayaking through mangrove canals and on peaceful lakes. You can also wade into murky knee-high waters among cypress domes on a rough-and-ready 'slough slog.'

There are sunrise strolls on boardwalks amid the awakening of birdsong, and moonlit glimpses of gators swimming gracefully along narrow channels in search of dinner. Backcountry camping, bicycle tours and ranger-led activities help bring the magic of this place to life. The biggest challenge is really just deciding where to begin.

WILDLIFE: THE BEST PLACES TO SEE...

Alligator Shark Valley (p139), Anhinga Trail (p134), Fakahatchee Strand Preserve (p139)

Crocodile Flamingo Marina (p140), 10,000 Islands (p146)

Manatee Flamingo Marina (p140), Gulf Coast Visitor Center (p142), Big Cypress Swamp Welcome Center (p142)

Bottlenose Dolphin 10,000 Islands (p146)

Birdlife Anhinga Trail (p134), Shark Valley (p139)

Florida Panther Everywhere and nowhere... Big Cypress National Preserve (p138), Florida Panther National Wildlife Refuge (p144)

⊙ Sights & Activities

⊙ Northern Everglades

As you fly over the northern Everglades on your approach into Miami International Airport, the incongruity of this extraordinary wilderness is impossible to miss. One minute, there are watery grasslands and barely a sign of human life as far as the eye can see. The next, you're in Miami, that poster child for Florida's all-consuming coastal development. Once on the ground, the Tamiami Trail/Hwy 41 cuts through the Everglades, from Calle Ocho in Miami's Little Havana to the Gulf of Mexico. All along this road, in whichever direction you're traveling, this trip traverses long landscapes of flooded forest, pine woods, gambling halls, swamp-buggy tours and roadside food shacks.

Ochopee VILLAGE
(38000 Tamiami Trail E; ⏱8-10am & noon-4pm Mon-Fri, 10-11:30am Sat) Drive to the hamlet of Ochopee (population about four), then pull over and break out the cameras: Ochopee's claim to fame is the country's smallest **post office**. It's housed in a former toolshed and set against big park skies; a friendly postal worker patiently poses for snapshots.

Big Cypress National Preserve PARK
(📞239-695-4758; www.nps.gov/bicy; 33000 Tamiami Trail E; ⏱24hr; P♿) 🎫 FREE The 1139-sq-mile Big Cypress National Preserve (named for the size of the park, not its trees) is the result of a compromise between environmentalists, cattle ranchers and oil-and-gas explorers. The area is integral to the Everglades' ecosystem: rains that flood the preserve's prairies and wetlands slowly filter down through the Glades. About 45% of the cypress swamp (actually mangrove islands, hardwood hammocks, orchid flowers, slash pine, prairies and marshes) is protected.

Skunk Ape Research Headquarters PARK
(📞239-695-2275; www.skunkape.info; 40904 Tamiami Trail E; adult/child $15/8; ⏱9am-5pm; P) This only-in-Florida roadside attraction is dedicated to tracking down southeastern USA's version of Bigfoot, the eponymous Skunk Ape (a large gorilla-man who supposedly stinks to high heaven). We never saw a Skunk Ape, but you can see a corny gift shop and, in the back, a reptile-and-bird zoo run by a true Florida eccentric, the sort of guy who wraps albino pythons around his neck for fun.

EVERGLADES IN...

One Day

If you only have a day in the Everglades, choose between a day in the north or a day in the south – where you start the day will most likely determine which works best. If you're in the north, consider driving the Loop Rd (p140), go for a short walk at the Kirby Storter Roadside Park (p133), or hike part of the Shark Valley Trail (p133) in the morning and then go kayaking with Everglades Adventures (p144) in the afternoon. If you're in the south, drive all the way to the Flamingo area, then hike the Anhinga Trail (p134), walk to the Pa-hay-okee Overlook (p141), and rent a kayak for an afternoon paddle.

Two Days

If you have two full days to dedicate to the park, spend one of the days exploring the northern reaches of the park, the other in the south – the order doesn't matter, but doing both will give you a good overview of the park and its possibilities.

Three Days

If you've done the main activities on days one and two, consider a deeper immersion for day three. If you're in the south, you could spend a whole day and into the evening getting out onto the water, hiking through the swamp, and taking a night walk with Garls Coastal Kayaking Everglades (p133). In the north, do the whole Shark Valley Trail, either on foot or by bike, and/or take a boat tour out toward the 10,000 Islands (p146), through the Gulf Coast Visitor Center (p142) or Smallwood Store Boat Tour (p146).

Shark Valley   PARK

(☎ 305-221-8776; www.nps.gov/ever/planyourvisit/svdirections.htm; 36000 SW 8th St; car/cyclist & pedestrian $30/15; ◷ 9am-5pm; P 🚻) 🖉 Shark Valley sounds like it should be the headquarters for the villain in a James Bond movie, but it is in fact a slice of National Park Service grounds heavy with informative signs and knowledgeable rangers. Shark Valley is located in the cypress, hardwood and riverine section of the Everglades, a more traditionally jungly section of the park than the grassy fields and forest domes surrounding the Ernest Coe visitor center.

If you don't feel like exerting yourself, the most popular and painless way to immerse yourself in the Everglades is via the two-hour **tram tour** (☎ 305-221-8455; www.sharkvalleytramtours.com; adult/child under 12yr/senior $25/19/12.75; ◷ departures 9:30am, 11am, 2pm, 4pm May-Dec, 9am-4pm Jan-Apr hourly on the hour) that runs along Shark Valley's entire 15-mile trail. If you only have time for one Everglades activity, this should be it, as guides are informative and witty, and you may see gators sunning themselves on the road. Halfway along the trail is the 50ft-high **Shark Valley Observation Tower**, an ugly concrete tower that offers dramatically beautiful views of the park.

Big Cypress Gallery   GALLERY

(☎ 239-695-2428; https://clydebutcher.com; 52388 Tamiami Trail; ◷ 10am-5pm; P) 🖉 This gallery showcases the work of Clyde Butcher, an American photographer who follows in the great tradition of Ansel Adams. His large-format black-and-white images elevate the swamps to a higher level. Butcher has found a quiet spirituality in the brackish waters. You'll find many gorgeous prints, which make fine mementos of the Everglades experience (though prices aren't cheap).

⭐ Fakahatchee Strand Preserve   PARK

(☎ 239-695-4593; www.floridastateparks.org/parks-and-trails/fakahatchee-strand-preserve-state-park; 137 Coastline Dr, Copeland; vehicle/pedestrian/bicycle $3/2/2; ◷ 8am-sunset; P 🚻) 🖉 The Fakahatchee Strand, besides having a fantastic name, also houses a 20-mile by 5-mile estuarine wetland that looks like something from the beginning of time. A 2000ft boardwalk traverses this wet and wild wonderland, where panthers still stalk their prey amid the black waters. While it's unlikely you'll spot any panthers, there's a great chance you'll see a large variety of blooming orchids, birdlife and reptiles ranging in size from tiny skinks to grinning alligators.

OFF THE BEATEN TRACK

DETOUR: LOOP ROAD

The 24-mile-long Loop Rd, off Tamiami Trail (Hwy 41), offers some unique sites.

➡ The homes of the Miccosukee, some of which have been considerably expanded by gambling revenue. You'll see some traditional *chickee*-style huts (wooden platforms above the waterline) and some trailer homes with massive add-on wings that are bigger than the original trailer – all seem to have shiny new pickup trucks parked out front.

➡ Great pull-offs for viewing flooded forests, where egrets that look like pterodactyls perch in the trees, and alligators lurk in the depths below.

➡ Houses with large 'Stay off my property' signs; these homes are as much a part of the landscape as the swamp.

➡ The short, pleasantly jungly **Tree Snail Hammock Nature Trail**. Though unpaved, the graded road is in good shape and fine for 2WD vehicles.

True to its name, the road loops right back onto the Tamiami; expect a leisurely jaunt on the Loop to add an hour or two to your trip.

Ah-Tah-Thi-Ki
Seminole Indian Museum   MUSEUM
(☑877-902-1113; www.ahtahthiki.com; Big Cypress Seminole Indian Reservation, 34725 West Boundary Rd, Clewiston; adult/child/senior $10/7.50/7.50; ☺9am-5pm) If you want to learn about Florida's Native Americans, come to the Ah-Tah-Thi-Ki Seminole Indian Museum, 17 miles north of I-75. All of the excellent educational exhibits on Seminole life, history and the tribe today were funded by gaming proceeds, which provide most of the tribe's multimillion-dollar operating budget.

The museum is located within a cypress dome cut through with an interpretive boardwalk, so from the start it strikes a balance between environmentalism and education. The permanent exhibit has several dioramas with life-sized figures depicting various scenes out of traditional Seminole life, while temporary exhibits have a bit more academic polish (past examples have included lengthy forays into the economic structure of the Everglades). There's an old-school 'living village' and re-created ceremonial grounds as well. The museum is making an effort to not be a cheesy Native American theme park, and the Seminole tribe has gone to impressive lengths to achieve this.

Miccosukee Indian Village   MUSEUM
(☑305-552-8365; www.miccosukee.com; Mile 70, Hwy 41; adult/child/child 5yr & under $15/8/free; ☺9am-5pm; P ⚑) Just west of the turnoff to Shark Valley, this 'Indian Village' is an informative open-air museum that showcases the culture of the Miccosukee via guided tours of traditional homes, a crafts gift store, dance and music performances, and an airboat ride (additional $20) into a hammock-cum-village of raised *chickee* (wooden platforms above the waterline) huts. The art and handmade crafts from the on-site art gallery make good souvenirs. There's a somewhat desultory restaurant as well, if you get hungry.

⊙ Southern Everglades

Head south of Miami to drive into the heart of the park and the biggest horizons of the Everglades. Plus there are plenty of side paths and canoe creeks for memorable detours. You'll also see some of the most quietly exhilarating scenery the park has to offer on this route.

Flamingo Marina   MARINA
(State Rd 9336) The chief draw here is taking either a boat tour or hiring a kayak or canoe – all arranged through Flamingo Everglades (p135), a short stroll from the visitor center (p142). Do spend some time hanging out near the water's edge. This is a great place for seeing manatees, alligators and even the rare American crocodile.

Ernest Coe Visitor Center   VISITOR CENTER
(☑305-242-7700; www.nps.gov/ever; 40001 State Rd 9336; ☺9am-5pm mid-Apr–mid-Dec, 8am-5pm mid-Dec–mid-Apr) Near the entrance to the Everglades National Park, this friendly visitor center has some excellent exhibits, including a diorama of 'typical' Floridians (the fisherman looks like he should join ZZ Top).

★ Pa-hay-okee Overlook
VIEWPOINT

State Rd 9336 cuts through the soft heart of the park, past long fields of marsh prairie, white, skeletal forests of bald cypress and dark clumps of mahogany hammock. Further on, the Pa-hay-okee Overlook is a raised platform that peeks over one of the prettiest bends in the River of Grass.

Royal Palm Visitor Center
PARK

(☎305-242-7237; www.nps.gov/ever/planyourvisit/royal-palm.htm; State Rd 9336; ☺9am-4:15pm) Four miles past Ernest Coe Visitor Center, Royal Palm offers the easiest access to the Glades in these parts. Two trails, the Anhinga (p134) and **Gumbo Limbo** (the latter named for the gumbo-limbo tree, also known as the 'tourist tree' because its bark peels like a sunburned tourist), take all of an hour to walk and put you face to face with a panoply of Everglades wildlife. There's a small information station and bookstore.

🛏 Sleeping & Eating

Options within the park, as opposed to the gateway towns, are largely restricted to camping, although 24 new and extremely comfortable cabins are slated to open in the southern Flamingo area of the park. Built from recycled shipping containers but repurposed to a hotel standard, they will be bookable through the national park website.

If you plan to camp in the park, make reservations months in advance. Otherwise, base yourself in Homestead or Florida City (both of which have dozens of hotels across all budgets) and visit the park during the day.

🛏 Northern Everglades

Monument Lake
CAMPGROUND $

(☎239-695-1205; www.recreation.gov; 50215 Tamiami Trail E; tent/RV sites $24/28) Reserve months ahead to book one of 10 tent sites (or 26 RV sites) at this appealing campground in the Big Cypress National Preserve. The lake looks quite enticing, but there's no swimming (alligators live here after all). There's plenty of greenery, but not a whole lot of shade.

Swamp Cottage
COTTAGE $$$

(☎239-695-2428; https://clydebutcher.com/bigcypress/vacation-rentals; 52388 Tamiami Trail; cottage $250-350; P🕱) 🍃 Want to get as close to the swamp as possible, without giving up on amenities? Book a bungalow or a two-bedroom cottage, tucked amid lush greenery behind the Big Cypress Gallery (p139). The

lodging is comfortably appointed, if not luxurious, and is certainly cozy, though the best feature is having one of America's great wetlands right outside your door.

Joanie's Blue Crab Cafe
AMERICAN $$

(☎239-695-2682; www.joaniesbluecrabcafe.com; 39395 Tamiami Trail E; mains $8-17; ☺11am-5pm Thu-Tue, closed seasonally, call to confirm; 🖋) This long-standing Everglades shack, east of Ochopee, with open rafters, shellacked picnic tables and alligator kitsch, serves filling food of the 'fried everything' variety on paper plates. Crab cakes are the thing to order. There's live music on some Saturdays and Sundays from 12:30pm and a rockabilly-loving jukebox at other times.

Glades Eats
AMERICAN $$

(☎305-894-2374; www.facebook.com/GladesEats; Tamiami Trail, Hwy 41; mains $12-16; ☺8am-4pm) Part of the Miccosukee complex of attractions along the Tamiami Trail close to the Shark Valley turnoff, Glades Eats does everything from Cuban sandwiches and quesadillas to BBQ spare ribs and a decent Wagyu beef burger.

🛏 Southern Everglades

Quality dining options are fairly sparse here, though there are some good, inexpensive Mexican restaurants in Florida City and Homestead.

NATIONAL PARK SERVICE CAMPING

There are campgrounds run by the National Park Service (NPS) located throughout the park. Sites are fairly basic, though there are showers and toilets. Depending on the time of year, the cold water can be either bracing or a welcome relief. The NPS information offices provide a map of all campsites, as does the park website. Visit www.nps.gov/ever/planyourvisit/camping.htm for more information.

There are also many backcountry tent sites ($2 per night). For these you'll also need a permit ($15) and to reserve ahead at one of the visitor centers. Sites are free during the off season (May to October). Note that these sites are accessible only by canoe or kayak (excepting one site that can be reached on foot from Flamingo).

WILDERNESS CAMPING

Three types of **backcountry campsites** (☎239-695-3311, 239-695-2945; www.nps.gov/ever/planyourvisit/backcamp.htm; permit Nov-Apr/May-Oct $15/free, plus per person per night $2; ⊙Flamingo & Gulf Coast Visitor Centers 8am-4:30pm) are available: beach sites on coastal shell beaches and in the 10,000 Islands; ground sites, which are basically mounds of dirt built up above the mangroves; and *chickees*, wooden platforms built above the waterline where you can pitch a freestanding (no spikes) tent. *Chickees*, which have toilets, are the most civilized – there's a serenity found in sleeping on what feels like a raft levitating above the water. Ground sites tend to be the most bug infested.

Warning: if you're paddling around and see an island that looks pleasant for camping but isn't a designated campsite, beware – you may end up submerged when the tides change.

From November to April, backcountry camping permits cost $15, plus $2 per person per night; from May to October sites are free, but you must still self-register at either Flamingo or Gulf Coast Visitor Centers or call 239-695-2945. And pick up the *Wilderness Trip Planner* brochure from Flamingo Visitor Center (p142); it has maps and information on campsites.

Some backcountry tips:

➡ Store food in a hand-sized, raccoon-proof container (available at gear stores).

➡ Bury your waste at least 10in below ground, but keep in mind some ground sites have hard turf.

➡ Use a backcountry stove to cook. Ground fires are only permitted at beach sites, and you can only burn dead or downed wood.

Flamingo Campground
CAMPGROUND **$**
(☎877-444-6777; www.nps.gov/ever/planyourvisit/flamdirections.htm; Flamingo Lodge Hwy; tent sites with/without hookups $20/30) There are over 200 campsites at the Flamingo Visitor Center, some of which have electrical hookups. Escape the RVs by booking a walk-in site. Reserve well ahead (via www.reserveamerica.com) for one of the nine waterfront sites.

Long Pine Key Campground
CAMPGROUND **$**
(☎305-242-7700; wwwnps.gov/ever/planyourvisit/camping.htm; Off State Rd 9336; tent & RV sites $20; ⊙closed Jun–mid-Nov) This is a good bet for car campers, just west of Royal Palm Visitor Center. It has 108 sites, available on a first-come basis (no reservations).

❶ Information

Shark Valley Visitor Center (☎305-221-8776; www.nps.gov/ever/planyourvisit/sv directions.htm; national park entry per vehicle/bicycle/pedestrian $25/8/8; ⊙9am-5pm) A good place to pick up information about the Everglades, including trails, wildlife watching and free ranger-led activities.

Gulf Coast Visitor Center (☎239-695-3311; www.nps.gov/ever; 815 Oyster Bar Lane, off Hwy 29, Everglades City; ⊙9am-4:30pm mid-Apr–mid-Nov, 8am-5pm mid-Nov–mid-Apr; ☔) This is the northwestern-most ranger station for Everglades National Park, and provides access to and information on the 10,000 Islands area.

Oasis Visitor Center (☎239-695-1201; www.nps.gov/bicy; 52105 Tamiami Trail E; ⊙9am-4:30pm; ☔) This visitor center, about 20 miles west of Shark Valley, has hands-on exhibits and info on nearby walks in the Big Cypress National Preserve. A platform overlooking a small water-filled ditch is a great spot to see alligators, particularly in the dry season (December to May).

Big Cypress Swamp Welcome Center (☎239-695-4758; www.nps.gov/bicy/plan yourvisit/big-cypress-swamp-welcome-center.htm; 33000 Tamiami Trail E; ⊙9am-4:30pm) About 2.5 miles east of the turnoff to Everglades City, this big visitor center is a good one for kids, with a small nature center where you can listen to recordings of different swamp critters. There's also a viewing platform overlooking a canal where you can sometimes spot manatees. Good spot for information on the reserve.

Flamingo Visitor Center (☎239-695-2945; www.nps.gov/ever; State Rd 9336; ⊙8am-4:30pm mid-Nov–mid-Apr) The visitor center is at the end of State Rd 9336. It's being rebuilt after sustaining hurricane damage, so they're operating out of a trailer until repairs are done.

❶ Getting There & Away

The largest subtropical wilderness in the continental USA is easily accessible from Miami. The Glades, which comprise the 80 southernmost miles of Florida, are bound by the Atlantic Ocean to the east and the Gulf of Mexico to the west. The Tamiami Trail (Hwy 41) goes east–west, parallel to the more northern (and less interesting) Alligator Alley (I-75).

ℹ️ Getting Around

You need a car to properly enter and explore the Everglades, or at least to get as far as the hiking trailheads or kayak jumping-off points. Once you're in, wearing a good pair of walking boots is essential to penetrate the interior. Having a canoe or a kayak helps as well; these can be rented from outfits inside and outside the park, or you can seek out guided canoe and kayak tours. Bicycles are well suited to the flat roads of Everglades National Park, particularly in the area between Ernest Coe and Flamingo Point. Road shoulders in the park tend to be dangerously small.

EVERGLADES CITY & CHOKOLOSKEE ISLAND

📞 239 / POP 426

On the edge of Chokoloskee Bay, you'll find this Old Florida fishing village of raised houses, turquoise water and scattershot emerald-green mangrove islands. 'City' is stretching it for Everglades City – this is really a friendly fishing town where you can easily disappear from the modern world for a day or three. You'll find some intriguing vestiges of the past here, including an excellent regional museum, as well as delicious seafood.

🔴 Sights

⭐ Museum of the Everglades   MUSEUM
(📞 239-252-5026; www.evergladesmuseum.org; 105 W Broadway, Everglades City; ⏰ 9am-4pm Mon-Fri, to 5pm Sat; 🅿️) FREE For a break from the outdoors, don't miss this small museum run by volunteers who have a wealth of knowledge on the region's history. Located in the town's former laundry house, the collection delves into human settlement in the area from the early pioneers of the 1800s to the boom days of the 1920s and its tragic moments (Hurricane Donna devastated the town in 1960), and subsequent transformation into the quiet backwater of today.

The most important player here is Barron Collier, Florida's largest landowner of the early 20th century, who essentially created the town from scratch to serve as the base for building the ambitious Tamiami Trail through the Everglades (completed in 1929). Photographs, models and films tell the story of this engineering marvel, as well as what life was like for the early settlers, the workers and the wealthy developers.

Smallwood Store   MUSEUM
(📞 239-695-2989; www.smallwoodstore.com; 360 Mamie St, Chokoloskee; adult/child $5/free; ⏰ 10am-5pm Dec-Apr, 11am-5pm May-Nov) Perched on piers overlooking Chokoloskee Bay, this wooden building dates back to 1906, when a pioneer by the name of Ted Smallwood opened his rustic trading post, post office and general store. The wooden shelves are lined with antiques and old artifacts, along with descriptions of events and characters from those rough and tumble days of life on a remote island frontier.

Don't miss the peaceful views (particularly around sunset) over the waterfront from the pier just below the store. You can also arrange boat tours here.

🎊 Festivals & Events

Everglades Seafood Festival   FOOD & DRINK
(www.evergladesseafoodfestival.org; 102 Copeland Ave; ⏰ Feb) In Everglades City, this three-day festival features plenty of feasting, as well as kids rides and live music. The star of the show is of course glorious seafood – stone crab, conch fritters, crab cakes, coconut shrimp, mussels, and calamari – though there's also fried gator, frog's legs, pulled-pork barbecue and key-lime pie on a stick!

🛏️ Sleeping

Reserve ahead, especially from December to March.

Outdoor Resorts of Chokoloskee   MOTEL $$
(📞 239-695-2881; www.outdoorresortsofchokolskee. com; 150 Smallwood Dr, Chokoloskee; r $125; ❄️🏊) At the northern end of Chokoloskee Island, this good-value place is a big draw due to its extensive facilities, including several swimming pools, hot tubs, tennis and shuffleboard courts, a fitness center and boat rentals. The fairly basic motel-style rooms have kitchenettes and a back deck overlooking the marina. It's popular with the RV crowd (there are 283 sites versus only eight motel units).

Parkway Motel & Marina   MOTEL $$
(📞 239-695-3261; www.parkwaymotelandmarina. net; 1180 Chokoloskee Dr, Chokoloskee; r $108-155; 🅿️❄️) A friendly couple runs this veritable testament to the old-school Floridian lodge: cute small rooms and one cozy apartment in a one-story motel building. It's in a peaceful spot on the island of Chokoloskee, and owners Bill and Geri have a wealth of knowledge on the region.

FLORIDA PANTHER NATIONAL WILDLIFE REFUGE

The critically endangered Florida panther is one of the Everglades' most charismatic characters and its most secretive – very few visitors see one here, although the chance of doing so animates any visit. The **Florida Panther National Wildlife Refuge** (☎ 239-657-8001; www.fws.gov/refuge/florida_panther; State Rd 29; ⊙ sunrise-sunset) FREE, north of Everglades National Park, covers 26,400 acres and is home to an estimated 12 to 16 of the 200 or so Florida panthers that remain in the wild. Also living on the refuge are bobcats, black bears and alligators.

Most of the refuge is off-limits to visitors, but there are two hiking trails where you can get a glimpse of the panther's habitat of hardwood hammocks, pine flatwoods, and flooded prairies. The trails run for 0.3 miles and 1.3 miles; watch for panther footprints along the longer trail in particular. Call ahead to check on trail conditions, as they can be impassable after heavy rains. Both trails are well signposted with brown signs on the west side of the road between a quarter- and a half-mile north of where State Road 29 intersects with I-75. Early morning and late afternoon are the best times to visit.

The refuge lies 20 miles east of Naples. Take I-75 South, then turn off at Exit 80.

Ivey House Bed & Breakfast
B&B $$

(☎ 877-567-0679; www.iveyhouse.com; 605 Buckner Ave N, Everglades City; inn $100-200, lodge $90-100, cottage $180-250; P ✳ 🛜 🛉) This friendly, family-run tropical inn offers a variety of well-appointed accommodations: bright spacious inn rooms overlooking a pretty courtyard, cheaper lodge rooms (with shared bathrooms) and a freestanding two-bedroom cottage with a kitchen and screened-in porch. The pool (covered in winter) is a great year-round option for a swim.

This is a top place to book nature trips with **Everglades Adventures** (www.iveyhouse.com/everglades-adventures; 107 Camellia St, Everglades City; 3-4hr tours adult/child from $99/59, canoe/kayak rental per day from $45/55) 🍃, from daytime paddles to six-day packages that include lodging, tours and some meals.

Everglades City Motel
MOTEL $$

(☎ 239-695-4224; www.evergladescitymotel.com; 309 Collier Ave, Everglades City; r from $149; P ✳ 🛜) With large rooms that have all the mod cons (flat-screen TV, fridge, coffeemaker) and friendly staff who can hook you up with boat tours, this motel provides good value for those looking to spend some time near the 10,000 Islands.

✖ Eating

Triad Seafood Cafe
SEAFOOD $

(☎ 239-695-0722; www.triadseafoodmarketcafe.com; 401 School Dr, Everglades City; mains $10-23, stone-crab meals $26-46; ⊙ 10:30am-6pm Sun-Thu, to 7pm Fri & Sat) Triad is famous for its stone-crab claws, but it serves up all kinds of coastal seafood that you can enjoy on picnic tables perched over the waterfront. Should you impress the friendly owners with your ability to devour crustaceans (or their claws, anyway), you get the dubious honor of having your picture hung on the Glutton Board.

★Havana Cafe
LATIN AMERICAN $$

(☎ 239-695-2214; www.havanacafeofthe everglades.com; 191 Smallwood Dr, Chokoloskee; breakfast $9-12, lunch mains $7-19; ⊙ 7am-4pm Sun-Thu, 5-8pm Fri & Sat mid-Oct–mid-Apr, closed mid-Apr–mid-Oct) The Havana Cafe is famed far and wide for its deliciously prepared seafood served with Latin accents. Lunch favorites include stone-crab enchiladas, blackened grouper with rice and beans, and a decadent Cuban sandwich. The outdoor dining amid palm trees and vibrant bougainvillea – not to mention the incredibly friendly service – adds to the appeal.

Reservations are essential on Friday and Saturday nights, when foodies from out of town arrive for stone-crab feasts. Order in advance the astonishingly good seafood paella or seafood pasta – both $50 but serving at least two people.

★Camellia Street Grill
SEAFOOD $$

(☎ 239-695-2003; www.facebook.com/camellia streetgrill; 202 Camellia St, Everglades City; mains $12-26; ⊙ 11am-9pm; 🍴) In a barnlike setting with fairy lights strung from the rafters and nautical doodads lining the walls, Camellia is an easygoing spot for a down-home seafood feast. Come before sunset to enjoy the pretty views from the waterfront deck. Don't miss the tender stone-crab claws in season.

ℹ Information

Everglades Area Chamber of Commerce
(☎239-695-3941; cnr Hwys 41 & 29 Everglades City; ☺9am-4pm) General information about the region.

ℹ Getting There & Away

There is no public transportation out this way. If you're driving, it's a fairly straight 85-mile drive west from Miami. The trip takes about 1¾ hours in good traffic.

HOMESTEAD & FLORIDA CITY

☎305 / POP 70,477 (HOMESTEAD), 12,077 (FLORIDA CITY)

Homestead and neighboring Florida City, 2 miles to the south, have little obvious appeal upon arrival – they're closer in spirit to Miami than the wild Everglades. Part of the ever-expanding subdivisions of South Miami, this bustling corridor can feel like an endless strip of big-box shopping centers, fast-food joints, car dealerships and gas stations. However, look beneath the veneer and you'll find much more than meets the eye: strange curiosities like a 'castle' built single-handedly by one lovestruck immigrant, an animal rescue center for exotic species, a winery showcasing Florida's produce (hint: it's not grapes), an up-and-coming microbrewery, and one of the best farm stands in America.

This area makes a great base for forays into the southern reaches of Everglades National Park.

◎ Sights

★ Coral Castle   CASTLE
(☎305-248-6345; www.coralcastle.com; 28655 S Dixie Hwy, Homestead; adult/senior/child $18/16/8; ☺9am-6pm Sun-Thu, to 7pm Fri & Sat) 'You will be seeing unusual accomplishment,' reads the inscription on the rough-hewn quarried wall. That's an understatement. There is no greater temple to all that is weird and wacky about South Florida. The legend goes that a Latvian man got snubbed at the altar, came to the US and settled in Florida, and hand-carved, unseen, in the dead of night, a monument to unrequited love.

Everglades Outpost   WILDLIFE RESERVE
(☎305-247-8000; www.evergladesoutpost.org; 35601 SW 192nd Ave, Homestead; adult/child $15/10; ☺10am-5:30pm Mon, Tue & Fri, 10am-6pm Sat & Sun) The Everglades Outpost houses, feeds and cares for wild animals that have been seized from illegal traders, abused, neglected or donated by people who could not care for them. Residents of the outpost include a lemur, wolves, a black bear, a zebra, cobras, alligators and a majestic tiger (who was bought by an exotic dancer who thought she could incorporate it into her act). Your money goes toward helping the outpost's mission.

Downtown Homestead   AREA
(☎305-323-6564; www.homesteadmainst.org; Krome Ave) You could pass a mildly entertaining afternoon walking around Homestead's almost quaint main street, which essentially comprises a couple of blocks of Krome Ave extending north and south of the **Historic Town Hall** (☎305-242-4463; www.townhallmuseum.org; 41 N Krome Ave; ☺1-5pm Wed-Sat). The town hosts one big monthly event from September to April, including concerts, food fests, holiday parades and other events at **Losner Park** (across the street from the Historic Town Hall).

Fruit & Spice Park   PARK
(☎305-247-5727; www.redlandfruitandspice.com; 24801 SW 187th Ave, Homestead; adult/child/child under 6yr $10/3/free; ☺9am-5pm; P) Set on the edge of the Everglades, this 35-acre public park grows all those great tropical fruits you usually have to contract dysentery to enjoy. The park is divided into 'continents' (Africa, Asia etc) and it makes for a peaceful wander past various species bearing in total around 500 different types of fruits, spices and nuts. Unfortunately, you can't pick the fruit, but you can eat anything that falls to the ground (go early for the best gathering!).

Schnebly Redland's Winery   WINERY
(☎305-242-1224; www.schneblywinery.com; 30205 SW 217th Ave, Homestead; wine tastings/tours $13/8; ☺noon-5pm Mon-Thu, noon-10pm Fri & Sat, 11am-5pm Sun) Given the climate, you won't find malbec, pinot noir or zinfandel – wines here are made of mango, passion fruit, lychee, avocado, coconut and other flavors from the tropics, and are surprisingly good. Tucked along a quiet farm road west of Homestead, Schnebly has the distinction of being the southernmost winery in America. You can stop in for tastings, available any time, or for a tour (weekends only, hourly 1pm to 5pm). There's also a good restaurant here, and a pretty back garden next to a small gurgling waterfall.

10,000 ISLANDS

One of the best ways to experience the serenity of the Everglades is by paddling the network of waterways that skirt the northwest portion of the park. Out here, apart from a few pleasure craft, other tourists are a rarity and they're easy to avoid in the labyrinth of islands and channels. The 10,000 Islands consist of tiny islands and a mangrove swamp that hugs the southwestern-most border of Florida. And there aren't really 10,000 of them, just a few hundred, but once you're among them it can feel like many more.

The 10,000 Islands run from Cape Romano, the southernmost tip of Marco Island, to the mouth of what's known as Lostman's River, close to Everglades City. In places it can be difficult to tell which are genuine islands (ie the tips of landscapes submerged in the shallow waters) and which are mangroves (plant life that grows between the point of high and low tide) that have grown atop oyster mounds; the mangroves occupy an estimated 230 sq miles, making it one of the most extensive areas of mangrove forest in the US. The southern islands fall within Everglades National Park.

Archaeologists have found evidence of Native American habitation from around 3500 years ago, although some of these sites have since disappeared beneath rising sea waters. You may also come across the remains of huts, occupied by pioneers who inhabited the islands in the 19th century. Chokoloskee Island, next to Everglades City, is the largest of the islands, and one of very few inhabited today. The absence of any nighttime light pollution makes the islands ideal for stargazing.

Exploring the Islands

Most travelers who explore the 10,000 Islands do so as part of a tour. Everglades Adventures (p144), operating out of Everglades City, is a recommended operator for kayak tours, while **Smallwood Store Boat Tour** (☎239-695-0016; www.smallwood storeboattour.com; 360 Mamie St, Chokoloskee; 1hr tour $40; 🚤) runs guided boat trips out into the islands from Chokoloskee Island; the latter operates one tour that follows the story of pioneers such as Edgar J Watson, the main (and real-life) protagonist in Peter Matthiessen's epic novel, *Shadow Country*, which was set in the region.

Getting around the 10,000 Islands is pretty straightforward if you're a competent navigator and you religiously adhere to National Oceanic & Atmospheric Administration (NOAA) tide and nautical charts. Going against the tides is the fastest way to make a miserable trip. The Gulf Coast Visitor Center (p142) sells nautical charts and gives out free tidal charts. You can also purchase charts prior to your visit – call 305-247-1216 and ask for charts 11430, 11432 and 11433.

👉 Tours

Hoosville Hostel offers fantastic tours of the eastern Everglades. You can either paddle into the bush, or if you don't mind getting a little damp, embark on a 'wet walk' into a flowered and fecund cypress dome, stepping through black water and around the edges of an alligator wallow. Half-day/full-day kayaking tours start from $135/160.

🛏 Sleeping

Aside from the excellent Hoosville Hostel in Florida City, unique lodging options are rare here. You will find plenty of chain hotels scattered along Rte 1 Krome Ave. Higher-end options tend to be close to the busy Ronald Reagan Turnpike.

⭐ **Hoosville Hostel**   HOSTEL **$**
(☎305-248-1122; www.hoosvillehostel.com; 20 SW 2nd Ave, Florida City; tent sites per person $18, dm $35, r $60-240; P🅿❄🅿🛜🅿🏊) Formerly the Everglades International Hostel, the Hoosville has kept the good-value dorms, private rooms and 'semi-privates' (you have an enclosed room within the dorms and share a bathroom with dorm residents). The creatively configured backyard is the best feature. There's a small rock-cut pool with a waterfall and a gazebo.

We should add the crowd is made up of free-spirited international types, and the hostel leads excellent tours into the Everglades.

Hotel Redland
HOTEL $

(☑305-246-1904; 5 S Flagler Ave, Homestead; r $110-150; ❀🐾) On the edge of Homestead's quaint downtown, the Hotel Redland is set in a 1904 building that has a warm, cozy feel thanks to its gracious hosts. The 12 rooms are comfortable, but dated in a charming, grand-motherly way (quilted bedspreads, floral curtains, old photos or framed paintings on the walls). There's a good restaurant here – which is just as well as the area feels deserted at night, so you'll need to get around by car.

✗ Eating & Drinking

★ Robert Is Here
MARKET $

(☑305-246-1592; www.robertishere.com; 19200 SW 344th St, Homestead; juices $7-10; ⊙8am-7pm) 🥭 More than a farmers stand, Robert's is an institution. This is Old Florida at its kitschy best, in love with the Glades and the agriculture that surrounds it. You'll find loads of exotic, Florida-grown fruits you won't get elsewhere – including black sapote, carambola (star fruit), dragon fruit, sapodilla, guanabana (soursop), tamarind, sugar apples, longans and passion fruit. The juices are fantastic.

There's also a petting zoo and a water-play area for kids (bring your own towels), live music on weekends, and plenty of home-made preserves and sauces.

Rosita's
MEXICAN $

(☑305-246-3114; www.rositasmexicanrestaurantfl. com; 199 W Palm Dr, Florida City; mains $8-13; ⊙8am-9pm) There's a working-class Mexican crowd here, testament to the sheer awe-someness of the tacos and burritos. Every-one is friendly, and the mariachi music adds to the authenticity.

Gator Grill
AMERICAN $

(☑786-243-0620; www.facebook.com/everglades gatorgrill; 36650 SW 192nd Ave, Homestead; mains $9-17; ⊙11am-6:30pm) A handy pit stop be-fore or after visiting the Everglades Na-tional Park, the Gator Grill is a white shack with picnic tables, where you can munch on all manner of alligator dishes. There are gator tacos, gator stir-fry, gator kabobs and straight-up fried alligator served in a basket.

Non-reptile eaters will find veggie burg-ers, pulled-pork sandwiches and grouper tacos, plus egg sandwiches (with or without gator) for breakfast.

White Lion Cafe
AMERICAN $$

(☑305-248-1076; www.whitelioncafe.com; 146 NW 7th St, Homestead; mains $12-26; ⊙11am-3pm & 5-10pm Tue-Sat) There's a comfy cabin vibe to this place near downtown Home-stead, with indoor and outdoor seating. The menu features American fare along the lines of meatloaf, crab cakes, fried chicken and fresh fruit cobbler.

Miami Brewing Company
BREWERY

(☑305-242-1224; www.miamibrewing.com; 30205 SW 217th Ave, Homestead; ⊙noon-6pm Sun-Wed, to 10pm Thu, to midnight Fri & Sat) You'll find first-rate craft brews in this enormous ware-house-style tasting room. The brewers here bring more than a hint of Floridian accents to beers like Shark Bait mango wheat ale, Big Rod coconut blond ale and Vice IPA with citrus notes.

There are big screens for game days, a pool table, outdoor picnic tables and live music (or DJs) on weekends.

AIRBOATS & SWAMP BUGGIES

Airboats are flat-bottomed skiffs that use powerful fans to propel themselves through the water. Their environmental impact has not been determined, but one thing is clear: airboats can't be doing much good, which is why they're not allowed in the park. Swamp buggies are large balloon-tired vehicles that can go through wetlands, creating ruts and damaging wildlife.

Airboat and swamp-buggy rides are offered all along US Hwy 41 (Tamiami Trail). Think twice before going on a 'nature' tour. Loud whirring fanboats and marsh jeeps are the antithesis of the Everglades' quiet serenity. If you do decide to take such a tour, **Cooper-town** (☑305-226-6048; www.coopertownairboats.com; 22700 SW 8th St; adult/child $23/11; ⊙9am-5pm; 🚸) is one of the longest-running airboat operators (since 1945) and is still one of the best. Friendly, knowledgeable guides have a knack for spotting wildlife and giving a good overview of this unique environment.

LOCAL KNOWLEDGE

GUARDIAN OF THE EVERGLADES

In a state known for iconoclasts, no one can hold a candle to **Marjory Stoneman Douglas** – not just for her quirks, but for her drive. A persistent, unbreakable force, she fueled one of the longest conservation battles in US history.

Born in 1890, Douglas moved to Florida after her failed first marriage. She worked for the *Miami Herald* and eventually as a freelance writer, producing short stories that are notable for both the quality of the writing and their progressive themes: *Plumes* (1930) and *Wings* (1931), published in the *Saturday Evening Post*, addressed the issue of Glades bird-poaching when the business was still immensely popular (the feathers were used to decorate ladies' hats).

In the 1940s Douglas was asked to write about the Miami River for the Rivers of America Series and promptly chucked the idea in favor of capturing the Everglades in her classic, *The Everglades: River of Grass*. Like all of Douglas' work, the book is remarkable for both its exhaustive research and lyrical, rich language.

River of Grass immediately sold out of its first print run, and public perception of the Everglades shifted from 'nasty swamp' to 'national treasure.' Douglas went on to be an advocate for environmental causes, women's rights and racial equality, fighting, for example, for basic infrastructure in Miami's Overtown.

Today she is remembered as Florida's favorite environmentalist. Always immaculately turned out in gloves, dress, pearls and floppy straw hat, she would bring down engineers, developers, politicians and her most hated opponents, sugar farmers; by force of her oratory alone. She kept up the fight, speaking and lecturing without fail, until she died in 1998 at the age of 108.

Today it seems every environmental institution in Florida is named for Douglas, but were she around, we doubt she'd care for those honors. She'd be too busy planting herself in the CERP office, making sure everything was moving along on schedule.

❶ Information

There are several info centers where you can get tips on attractions, lodging and dining.

Chamber of Commerce (☑ 305-247-2332; www.southdadechamber.org; 455 N Flagler Ave, Homestead; ⊙ 9am-5pm Mon-Fri)

Tropical Everglades Visitor Association (☑ 305-245-9180; www.tropicaleverglades.com/homestead.php; 160 N 1st St, Florida City; ⊙ 8am-5pm Mon-Sat, 10am-2pm Sun)

❶ Getting There & Away

From December or January until April, Homestead runs a free weekend **trolley bus service** (☑ 305-224-4457; www.cityof homestead.com; ⊙ Sat & Sun Dec or Jan-Apr), which takes visitors from Losner Park (downtown Homestead) out to the Royal Palm Visitor Center (p141) in Everglades National Park. It also runs between Losner Park and Biscayne National Park. Call for the latest departure times.

BISCAYNE NATIONAL PARK

Just to the east of the Everglades and right on Miami's southern doorstep is **Biscayne National Park** (☑ 305-230-1144, boat tours 786-335-3644; www.nps.gov/bisc; 9700 SW 328th St, Homestead; ⊙ 7am-5:30pm) **FREE**, 95% of which is made up of the waters of Biscayne Bay and the Atlantic. A portion of the world's third-largest reef sits here off the coast of Florida, along with mangrove forests and the northernmost Florida Keys. This is some of the best reef viewing and snorkeling you'll find in the USA, outside Hawaii and nearby Key Largo.

This unique 300-sq-mile park is easy to explore independently with a canoe, or via a boat tour. Generally summer and fall are the best times to visit the park. The offshore Keys, accessible only by boat, offer pristine opportunities for camping. There is no park fee for day admission to the park.

🏃 Activities

Long **Elliott Key** has picnicking, campsites and hiking among mangrove forests; tiny **Adams Key** has only picnicking; and equally tiny **Boca Chita Key** has an ornamental lighthouse, picnicking and campsites. These little islands were settled under the Homestead Act of 1862, which gave land freely to anyone willing to spend five years turning a scratch of the tropics into a working pineapple and key-lime farm.

Boating & Kayaking

Boating is naturally very popular, but you'll need to get some paperwork in order. Boaters will need to get tide charts from the park (ask at Dante Fascell Visitor Center or download them from www.nps.gov/bisc/planyourvisit/tide-predictions.htm). Make sure you comply with local slow-speed zones, designed to protect the endangered manatee. If you'd rather be taking in the scenery than be at the helm, take one of the park-led tours run by the Biscayne National Park Institute.

If you end up on Boca Chita Key, allow time to walk part of the 6-mile trail and look for the 65-foot-high lighthouse. Other highlights include **Jones Lagoon**, with its rich marine life and bird rookeries, and **Sands Key**, another rarely visited lagoon.

Diving & Snorkeling

The **Maritime Heritage Trail** (www.nps.gov/bisc/learn/historyculture/maritime-heritage-trail.htm) takes visitors through one of the only trails of its kind in the US. If you want to explore a sunken ship, this may well be the best opportunity in the country. Six are located within the park grounds; the trail experience involves taking visitors out, by boat, to the site of the wrecks where they can swim and explore among derelict vessels and clouds of fish.

There are even waterproof information site cards placed among the ships. Three of the vessels are suited for scuba divers, but the others – particularly the *Mandalay*, a lovely two-masted schooner that sank in 1966 – can be accessed by snorkelers.

Biscayne National Park Institute also offers snorkeling opportunities.

Wherever you go, there's plenty to see – Biscayne National Park has shipwrecks, more than 500 different kinds of fish (including parrotfish, angelfish, wrasses and butterfly fish) as well as sea cucumbers and the gloriously named Christmas tree worm.

👉 Tours

The **Biscayne National Park Institute** (📞 786-335-3644; www.biscaynenationalpark institute.org; Convoy Point; tours per person $44-159) is the hub for activities and tours within the park. Options include a three-/four-hour boat cruise ($44/70), 3¼-hour snorkeling trip ($64) and six-hour boat trips ($159). Most adventures begin at Convoy Point.

🛏 Sleeping & Eating

Primitive campsites are available on Elliott and Boca Chita Keys, though you'll need a boat to get there. No-see-ums (tiny flies) are invasive, and their bites are nasty. Make sure your tent is devoid of minuscule entry points.

Tent sites cost $25 per night from October to April, but are free the rest of the year. Visit www.nps.gov/bisc/planyourvisit/camping.htm for more information.

ℹ Information

Dante Fascell Visitor Center (📞 305-230-7275; www.nps.gov/bisc; 9700 SW 328th St, Homestead; ⊙ 9am-5pm) Located at Convoy Point, this center shows a great introductory film for an overview of the park, and has maps, information and excellent ranger activities. The grounds around the center are a popular picnic spot on weekends and holidays, especially among families from Homestead. Also showcases local artwork.

ℹ Getting There & Away

To get here, you'll have to drive about 9 miles east of Homestead (the way is pretty well signposted) on SW 328th St (North Canal Dr) into a long series of green-and-gold flat fields and marsh.

The Everglades Environment

The Everglades is one of the most important wilderness areas in the Lower Forty Eight, a fragile ecosystem rich in astonishing wildlife that is also under existential threat from human-led and natural causes. Charismatic wildlife is an Everglades specialty, from alligators and manatees to bobcats, river otters and, if you're *really* lucky, the Florida panther. Whether the Everglades can be protected from the many things that threaten it will be a bellwether for the future of the US environment.

Everglades Wildlife

The Everglades provides rich habitat for a wide range of animals. These include more than 40 species of mammals, 50 different reptiles, 300 fish species, 700 different plants and more than 360 bird species. Of these, one species of snake, four turtles, and one bat species, as well as the Florida panther and West Indian manatee, are among those species considered to be endangered.

Alligators

Alligators are the most commonly seen large animal in the park, although not so much in the 10,000 Islands, as they tend to avoid salt water. They are a keystone species in the Everglades, where they play an important role in the ecosystem – alligator dens, for example, are often used later by other species. More than 200,000 are thought to inhabit the Everglades (the Florida-wide gator population is around 1.5 million).

American alligators (*Alligator mississippiensis*) love freshwater swamps, lakes and rivers, although they can inhabit salt water for short periods; unlike crocodiles, they don't possess a gland that gets rid of the salt.

Female alligators in the Everglades rarely exceed 10ft. They dig dens, where they then give birth, but due to the dangers of flooding, these dens are usually above the waterline and can be up to 3.5ft high. They also use them for shelter when temperatures fall. Eggs usually take around two months to hatch. If the eggs incubate at temperatures between 90°F and 93°F (around 32°C to 34°C), baby male alligators emerge. Female babies are produced when incubation temperatures range between 82°F and 86°F (27.7°C and 30°C). Mixed litters are born when temperatures are between these two ranges during incubation. Once the eggs hatch, the mother carries up to 10 babies at a time on her tongue and then releases them into the water. Young alligators remain close to their mother for between one and three years.

Males in the Everglades generally grow to around 13ft to 15ft. Younger alligators have bright yellow bands across their backs which, when combined with their black base color, provides a form of camouflage during the early years when they are at their most vulnerable.

Young alligators feed on insects, small fish and frogs, but they graduate to larger fish, turtles, mammals, birds and

Top: Alligator
Bottom: Florida panther (p152)

other reptiles when they become adults. When temperatures drop below 68°F (20°C), alligators stop feeding and cease most activities. Even their color – from olive to brown to nearly black – depends on their surroundings: in waters with a high algae content they tend toward green, while skin colors are darker where there are lots of overhanging trees.

If you do see an alligator, it probably won't bother you unless you do something overtly threatening or angle your boat between it and its young. If you hear an alligator making a loud hissing sound, get the hell out of Dodge. That's a call to other alligators when a young gator is in danger. Finally, never feed an alligator – it's dangerous and illegal.

Crocodiles

The American crocodile (*Crocodylus acutus*) was once found across the southern US. Although they have been sighted further north in Florida and as far north as the South Carolina coast, only a few hundred remain in the US, and only in any numbers in Florida's far south. There are also populations across Central and northern South America. Crocodiles are less commonly seen in the Everglades,

as they prefer coastal and predominantly saltwater habitats, including islands; they're commonly seen in the 10,000 Islands and around Flamingo Marina.

Males can grow up to 20ft in length and weigh up to 880lb. They are more aggressive than alligators.

Marine Mammals

If you're traveling along the coastal sections of the Everglades, including the 10,000 Islands, look out for **bottlenose dolphins**. Beautiful, streamlined creatures, they are usually between 10ft and 14ft in length and have smooth gray skin. They live in highly complex social groups and are considered among the smartest of all mammals.

The **West Indian manatee** is a common sight in the warm waters along the coast of Florida. Manatees are shy, utterly peaceful mammals that look like obese seals with vaguely elephantine noses. Despite weighing between 1500lb and 1800lbs, they're surprisingly graceful, able to swim at around 15mph for short periods. But typically, they drift around, feeding on vegetation just below the water's surface (hence their none-too-flattering nickname of 'sea cow'). After grabbing a bite, manatees come up for air and often float just beneath the surface.

Another charismatic Everglades presence is the playful **river otter**, sometimes known as the 'playboy of the Everglades.' River otters are rarely out of the water during daylight hours – their webbed feet, sleek design and powerful jaws combine to make them swift swimmers and excellent hunters of turtles, fish and even baby alligators; the latter are relatively easy prey if caught alone. Your best chance of seeing a river otter is along the Anhinga Trail (p134) and in the waterways of Shark Valley (p139).

Florida Panthers

The critically endangered Florida panther is the state's official animal. As recently as the early 1990s, the Florida panther was in deep trouble, with as few as 10 (and no more than 30) left in the wild. There were, and remain, no other known populations of mountain lions (also known as cougars, pumas and, here in

ALLIGATOR OR CROCODILE?

Alligators and crocodiles are closely related, but how can you tell the difference between them?

For a start, if you're in the Everglades' freshwater channels, swamps and lakes (which make up most of the subcoastal areas of the national park), it's more than likely that you're looking at an alligator. Crocodiles are more likely to be seen in coastal, saltwater areas.

Secondly, the alligator's long snout has more of a 'U' shape, while crocodile snouts have a long, pointier 'V' shape.

When an alligator's mouth is closed, the upper jaw is wider than the lower jaw and no teeth are visible. In contrast, the fourth tooth from the front on each side of a crocodile's mouth sticks out when it's closed.

River otter

Florida, the Florida panther) east of the Mississippi. Those that did inhabit southwestern Florida had already developed a number of genetic problems (including heart defects) that came from close inbreeding. In the mid-1990s, scientists brought in eight female mountain lions from Texas. The population in Florida began to grow, the genetic flaws began to disappear, and estimates of the number of Florida panthers now range between 130 and 200. In November 2016, a female panther became the first of her kind to cross the Caloosahatchee River; although males had crossed the river before, the female, who soon had cubs, represented an important milestone for the species.

Many challenges remain, however. As usual, humans have been the culprits behind this predator's demise. Widespread habitat reduction (ie the arrival of big subdivisions) is the major cause of concern. Breeding units (one male and two to five females) require about 200 sq miles, and that often puts panthers in the way of one of Florida's most dangerous beasts: drivers. Some 31 panthers were killed by cars in 2016, with 26, 24 and 23 killed in the following three years. Underpasses have been critical in reducing road fatalities. Planned major new roads, including one between Orlando and Naples, will cut through habitat considered essential if the Florida panther population is to grow.

Florida panthers are rather magnificent golden-brown hunting cats. They are extremely elusive and only inhabit 5% of their historic range. They're found in the northern Everglades region, with denser concentrations in Big Cypress National Preserve (p138) and Florida Panther National Wildlife Refuge (p144). Sightings are also possible in **Corkscrew Swamp Sanctuary** (☏239-348-9151; www.corkscrew.audubon.org; 375 Sanctuary Rd W; adult/child 6-18yr $14/4; ☺7am-5:30pm, last entry 4:30pm).

To learn more about the battle to save the panther, track down *Cat Tale* (Craig Pittman; 2020).

Raccoon

Other Mammals

One of the Everglades' most commonly seen mammals is the **white-tailed deer**. Deer in the Everglades have no need for the extra layer of fat that protects deer from winter cold elsewhere. Here, they're often seen grazing on saw grass in open prairie. During spring, watch for recently born fawns (with white spots for camouflage).

If you're *really* lucky, you might just see a **bobcat** lurking in the mangroves. Found throughout the continental United States, the bobcat is a member of the lynx family, and has beautiful markings, with black spots and streaks against a gray to brown undercoat, as well as affecting tufts on the ears. One of the most adaptable of all wild cat species, it is found anywhere from the desert regions of the American West to the Everglades subtropical swamps, and is an opportunistic hunter, killing fish, small mammals and birds; in 2015 one enterprising bobcat was even photographed pulling a shark from the ocean shallows...

Other mammals include **raccoon**, dwindling numbers of **marsh rabbit**, and the Everglades' only pouched marsupial, the **opossum**. The **gray fox** of the Everglades is the only fox species known to climb trees.

BURMESE PYTHONS

As the name would suggest, the Burmese python (*Python bivittatus*) belongs in tropical Asia, not subtropical Florida. How they came to be in Florida is simple: Burmese pythons make popular pets – their beautiful, traditional python markings make them one of the prettier snakes in the pet-snake market. However, the small young pythons sold by pet stores and importers of exotic pets have a tendency to just keep growing – the longest Burmese python recorded in Florida reached 17.5ft in length. Burmese pythons are one of the five largest snake species in the world and can grow up to 23ft in length. And so many pet owners who couldn't take care of such a massive creature with a ravenous appetite dumped the animals into the swamp.

Burmese pythons first began turning up in the Everglades in the 1980s. The latest estimates suggest that at least 30,000, but possibly as many as 300,000, may now live in the wild in southern Florida. It has been illegal to import Burmese pythons into the US since 2012, although at this point it is of course too late to turn back the clock.

As an invasive species, the Burmese python has had a devastating impact on the Everglades environment. A female python can lay up to 50 eggs and live for 20 years. The pythons have also preyed on a whole range of species – marsh rabbits have been nearly wiped out from the Everglades, while populations of everything from raccoon and fox to bobcat have been devastated. In 2017 one *Palm Beach Post* reporter even stumbled upon a large python devouring an alligator just off Loop Rd.

Programs to reduce the number of Burmese pythons in the Everglades have ranged from hunting using dogs right through to offering bounties and biological methods, but have had very limited effect.

Threats to the Everglades

Unfortunately, the whole 'River of Grass' needs the river to survive and the Everglades acts as a hurricane barrier and kidney. Kidney? All those wetlands leached out pollutants from the Florida Aquifer (the state's freshwater supply). But when farmland wasn't diverting the sheet flow, it was adding fertilizer-rich wastewater to it. Result? Bacteria, and eventually plant life, bloomed at a ridiculous rate (they call it fertilizer for a reason), upsetting the fragile balance of resources vital to the Glades' survival.

Despite the tireless efforts of environ-mentalists, today the Florida Aquifer is in serious danger of being contaminated and drying up. The number of wading birds nesting has declined by 90% to 95% since the 1930s. Currently there are more than 60 threatened and endangered plant and animal species in the park.

The diversion of water away from the Glades and runoff pollution are the main culprits. This delicate ecosystem is the neighbor of one of the fastest-growing urban areas in the US. The current water-drainage system in South Florida was built to handle the needs of two million people; the local population is now closer to 10 million. Scientists estimate the wetlands have been reduced to as little as a quarter of their original size.

Nature has done some damage as well. During 2005's Hurricane Wilma, for example, six storm water treatment areas (artificial wetlands that cleanse excess nutrients out of the water cycle) were heavily damaged by powerful winds. Without these natural filtration systems, the Glades are far more susceptible to nutrient blooms and external pollution. In 2016 nearly 4000 acres went up in flames in wildfires near Long Pine Key. And, of course, rising sea levels associated with climate change could also have a devastating impact on the Everglades.

PROTECTING MANATEES

The manatee has become the poster child of Floridian environmentalism. Pollution is a big problem, but their biggest killers are pleasure boaters.

Manatees seek warm, shallow water and feed on vegetation. South Florida is surrounded by just such an environment, but it also has one of the highest concentrations of pleasure boats in the world. Despite pleas from environmental groups, wildlife advocates and the local, state and federal governments, which have declared many areas 'Manatee Zones,' some pleasure boaters routinely exceed speed limits and ignore simple practices that would help protect the species.

Manatees spend a lot of their time grazing gently just below the water's surface. When speedboats zoom through the area, manatees are hit by the hulls and either knocked away or pushed under the boat, whose propeller then gashes the mammal as the boat passes overhead. Few manatees get through life without propeller scars, and many are killed.

Save the Manatee (www.savethemanatee.org) works with teams from the Dolphin Research Center to respond to reports of injured manatees, dolphins and whales, but they're fighting a losing battle. The Florida Fish & Wildlife Commission reported that 136 manatees were killed by watercraft in 2019 – an all-time high. The commission also reported a five-year average of nearly 100 manatees killed by watercraft every year.

Restoration of the Everglades

Efforts to save the Everglades began in the late 1920s, but were sidelined by the Great Depression. In 1926 and 1928 two major hurricanes caused Lake Okeechobee to overflow; the resulting floods killed hundreds. The Army Corps of Engineers did a really good job of damming the lake. A bit too good: the Glades were essentially cut off from their source, the Kissimmee watershed.

In the meantime, conservationists began donating land for protection, starting with 1 sq mile of land donated by a garden club. The Everglades was declared a national park in 1947, the same year Marjory Stoneman Douglas' *The Everglades: River of Grass* was published.

By draining the wetlands through the damming of the lake, the Army Corps made huge swaths of inland Florida inhabitable. But the environmental problems created by shifting water's natural flow, plus the area's ever-increasing population, now threaten to make the whole region uninhabitable. The canal system sends, on average, more than 1 billion gallons of water into the ocean every day. At the same time, untreated runoff flows unfiltered into natural water supplies.

Clean water is disappearing from the water cycle while South Florida's population gets bigger by the day.

The **Comprehensive Everglades Restoration Plan** (CERP; www.evergladesrestoration.gov) is designed to address the Everglades' water problems. The plan is to unblock the Kissimmee, restoring Everglades lands to predevelopment conditions, while maintaining flood protection, providing fresh water for South Florida's populace and protecting regions against urban sprawl. Political battles, cost overruns and bureaucratic red tape have significantly slowed the implementation of CERP.

A major portion of CERP is the **Central Everglades Planning Project** (CEPP), the rare public works project that is supported by environmentalists and industry alike. The CEPP's aim is to clean polluted water from Florida's agricultural central heartland and redirect it toward the Everglades. The River of Grass would be rewatered, and toxic runoff would no longer flow to the sea. In 2016 the US Congress approved $976 million of funding for CEPP as part of its Water Infrastructure Improvements for the Nation Act. Congress authorized a further $111 million for restoration projects in 2018 and 2019, with $200 million allocated in the 2020 budget.

Black vulture

POPULATION
79,000

**NUMBER OF
ISLANDS**
1700

**BEST
MICROBREWERY**
Florida Keys Brewing
Company (p172)

BEST KEY LIME PIE
Blue Heaven (p190)

BEST CABARET
La Te Da (p194)

WHEN TO GO

Dec–Mar
The dry, sunny days
are perfect, though
lodging is at its most
expensive.

Apr–Jun
Sea breezes help
keep summer heat
down, and hotel rates
drop precipitously.

Jul–Nov
There's some
rain (and maybe
hurricanes), but also
unbeatable low-
season prices.

Bahia Honda State Park (p176)
ANNA KRASNOPEEVA/SHUTTERSTOCK ©

Florida Keys & Key West

Curving beneath Southern Florida, this 113-mile-long archipelago is a land of mangrove and sandbar islands, teal waters and magnificent sunsets. A memorable journey down the Overseas Highway takes you from the bustle of Key Largo to Key West, passing arts-loving villages, old-fashioned roadside eateries and stretches of verdant hardwood forest, crossing some 42 bridges along the way (including one that stretches 7 miles across open waters).

Paddling across mirror-like coves and joining the free-spirited party people in Key West is just a sample of the great Florida Keys experience. You can also take in the unusual plant and animal life (manatees, endangered Key Deer and the world's third largest coral reef) and explore the fascinating history still visible on these shores – from abandoned railroad trestles built in the early 20th century to grand homes and museums filled with treasures (much of which was discovered by the region's once-thriving salvaging industry).

Florida Keys & Key West Highlights

1 **Key West** (p179)
Shopping and dining amid the pastel-hued cottages of the Bahamian Village, followed by drinks on Duval St.

2 **John Pennekamp Coral Reef State Park** (p166) Diving around the rainbow reefs.

3 **Indian Key Historic State Park** (p170) Paddling

out to this eerie, lonely, beautiful park.

4 **Bahia Honda State Park** (p176) Basking on the sands of one of South Florida's prettiest beaches.

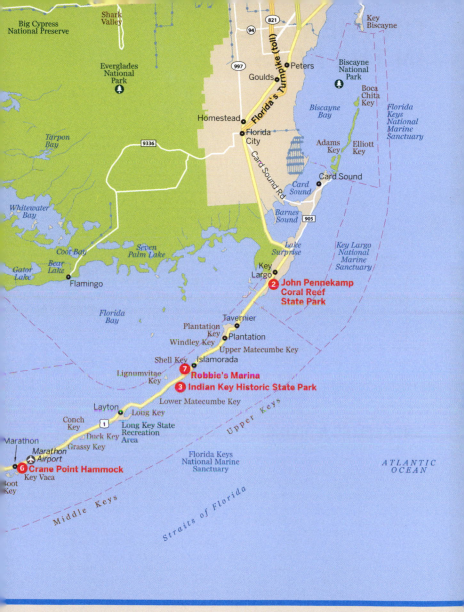

Big Cypress National Preserve

Shark Valley

Everglades National Park

Tarpon Bay

Whitewater Bay

Coot Bay

Seven Palm Lake

Gator Lake

Bear Lake

Flamingo

Florida Bay

Lignumvitae Key

Shell Key

Layton

Conch Key

Duck Key

Grassy Key

Marathon

Marathon Airport

Key Vaca

Boot Key

Middle Keys

Long Key

Long Key State Recreation Area

Lower Matecumbe Key

Straits of Florida

Florida Keys National Marine Sanctuary

ATLANTIC OCEAN

Upper Keys

Plantation Key

Windley Key

Plantation

Tavernier

Upper Matecumbe Key

Islamorada

Peters

Goulds

Homestead

Florida City

Card Sound Rd

Card Sound

Barnes Sound

Lake Surprise

Key Largo

Biscayne Bay

Biscayne National Park

Key Biscayne

Boca Chita Key

Adams Key

Elliott Key

Card Sound

Florida Keys National Marine Sanctuary

Key Largo National Marine Sanctuary

Florida's Turnpike (toll)

94
821
95
997
9336
905
1

2 **John Pennekamp Coral Reef State Park**

7 **Robbie's Marina**

3 **Indian Key Historic State Park**

6 **Crane Point Hammock**

5 **Big Pine Key** (p176)
Looking for tiny Key Deer and other wildlife on nature trails near the Blue Hole.

6 **Crane Point Hammock** (p173) Strolling through the palm hammock, mangroves and gorgeous shoreline near Marathon.

7 **Robbie's Marina** (p171) Feeding the giant tarpon, then hiring a kayak for a paddle to forest-covered Lignumvitae Key.

8 **Dry Tortugas National Park** (p195) Making an island-hopping day trip or detour.

ON THE WATER IN THE KEYS

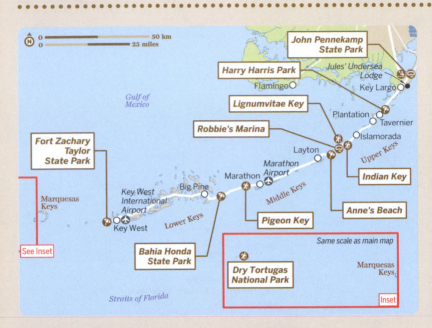

John Pennekamp State Park

Harry Harris Park

Jules' Undersea Lodge

Flamingo

Key Largo

Gulf of Mexico

Lignumvitae Key

Plantation

Tavernier

Robbie's Marina

Islamorada

Fort Zachary Taylor State Park

Layton

Upper Keys

Indian Key

Marathon Airport

Marquesas Keys

Key West International Airport

Big Pine

Marathon

Middle Keys

Anne's Beach

Lower Keys

Pigeon Key

Key West

Bahia Honda State Park

See Inset

Same scale as main map

Dry Tortugas National Park

Marquesas Keys

Straits of Florida

Inset

0 — 50 km
0 — 25 miles

SNORKELING & DIVING

Colorful coral reefs are within a short boat trip from the Keys. Key Largo makes a great base for exploring offshore wonders. True to its name, **John Pennekamp Coral Reef State Park** (p166) draws visitors more for its underwater attractions than its shoreline trails. For snorkeling enthusiasts, this should figure high on an itinerary. Trips depart regularly, and on calm days, you might have the opportunity to snorkel above the open-armed Christ of the Abyss – a massive statue sunk in 25ft of water and surrounded by reefs. Divers can also plan trips in the area, though you'll have to charter your own vessel. It's easier to join trips (or take classes) offered by the well-run **Looe Key Dive Center** (p178) in the Lower Keys. Avid divers can even overnight in the **Jules' Undersea Lodge** (p168), located in 30ft of water in a protected lagoon.

Near Islamorada, **Robbie's Marina** (p171) offers snorkeling trips as well as myriad other activities.

KAYAKING

There are paddling hot spots up and down the keys. Many hotels include kayak rental with accommodation, making it easy to head off on some DIY exploring when the water is calm. Keep an eye out for manatees, sting rays and sharks, plus winged residents like cormorants, frigate birds, herons and ospreys. With its protected mangroves, **John Pennekamp Coral Reef State Park** (p166) is a superb place for kayaking.

For something more immersive, consider booking a guided backcountry tour. On a memorable outing, you'll make your way across grass flats and through mangrove-filled inlets, spotting wildlife along the way. One of the best operators in the business is **Big Pine Kayak Adventures** (p177) in the Lower Keys. You can arrange customized tours with experienced paddler Bill Keogh, who wrote the iconic guide to paddling in the Florida Keys.

Paddling through sun-dappled mangroves, walking the shorelines of forest-covered islands and setting off on a sunset cruise: there are many ways to experience the life aquatic in the Florida Keys.

MARIDAV/SHUTTERSTOCK ©

Above: Kayaking, Islamorada (p169)

Left: Molasses Reef, Key Largo (p166))

OFF AXIS PRODUCTION/SHUTTERSTOCK ©

Flying tours, Dry Tortugas National Park (p196)

BOATING & SAILING

Key West is one of the great boating capitals of South Florida. You can head off for a kitschy pirate-themed tour on the **Jolly Rover** (p185), or hire a Hobie Cat for sailing adventures off **Smathers Beach** (p184). There are loads of options – dinner cruises, sunset trips and dolphin-watching tours. The waterfront along Key West Bight is where many agencies dock.

Elsewhere, you'll find some gems: you can step back in time by booking passage on the **African Queen** (p167), the small steamboat depicted in the 1951 Humphrey Bogart and Katharine Hepburn film. Docked in Key Largo, it makes regular forays through the Port Largo canals, with guides (slightly less wisecracking than Bogart) sharing historical details along the way. For something completely different, sign up for a glass-bottom boat tour in the **John Pennekamp Coral Reef State Park** (p166).

BEACHES

The Keys aren't known for their sandy shores, but there are still a handful of small but captivating stretches of coastline where you can enjoy a waterside afternoon in between island-hopping. Chief among them, **Bahia Honda State Park** (p176) has one of the most alluring stretches of beachfront anywhere in Florida. **Harry Harris Park** (p167) is a local favorite in Tavernier for its small but photogenic lagoon. **Anne's Beach** (p170), near Islamorada, has a sandy beach and a boardwalk stretching through mangroves. In Marathon, **Sombrero** (p174) is another obligatory stop for beach lovers.

Key West has its share of sandy seduc-tion: at **Fort Zachary Taylor State Park** (p183) you can swim, snorkel, stretch out under palm trees, join an outdoor yoga class or watch a (usually) spectacular sunset.

ISLAND ADVENTURES

You'll get a far different perspective of the Keys when you leave behind the busy main highway and head out to explore one of many islands reachable only by boat.

Near Islamorada, you can visit two very different islands – both state parks – that make for fascinating exploring. The larger of the two, **Lignumvitae Key** (p170), is home to old-growth tropical hardwood hammock and a solution hole (good for spying bird life), with rangers leading guided tours several times a week. At **Indian Key** (p170), you can slip into the past while looking for ruins on

a walk across the 11-acre island. In the 1830s, this was once a bustling community based on salvaging cargo from shipwrecks. Reach either island by kayak, which you can hire from **Robbie's Marina** (p171) in Islamorada.

Pigeon Key (p173) gives a first-hand glimpse of what life was like for the workers who built the Overseas Railway (completed in 1912). Tours take in the restored structures that once made up the work camp (later used by railway maintenance), with downtime on the small beach afterwards.

Far beyond Key West, the **Dry Tortugas National Park** (p195) isn't easy to reach. But those who make the effort can snorkel coral reefs, lounge on the beach and explore a historic 19th-century fortress. You'll have to book well in advance for a spot on a boat or a seaplane that makes the journey out. You can also camp on the island.

❶ Getting There & Away

Getting here can be half the fun – or, if you're unlucky, inject a whopping dose of frustration. On a good day, driving along the Overseas Hwy with the windows down – the wind in your face and the twin sisters of Florida Bay and the Atlantic stretching on either side – is the US road trip in tropical perfection. On a bad day, you end up sitting in gridlock behind a midlife-crisis Harley.

Greyhound (www.greyhound.com) buses serve all Keys destinations along Hwy 1 and depart from Downtown Miami and Key West; you can pick up a bus along the way by standing on the Overseas Hwy and flagging one down. If you fly into Fort Lauderdale or Miami, the **Keys Shuttle** (☑ 305-289-9997; www.keysshuttle.com) provides door-to-door service to most of the Keys ($70/80/90 to the Upper and Middle Keys/Lower Keys/Key West). Reserve 48 hours in advance.

UPPER KEYS

The huge blanket of mangrove forest that forms the South Florida coastline spreads like a woody morass into Key Largo; little differentiates the island from Florida proper. Keep heading south and the mangroves give way to wider stretches of road and ocean, until all of a sudden you're in Islamorada and the water is everywhere. If you want to avoid traffic on US 1 south of Florida City, you can try the less trafficked FL 997 and Card Sound Rd to FL 905 (toll $1), which passes Alabama Jack's (p169).

Key Largo & Tavernier

Key Largo (both the name of the town and the island) is slightly underwhelming at a glance. As you drive onto the islands, Key Largo resembles a long line of low-lying hammock and strip development. But head down a side road and duck into this warm little bar, or that converted Keys plantation house, and the island idiosyncrasies become more pronounced.

The 33-mile-long Largo, which starts at Mile Marker 106, is the longest island in the Keys, and those 33 miles have attracted a lot of marine life, all accessible from the biggest concentration of dive sites in the islands. The town of Tavernier (Mile Marker 93) is just south of the town of Key Largo.

◎ Sights

★ John Pennekamp Coral Reef State Park STATE PARK

(☑ 305-451-6300; www.pennekamppark.com; Mile 102.6 oceanside; car with 1 person/2 people $4.50/9, cyclist or pedestrian $2.50; ⏱ 8am-sunset, aquarium to 5pm; P 🚻) 🐾 John Pennekamp has the singular distinction of being the first underwater park in the USA. There's 170 acres of dry parkland here and more than 48,000 acres (75 sq miles) of wet: the vast majority of the protected area is the ocean. Before you get out in that water, be sure to take in some pleasant beaches and stroll along the nature trails.

The **Mangrove Trail** is a good boardwalk introduction to this oft-maligned, ecologically awesome species (the trees, often submerged in water, breathe via long roots that act as snorkels). Stick around for nightly campfire programs and ranger discussions. The visitor center is well run and informative, and has a small saltwater **aquarium** and nature films that give a glimpse of what's under those waters. To really get beneath the surface, you should take a 2½-hour **glass-bottom boat tour** (adult/child $24/17). You'll be brought out in a safe, modern 38ft catamaran to the splendid Molasses Reef, where you'll see filigreed flaps of soft coral, technicolor schools of fish, dangerous-looking barracuda and perhaps massive, yet graceful, sea turtles.

The park's most famous attraction is the coral-fringed *Christ of the Abyss*, an 8.5ft, 4000lb bronze sculpture of Jesus – a copy of a similar sculpture off the Portofino Peninsula in northern Italy. On calm days, the park offers **snorkeling trips** (adult/child $30/25, plus equipment rental) to the statue, which is six miles offshore. You can also arrange **diving excursions** (six-person charter from $500). DIY-ers may want to take out a canoe ($20 per hour), kayak (from $12/30 per hour/half day) or stand-up paddleboard (from $25/50 per hour/half day) to journey through a 3-mile network of trails. Phone for boat-rental information.

Laura Quinn Wild Bird Sanctuary WILDLIFE RESERVE

(☑ 305-852-4486; www.keepthemflying.org; 93600 Overseas Hwy, Mile 93.6; donations accepted; ⏱ sunrise-sunset; P 🚻) 🐾 This 7-acre sanctuary serves as a protected refuge for a wide variety of injured birds. A boardwalk leads through various enclosures where you can learn a bit about some of the permanent residents – those unable to be released back in the wild. The species here include masked boobies, great horned owls, green herons, brown pelicans, double-crested cormorants and others.

Keys Meads   DISTILLERY
(☑ 305-204-4596; www.keysmeads.com; 99353 Overseas Hwy; mead tasting $8; ☺ noon-7pm Tue-Sat, to 6pm Sun) For something completely different, stop in for a tasting at this artisanal, family-run mead producer which opened back in 2017. Owner Jeff Kesling has an encyclopedic knowledge of all things mead related, and has created many unique varieties of his award-winning libation (one of the world's oldest alcoholic drinks), all made from locally sourced honey.

During a tasting, you can try up to 12 different meads (small pours since the alcohol content ranges from 7% to 14%), with a regularly changing lineup including a spicy habanero, Jamaican cherry and star fruit. Bottles (from $16) make fine gifts.

Harry Harris Park   PARK
(50 East Beach Rd, Mile 92.6, Tavernier; Mon-Fri free, Sat, Sun & holidays $5; ☺ 7:30am-sunset; 🚻🏊) This small park is a good place to take the kids – there's a playground, picnic tables, grills for barbecuing, basketball courts and ball fields. Unusually for the Keys, there's also a good patch of white sand fronting a warm lagoon that's excellent for swimming.

🏃 Activities

Key Largo Bike and Adventure Tours   CYCLING
(☑ 305-395-1551; www.keylargobike.com; 90775 Old Hwy, Tavernier; 3hr tour $75) This outfit offers various tours, including three-hour jaunts around Islamorada and two-day tours from Key Largo to Key West ($575). It also hires out bikes for those who want to go it alone – the $375 package includes one-way bike rental to Key West (the staff will transfer your bags for you and pick up the bike when you finish).

Key Largo Princess   BOATING
(☑ 305-451-4655; Key Largo Holiday Inn, 99701 Overseas Hwy; adult/child from $37/21; ☺ cruises 10am, 1pm & 4pm; 🚻) Get a glimpse of the Key's undersea beauty on a glass-bottom boat tour. Popular with families, these 75ft, 129-passenger vessels give you the opportunity to see lots of colorful coral, plus sea fans, sharks, tropical fish and the odd sea turtle winging along.

African Queen   BOATING
(☑ 305-451-8080; www.africanqueenflkeys.com; Key Largo Holiday Inn, 99701 Overseas Hwy; cruises from $59) The steamboat used in the 1951 movie starring Humphrey Bogart and Katharine Hepburn has been restored to its former splendor, and offers cinematic tours through the Port Largo canals and out to the ocean. It was built in England in 1912 and used in Africa to transport goods, missionaries and hunters, before becoming a movie star.

Jacob's Aquatics Center   WATER PARK
(☑ 305-453-7946; www.jacobsaquaticcenter.org; 320 Laguna Ave, Mile 99.6; adult/child/student/family weekday $10/6/8/25, weekend $12/8/10/30; ☺ 10am-6pm; 🚻) Jacob's is a complex filled with all kinds of aquatic fun. There's an eight-lane pool for lap and open swimming, an accessible therapy pool and water aerobic courses. For the kids there's a small waterpark with waterslides, a playground and, of course, kiddie-sized pools.

🛏 Sleeping

John Pennekamp Coral Reef State Park   CAMPGROUND $
(☑ information 305-676-3777, reservations 800-326-3521; www.reserveamerica.com; 102601 Overseas Hwy; tent & RV sites $38.50; 🅿) You don't even have to leave Pennekamp at closing time if you opt for tent or RV camping, but you'll need to make a reservation well in advance (up to 11 months ahead), as the 47 sites fill up fast. Leashed, well-behaved pets are welcome.

Bay Harbor Lodge   MOTEL $$
(☑ 305-852-5695; www.bayharborkeylargo.com; 97702 Overseas Hwy, bayside; r $150-350; 🚻🏊) This lush 2.5-acre property has its own private beach (and free kayaks), a temperature-controlled pool and tropical gardens alive with birdsong. The spacious and comfortable cottage-style rooms are painted in cheery colors and come with small kitchen units and outdoor seating areas. The homemade scones (available in the morning along with freshly brewed coffee) are all the rage. Excellent value.

MB at Key Largo   HOTEL $$
(☑ 305-852-6200; www.mbatkeylargo.com; 147 Seaside Ave; r $175-400; 🅿🚻) This mid-sized hotel fronting the Atlantic Ocean offers bright rooms that have an old-school tropical

vibe with lemon-hued walls, wood and rattan furniture and earth-hued carpeting. Some rooms have small balconies that catch a fine breeze. It's a family-friendly spot and you can borrow bikes and kayaks or just lounge away by the seaside pool.

Kona Kai Resort & Gallery RESORT $$$

(☎305-852-7200; www.konakairesort.com; Mile 97.8 bayside; r $320-530; ⓅⓈⓈ) This hideaway is one of the only botanical gardens we can think of that integrates a hotel onto its grounds – or is that the other way around? Either way, this spot, backing onto peaceful waterfront, is lush. The 13 airy rooms and suites (some with full kitchens) are all bright and comfortable, with good natural light and an attractive modern design.

Jules' Undersea Lodge HOTEL $$$

(☎305-451-2353; www.jul.com; 51 Shoreland Dr, Mile 103.2 oceanside; s/d/tr $675/800/1050) If you fancy diving to your hotel, this place is for you. Once a research station, this module has been converted into a delightfully cheesy Keys motel, but wetter. In addition to two private guest rooms, there are common rooms, a kitchen-dining room and a wet room with hot showers and gear storage. Telephones and an intercom connect guests with the surface.

✕ Eating

Harriette's AMERICAN $

(☎305-852-8689; www.facebook.com/Harriettes Restaurant; 95710 Overseas Hwy, bayside; mains $8-15; ⓈⓈ6am-3pm) This sweet, breadbox-sized eatery is famed far and wide for its utterly addictive key lime muffins (so big you'll need a knife and fork to eat them). There's also classic American fare – pancakes, bacon and eggs, and not-to-be-missed fluffy biscuits for breakfast, which is the best time to come.

★ Key Largo Fisheries SEAFOOD $$

(☎305-451-3782; www.keylargofisheries.com; 1313 Ocean Bay Dr; mains $12-24; ⓈⓈ10am-5:30pm Tue-Sat) At this laid-back dockside spot, you can sit at picnic tables and watch the boats bobbing in the marina while tucking into scrumptious seafood caught the same day. Famous fish sandwiches (like the blackened mahimahi) are massive and pair nicely with local microbrews. The on-site market has a good selection of fresh catch if you're self-catering.

Fish House SEAFOOD $$

(☎305-451-4665; www.fishhouse.com; Mile 102.4 oceanside; mains lunch $13-21, dinner $23-30; ⓈⓈ11:30am-10pm; Ⓟ) The Fish House delivers on the promise of its title – very good fish, bought from local fishers and prepared fried, broiled, jerked, blackened or chargrilled. Because the Fish House only uses fresh fish, the menu changes daily based on what is available.

Key Largo Conch House FUSION $$

(☎305-453-4844; www.keylargoconchhouse.com; Mile 100.2 oceanside; mains lunch $11-18, dinner $18-30; ⓈⓈ8am-10pm; ⓅⓈⓈⓈ) This innovative kitchen likes to freshen up local classics (grilled mahimahi stuffed with blue crab and mango, or yellowfin tuna with coconut and sesame served with Sriracha rice cake and seaweed).

Set in a restored old-school Keys mansion wrapped in a *Gone With the Wind* veranda, it's hard not to love the way the period architecture blends in seamlessly with the local tropical flora.

Mrs Mac's Kitchen AMERICAN $$

(☎305-451-3722; www.mrsmacskitchen.com; Mile 99.4 bayside; mains breakfast & lunch $9-21, dinner $16-30; ⓈⓈ7am-9:30pm Mon-Sat; ⓅⓈ) When Applebee's stuffs its wall full of license plates, it's tacky. When Mrs Mac's does it, it's homey. Probably because the service is warm and personable, and the meals are delicious. Plus the food packs in the locals, tourists, their dogs and pretty much everyone else on the island (plus, admittedly, a fair few calories, but that's why it tastes good).

Sal's Ballyhoo's SEAFOOD $$$

(☎305-852-0822; www.ballyhoosrestaurant.com; 97860 Overseas Hwy; mains $23-37; ⓈⓈ11am-10pm; Ⓢ) A rather ho-hum looking building along the highway serves up outstanding seafood dishes. This is the place for decadent yellowtail Hemingway (parmesan-crusted snapper topped with crab meat and key-lime butter) or pasta loaded with scallops, mussels, mahimahi and shrimp. There's also stone crabs in season (mid-October to mid-May) and vegetarian options (sweet-potato burgers, black-bean tacos, vegan grilled cheese).

On clear nights, grab an outdoor table on the front patio.

🍷 Drinking & Nightlife

Sundowners BAR
(☎305-451-4502; www.sundownerskeylargo.com; 103900 Overseas Hwy; ☺11am-10pm; 🐾) The best place in town to watch the sunset is the buzzing bar and restaurant sitting pretty on the Florida Bay. There's ample outdoor seating, good happy hour drink specials (from 4pm to 7pm), live music most nights and a first-rate pub grub and seafood menu (mains $14 to $38). There's also a glass-walled dining room if you need to escape the elements.

Alabama Jack's BAR
(☎305-248-8741; 58000 Card Sound Rd; ☺11am-7pm) Welcome to your first taste of the Keys: zonked-out fishers, exiles from the mainland and Harley heads swilling beers on a mangrove bay. This is the line where Miami-esque South Florida gives way to the countrified American South. The laid-back vibe is the perfect setting for conch fritters, crab cakes and mahimahi tacos, among other favorites (mains $11 to $20).

Just watch out for dive-bombing gulls along the deck (though the oversized red buoys seem to keep them away), and the evening onslaught of mosquitoes – which is why Alabama Jack's closes at 7pm every night. Country bands take the stage on Saturday (2pm to 5pm) and Sunday (2pm to 7pm). It's located just before the tollbooth over the Card Sound Bridge.

ℹ Information

Mariners Hospital (☎305-434-3000; www.baptisthealth.net; Mile 91.5 bayside, Tavernier; ☺24hr) The best hospital in the area with a 24-hour emergency room. If you're diving, this is the only place in the Keys that has a hyperbaric chamber.

ℹ Getting There & Away

The Greyhound bus stops at Mile Marker 99.6 oceanside. It stops twice a day traveling between Miami and Key West.

Islamorada
📞 305 / POP 6400

🎯 Sights

★ Keys History & Discovery Museum MUSEUM
(☎305-922-2237; www.keysdiscovery.com; 82100 Overseas Hwy, Islander Resort; adult/child $15/6; ☺10am-5pm Wed-Sun) It's easy to spend a few hours at this fascinating interactive museum that delves into the people and major events that have shaped the Keys' past. The first floor takes in coral reefs (with several aquariums boasting live coral as well as elegant angelfish, butterfly fish and otherworldly lionfish), aboriginal peoples and Spanish treasure fleets (and the salvagers and pirates who thrived off of them).

FLORIDA KEYS & KEY WEST ISLAMORADA

FLORIDA KEYS OVERSEAS HERITAGE TRAIL

One of the most rewarding ways to see the Keys is by bicycle. The flat elevation and ocean breezes are perfect for cycling, and the Florida Keys Overseas Heritage Trail (☎305-853-3571; www.floridastateparks.org/trail/Florida-Keys) gives gorgeous vantage points along the way. Around 90 miles (out of 106 miles) of this multiuse trail are finished. A complete, safe bike trail covering the entire length of the Keys is still a distant dream (damage from Hurricane Irma in 2017 brought expansion to a close, though work may resume in the years ahead).

If you are keen to ride, it's currently possible to bike through the Keys along portions of this trail, though it's not always easy to follow (sometimes crossing from bayside to oceanside and back). In the incomplete parts of the trail, you can ride along the shoulder of the highway if you don't mind traffic whizzing by at 50mph (crossing the Seven-Mile Bridge is particularly harrowing; taxis in Marathon have bike racks, saving you the stress). Bring plenty of spares (road debris makes quick work of non-Kevlar-lined tires). You can download a map on www.floridastateparks.org.

Among the most peaceful stretches are the Old Road from Mile Marker 90 to 80 in Islamorada, the historic 2.2-mile Long Key Bridge (near Mile Marker 66), and the fine coastal scenery from Mile Markers 15 to 5 near Key West.

For two-day biking trips between Key Largo and Key West, book a tour with Key Largo Bike and Adventure Tours (p167), which leads a range of bike outings. It also rents out bikes for those who want to go it alone – the staff will transfer your luggage for you on the way, then pick up your bike in Key West ($375 for the package).

There's also a handsome scale model of Indian Key (which was a small flourishing village in the 1830s), and stories of the homesteaders, fisherfolk, botanists and hermit artists who settled here over the years. Upstairs, a comfy theater screens a number of worthwhile films that capture the incredible challenges of building Henry Flagler's Overseas Railway (completed in 1912) and survivors' accounts of the horrific 1935 Labor Day Hurricane.

The museum also hosts a lecture series (admission $10) on topics like reef restoration, pirate stories and underwater exploration. It happens twice monthly from October to April.

★ **Anne's Beach**   BEACH

(Mile 73.5 oceanside; ♿) **FREE** Named after local environmentalist Anne Eaton, this tiny beach is one of the finest seascapes in these parts. The small ribbon of sand opens onto a sky-bright stretch of tidal flats and a green tunnel of hammock and wetland. A short (quarter-mile) boardwalk leads through the mangroves with lookouts and picnic tables along the way.

Florida Keys History
of Diving Museum   MUSEUM

(📞305-664-9737; www.divingmuseum.org; Mile 83; adult/child $15/7; ⊙10am-5pm, to 6:45pm 3rd Wed of month; P♿) You can't miss the diving museum – it's the building with the enormous mural of whale sharks on the side. This journey 'under the sea' covers 4000 years, with fascinating pieces like the 1797 Klingert's copper kettle diving machine, a whimsical room devoted to Jules Verne's Captain Nemo, massive deep-diving suits and an exquisite display of diving helmets from around the world. These imaginative galleries reflect the charming quirks of the Keys.

Windley Key Fossil
Reef Geological State Site   STATE PARK

(📞305-664-2540; www.floridastateparks.org; Mile 85.5 oceanside; admission $2.50, tour $2; ⊙8am-5pm Thu-Mon) To get his railroad built across the islands, Henry Flagler had to quarry out some sizable chunks of the Keys. The best evidence of those efforts can be found at this former quarry-turned-state park. Windley has leftover quarry machinery scattered along an 8ft former quarry wall, with fossilized evidence of brain, star

and finger coral embedded right in the rock. The wall offers a cool (and rare) public peek into the stratum of coral that forms the substrate of the Keys.

There are also various short trails through tropical hardwood hammock that make for a pleasant glimpse into the Keys' wilder side. Borrow a free trail guide from the visitor center. From December to April, ranger-led tours are offered at 10am and 2pm Friday to Sunday for $2 per person.

Rain Barrel Village   ARTS CENTER

(📞305-521-2043; www.rainbarrelvillage.com; 86700 Overseas Hwy; ⊙9am-5pm) Once you see the giant spiny lobster, you know you've arrived. Welcome to the Rain Barrel, a craft emporium that is packed with souvenir-y tourist tat, beach wear, island-themed artwork, pottery, glasswork and plenty of other eye candy – though not everything is made locally.

Indian Key Historic State Park   ISLAND

(📞305-664-2540; www.floridastateparks.org/indiankey; Mile 78.5 oceanside; $2.50; ⊙8am-sunset) This quiet island was once a thriving city, complete with a warehouse, docks, streets, a hotel and about 40 to 50 permanent residents. There's not much left at the historic site – just the foundation, some cisterns and jungly tangle. Arriving by boat or kayak is the only way to visit. Robbie's Marina hires out kayaks for the paddle out here – around 30 minutes one way in calm conditions.

Lignumvitae Key
Botanical State Park   ISLAND

(📞305-664-2540; www.floridastateparks.org/lignumvitaekey; admission/tour $2.50/2; ⊙8am-5pm Thu-Mon, guided tours (1¼hrs) 10am & 2pm Fri-Sun Dec-Apr) This key, only accessible by boat, encompasses a 280-acre island of virgin tropical forest ringed by alluring waters. The official attraction is the 1919 **Matheson House**, with its windmill and cistern; the real draw is a nice sense of shipwrecked isolation. You'll have to get here via Robbie's Marina; you can hire kayaks from there (it's about an hour's paddle).

Strangler figs, mastic, gumbo-limbo, poison wood and lignum vitae trees form a dark canopy that feels more South Pacific than South Florida. Prepare for fierce mosquitoes outside of winter.

DOLPHINS IN CAPTIVITY

Aquariums and marine life centers are popular destinations in Florida, particularly those with shows featuring dolphins and other marine mammals. Some even offer one-on-one interaction with dolphins. While swimming across a pool being towed by Flipper may sound like a memorable photo op, such practices raise deep ethical concerns.

The harsh reality of life for dolphins in captivity is hidden from visitors. Dolphins are highly intelligent and complex animals, and an artificial environment prevents them from communicating, hunting, playing and mating as they would in the wild. The stress of living in captivity often leads to a greater incidence of illness, disease and behavioral abnormalities. As a result, dolphins in captivity often live much shorter lives than those in the wild. Those dolphins that remain 'voluntarily' in captivity often do so simply to remain close to food.

You can read more about captive marine life at **World Animal Protection** (www.worldanimalprotection.us), **Whale and Dolphin Conservation** (www.whales.org/issues/swimming-with-dolphins) and the **World Cetacean Alliance** (www.worldcetaceanalliance.org).

Activities

★ Robbie's Marina BOATING

(☎305-664-8070; https://robbies.com; Mile 77.5 bayside; kayak & stand-up paddleboard rentals $50-80; ⏰7am-8pm; 👪) Robbie's covers all the bases – it's a local flea market, tacky tourist shop, sea pen for tarpons (massive fish), waterfront restaurant and jumping-off point for fishing expeditions, all wrapped into one driftwood-laced compound. Boat rental and tours are also available. You can quickly escape the mayhem by hiring a kayak for a peaceful paddle through nearby mangroves, hammocks and lagoons.

You can also book a snorkeling trip ($36), which takes you out on a very smooth-riding Happy Cat vessel for a chance to bob amid coral reefs. If you don't want to get on the water, you can feed the freakishly large tarpons from the dock ($4 per bucket, $2.25 to watch).

Sleeping

Ragged Edge Resort RESORT $$

(☎305-852-5389; www.ragged-edge.com; 243 Treasure Harbor Dr; apt $160-330; P❄📶🏊) This low-key and popular apartment complex, far from the maddening traffic jams, has 10 quiet units (all renovated in 2018) and friendly hosts. The larger studios have screened-in porches, and the entire vibe is happily comatose. There's no beach, but you can swim off the dock and in the heated pool.

There are also kayaks, bikes and hammocks for guest use.

Sunset Inn MOTEL $$

(☎305-664-3454; www.sunsetinnkeys.com; 82200 Overseas Hwy; r $150-300; P❄📶🏊) After a stylish makeover, this once boxy motel along the highway has earned a new following for its bright, spacious rooms and appealing amenities. Oversized TVs, Keurig coffee makers, refrigerators and attractive bathrooms (brass fixtures, subway tiles) come standard in the rooms, and old photos of bygone days channel Keys nostalgia.

You can also borrow bikes, use the outdoor games (table tennis, giant Jenga and chess) or fire up the barbecue.

Lime Tree Bay Resort Motel MOTEL $$$

(☎305-664-4740; www.limetreebayresort.com; Mile 68.5 bayside; r $250-480; ❄📶🏊) Hammocks and lawn chairs provide front-row seats for the spectacular sunsets at this 2.5-acre waterfront hideaway. The rooms are comfortable, airy and elegant, with wood floors and decorative rope details – the best have balconies overlooking the water. The extensive facilities include use of tennis courts, bikes, kayaks and stand-up paddleboards, plus a pool and Jacuzzi.

Casa Morada HOTEL $$$

(☎305-664-0044; www.casamorada.com; 136 Madeira Rd, off Mile 82.2; ste incl breakfast $440-710; P❄📶🏊) Contemporary chic comes to Islamorada, but it's not gentrifying away the village vibe. Rather, Casa Morada adds a welcome dash of sophistication to Conch chill: a keystone standing circle, freshwater pool, artificial lagoon – plus a *Wallpaper*-magazine-worthy bar that overlooks Florida Bay – all make this 16-suite boutique hotel worth a reservation. Go to the bar to catch a drink and a sunset.

Ask about yoga on the pier, private sunset sails on a 30ft Skipjack, and free use of kayaks and/or stand-up paddleboards.

✕ Eating

Bad Boy Burrito   MEXICAN $
(☎305-509-7782; www.badboyburritoislamorada.com; 103 Mastic St, Mile 81.8 bayside; mains $8-24; ⏰10am-9pm Mon-Sat; ▨) Tucked away in a small shopping plaza complete with gurgling fountain, orchids and swaying palms, Bad Boy Burrito whips up superb fish tacos and its namesake burritos – with quality ingredients (skirt steak, duck confit, zucchini and squash) and all the fixings (shaved cabbage, chipotle mayo, house-made salsa). Top it off with a hibiscus tea or a fruit smoothie and some chips and guacamole.

Midway Cafe   CAFE $
(☎305-664-2622; www.midwaycafecoffeebar.com; 80499 Overseas Hwy; mains $6-11; ⏰7am-3pm Mon-Sat, to 2pm Sun; ℗🛜♿) A homey cafe that is a favorite stopover on the journey to the Keys for its excellent coffee and good sandwiches, wraps, salads and omelets. The lovely folks who run this cafe roast their own beans and make delectable baked goods, and everything is best enjoyed on the tiny patio beside the cafe.

★Lazy Days   SEAFOOD $$
(☎305-664-5256; www.lazydaysislamorada.com; 79867 Overseas Hwy, oceanside; mains lunch $12-24, dinner $20-35; ⏰11am-9:30pm Sun-Thu, to 11pm Fri & Sat; ▨♿) One of Islamorada's culinary icons, Lazy Days has a stellar reputation for its fresh seafood plates. Start off with a conch chowder topped with a little sherry (provided), before moving on to a decadent grouper Lorenzo (fish topped with crab cake, key-lime butter and béarnaise sauce) or the creative Key West salad (spinach, coconut shrimp, sliced peaches, oranges and toasted almonds).

★Square Grouper Islamorada   SEAFOOD $$
(☎786-901-5678; www.squaregrouperislamorada.com; 80460 Overseas Hwy; mains lunch $12-31, dinner $18-39; ⏰11am-2:30pm & 5-10pm Wed-Mon; ℗▨) In a peaceful spot overlooking a small marina, Square Grouper serves up beautifully executed appetizers (such as seared tuna with ponzu sauce), mouthwatering seafood platters, as well as creative salads and jasmine rice bowls topped with lobster tails,

portobello mushrooms, scallops or other delicacies.

The elegant setting invites a long, lingering meal – particularly out on the deck, where you can watch pelicans winging past and contemplate the distant mangroves.

Bayside Gourmet   AMERICAN $$
(☎305-735-4471; www.baysidegourmet.com; Mile 82.7 bayside; mains breakfast $8-10, lunch & dinner $10-22; ⏰6am-9:30pm Mon-Sat, 11am-9pm Sun) This friendly deli and restaurant is a family-run affair and adds a dash of style to the average Keys seafood shack. The diverse menu serves up something for all palates: from pancakes and breakfast burritos to grouper sandwiches, lasagna and delicious thin-crust pizzas. There's outdoor dining in the palm-fringed back courtyard and old-school arcade games up front.

Beach Café & Bar
at Morada Bay   AMERICAN $$$
(☎305-664-0604; www.moradabaykeys.com/dining/beach-cafe/; Mile 81.6 bayside; mains lunch $17-42, dinner $20-38; ⏰11:30am-10pm Sun-Thu, to 11pm Fri & Sat; ℗) The Beach Café & Bar has a lot going for it, namely a lovely, laid-back Caribbean vibe, a powder-white sandy beach, nighttime torches, tapas and outstanding seafood. It's also a good place to bring the kids, with room to run around, and the adults can come back for a monthly full-moon party, with live music, special cocktails and a beach barbecue.

🍷 Drinking & Nightlife

★Florida Keys
Brewing Company   MICROBREWERY
(☎305-916-5206; www.floridakeysbrewingco.com; 81611 Old Hwy; ⏰11am-10pm) Locally owned and operated, Florida Keys brews innovative, well-balanced beers with a hint of the tropics (including flavor notes like hibiscus, star fruit and key lime). Come in to the friendly tap room, order a flight and have a chat with one of the knowledgeable bartenders.

You can relax in the back garden, catch live music several nights a week, or join in another of the brewery's regular events like movie nights and trivia quizzes.

🛍 Shopping

Old Road Gallery   ARTS & CRAFTS
(☎305-852-8935; www.oldroadgallery.com; Mile 88.8 oceanside; ⏰10am-5pm Thu-Tue) Specializing in pottery and sculpture, the Old Road

Gallery embodies the Key's most creative side. After browsing the ceramics, jewelry and bronze works in the shop, take a stroll along the winding forested path to the cottage – a house built by the Red Cross in the aftermath of the 1935 Labor Day Hurricane, and home to yet more works of art.

❶ Getting There & Away

The Greyhound bus stops at the Burger King at Mile Marker 82.5 oceanside. It goes twice daily to both Key West and Miami.

MIDDLE KEYS

On this stretch of the Keys, the bodies of water get wider, and the bridges get more impressive. This is where you'll find the famous Seven Mile Bridge, one of the world's longest causeways and a natural divider between the Middle and Lower Keys. In this stretch of islands you'll cross specks like Conch Key and Duck Key; green, quiet Grassy Key; as well as Key Vaca, where Marathon, the second-largest town and most Key-sy community in the islands, is located.

Grassy Key

Curry Hammock State Park　　STATE PARK
(☑305-289-2690;　　www.floridastateparks.org; Mile 56.2 bayside; car/cyclist $5.50/2.50; ⊘8am-sunset; ℗🅷) ✐ Curry Hammock is a popular spot for paddling through some lovely coastal scenery: you can rent a kayak (single/double for two hours $18/22) or stand-up paddleboard ($22 for two hours). You can also hike a 1.5-mile trail amid preserved tropical hardwood and mangrove habitats. The trailhead is one mile past the park's main entrance on the bayside (heading towards Marathon); look for the parking area on the right.

Rainbow Bend　　HOTEL $$$
(☑305-289-1505; www.rainbowbend.com; Mile 58 oceanside; r $260-480; ℗🛜🅯) You'll be experiencing intensely charming Keys-kitsch in these big pink cabanas, which have all been renovated following a big hit from Hurricane Irma in 2017. Inside, the 23 rooms are modern and attractively furnished, with cheerful color schemes and extras like small kitchen units in the bigger suites. The beachfront location and fine-dining restaurant add to the appeal.

SS Wreck Galley & Galley Grill　　AMERICAN $$
(☑305-517-6484; www.wreckgalleygrill.com; Mile 59 bayside; mains $12-28; ⊘11am-9pm Sun & Tue-Thu, to 10pm Fri & Sat; ℗) The SS Wreck is a Keys classic, where fisherfolk types knock back brews and feast on wings. It's definitely a local haunt, where island politicos like to prattle on about the issues (fishing). The food is excellent: it grills one of the best burgers in the Keys, and fires up satisfying daily specials.

Marathon
☑ 305, 786 / POP 8700

◎ Sights

★**Crane Point Hammock**　　NATURE RESERVE
(☑305-743-9100; www.cranepoint.net; Mile 50.5 bayside; adult/child $15/10; ⊘9am-5pm Mon-Sat, from noon Sun; ℗🅷🅐) ✐ For a look at a Keys ecosystem in a near pristine state, don't miss a visit to this 63-acre reserve encompassing dense tropical hammock, solution holes, mangroves, a butterfly meadow and a lovely stretch of coastline. A looping 1.5-mile trail with various boardwalk detours transports you quickly into the wild side.

Highlights along the way include the restored Adderley House (built by Bahamian immigrants in 1903), the jungle-like palm hammock (which only grows between Mile Markers 47 and 60), and a wild bird center (where injured birds are nursed back to health). Start off with a short film that gives an overview of the park, and have a look at the natural history museum (featuring dugout canoes, pirate exhibitions and a simulated coral reef). It's a great spot for kids.

Pigeon Key National Historic District　　ISLAND
(☑305-743-5999; www.pigeonkey.net; Mile 47 oceanside; adult/child $12/9; ⊘tours 10am, noon & 2pm) For years tiny Pigeon Key, located 2 miles west of Marathon (basically below the Old Seven Mile Bridge), housed the rail workers and maintenance men who built the infrastructure that connected the Keys. Today you can tour the structures of this National Historic District or relax on the beach and get in some snorkeling. Buy tickets from the **visitor center** (2010 Overseas Hwy; ⊘9:30am-4pm) at Mile 47.5 on the main highway; boats leave from the pier in back – parking is available at the Hyatt Place next door.

Restoration is underway on the 2-mile stretch of the Old Seven Mile Bridge that connects Marathon to Pigeon Key. Once complete, visitors will be able to walk or bike to the island along this historic former rail line.

Florida Keys
Aquarium Encounters
AQUARIUM

(☑305-407-3262; www.floridakeysaquarium encounters.com; 11710 Overseas Hwy, Mile 53.1 bayside; adult/child $25/18, animal encounters from $30; ☺9am-5pm; ⛟) A visit to this small, interactive aquarium starts with a free guided tour of some fascinating marine ecosystems. There are also more immersive experiences, where you snorkel in the coral reef aquarium or the tropical fish–filled lagoon.

Some of the ecosystems you will encounter include a mangrove-lined basin full of tarpon, a tidal pool tank with queen conch and horseshoe crabs, and a 200,000-gallon coral reef tank with moray eels, grouper and several different shark species.

You can also observe mesmerizing lionfish, a pig-nosed turtle, juvenile alligators and various fish species from the Everglades, plus snowy egrets and little blue herons that come by for a visit.

Slightly more controversial are the 'touch tanks' and 'stingray encounters' where you can handle shallow-water marine species and touch stingrays (the barbs have been trimmed). Please note that the stress of human interaction can be detrimental to the well-being of aquatic creatures.

Sombrero Beach
BEACH

(Sombrero Beach Rd, off Mile 50 oceanside; ☺7:30am-dusk; ⓟ ⛟ ⛟) One of the few white-sand, mangrove-free beaches in the Keys. It's a good spot to lounge on the sand or swim, and there's also a small playground.

Turtle Hospital
WILDLIFE RESERVE

(☑305-743-2552; www.theturtlehospital.org; 2396 Overseas Hwy; adult/child $27/13; ☺9am-6pm; ⓟ ⛟) ✦ Be it a victim of disease, boat propeller strike, flipper entanglement with fishing lines or any other danger, an injured sea turtle in the Keys will hopefully end up in this motel-sanctuary. It's sad to see the injured and sick ones, but heartening to see them so well looked after. Ninety-minute tours are educational, fun and offered on the hour from 9am to 4pm.

NATURAL WONDERS OF THE KEYS

It's easy to think of the Keys, environmentally speaking, as a little boring. The landscape isn't particularly dramatic (with the exception of those sweet sweeps of ocean visible from the Overseas Hwy); it tends toward low brush and...well, more low brush.

Hey, don't judge a book by its cover. The Keys have one of the most remarkable, sensitive environments in the USA. The difference between ecosystems here is measured in inches, but once you learn to recognize the contrast between a hammock and a wetland, you'll see the islands in a whole new tropical light. Some of the best introductions to the natural Keys can be found at Crane Point Hammock (p173) and the Florida Keys Eco-Discovery Center (p183).

But we want to focus on the mangroves – the coolest, if not most visually arresting, habitat in the islands. They rise from the shallow shelf that surrounds the Keys (which also provides that lovely shade of Florida teal), looking like masses of spidery fingers constantly stroking the waters. Each mangrove traps the sediment that has accrued into the land your tiki bar stool is perched on. That's right, no mangroves = no Jimmy Buffett.

The three different types of mangrove trees are all little miracles of adaptation. Red mangroves, which reside on the water's edge, have aerial roots, called propagules, allowing them to 'breathe' even as they grow into the ocean. Black mangroves, which grow further inland, survive via 'snorkel' roots called pneumatophores. Resembling spongy sticks, these roots grow out from the muddy ground and consume fresh air. White mangroves grow furthest inland and actually sweat out the salt they absorb through air and water to keep healthy.

The other tree worth a mention here isn't a mangrove. The lignum vitae, which is limited to the Keys in the USA, is also intriguing. Its sap has long been used to treat syphilis, hence the tree's Latin name, which translates to 'tree of life.'

🏃 Activities

Keys Kayak   KAYAKING
(📞 305-743-8880; www.keyskayakllc.com; 10499 Overseas Hwy; tour $50-70; ⏰8:30am-5:30pm) This professional outfit runs highly rated two- to three-hour kayaking tours, including paddles through the mangroves off Sombrero Beach and sunset trips off Grassy Key. If you prefer DIY adventures, you can rent kayaks (single/double $30/55 per day) and stand-up paddleboards ($50 per day).

Tilden's Scuba Center   DIVING
(📞 305-743-7255; www.tildensscubacenter.com; 4650 Overseas Hwy; snorkel/dive trip $60/85, full scuba gear hire $120-150, snuba trip $165; ⏰8am-6pm) This knowledgeable and respected outfit offers snorkeling and diving expeditions through nearby sections of the coral reef. Reef trips typically depart twice daily at 8am and 1pm. Inexperienced divers can try snuba, allowing you to dive to depths of 20ft, while breathing through an air hose tethered to the surface.

🛏 Sleeping

Ranch House Motel   MOTEL $$
(📞 305-743-2217; www.theranchhousemotel.com; 7251 Overseas Hwy; r $130-230; P ❄ 🛜) For the money, this friendly, family-run place right off the highway is one of the best-value lodging options in the Keys. The owners go the extra mile to make guests feel at home. The rooms are clean and well maintained, with wood-paneled walls, comfy beds, fluffy towels (and modern bathrooms), wall-mounted TVs, and a fridge and microwave in each.

Sea Dell Motel   MOTEL $$
(📞 305-743-5161; www.seadellmotel.com; 5000 Overseas Hwy; r $180-250; P ❄ 🛜 🏊) The Sea Dell is a Keys classic: bright, low-slung rooms with a pastel color scheme and floral bedspreads. The rooms are well equipped (coffeemaker, fridge and microwave), and can comfortably accommodate small families. The small pool entices after a day of exploring.

Seascape Motel & Marina   MOTEL $$$
(📞 305-743-6212; www.seascapemotelandmarina.com; 1075 75th St Ocean E, btwn Mile 51 & 52; r $290-550; P ❄ 🛜 🏊) The understated luxury of this B&B manifests in its 12 rooms, with their minimalist and sleek decor. There is a waterfront pool, kayaks, stand-up paddleboards and bikes for guests to use, and its secluded setting will make you feel like you've gotten away from it all. Seascape also offers guests complimentary wine and beer at 5pm.

Tranquility Bay   RESORT $$$
(📞 305-289-0667; www.tranquilitybay.com; Mile 48.5 bayside; r $320-970; P ❄ 🛜 🏊) If you're serious about going upscale, you should book in here. Tranquility Bay is a massive condo-hotel resort with plush townhouses, a lagoon-style pool (as well as two others), a waterfront tiki bar, fitness room, and a top-notch restaurant – while the inviting, palm-studded beach is just steps away from your bed. The grounds are enormous and activity-filled; they really don't want you to leave.

🍴 Eating

Wooden Spoon   AMERICAN $
(7007 Overseas Hwy; mains $6-12; ⏰5:30am-1pm; P) Never mind the sometimes surly service, the Wooden Spoon whips up the best breakfast for miles around, and always warrants a visit. The fluffy pancakes (ideally with blueberries) are outstanding, and you can also opt for perfectly baked biscuits covered in thick sausage gravy, a spicy Mexican omelet and other favorites. The down-at-the-heels diner ambience is a Keys classic.

⭐ Keys Fisheries   SEAFOOD $$
(📞 866-743-4353; www.keysfisheries.com; 3502 Louisa St; mains $14-33; ⏰11am-9pm; P 🍴) The lobster Reuben is the stuff of legend. Sweet, chunky, creamy – so good you'll be daydreaming about it afterward. But you can't go wrong with any of the excellent seafood here, all served with sass. Expect some seagull harassment as you dine on a working waterfront.

The rambling waterfront property also includes an upstairs bar with cold beer, oysters and sweeping views over the marina.

Sunset Grille   AMERICAN $$
(📞 305-396-7235; www.sunsetgrille7milebridge.com; 7 Knights Key Blvd, Mile 47 oceanside; mains lunch $12-17, dinner $20-35; ⏰8am-10pm; 🍴) Overlooking the Seven Mile Bridge, this huge, festive spot has an unbeatable location (it's not called Sunset for nothing) and wide-ranging appeal: namely a huge menu of seafood and grilled meat dishes, plus a raw bar, sushi and plenty of kid-friendly options. There's also an appealing swimming pool (heated in winter) that's free and open to all.

Burdines Waterfront
AMERICAN $$

(☎ 305-743-9204; www.burdineswaterfront.com; 1200 Oceanview Ave, end of 15th St, Mile 48 oceanside; mains $10-19; ⊙11am-9pm; 🅿) For a taste of old-school Marathon, head to this barn-like upper-story shack on the waterfront. It's a much-loved local haunt where you can take a seat around the thatch-roof bar or at a picnic table and take in the breezy views while munching on mahimahi Reuben sandwiches, fresh tuna melts and the best burgers (and hand-cut fries) in the Keys.

🍷 Drinking & Nightlife

Sparky's Landing
BAR

(☎ 305-363-2959; www.sparkyslanding.com; 13205 Overseas Hwy; ⊙11am-10pm) Newly re-born after being wiped off the face of the earth by Hurricane Irma in 2017, Sparky's is the go-to spot for easygoing waterfront drinking no matter the time of day. There's live music most nights, a buzzing happy hour (4pm to 6pm) and a first-rate food menu (fish tacos, pizza, seafood platters).

It's hidden behind a ho-hum Holiday Inn Express. Look for the steep thatched roof.

Hurricane
BAR

(☎ 305-743-2200; www.facebook.com/Hurricane GrilleMarathon; Mile 49.5 bayside; ⊙11am-midnight) Locals, tourists, mad fisherfolk and rednecks saddle up here for endless Jägerbombs before dancing the night away to any number of consistently good live acts. With sassy staff and heartwarming (strong) drinks, this is one of Marathon's best dive bars.

Island Fish Company
BAR

(☎ 305-743-4191; www.islandfishco.com; Mile 54 bayside; ⊙8am-10pm) The Island has a friend-ly staff pouring strong cocktails on a sea-breeze-kissed tiki island overlooking Florida Bay. Chat with your friendly bartender – tip well, and they may top up your drinks with-out you realizing it. The laid-back, by-the-water atmosphere is quintessentially Keys. Pretty sunsets, great seafood plates and a raw bar add to the allure.

☆ Entertainment

Marathon Cinema & Community Theater
CINEMA

(☎ cinema 305-743-0288, theater 305-743-0994; www.marathontheater.org; 5101 Overseas Hwy) An iconic single-stage theater that shows plays and movies in big reclining seats (with even bigger cup holders); the snack bar serves wine and beer.

❶ Information

Fishermen's Hospital (☎ 305-743-5533; 3301 Overseas Hwy; ⊙24hr) Has a major emergency room, as well as a walk-in clinic for less severe health issues.

❶ Getting There & Away

Only chartered planes currently fly into **Marathon Airport** (☎ 305-289-6060; Mile 50.5 bayside), which is in the center of the island – and serves as the Greyhound bus stop. There's also a regular bus service to Key West on **Key West Transit** (☎ 305-600-1455; www.kwtransit.com; day pass $4-8).

LOWER KEYS

The people of the Lower Keys vary between winter escapees and native Conchs. Some local families have been here Keys castaways for generations, and there is somewhat of a more insular feel than other parts of the Overseas Hwy. The islands get at their most isolated and rural before opening onto (rel-atively) cosmopolitan, heterogeneous and free-spirited Key West.

People aside, the big draw in the lower Keys is nature. You'll find the loveliest state park in the Keys here, and one of its rarest species. For paddlers, there is a great man-grove wilderness to explore in a photogenic and pristine environment.

Big Pine Key, Bahia Honda Key & Looe Key

Big Pine is home to endless stretches of quiet roads, Key West employees who found a way around astronomical real-estate rates, and packs of wandering Key deer. Bahia Honda has everyone's favorite sandy beach, while the coral-reef system of Looe offers amazing reef-diving opportunities.

◎ Sights

★ Bahia Honda State Park
STATE PARK

(☎ 305-872-3210; www.bahiahondapark.com; Mile 37; car $4.50-8.50, cyclist & pedestrian $2.50; ⊙8am-sunset; 🅿) 🐾 This park, with its long, white-sand (and at times seaweed-strewn) beach, named Sandspur Beach by locals, is the big attraction in these parts. As Keys beaches go, this one is probably the best natural stretch of sand in the island chain. There's also the novel experience of walking on the **old Bahia Honda Rail Bridge**, which offers nice views of the surrounding islands. Heading out on kayaking adventures (from $12/36 per hour/half day) is another great way to spend a sun-drenched afternoon.

You can also check out the nature trails and science center, where helpful park employees can assist you to identify stone crabs, fireworms, horseshoe crabs and comb jellies. The park concession offers daily 1½-hour snorkeling trips at 9:30am and 1:30pm (adult/child $30/25). Reserve ahead in high season. Many parts of the park were badly damaged by Hurricane Irma (2017), but the park should be fully operational again soon.

No Name Key   ISLAND
Perhaps the best-named island in the Keys, No Name gets few visitors, as it's basically a residential island. It's one of the most reliable spots for Key deer watching. From Overseas Hwy, go on to Watson Blvd, turn right, then left onto Wilder Blvd. Cross Bogie Bridge and you'll be on No Name.

There are several barely signed trails here, including one off to the right about 0.8 miles after crossing Bogie Bridge. It leads through mangrove forest (badly damaged by Hurricane Irma) and out to the waterfront, passing an old rock quarry with abandoned machinery along the way.

National Key Deer
Refuge Headquarters   WILDLIFE RESERVE
(☏305-872-0774; www.fws.gov/refuge/National_Key_Deer_Refuge/; 30587 Overseas Hwy; ☺10am-3pm Mon-Sat; ♿) What would make Bambi cuter? Mini Bambi. Introducing the Key deer, an endangered subspecies of white-tailed deer that prance about primarily on Big Pine and No Name Keys. The folks here are an incredibly helpful source of information on the deer and all things Keys related. The refuge sprawls over several islands, but the sections open to the public are on Big Pine and No Name.

The headquarters also administers the **Great White Heron National Wildlife Refuge** – 200,000 acres of open water and mangrove islands north of the main Keys that is only accessible by boat. There's no tourism infrastructure in place to get out here, but you can inquire about nautical charts and the herons themselves at the office.

Blue Hole   LAKE
(Key Deer Blvd, off Mile 30.5) This little pond (and former quarry) is now the largest freshwater body in the Keys. That's not saying much, but the hole is a pretty little dollop of blue (well, algal green) surrounded by a small path and information signs. The water is home to turtles, fish, wading birds and the odd alligator. A quarter-mile further along the same road is **Watson's Nature Trail** (less than 1 mile long) and **Watson's Hammock**, a small Keys forest habitat.

Looe Key National Marine Sanctuary   PARK
(☏305-809-4700;   www.floridakeys.noaa.gov) Looe (pronounced 'loo') Key, located 5 nautical miles off Big Pine, isn't a key at all but a reef, and is part of the Florida Keys National Marine Sanctuary. This is an area of some 2800 sq nautical miles of 'land' managed by the National Oceanic & Atmospheric Administration. The reef here can only be visited on a specially arranged charter-boat trip, best arranged through any Keys diving outfit, the most convenient one being Looe Key Dive Center (p178).

Big Pine Flea Market   MARKET
(www.bigpinefleamarket.com; Mile 30.5 oceanside; ☺8am-2pm Sat & Sun late Nov-May; ℗) This market, which attracts folks from across the Keys, rivals local churches for weekly attendance. This is an extravaganza of locally made crafts, antiques, vintage clothes, handbags, sunglasses, souvenir T-shirts and beach towels, wood carvings, wind chimes and hand tools – plus all the secondhand gear you might need for a fishing trip.

🏃 Activities

★ Big Pine Kayak Adventures   KAYAKING
(☏305-872-7474; www.keyskayaktours.com; tours depart from 1791 Bogie Dr; half-day backcountry tour per person from $150) For backcountry paddling tours in the Keys, there's no better operator than the highly regarded Big Pine Kayak Adventures. It's run by Bill Keogh, a highly experienced naturalist guide who has written the book on South Florida aquatic tours (literally – check out his extensively researched *Florida Keys Paddling Guide*, published in 2004).

Whether you go with Bill or another of Big Pine's guides, you're in for a treat. You'll paddle across pristine coves with mirror-like waters, through mangrove forests, and sponge and grass flats while looking for wildlife (Key deer, starfish, jellyfish, sponges, herons and loads of other bird life). Tours depart from the Old Wooden Bridge Resort & Marina (p178). Book ahead.

Old Wooden Bridge Resort & Marina
BOATING

(☎ 305-872-2241; www.oldwoodenbridge.com; 1791 Bogie Dr; 2hr single/double kayak ride $25/35, motorboat half-/full-day rental from $150/200; ⊙ 8:30am-5pm) At the foot of the bridge that takes you over to No Name Key, you can hire kayaks and small motor boats for the day (multiday discounts available). This is a lovely area to explore.

Looe Key Dive Center
DIVING

(☎ 305-872-2215; www.diveflakeys.com; 27340 Overseas Hwy, Ramrod Key; snorkel/dive from $40/70; ⊙ 8am-7pm) Located in a resort of the same name, the Looe Key Dive Center on Ramrod Key runs recommended day trips out to Looe Key departing in the morning (at 8am) and afternoon (12:45pm). This two-tank/two-location dive is $70 plus gear for scuba divers, $40 plus gear for snorkelers, and $25 for 'bubblewatchers' who want to come along for the ride.

📛 Sleeping

Bahia Honda State Park Campground
CAMPGROUND $

(☎ 800-326-3521; www.reserveamerica.com; Mile 37, Bahia Honda Key; campsites/cabins $50/175; P 🛜) 🍴 Bahia Honda has the best camping in the Keys. There's nothing quite like waking up to the sky as your ceiling and the ocean as your shower (and: Ow! Sand flies. OK, it's not paradise...). The park has six cabins, each sleeping four to six people, and 80 campsites a short distance from the beach. Reserve months in advance.

⭐ Deer Run on the Atlantic
B&B $$$

(☎ 305-872-2015; www.deerrunontheatlantic.com; 1997 Long Beach Dr, Big Pine Key, off Mile 33 oceanside; r from $355; P ✳ @ 🛜 🐾) 🍴 This state-certified green lodge and pet-friendly B&B is isolated on a lovely stretch of Long Beach Dr. One of the hardest hit places by Hurricane Irma, Deer Run has gone through an extensive restoration inside and out since 2017. The four bright, ecofriendly rooms have sparkling views over the water, and guests have free use of bikes and kayaks.

The helpful owners have a wealth of information about the area and whip up delicious vegan meals.

🍴 Eating

Good Food Conspiracy
VEGETARIAN $

(☎ 305-872-3945; www.goodfoodconspiracy.com; 30150 Overseas Highway, Big Pine Key, Mile 30 oceanside; sandwiches $9-15; ⊙ 10am-6pm Mon-Sat; P 🚗) 🍴 Rejoice, health-food lovers: all the greens, sprouts, herbs and tofu you've been dreaming about during that long, fried-food-studded drive down the Overseas Hwy are available at this friendly little macrobiotic organic shop. There is a good sandwich and fresh-juice bar on-site, where you can get avocado melts, fresh salads, veggie burgers, homemade soup and fruit smoothies.

No Name Pub
PIZZA $$

(☎ 305-872-9115; www.nonamepub.com; N Watson Blvd, Big Pine Key, off Mile 30.5 bayside; mains $13-27; ⊙ 11am-10pm; P) The No Name's one of those off-the-track places that everyone seems to know about. Despite the isolated location, folks come from all over to this divey spot to add their dollar bills to the walls, drink locally brewed beer, enjoy some classic rock playing overhead, and feast on pizzas, burgers and pub grub.

Take in the kooky ambience from a bar stool or head out back to a shaded yard full of picnic tables. Note: the name of this place implies that it is located on No Name Key, but it is on Big Pine Key, just over the causeway.

🍷 Drinking & Nightlife

Kiki's Sandbar
BAR

(☎ 305-872-4500; www.kikissandbar.com; 183 Barry Ave, Mile 28.3 bayside; ⊙ 11am-midnight) For drinks with a view, Kiki's is hard to beat. You can have a chat around the bar or retreat for a bit of sunset watching or stargazing from one of the picnic tables on the waterfront lawn – or better yet stroll to the pier, which can be a magical setting when the moon is on the rise.

ℹ Getting There & Away

Greyhound (www.greyhound.com) has two buses daily that stop in Big Pine Key on the run between Miami and Key West (one way from $12).

Key West Transit (p176) runs nine buses daily between Key West and Marathon, stopping in Big Pine Key. The one-way fare is $4.

Sugarloaf Key & Boca Chica Key

This is the final stretch before the holy grail of Key West. There's not much going on – just bridges over lovely swaths of teal and turquoise and a few good dining options, including longtime Key classics, and a newer hot spot serving cutting-edge fare.

This lowest section of the Keys goes from about Mile Marker 20 to the start of Key West.

Sleeping & Eating

Sugarloaf Lodge
MOTEL $$
(☎305-745-3211; www.sugarloaflodge.net; Sugarloaf Key, Mile 17; r $180-280; P✳︎☎︎☎︎) The 55 motel-like rooms with wood paneling are nothing special, though every single one has a bay view from the balcony or patio (1st floor), and the service is friendly. There's plenty of extras on hand including an excellent restaurant, an appealing tiki bar and a neighboring marina, where you can hire kayaks and arrange fishing charters.

Baby's Coffee
CAFE $
(☎305-744-9866; www.babyscoffee.com; Mile 15 oceanside; ☉6:30am-6pm) This very cool coffee counter has an on-site bean-roasting plant and sells bags of the aromatic stuff along with excellent hot and cold java brews. Other essentials are sold, from yummy baked goods to fruit smoothies.

Mangrove Mama's
CARIBBEAN $$
(☎305-745-3030; www.mangrovemamas20.com; Mile 20 bayside; mains $15-32; ☉11am-10pm; P☎︎⛭) This groovy roadside eatery serves globally inspired seafood – scallops with linguine, plantain-crusted hogfish, blackened mahimahi tacos – best enjoyed on the backyard patio and accompanied by a little live music (daily 6pm to 9pm).

Square Grouper
MODERN AMERICAN $$$
(☎305-745-8880; www.squaregrouperbarandgrill.com; Mile 22.5 oceanside, Cudjoe Key; mains lunch $13-31, dinner $18-39; ☉11am-2:30pm & 5-10pm Tue-Sat; ☎︎) ⊘ Reason enough to venture out of Key West, the Square Grouper hits all the right notes with fresh, locally sourced ingredients, innovative recipes and great service, all dished up in one elegant but unpretentious dining room. Local fish-of-the-day tacos, seared sesame-encrusted tuna loin and a rich seafood stew are among the highlights, though it's worth investigating daily specials.

Reserve ahead. And don't forget to have a pre- or post-dinner drink in the upstairs lounge My New Joint.

Drinking & Nightlife

★ My New Joint
COCKTAIL BAR
(☎305-745-8880; www.mynewjoint420lounge.com; Mile 22.5, Cudjoe Key; ☉4:20pm-11pm Tue-Sat) My New Joint brings a serious dash of style to the Lower Keys. This spacious, warmly lit lounge has artfully made cocktails, excellent brews on tap (including local varieties), great tapas plates and platters of oysters, and live music most nights (from 7pm). Nibble on house-smoked fish, charred Brussels sprouts, soft-shell crab steamed buns and other gourmet sharing plates.

ⓘ Getting There & Away

Key West Transit (p176) runs nine buses a day between Key West and Marathon, stopping in both Boca Chica and Sugarloaf Key. The one-way fare is $4.

KEY WEST
☎ 305, 786 / POP 24,600

◉ Sights

★ Museum of Art & History at the Custom House
MUSEUM
(☎305-295-6616; www.kwahs.com; 281 Front St; adult/child $12/5; ☉9:30am-4:30pm) This excellent museum, set in a grand 1891 red-brick building that once served as the Custom House, covers Key West's history. Highlights are the archival footage from the building of the ambitious Overseas Hwy (and the hurricane that killed 400 people), a model of the ill-fated USS *Maine* (sunk during the Spanish–American War), exhibitions on the role of the navy (once the largest employer in Key West) and the 'wreckers' of Key West, who scavenged sunken treasure ships.

★ Key West Butterfly & Nature Conservatory
WILDLIFE RESERVE
(☎305-296-2988; www.keywestbutterfly.com; 1316 Duval St; adult/child $15/11; ☉9am-5pm; ⛭) This huge domed conservatory lets you stroll through a lush, enchanting garden of flowering plants, tiny waterfalls, colorful birds (including flamingos) and up to 1800 fluttering butterflies comprising some 50 different species – all live imports from around the globe. The shimmery blue morpho butterflies winging past are particularly captivating. Don't miss the small viewing area,

Key West

Latitudes (0.25mi)

Key West Bight

Land's End Marina

Sunset Key

Historic Seaport

Schooner Wharf

58

Front St

54
19
8
18
11
65

Greene St

39

William St

Dey St
68

Museum of Art & History at the Custom House

Key West Chamber of Commerce

Caroline St

Ann St
53
23

Elizabeth St

2

12

42 56

Duval St

62
16
67
30
21
13

Whitehead St

52
31

Front St

10

27
63
49
28

Fleming St

14 48
64 55
3

Pier B

Bahama St

Submarine Basin

Emma St

Truman Waterfront Park

57
BAHAMA VILLAGE
Whitehead St
50 25
51

Angela St

35
66
59
32

Gay Key West Business Guild

38
60
47

Petronia St

6
9

4

Fort St

Olivia St

Thomas St

Julia St

Angela St

Emma St

Howe St

P

5

Naval Air Station – Truman Annex

Fort Zachary Taylor State Park

20

Whitehead Spit

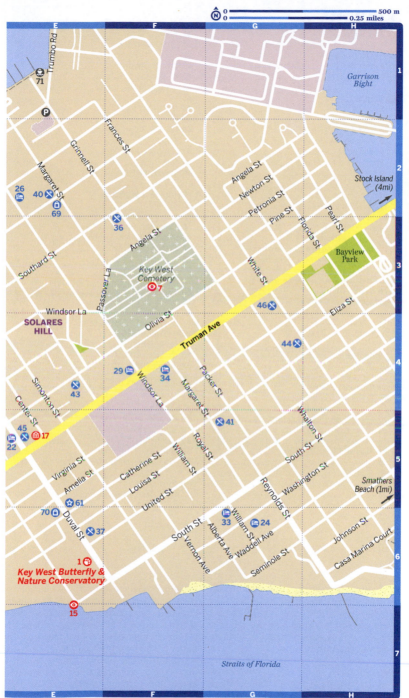

0
N
0
500 m
0.25 miles

Trumbo Rd

71

Garrison
Bight

Stock Island
(4mi)

Grinnell St

Frances St

Margaret St

26
40
69

36

Angela St
Newton St
Petronia St
Pine St

Pearl St

Florida St

Bayview
Park

Angela St

Key West
Cemetery

7

White St

46

Southard St

Passover La

Windsor La

**SOLARES
HILL**

Olivia St

Truman Ave

44

Eliza St

Simonton St

Center St

29
34

Windsor La

Packer St

Margaret St

43

45
22
17

Virginia St

Amelia St

Catherine St

Louisa St

United St

William St

Royal St

41

South St

Washington St

Reynolds St

Whalton St

Smathers
Beach (1mi)

61

70

Duval St

37

33

William St

Alberta Ave

Waddell Ave

24

South St

Vernon Ave

Seminole St

Johnson St

Casa Marina Court

1

**Key West Butterfly &
Nature Conservatory**

15

Straits of Florida

Key West

where butterflies emerge from their chrysalises (most frequently in the morning).

A tiny exhibition center has intriguing videos and displays describing the life cycle, anatomy and migratory patterns of these wondrous creatures.

Mallory Square
SQUARE

(www.mallorysquare.com; P 🚻) Take all those energies, subcultures and oddities of Keys life and focus them into one torchlit, family-friendly (but playfully edgy), sunset-enriched street party. The result of all these raucous forces is Mallory Sq: a cinematic, if tourist-clogged, show that starts in the hours leading up to dusk, the sinking sun a signal to bring on the madness. Watch a dog walk a tightrope, a man swallow fire, and British acrobats tumble and sass each other.

Hemingway House
HOUSE

(☎305-294-1136; www.hemingwayhome.com; 907 Whitehead St; adult/child $15/6; ⊙9am-5pm) Key West's biggest darling, Ernest Hemingway, lived in this gorgeous Spanish Colonial house from 1931 to 1940. Papa moved here with his second wife, a *Vogue* fashion editor and (former) friend of his first wife (he left the house when he ran off with his third wife). *The Short Happy Life of Francis Macomber* and *The Green Hills of Africa* were produced here, as well as many cats, whose descendants basically run the grounds.

Nancy Forrester's Secret Garden
GARDENS

(www.nancyforrester.com; 518 Elizabeth St; adult/child $10/5; ⊙10am-3pm; ⊕) Nancy, an environmental artist and fixture of the Keys community, invites you into her backyard oasis where chatty rescued parrots and macaws await visitors. She gives an overview of these marvelously intelligent and rare birds ('Parrot 101' as she calls it) between 10am and 11am daily. It's a great place for kids, who often leave inspired by the hands-on interactions. Musicians are welcome to bring their instruments to play in the yard. The birds love it – particularly flutes!

Duval Street
AREA

Key West locals have a love-hate relationship with the most famous road in Key West (if not the Keys). Duval, Old Town Key West's main strip, is a miracle mile of booze, tacky everything and awful behavior – but it's a lot of fun. The 'Duval Crawl' is one of the wildest pub crawls in the country. The mix of neon drink, drag shows, T-shirt kitsch, local theaters, art studios and boutiques is more charming and entertaining than jarring.

Florida Keys Eco-Discovery Center
MUSEUM

(☎305-809-4750; https://floridakeys.noaa.gov/eco_discovery.html; 35 East Quay Rd; ⊙9am-4pm Tue-Sat; P ⊕) 🅿 FREE This 6000-sq-ft center is one of the best places in the Keys to learn about the extraordinary marine environments of South Florida. Start off with the 20-minute film which has some beautiful footage of life among the reefs, hardwood hammocks, seagrass beds and mangroves. Continue to the exhibits of life above the waterline, then look at sea creatures in the small aquarium tanks that make up the 'Living Reef' section.

Studios of Key West
GALLERY

(TSKW; ☎305-296-0458; www.tskw.org; 533 Eaton St; ⊙10am-4pm Tue-Sat) FREE This nonprofit showcases about a dozen artists' studios in a three-story space, and hosts some of the best art openings in Key West on the first Thursday of the month. Besides its public visual-arts displays, it also hosts readings, literary and visual workshops, concerts, lectures and community discussion groups. Don't miss Hugh's Views, a new rooftop deck that opened in 2020, and offers a fine perspective over town.

Key West Cemetery
CEMETERY

(www.friendsofthekeywestcemetery.com; cnr Margaret & Angela Sts; ⊙7am-6pm; ⊕) A darkly alluring Gothic labyrinth beckons at the center of this pastel town. Built in 1847, the cemetery crowns Solares Hill, the highest point on the island (with a vertigo-inducing elevation of 16ft). Some of the oldest families in the Keys rest in peace – and close proximity – here. With body space at a premium, mausoleums stand practically shoulder to shoulder. Island quirkiness penetrates the gloom: seashells and macramé adorn headstones with inscriptions like, 'I told you I was sick.'

Get chaperoned by a guide from the **Historic Florida Keys Foundation** (☎305-292-6718), with guided tours ($20 per person) offered periodically. Call to reserve a spot.

Fort Zachary Taylor State Park
STATE PARK

(☎305-292-6713; www.fortzacharytaylor.com; 601 Howard England Way; vehicle/pedestrian/bicycle $7/2.50/2.50; ⊙park 8am-sunset, fort 8am-5pm) 'America's Southernmost State Park' is home to an impressive fort, built in the mid-1800s, that played roles in the American Civil War and in the Spanish–American War. The **beach** here is the best one Key West has to offer – it has white sand to lounge on (but is rocky in parts), water deep enough to swim in and tropical fish under the waves. It's also a fine spot for sunset viewing. Learn more about the fort on free guided tours offered at 11am.

There's a fine cafe on-site, and you can hire lounge chairs and umbrellas, as well as snorkeling gear for aquatic activities. If coming by foot, it's about a half-mile walk (12 minutes) from the entrance to the beach.

Mel Fisher Maritime Museum   MUSEUM

(www.melfisher.org; 200 Greene St; adult/child/student $16/7/14; ⊙8:30am-5pm Mon-Fri, from 9:30am Sat & Sun) For a fascinating glimpse into Key West's complicated history, pay a visit to this popular museum near the waterfront. It's best known for its collection of gold coins, rare jewels and other treasures scavenged from Spanish galleons by Mel Fisher and crew. More thought-provoking is the exhibition devoted to the slave trade, with artifacts from the wreck of the *Henrietta Marie,* a merchant slave ship that sank in 1700.

Key West First Legal Rum   DISTILLERY

(⌨305-294-1441; www.keywestlegalrum.com; 105 Simonton St; ⊙10am-8pm Mon-Fri, 11am-7pm Sat, 10am-6pm Sun, tours 1pm, 3pm & 4pm Mon-Sat, 1pm & 3pm Sun) Opened back in 2013 by a kitesurfing pioneer, this distillery makes some mighty fine rums, which are made with Florida sugarcane and infused with coconut, vanilla and key lime. Try up to eight rums in the shop by buying a shot glass ($10 to $18). The entertaining chef-guided tours in the production room include a tasting.

Fort East Martello
Museum & Gardens   MUSEUM

(⌨305-296-3913; www.kwahs.org/museums/fort-east-martello/history; 3501 S Roosevelt Blvd; adult/child $12/5; ⊙9:30am-4:30pm) This old fortress was built to resemble an old Italian Martello-style coastal watchtower, a design that quickly became obsolete with the advent of the explosive shell. Now the fort serves a new purpose: preserving the past. There's historical memorabilia exploring Key West's role in the Civil War, its heyday in the wrecking and cigar industry, plus the folk art of Mario Sanchez and 'junk' sculptor Stanley Papio, who worked with scrap metal.

Perhaps the most haunted thing in Key West, 'Robert the Doll' is a terrifying child's toy from the 19th century who reportedly causes much misfortune to those who question his powers (get the backstory on www.robertthedoll.org). Indeed, he looks like something out of a Stephen King novel. Creepy music playing overhead adds to the sense of unease.

Little White House   HISTORIC BUILDING

(⌨305-294-9911; www.trumanlittlewhitehouse.com; 111 Front St; adult/child $23/11; ⊙9am-5pm) This sprawling 1890s mansion (a former naval officer's residence) is where President Harry S Truman used to vacation when he wasn't molding post-WWII geopolitics. It's beautifully preserved and open only for guided tours, although you are welcome to visit one small gallery with photographs and historical displays (and a short video) on the ground floor.

Tennessee Williams Museum   MUSEUM

(⌨305-204-4527; www.kwahs.org; 513 Truman Ave; $7; ⊙9:30am-4:30pm) Tennessee Williams, who lived in Key West for more than three decades, was one of the great playwrights of the 20th century. Although he actually lived a mile away (at 1431 Duncan St), this small museum is a great place to learn about his contributions to the literary and theatrical world. On display are photos, manuscripts, one of Williams' typewriters, newspaper articles and a dollhouse-sized model of his one-story home.

Key West Lighthouse   LIGHTHOUSE

(⌨305-294-0012; www.kwahs.org; 938 Whitehead St; adult/child/senior $12/5/9; ⊙9:30am-4:30pm) You can climb up 88 spiraling steps to the top of this snowy white lighthouse, opened in 1848, for a decent view (perhaps not as striking as it was in the days when a men's clothing-optional resort was next door. You can also visit the lighthouse keeper's cottage, which has photographs and artifacts with historical tidbits on the lives of the keepers of the light.

Southernmost Point   LANDMARK

(cnr South & Whitehead Sts) This is the most-photographed spot on the island. The red-and-black buoy isn't even the southernmost point in the USA (that's in the off-limits naval base around the corner). Worth a quick snapshot if you happen to be walking past.

🏃 Activities

Yoga on the Beach   YOGA

(⌨508-737-3211; www.yogaonbeach.com; Fort Zachary Taylor State Park; class $18; ⊙8:15am-9:45am) If you're a yoga fan, you won't want to miss a session on the beach at Fort Zachary Taylor State Park (p183). The daily 90-minute class, held on the sands overlooking gently lapping waves, is simply exhilarating. The class fee includes park admission for the day, and mats are available.

Sunset Watersports   OUTDOORS

(⌨855-378-6386; Smathers Beach, S Roosevelt Blvd; kayak/paddleboard/windsurfer/Hobie Cat per hr from $25/25/35/50; ⊙9am-5pm) For a down day on Smathers Beach, this outfit rents out all the essentials: chairs and umbrellas, kayaks, paddleboards, windsurfing gear and Hobie Cats for a sailing adventure. The same company also runs snorkeling trips, sunset cruises and other outings from the dock at 201 William St.

Jolly Rover   CRUISE
(📞305-304-2235; www.schoonerjollyrover.com; Schooner Wharf, cnr Greene & Elizabeth Sts; day cruise adult/child $45/25, sunset cruise $65/34) This outfit has a gorgeous, tanbark (reddish-brown) 80ft schooner that embarks on daily two-hour cruises under sail. It looks like a pirate ship and has the cannons to reinforce the image. You can bring your own food and drink (including alcohol) – small coolers only.

👉 Tours

Key West Food Tours   FOOD & DRINK
(📞305-570-2010; www.keywestfoodtours.com; food tour adult/child $75/50) Created by a born-and-raised Conch with a passion for Key West, these three-hour walking tours celebrate the island's food and culture. You'll learn about Key West's Cuban and Caribbean connections, while stopping for fish tacos, conch fritters, key-lime pie and other delights. The same outfit also runs an evening pub crawl, taking you to alternative spots well off the Duval St strip.

Conch Tour Train   TOURS
(📞888-916-8687; www.conchtourtrain.com; cnr Front & Duval Sts; adult/child $35/20; ⊙tours 9am-4:30pm; 🚐) This tour outfit seats you in breezy linked train cars on a 70-minute narrated tour; there are three stops (including one near the Hemingway House), where you can hop off and take a later train. Offers discounted admission to the Hemingway House as well as Ghosts and Graveyards night tours. The best place to board is at the Front St depot.

Key West Ghost & Mysteries Tour   TOURS
(📞305-292-2040; www.keywestghostandmysteries tour.com; adult/child $23/15; ⊙tours 9pm; 🚐) A playfully creepy ghost tour that's as family-friendly as this sort of thing gets – in other words, no big chills or pop-out screaming. Tours depart near the corner of Duval and Caroline Streets.

✨ Festivals & Events

Key West Literary Seminar   LITERATURE
(www.kwls.org; ⊙Jan) A feast for the literary minded, this annual four-day event draws top novelists, poets and historians from around the country (although it costs more than $700 to attend). Most book signings and presentations take place in the San Carlos Institute (Map p180; 📞305-294-3887; www. institutosancarlos.org; 516 Duval St; ⊙noon-5pm Fri-Sun). Year-round, you can catch one of its literary-themed walking tours ($30), held on Friday at 5pm and Saturday at 10am.

Conch Republic Independence Celebration   CULTURAL
(www.conchrepublic.com; ⊙Apr) A 10-day tribute to Conch Independence; vie for (made-up) public offices and watch a drag-queen footrace.

Hemingway Days Festival   CULTURAL
(www.fla-keys.com/hemingwaymedia; ⊙Jul 21) Held on days surrounding the author's birthday, this long-running fest brings parties, a 5km run, a fishing tournament, arm-wrestling contests, a 'Papa' look-alike contest and the running of the bulls (with mock animals pulled on wheels).

Womenfest   LGBTQI+
(www.gaykeywestfl.com/womenfest; ⊙Sep) One of North America's biggest lesbian celebrations, Womenfest is four days of merry-making, with pool parties, art shows, roller derby, drag brunches, sunset sails, flag football, and a tattoo and moustache bicycle ride. It's great fun, with thousands descending on Key West from all corners of the USA and beyond.

★ Fantasy Fest   CULTURAL
(www.fantasyfest.com; ⊙late Oct) Akin to New Orleans' riotous Mardi Gras revelry, Fantasy Fest is 10 days of burlesque parades, parades, street fairs, concerts and loads of costumed events. Bars and inns get competitive about decorating their properties, and everyone gets decked out in the most outrageous costumes they can cobble together (or get mostly naked with daring body paint).

Goombay Festival   CULTURAL
(⊙late Oct; 🚐) Held during the same out-of-control week as Fantasy Fest, this is a Bahamian celebration of food, crafts and culture. The family-friendly event runs over two days (typically a Friday and Saturday).

THE CONCH REPUBLIC: ONE HUMAN FAMILY

A Conch (pronounced 'conk' as in 'bonk') is someone born and raised in the Keys. It's a rare title to achieve. Even transplants can only rise to the rank of 'freshwater Conch.' You will hear reference to, and see the flag of, the Conch Republic everywhere in the islands, which brings us to an interesting tale.

In 1982 US border patrol and customs agents erected a roadblock at Key Largo to catch drug smugglers and illegal aliens. As traffic jams and anger mounted, many tourists disappeared. They decided they'd rather take the Shark Valley Tram in the Everglades, thank you very much. To voice their outrage, a bunch of fiery Conchs decided to secede from the USA. After forming the Conch Republic, they made three declarations (in this order): secede from the USA; declare war on the USA and surrender; and request $1 million in foreign aid. The roadblock was eventually lifted, and every February, Conchs celebrate the anniversary of those heady days with nonstop parties, and the slogan 'We Seceded Where Others Failed.'

Today the whole Conch Republic thing is largely a marketing gimmick, but that doesn't detract from its official motto: 'One Human Family.' This emphasis on tolerance and mutual respect has kept the Keys' head and heart in the right place, accepting peoples of all backgrounds, sexual orientations and religions.

🛏 Sleeping

There's a glut of boutique hotels, cozy B&Bs and four-star resorts here at the end of the USA. Unfortunately, the one thing lacking is inexpensive lodging. Aside from sleeping in the town's only hostel, it's not easy to find a bed for less than $300 a night during the high season. During low season (June to November, excluding big festivals), prices listed here can drop by up to 50%.

Seashell Motel & Key West Hostel
HOSTEL $

(☎305-296-5719; www.keywesthostel.com; 718 South St; dm $74; P ❄ 🛜) This place isn't winning any design awards, but the staff are kind, and the dorms are some of the only lower-priced choices on the island. The Seashell also offers much pricier double rooms (starting at $265 in high season). Wherever you stay, you'll find white tile floors, a cheery paint job, and a back patio where you can meet other travelers.

There's also a kitchen for guests, laundry service and bikes for hire.

El Patio
MOTEL $$

(☎305-296-6531; www.elpatiomotel.com; 800 Washington St; r $200-330; ❄ 🛜 🏊) One of Key West's more affordable options, El Patio has spacious rooms set in a two-story art-deco building on a quiet residential street. Rooms are simple with a rather old-fashioned Floridian design, but the beds are comfy and the mini-fridges are a nice touch (some rooms have kitchens). There's also ample (free) parking, a rooftop deck, pool and bike rental.

⭐ Mermaid & the Alligator
GUESTHOUSE $$$

(☎305-294-1894; www.kwmermaid.com; 729 Truman Ave; r winter $370-430, summer $270-330; P ❄ 🛜 🏊) It takes a real gem to stand out amid Key West's grand guesthouses, but this converted 1904 mansion never fails to impress. Lush tropical gardens designed by a landscape architect are set with a trickling fountain, plunge pool and enticing hammocks (there's also a cabana for massages). Each of the nine individually designed rooms boasts a mix of modern comfort and artful details.

Guests can enjoy cookies and lemonade at 3pm and wine and cheese at 5pm. The breakfasts (included) are outstanding – not surprising since the owner is a trained chef (and a great resource on Key West's dining scene).

Saint Hotel
BOUTIQUE HOTEL $$$

(☎305-294-3200; www.sainthotels.com/key-west; 417 Eaton St; r $465-730; ❄ 🛜 🏊) Despite its proximity to Duval St, the Marriott-owned Saint feels like a world removed with its plush rooms – which play with the ideas of 'Saint' and 'Sinner' – chic minimalist lobby, photogenic pool with small cascading waterfall, and artfully designed bar. The best rooms have balconies overlooking the pool. Book well in advance.

Tropical Inn
BOUTIQUE HOTEL **$$$**

(☑888-611-6510; www.tropicalinn.com; 812 Duval St; r $300-500; ❄☎🏊) The Tropical Inn has excellent service and a host of individualized rooms spread out over a historic home property. Each room comes decked out in bright pastels and shades of mango, lime and seafoam. A delicious breakfast is included and can be enjoyed in the jungly courtyard next to a lovely sunken pool.

Gardens Hotel
HOTEL **$$$**

(☑305-294-2661; www.gardenshotel.com; 526 Angela St; r $440-780; P❄☎🏊) This boutique, environmentally friendly property lives up to its name with extravagant greenery surrounding lavish rooms and cottages. Shaded walkways meander past palms, orchids, a koi pond, an aviary and fountains with peaceful seating areas to relax. Inside, Caribbean accents mesh with antique furniture, polished wood floors, designer linens and marble bathrooms to create some of Key West's most enticing rooms.

Artist House
B&B **$$$**

(☑305-296-3977; www.artisthousekeywest.com; 534 Eaton St; r $330-420; ❄☎) A picture-perfect Queen Anne Victorian a short hop from Duval Street, this 1890s mansion has attractive rooms with tall ceilings, polished wood floors and a dash of originality (large paintings in some, vintage wallpaper in others). Breakfast is served on the palm-shaded back terrace, and there's also a complimentary happy hour.

The historic property was once the residence of the painter Robert Eugene Otto and his creepy sidekick, Robert the Doll (the artist named it after himself), which today casts its curses inside the Fort East Martello Museum (p184).

Casablanca Key West
GUESTHOUSE **$$$**

(☑305-296-0815; www.keywestcasablanca.com; 900 Duval St; r $275-725; ❄☎🏊) On the quieter end of Duval St, the Casablanca is a friendly guesthouse with eight bright rooms, all with polished wood floors and comfy beds; some have small balconies. This lush, tropical and elegant inn, once a private house, was built in 1898.

Old Town Manor
BOUTIQUE HOTEL **$$$**

(☑305-292-2170; www.oldtownmanor.com; 511 Eaton St; $330-485; ❄☎🏊) While it bills itself as a B&B (and breakfast is included), the Old Town feels more like a boutique operation that offers a variety of rooms spread throughout lush gardens. The digs come in a subdued, tropically inspired palette, with quality furnishings (four-poster beds in some) and thoughtful extras like coffee-makers and mini-fridges. The best rooms open onto verandas.

L'Habitation
GUESTHOUSE **$$$**

(☑305-293-9203; www.lhabitation.com; 408 Eaton St; r $292-410; ❄☎) A beautiful, classical Keys cottage, L'Habitation has fine rooms kitted out in light tropical shades, with cozy quilts and lamps that look like contemporary art pieces. The friendly bilingual owner welcomes guests in English or French. The front porch, shaded by palms, is a perfect place to stop and engage in Keys people-watching.

Key West Bed & Breakfast
B&B **$$$**

(☑305-296-7274; www.keywestbandb.com; 415 William St; r $350, with shared bathroom $125-230; ❄☎) Sunny, airy and full of artistic touches, this adults-only B&B has 10 unique rooms, each bursting with personality. Some rooms are lined with Dade County pine, others have mahogany four-poster beds, antique furniture, or access to a private deck. If you're on a budget, book early to score one of four rooms with shared bathrooms. The kindhearted host has loads of great travel tips.

There's also a tiny single (the so-called Nun's Room) that's a steal at $125.

Seascape Tropical Inn
B&B **$$$**

(☑305-296-7776; www.seascapetropicalinn.com; 420 Olivia St; r $250-460; ❄☎🏊) Had this B&B existed back in the day, Hemingway could have stumbled into it after one of his epic drinking binges – it's within hollering distance of his old house. Now you can crash in one of seven rooms, each uniquely designed with floral comforters and artwork on the walls. The best rooms have French doors opening onto private terraces.

Silver Palms Inn
BOUTIQUE HOTEL **$$$**

(☑305-294-8700; www.silverpalmsinn.com; 830 Truman Ave; r $475-610; P❄☎🏊) 🌿 Royal blues, sweet teals, bright limes and lemon-yellow color schemes pervade the interior of this boutique property, which also boasts bicycle rentals, a saltwater swimming pool and a green certification from the Florida Department of Environmental Protection. Overall, the Silver Palms offers more of a modern, large-hotel vibe with a candy-colored dose of Keys tropics attitude.

STOCK ISLAND

Just east of Key West, Stock Island is home to boatyards, fishing marinas and grid-like housing strips favored by Key West's largely immigrant workforce. While most visitors pass quickly over the island, it's well worth making a detour here to discover a bit of vintage South Florida coupled with some recent revitalization.

Sheriff's Animal Farm (Monroe County Sheriff's Office Animal Farm; ☑ 305-293-7300; www.facebook.com/KeysAnimalFarm/; 5501 College Rd, Stock Island; ⊙ 1-3pm 2nd & 4th Sun of the month or by appointment; ℗ ⊞) ⊘ FREE is a longtime favorite with Key West families. This Monroe County shelter houses miniature horses, pot-bellied pigs, sloths, birds, snakes, alpacas, an ostrich, lemurs and some massive tortoises.

Drawn to the (slightly) cheaper rents and bigger spaces, artists continue to colonize abandoned spaces on the island. There are a growing number of creative spaces, including **Art Shack** (www.facebook.com/TheArtShackKeyWest; 6404 Front St; ⊙ 11am-7pm Tue-Sun), a collective of galleries and studios, and also a venue for live music, painting classes and other periodic events. A great time to take in Stock Island's cultural scene is during the Art Stroll, held on the second Saturday of every month, from 11am to 4pm (find other upcoming events at www.ilovestockisland.org).

There are several good restaurants on the island. The long-running **Hogfish Bar & Grill** (☑ 305-293-4041; www.hogfishbar.com; 6810 Front St; mains $15-30; ⊙ 11am-midnight Mon-Sat, from 9am Sun) is a charmingly ramshackle eatery perched over Safe Harbor Marina that serves excellent seafood. It's also the favored watering hole for Stock Island's shrimpers, fisherfolk, artists and other assorted characters. For a more cutting-edge culinary experience, reserve a spot for the **Lost Kitchen Supper Club** (www.lostkitchenkeywest.com), held monthly at Hogfish.

Though it opened the same year Hurricane Irma hit in 2017, the architecturally striking **Perry Hotel** (☑ 305-296-1717; www.perrykeywest.com; 7001 Shrimp Road, Stock Island Marina; r $395-600; ⊙ restaurant 8am-2pm & 6-10pm; ℗ ✱ ⊛ ⊠) was spared from destruction. Bright, stylishly furnished rooms afford fine views over the waterfront, and the amenities are top notch. Even if you don't stay here, it's worth booking a table at its award-winning **Matt's Stock Island Kitchen & Bar** (mains $24 to $38) for an outstanding meal.

Mango Tree Inn
B&B $$$

(☑ 305-293-1177; www.mangotree-inn.com; 603 Southard St; r $250-420; ✱ ⊛ ⊠) This down-to-earth B&B offers a courtyard pool and attractive accommodation in a number of airy rooms, each decorated with swaths of tropical-chic accoutrements, from rattan furniture to flowering hibiscus. Rates dip as low as $160 in the low season.

Curry Mansion Inn
HOTEL $$$

(☑ 305-294-5349; www.currymansion.com; 511 Caroline St; r $290-400; ℗ ✱ ⊛ ⊠) In a city full of stately 19th-century homes, the Curry Mansion is especially handsome. All the elements of an aristocratic American home come together here, from plantation-era Southern colonnades to a New England–style widow's walk and, of course, bright Floridian rooms with canopied beds. Enjoy bougainvillea and breezes on the veranda.

✗ Eating

BO's Fish Wagon
SEAFOOD $

(☑ 305-294-9272; www.bosfishwagon.com; 801 Caroline St; mains $12-20, lunch specials $12-18; ⊙ 11am-9:30pm) Looking like a battered old fishing boat that smashed onto the shore, BO's is awash with faded buoys, lifesavers and rusting license plates strung from its wooden rafters (in some spots you needn't step outside to peer up at the moon). Regardless, the seafood is fantastic – with rich conch fritters, soft-shell crab sandwiches and tender fish tacos.

Date & Thyme
HEALTH FOOD $

(☑ 305-296-7766; www.dateandthyme.com; 829 Fleming St; mains $6-15; ⊙ cafe 8am-4pm, market to 6pm; ⊘) ⊘ Equal parts market and cafe, Date & Thyme whips up deliciously guilt-free breakfast and lunch plates, plus energizing smoothies and juices. Try the açaí bowl with blueberry, granola and coconut milk for breakfast, or lunch favorites like Thai coconut curry with mixed vegetables and quinoa. There's a shaded patio in front, where roaming chickens nibble underfoot (don't feed them).

5 Brothers Grocery & Sandwich Shop
DELI $

(☑305-296-5205; www.5brotherskw.com; 930 Southard St; sandwiches $6-10; ⊙grocery 6:30am-3pm, kitchen 7am-3pm Mon-Sat) A Key West icon, this tiny grocery store has a loyal local following who come for first-rate Cuban-style espresso. Stop in for early-morning *café con leche*, guava pastries and bacon and egg rolls, or come later for delectable roast pork sandwiches.

Garbo's Grill
FUSION $

(☑305-304-3004; www.garbosgrillkw.com; 409 Caroline St; mains $10-15; ⊙11am-10pm Mon-Sat, noon-6pm Sun) Just off the beaten path, Garbo's whips up delicious tacos with creative toppings like mango ginger habanero-glazed shrimp, Korean barbecue, and fresh mahimahi with all the fixings, as well as gourmet burgers and hot dogs. It's served out of a sleek Airstream trailer, which faces onto a shaded brick patio dotted with outdoor tables.

Pierogi Polish Market
EASTERN EUROPEAN $

(☑305-292-0464; www.facebook.com/Pierogi PolishMarket; 1008 White St; mains $6-12; ⊙10am-7pm Mon-Sat; P☑) The Keys has an enormous seasonal population of temporary workers largely drawn from Central and Eastern Europe. This is where those workers can revisit their homeland, via pierogies, dumplings, blinis and a great sandwich selection. The market is a good place to assemble a picnic with smoked fish, sausages, rye bread and quality Czech beer.

★ Santiago's Bodega
SPANISH $$

(☑305-296-7691; www.santiagosbodega.com; 207 Petronia St; tapas $8-16, meals for 2 $48-90; ⊙11am-10pm; ☑) A much-loved local icon, Santiago's has easygoing front porch tables, an elegant dining room filled with whimsical artwork, and a zigzagging wooden bar in back that you won't want to miss during happy hour. Small plates are ideal for sharing, with standouts like prosciutto-wrapped dates stuffed with goat cheese, yellowfin tuna ceviche, and blue-cheese-topped beef tenderloin. There is a good selection of wines by the glass.

Stop in from 3pm to 6pm for wine and sangria specials, and a $5 tapa that changes daily.

Thirsty Mermaid
SEAFOOD $$

(☑305-204-4828; www.thirstymermaidkeywest. com; 521 Fleming St; mains $17-33; ⊙11am-10pm; ☑) The lovely Thirsty Mermaid serves outstanding seafood in an elegant, easygoing space. The menu is a collection of sea-life culinary treasures such as an oyster bar, ceviche, middleneck clams and caviar. Among the main courses, seared diver scallops or spiced tuna with jasmine rice and lemon aioli are outstanding. There are also luxurious sandwiches with lobster, fried oysters or local snapper fillings.

The Café
FUSION $$

(☑305-296-5515; www.thecafekw.com; 509 Southard St; mains $13-24; ⊙9am-10pm; ☑) The oldest (mostly) vegetarian spot in Key West is a sunny luncheonette by day that morphs into a buzzing, low-lit eating and drinking spot by night. The cooking is outstanding, with an eclectic range of dishes: spicy Szechuan stir fries, grilled portobello salads, udon noodle bowls, pizza with shaved Brussels sprouts, and a famous veggie burger.

Banana Cafe
FRENCH $$

(☑305-294-7227; www.bananacafekw.com; 1215 Duval St; mains breakfast & lunch $10-21, dinner $17-29; ⊙7:30am-10pm; ☎☑) One of the best places in town to start off the day, the sun-drenched two-story Banana Cafe serves up creatively topped eggs Benedict (try it with blackened shrimp or Florida lobster), fluffy omelets and delicious savory or sweet crepes.

For lunch and dinner, the antique- and vintage-poster-filled eatery leans heavily toward French cooking, with mussels and *frites*, tuna Niçoise (with blackened yellowfin), baked *escargots* as well as satisfying comfort fare like fish and chips and baguette sandwiches.

El Siboney
CUBAN $$

(☑305-296-4184; www.elsiboneyrestaurant.com; 900 Catherine St; mains $12-20; ⊙11am-9:30pm) This is a rough-and-ready Cuban joint where the portions are big and there's no messing around with high-end embellishment or bells and whistles. It uses classic ingredients: rice, beans, grilled grouper, roasted pork, barbecue chicken, sweet plantains – all cooked with pride to belly-filling satisfaction.

Point5
FUSION $$

(☑305-296-0669; www.915duval.com/point5; 915 Duval St; mains $14-22, small plates $8-16; ⊙6pm-midnight; ☑) This sophisticated upstairs hideaway with well-placed balcony tables trades in fusion-style tapas with a global influence: think Greek flatbread with lamb and feta, walnut pistachio tacos, shishito peppers and marinated octopus salad. All go nicely with wines by the glass and creative cocktail selections.

Heartier plates include seafood risotto, lobster ravioli and fall-off-the-bone Mongolian ribs.

Mo's Restaurant
CARIBBEAN $$

(☑305-296-8955; 1116 White St; mains $12-24; ⊙11am-10pm Mon-Sat) The words 'Caribbean' and 'home cooking,' when used in conjunction, are generally always enough to impress. But it's not just the genre of cuisine that wins us over at Mo's – it's the execution. The dishes are mainly Haitian, and they're delicious – the spicy pickles will inflame your mouth, which you can then cool down with a rich vegetable 'mush' over rice, or try the incredible signature snapper.

★ Little Pearl
SEAFOOD $$$

(☑305-204-4762; www.littlepearlkeywest.com; 632 Olivia St; mains $24-42; ⊙5-10pm) The same team behind the Thirsty Mermaid opened this vaguely nautical-themed restaurant (and four-seat bar) to much acclaim back in 2018.

Sink into a cerulean blue banquette and let the evening unfold while indulging in Asian-accented dishes like king crab and papaya salad, Bangkok octopus (with mint and basil), seared diver scallops with baby bok choy slaw, or (for the nonpescatarians) duck breast with cognac shallot butter.

★ Blue Heaven
AMERICAN $$$

(☑305-296-8666; www.blueheavenkw.com; 729 Thomas St; mains breakfast & lunch $13-25, mains dinner $24-42; ⊙8am-10:30pm; ☑) This is one of the quirkiest venues on an island of oddities – customers, together with free-ranging fowl, flock to dine in the ramshackle, tropical-plant-filled garden where Hemingway once officiated boxing matches. This place gets packed with customers who come for the delectable breakfasts (blueberry pancakes) and Keys cuisine with French touches (like yellowtail snapper with citrus *beurre blanc*). Entrance on Petronia St.

Nine One Five
FUSION $$$

(☑305-296-0669; www.915duval.com; 915 Duval St; mains lunch $14-26, dinner $26-45; ⊙5-11pm Mon & Tue, 11:30am-11pm Wed-Sun; ☑) Classy Nine One Five certainly stands out from the Duval dens of drunkenness and '80s cover bands. Ignore all that and enter this modern and elegant space, which serves a creative, changing New American menu with global accents. It's all quite rich – imagine yellowtail snapper with Thai chili sauce and basmati rice, mojito-cured salmon tartare or duck confit with parsley pesto.

Latitudes
SEAFOOD $$$

(☑305-292-5300; www.sunsetkeycottages.com; Sunset Key; mains lunch $18-28, dinner $32-56; ⊙7am-2:15pm & 5-10pm) For a memorable meal on your own private island (well, plus the other diners and resort guests), Latitudes is hard to top. The palm-studded 27-acre key sits around 546 yds (500m) off Key West, and offers gorgeous views over the water and breathtaking sunsets (time your visits well). The seafood is excellent, but pricey (it's the unrivaled location you're paying for).

The ferry dock to the island is tucked behind a parking garage on Front St (just south of the Mel Fisher Maritime Museum). For a long, leisurely lunch without the rush, book a 1:15pm or 1:45pm reservation.

🍷 Drinking & Nightlife

Duval St is the famed nightlife strip, which is lined with all manner of drinking dens – from frat-boy party hubs to raucous drag-loving cabarets. Live music is a big part of the equation.

★ Green Parrot
BAR

(☑305-294-6133; www.greenparrot.com; 601 Whitehead St; ⊙10am-4am) The oldest bar on an island of bars – 'A sunny place for shady people' being one of its mottos – this rogues' cantina opened in the late 19th century and has kept going. Its ramshackle interior, with local artwork on the walls and a parachute stretched across the ceiling, only adds to the atmosphere, as does the fun-loving, colorful crowd.

The Green Parrot books some of the best bands – playing funk-laden rock, brassy jazz, juke-joint blues and Latin grooves – that hail from Miami, New Orleans, Atlanta and other places. There's never a cover charge.

Cuban Coffee Queen
CAFE

(305-294-7787; www.cubancoffeequeen.com; 5 Key Lime Square; ⏰ 7am-7pm) Key West's best coffee is served at this open-sided cafe (one of several branches in town), tucked down a tiny lane behind Duval St. The *café con leche* (coffee with steamed milk) is simply perfection, though there are plenty of other options including iced coffee (the ice cubes are also made of coffee) and the delicious, caffeine-free, Ayurvedi turmeric *con leche.*

Lagerheads
BAR

(305-509-7444; www.lagerheadsbeachbar.com; 0 Simonton St; ⏰ 9am-sunset) Walk to the end of Simonton St to find this peaceful beach bar, with umbrella-shaded lounge chairs for hire in the sand, and a small swimming area where you can cool off. It's a great spot for cold drinks, conch salad and a legendary smoked fish dip – particularly around sunset, for fine views without the Mallory Square mob.

Burgundy Bar
BAR

(305-294-3200; www.sainthotels.com/bite-sip; 417 Eaton St; ⏰ 1-11pm) Inside the Saint Hotel, this small, convivial bar deserves special mention for its outstanding Bloody Marys – among the best you'll find in this country. It's also a fine setting for a cocktail and high-end pub grub – and feels secreted away from the chaos of nearby Duval St.

Vinos on Duval
WINE BAR

(305-294-7568; www.vinosonduval.com; 810 Duval St; ⏰ 2pm-12:30am Mon-Wed, from noon Thu-Sun) On the less rowdy end of Duval St, Vinos pours a good selection of wines from around the globe – Spanish tempranillos, Argentine malbecs, Californian cabs – in a cozy setting with a touch of Key West eccentricity. Grab a seat at the bar and have a chat with the knowledgeable staff, or retreat to one of the tables on the porch.

Captain Tony's Saloon
BAR

(305-294-1838; www.capttonyssaloon.com; 428 Greene St; ⏰ 10am-2am) Propagandists would have you believe the nearby megabar complex of Sloppy Joe's was Hemingway's original bar, but the original spot where the old man famously drank was right here, the original Sloppy Joe's location (before it was moved onto Duval St and into frat-boy hell). According to legend, Martha Gellhorn, Hemingway's third wife, seduced him in this very bar.

Conch Republic
BAR

(305-294-4403; www.conchrepublicseafood.com; 631 Greene St; ⏰ 11:30am-midnight) Overlooking the waterfront, this sprawling, open-sided eatery and drinking space is a fun place to get you in the Key West spirit. The allure: a festive happy hour, a chatty laid-back crowd, island breezes and live music (nightly from 5:30pm to 9pm, plus noon to 4pm on Saturday and Sunday). The seafood is also quite good (mains $16 to $32).

Viv
WINE BAR

(305-517-6799; www.vivez-joyeux.com; 300 Petronia St; ⏰ noon-11pm) This French-run wine bar is tiny but utterly charming, with velvety red wines by the glass or bottle from an impressive rotation of French and American wine growers. You can pair those wines with first-rate cheese, charcuterie and other snacks. The same owners also run the very charming crêperie next door.

Bourbon St Pub
GAY & LESBIAN

(305-293-9800; www.bourbonstpub.com; 724 Duval St; ⏰ 10am-4am) A celebratory crowd, great DJs and striking male dancers (who shimmy on top of the bar from 10pm onward) keep the party going at this iconic spot on Duval St. The garden bar in back, with pool and Jacuzzi, is open to men only, and occasionally hosts clothing-optional afternoon parties. Tuesday nights are for the girls.

Garden of Eden
BAR

(224 Duval St; ⏰ noon-4am) Take the stairs to the rooftop to discover Key West's own clothing-optional drinking patio. Lest you get too excited, cameras aren't allowed and most people forego the striptease. Regardless, the views over town are great, the mixed crowd is up for a fun time, and it's an obligatory stop when bar-hopping along Duval.

If you go, don't be a voyeuristic wallflower. Get out there and dance!

Aqua
GAY & LESBIAN

(305-294-0555; www.aquakeywest.com; 711 Duval St; ⏰ 3pm-2am) Aqua hosts some of the best drag shows on the island and attracts people of all ages and sexual orientations – including couples and groups – all wanting to see what the excitement is about. Shows happen nightly at 9pm, plus 7pm on Thursday, and 7pm and 11pm on Friday and Saturday.

LAZY DAYS IN KEY WEST

With its walkable town center, easygoing bars and friendly locals happy to share a story or two, Key West seems like it was made for lazy days. After you've seen the sights, take a day for seaside relaxing and enjoying the Keys' lesser-known charms.

BEACH LOUNGING

Although not known as a beach destination, Key West has some pretty spots for a day by the ocean. **Fort Zachary Taylor State Park** (p183) has a palm-backed stretch of white sand and clear water, plus snorkel gear for hire and a peaceful cafe.

BRUNCH & COCKTAILS

The classic way to start the day in Key West is over a long, leisurely brunch. You can join the roosters for a bit of backyard nibbling at **Blue Heaven** (p190), or linger over America's finest Bloody Mary at **Burgundy Bar** (p191).

BACKYARD OASIS

At **Nancy Forrester's Secret Garden** (p183), Nancy happily introduces visitors to her remarkable parrots and macaws, all with unique personalities. If you play an instrument, these birds always enjoy a concert!

NO NAME KEY

An easy 45-minute drive from Key West is **No Name Key** (p177), where endangered Key deer feed in the forests near the road. You can take some short walks in the **National Key Deer Refuge** (p177) and stop for a meal at the famous **No Name Pub** (p178).

MIA2YOU/SHUTTERSTOCK ©

1. Key deer, National Key Deer Refuge (p177)
2. Fort Zachary Taylor State Park (p183)
3. Blue Heaven (p190), South Beach

⭐ Entertainment

La Te Da
CABARET

(📞305-296-6706; www.lateda.com; 1125 Duval St; tickets $33; ⊘piano bar shows 8:30pm daily, cabaret 9pm Mon-Sat) While the outside bar is where locals gather for mellow chats over beer, you can catch high-quality drag acts – big names come here from around the country – upstairs at the fabulous Crystal Room on weekends. More low-key cabaret acts grace the downstairs piano bar (admission free). The Sunday tea dance – an afternoon dance party (4pm to 6:30pm) by the pool – is great fun.

Virgilio's
LIVE MUSIC

(📞305-296-8118; www.latrattoria.us/index.php/virgilios; 524 Duval St; ⊘6pm-3am) This barstage is as 'un-Keys' as they come, and frankly, thank God for a little variety. This town needs a dark, candlelit martini lounge where you can chill to blues or jazz and get down with some salsa, which Virgilio's handsomely provides. Enter on Applerouth Lane.

Tropic Cinema
CINEMA

(📞305-396-4944; www.tropiccinema.com; 416 Eaton St) Great art-house movie theater with deco frontage.

Waterfront Playhouse
THEATER

(📞305-294-5015; www.waterfrontplayhouse.org; 407 Wall St, Mallory Sq) Catch high-quality musicals and dramas from the oldest-running theater troupe in Florida. The season generally runs from October through early June.

Red Barn Theatre
THEATER

(📞305-296-9911; www.redbarntheatre.com; 319 Duval St; ⊘box office 1-8pm Tue-Fri, 4-8pm Sat & Sun) An occasionally edgy and always fun local playhouse, the quaint Red Barn Theatre stages indie productions like *Tiny Beautiful Things* by Cheryl Strayed or Steve Martin's *Meteor Shower*. The season runs from December through April.

🛍 Shopping

Salt Island Provisions
GIFTS & SOUVENIRS

(305-517-6088; www.saltislandprovisions.com; 830 Fleming St; ⊘10am-5pm) This crafty little shop is a fun place to browse for gift ideas. You'll find delicate jewelry made by local artisans, beeswax candles, honey and, of course, salt in its many incarnations: namely salt scrubs and gourmet cooking salts in infusions of merlot, sriracha, curry and white truffle.

The Green Pineapple
FASHION & ACCESSORIES

(📞305-509-7378; www.facebook.com/TheGreen Pineapple; 1130 Duval St; ⊘9am-8pm Mon-Sat, to 6pm Sun) 🖊 An inviting and sustainably minded boutique with handmade jewelry, skincare products and beautifully made apparel, as well as sunglasses, wide-brimmed hats, sandals and other South Florida essentials. The Green Pineapple also offers yoga classes and has a cafe on-site for smoothies, light organic meals and glasses of wine, with happy hour specials (you're still in Key West, after all).

Books & Books
BOOKS

(📞305-320-0208; www.booksandbookskw.com; 533 Eaton St; ⊘10am-6pm) Miami's best indie bookshop has a branch in Key West, and it's a magnet for the literary minded. You'll find plenty of titles of local interest (particularly on Key West and Cuba), great staff picks and thought-provoking new releases. Regular book signings and author readings take place throughout the year.

The Key West branch was founded by children's book author Judy Blume and her writer husband George Cooper, who often work in the store.

Bésame Mucho
GIFTS & SOUVENIRS

(📞305-294-1928; www.besamemucho.net; 315 Petronia St; ⊘10am-6pm Mon-Sat, to 4pm Sun) It's hard not to be lured inside this handsomely designed boutique with its old-world charm (gilt-framed mirrors, exposed brick, antique display counters) in the Bahama Village. There's a wide range of temptations, including high-end bath, fragrance and skincare products, antique-inspired jewelry, sustainably sourced clothing and eye-catching ceramics and other housewares.

Kermit's
FOOD

(www.keylimeshop.com; 200 Elizabeth St; ⊘9am-9:30pm) Satisfy your innermost cravings for all things key-lime-related at this long-running institution near the waterfront. You'll find salsa, barbecue sauce, candies, ice cream, dog biscuits and even wine bearing that distinctive key-lime flavor. Purists may prefer to settle for a pie (mini pies available) or perhaps a chocolate-dipped key-lime Popsicle.

ℹ Information

Gay Key West Business Guild (Map p180; 📞305-294-4603; www.gaykeywestfl.com; 808 Duval St; ⊘9am-5pm Mon-Sat) Serves as a welcome center for LGBTQI+ travelers. Loads of great tips on restaurants, bars, lodging and outdoor activities in Key West.

Key West Chamber of Commerce (Map p180; ☎ 305-294-2587; www.keywestchamber.org; 510 Greene St; ⏱ 9am-5:30pm) An excellent source of information.

Lower Keys Medical Center (☎ 305-294-5531; www.lkmc.com; 5900 College Rd, Mile 5, Stock Island) Has a 24-hour emergency room.

ⓘ Getting There & Away

Key West International Airport (EYW; ☎ 305-809-5200; www.eyw.com; 3491 S Roosevelt Blvd) is off S Roosevelt Blvd on the east side of the island. You can fly into Key West from some main US cities, such as Miami, Chicago, Atlanta, Charlotte and Newark. From Key West airport, a quick and easy taxi ride into Old Town costs a fixed $9 per person (solo travelers pay the meter, usually less than $20).

Greyhound (☎ 305-296-9072; www.greyhound. com; 3439 S Roosevelt Blvd; ⏱ 7:30-9am & 4:30-6pm) has two buses daily between Key West and Downtown Miami. Buses leave Miami for the 4½-hour journey at 12:25pm and 6:25pm and Key West at 8.30am and 5:45pm going the other way (from $20 to $44 each way).

You can take a boat ride from Fort Myers to the Keys on the **Key West Express** (☎ 239-463-5733; www.seakeywestexpress.com; 100 Grinnell St, Key West; adult/child/junior/senior/round-trip $155/62/92/145, one way $95/31/68/95), which departs from Fort Myers beach daily at 8am and does a 3½-hour cruise to Key West. Returning boats depart the seaport at 6pm.

ⓘ Getting Around

Once you're in Key West, the best way to get around is by bicycle (rentals from the Duval St area, hotels and hostels cost from $10 a day). For transportation within the Duval St area, the free Duval Loop shuttle (www.carfreekeywest. com/duval-loop) runs from 6am to midnight.

Other options include Key West Transit (p176), with color-coded buses running about every 15 minutes; mopeds, which generally cost from $35 per day ($60 for a two-seater); or the open-sided electric tourist cars, aka 'Conch cruisers,' which travel at 35mph and cost about $140/200 for a four-/six-seater per day.

A&M Scooter Rentals (☎ 305-896-1921; www.amscooterskeywest.com; 523 Truman Ave; bicycle/scooter/electric car per day from $10/35/140; ⏱ 9am-7pm) rents out scooters and bicycles, as well as open-sided electric cars that can seat two to six people, and offers free delivery.

Parking can be tricky in town. There's a free **parking lot** on Fort St off Truman Ave.

DRY TORTUGAS NATIONAL PARK

After all those keys, connected by that convenient road, the nicest islands in the archipelago require a little extra effort – the **Dry Tortugas** (☎ 305-242-7700; www.nps.gov/drto) are accessible only by boat or plane.

The park is open for day trips and overnight camping, which provides a rare phenomenon: a quiet Florida beach. Reserve months in advance through the **Yankee Freedom III** (☎ 800-634-0939; www.dry tortugas.com; Key West Ferry Terminal, 100 Grinell St; adult/child/senior $180/125/170), which provides ferry service to the island. The sparkling waters offer excellent snorkeling and diving opportunities. A **visitor center** is located within fascinating Fort Jefferson.

In March and April, there is stupendous bird-watching, including aerial fighting. Stargazing is mind-blowing any time of the year.

⊙ Sights

Dry Tortugas National Park is America's most inaccessible national park. Reachable only by boat or seaplane, it rewards you for your effort in getting there with amazing snorkeling amid coral reefs full of marine life. You'll also get to tour a beautifully preserved 19th-century brick fort, one of the largest such fortifications in the USA despite its location 70 miles off the coast of Key West.

On paper, the Dry Tortugas covers an extensive area – more than 70 sq miles. In reality, only 1% of the park (about 143 acres) consists of dry land, so much of the park's allure lies under the water. The marine life is quite rich here, with the opportunity to see tarpon, sizable groupers and lots of colorful coral and smaller tropical fish, plus the odd sea turtle gliding through the sea.

Explorer Ponce de León named this seven-island chain Las Tortugas (The Turtles) for the sea turtles spotted in its waters. Thirsty mariners who passed through and found no water later affixed 'dry' to the name. In subsequent years, the US Navy set an outpost here as a strategic position into the Gulf of Mexico. But by the Civil War, **Fort Jefferson**, the main structure on the islands, had become a prison for Union deserters and at least four other people, among them Dr Samuel Mudd, who had been arrested for complicity in the assassination of Abraham Lincoln. Hence a new nickname: Devil's Island. The name was prophetic; in 1867 a yellow-fever outbreak killed 38 people, and after an 1873 hurricane the fort was abandoned. It reopened in 1886 as a quarantine station for smallpox and cholera victims, was declared a national monument in 1935 by President Franklin D Roosevelt, and was upped to national park status in 1992 by George Bush Sr.

Today, the Dry Tortugas are a national park under the control of the National Park Service.

🛏 Sleeping

There's no lodging on the island, but you can camp here if you plan well in advance. Garden Key has 10 campsites ($15 per person, per night), which are given out on a first-come, first-served basis. You'll need to reserve eight to 12 months ahead on the ferry *Yankee Freedom III* (p195), which takes only 10 campers per day to and from the island. There are toilets, but no freshwater showers or drinking water; bring everything you'll need. You can stay up to three nights.

❶ Getting There & Away

If you have your own boat, the Dry Tortugas are covered under National Ocean Survey chart No 11438. Otherwise, the *Yankee Freedom III* (p195) operates a fast ferry between Garden Key and the Historic Seaport (at the northern end of Margaret St). The round-trip fare (2¼ hours each way) costs per adult/child $180/125. Reservations are essential. Continental breakfast, a lunch buffet, snorkeling gear, a 45-minute tour of the fort and park admission fee are all included.

Key West Seaplanes (☎305-293-9300; www.keywestseaplanecharters.com; half-day trip adult/child $361/288, full-day trip $634/508) can take up to 10 passengers (flight time 40 minutes each way). The half-day tour is four hours, allowing 2½ hours on the island. The eight-hour full-day excursion gives you six hours on the island. Again, reserve at least a week in advance. Passengers over age 16 arriving by plane also need to pay an added $10 park admission fee (cash only). Flights depart from Key West International Airport.

Understand Miami & the Keys

History

South Florida was built on a cycle of boom and bust, by dreamers who took advantage of nice weather and opportunists who took advantage of natural disasters – nothing clears out old real estate like a hurricane, after all. Every chapter of the region's saga has been closed by a hurricane, building boom or riot. South Florida has historically treated slow growth with contempt, and this attitude has paid with huge financial dividends on the one hand, and economic and environmental catastrophes on the other.

Spain, Britain & Spain Again

The Spanish settled Florida in 1565, several decades before Pilgrims landed on Plymouth Rock and English aristocrats starved in Jamestown, Virginia. The territory changed hands from Spain (until 1763) to Britain (1763–83) and back to Spain again (1783–1821). And then came American Independence. The Spanish had to deal with a big, land-hungry new nation lying just to the north.

Relations chilled when escaped American slaves made for Spanish Florida, where slavery was illegal and freed slaves were employed as standing militia members. White American Southerners saw armed black militia and started sweating the notion of slave revolts in their back plantation yard. By 1821 the USA had purchased Florida from Spain; concurrently, businessman John W Simonton bought the island of Key West from Spanish artillery officer Juan Pablo Salas.

The island was deemed the 'Gibraltar of the West' for its command of the Straits of Florida, which sit between the Atlantic Ocean and the Gulf of Mexico. In 1823 Commodore David Porter of the US Navy took over the island, administering it as a base from which to track down illegal slave ships.

The Unconquered People

In the late 18th century, elements of the Creek nation in Georgia and other tribes from the north migrated to Florida. These tribes intermingled and intermarried, and in the late 1700s were joined by runaway black slaves. Black newcomers were generally welcomed into Native American society

TIMELINE	10,000 BCE	2000 BCE	500 BCE
	After crossing the Bering Strait from Siberia some 50,000 years earlier, humans arrive in Florida, hunting mastodon and saber-toothed tigers at the end of the last ice age.	The earliest period in which archaeologists can find evidence of the creation of fired pottery in the state of Florida.	Pottery from this period is attributed to the Glades Culture, which stretches from the Keys to present-day Martin county, north of Miami. The Glades Culture does not survive European contact.

though were occasionally kept as slaves, although this slavery was more akin to indentured servitude (slaves, for example, had their own homes that they inhabited with their families).

At some point, these fugitive, mixed peoples occupying Florida's interior were dubbed 'Seminoles,' a corruption of the Spanish word *cimarrones,* meaning 'free people' or 'wild ones.' Defying European rule and ethnic category, they were soon considered too free for the newly independent United States, which coincidentally was growing hungrier for land.

When the majority of the Creek were forced west across the Mississippi River in 1817, Americans figured everything east of that body of water was now theirs for the settling. But the Seminoles had no intention of leaving their homes.

Bad blood and sporadic violence between Americans and Seminoles eventually gave the USA the excuse it needed to make a bid for Florida, which was finally bought from Spain in 1821. Before and after that the US military embarked on several campaigns against the Seminoles and their allies, who took to the swamps, fought three guerrilla wars, and scored a respectable amount of victories against an enemy several times their size. In fact, the Second Seminole War (1835–42) was the longest in American history between the American Revolution and the Vietnam War.

Indeed, operationally the Seminole wars were a 19th-century version of Vietnam, a never-ending parade of long, pointless patrols into impenetrable swamps, always searching for an ever-invisible enemy. By 1830 Congress came up with the shocking Removal Act, a law that told Native Americans to pack up their things and move across the country to Oklahoma. Seminole Chief Osceola and his band (never exceeding more than 100 warriors) refused to sign the treaty and fled into the Everglades. After keeping thousands of soldiers jumping at the barest hint of his presence for years, Osceola was captured under a false flag of truce in

Native American Resources

Ah-Tah-Thi-Ki Museum (www.ahtahthiki.com)

Tequesta Indians (www.floridiannature.com/tequesta.htm)

Miccosukee Tribe (www.miccosukee.com/tribe)

HISTORY THE UNCONQUERED PEOPLE

TEQUESTA INDIANS

In 1998, 24 holes, inscribed in bedrock and arranged in the shape of a perfect circle, were found in Downtown Miami. The 'Miami Circle,' as it was dubbed, is thought to be the foundations of a permanent structure and, at some 2000 years old, it's the oldest such structure of its kind on the US East Coast.

Archaeologists think the Circle was built by Miami's earliest known inhabitants, the Tequesta (Tekesta) Indians, who are otherwise a mystery. The tribe was mostly wiped out by Spanish first contact, which brought violence and disease, and survivors likely melted into the Miccosukee and Seminole nations.

500 CE	1513	1702	1763
The Caloosahatchee Culture develops and thrives in the area that now includes the western Everglades and 10,000 Islands. This complex society lasts till 1750.	Ponce de León 'discovers' Florida, landing south of Cape Canaveral, believing it to be an island. Since it's around Easter, he names it La Florida, 'The Flowery Land' or 'Feast of Flowers.'	In their ongoing struggle with Spain and France over New World colonies, the British burn St Augustine to the ground; two years later they destroy 13 Spanish missions in Florida.	The mixed Spanish–Native American community in Key West is resettled in Havana after the island is seized by the British. For years, Key West has little real authority.

1837. Yet resistance continued, and while the Seminoles gave up fighting, the government gave up on moving them west.

By 1842 the warring had ended, but no peace treaty was ever signed, which is why the Seminoles to this day call themselves 'the unconquered people.' Those Seminoles who remained in Florida are now organized under a tribal government and run the Ah-Tah-Thi-Ki Museum and the Hard Rock Cafe. Not one Hard Rock Cafe: the entire chain, bought for $965 million in 2007 with money made from gambling revenue. The Seminoles were the first Native American tribe to cash in on gambling, starting with a bingo hall in 1979 that has since expanded to a multibillion-dollar empire. Not bad for a Seminole population of a little over 3000.

A Freeze Brings Flagler & the Railway

For decades, Florida was farming country: sugar, citrus and drained swamps. In 1875 Julia Tuttle and her tubercular husband arrived in this agricultural empire from Cleveland, Ohio. After his death she moved to South Florida to take over the land she had inherited as a widow. Proving her worth as a true Floridian, over the next 20 years she proceeded to buy more and more property.

In the meantime, Henry Morrison Flagler, a business partner of John D Rockefeller, realized Florida's tourism potential. Flagler had been busy developing the northern Florida coast in St Augustine and Palm Beach, and he also built the Florida East Coast Railroad, which extended down as far as Palm Beach. Tuttle saw a business opportunity and contacted Flagler with a proposition: if he would extend his railroad to Miami, Tuttle would split her property with him. Miami? Way down at the end of nowhere? Flagler wasn't interested.

Then, in 1895, a record freeze enveloped most of Florida (but not Miami), wiping out citrus crops and sending vacationers scurrying. Legend has it that Tuttle – who is said to have been rather quick both on the uptake and with an 'I told you so' – went into her garden at Fort Dallas on the Miami River, snipped off some orange blossoms and sent them to Flagler, who hightailed it down to Miami to see for himself.

Flagler was hooked. He and Tuttle came to terms, and all those Floridians whose livelihoods had been wiped out by the freeze followed Flagler south. Passenger-train services to Miami began on April 22, 1896, the year the city of Miami became incorporated. Incidentally, this was the same year John S Collins began selling lots out of a 5-mile strip between the Atlantic and Biscayne Bay, or what is now 14th to 67th Sts on Miami Beach (ie most of the city).

Of Miami's 502 original inhabitants, 100 of them were black, conscripted for hard labor and regulated to the northwest neighborhood of Colored Town.

Miami Histories

Miami
(1987; Joan Didion)

The Corpse Had a Familiar Face
(1987; Edna Buchanan)

Black Miami in the Twentieth Century (1997; Marvin Dunn)

This Land Is Our Land: Immigrants and Power in Miami (2003; Alex Stepick)

Miami, USA
(2000; Helen Muir)

1776	Late 1700s	1818	1822
The American Revolution begins, but Florida's two colonies don't rebel. They remain loyal to the British crown, and soon English Tories flood south into Florida to escape the fighting.	Elements of the Creek nation, supplemented by black runaway slaves and their descendants, begin settling in South Florida, displacing local Calusa and Mayaimi Indians.	Andrew Jackson invades Western Florida after violence between settlers and a coalition of Native Americans and blacks. The First Seminole War essentially ends when the USA buys Florida from Spain.	Commodore Matthew C Perry lands on Key West and plants the American flag, claiming the entire Keys island chain for the USA.

During this period, a frenzy of activity was underway to prepare South Florida for extensive settlement. In 1900 Governor Napoleon Bonaparte Broward, envisioning an 'Empire of the Everglades,' set in motion a frenzy of canal building. Over the next 70 years some 1800 miles of canals and levees were etched across Florida's porous limestone. These earthworks drained about half the Everglades (about 1.5 million acres) below Lake Okeechobee, replacing it with farms, cattle ranches, orange groves, sugarcane and suburbs.

Caribbeans & Confederates

For most of the second half of the 19th century, Key West was the largest, wealthiest city in Florida. How did the little island do so well? Wrecking and sponges. Wrecking is the art of salvaging shipwrecks; local boosters liked to make out this was an altruistic act, and many sailors were pulled from the sea, but the cargo on their boats was sold by Keys merchants. Sponges are just that – undersea sponges that became the backbone of the actual American sponge industry for decades.

The population of the island consisted largely of Caribbean émigrés, but mainland Floridians attracted by business opportunities also made their way here. While the presence of a US Naval Base kept Key West in the Union during the American Civil War, many island residents overtly sympathized with the Confederacy.

The First Big Booms

The promise of money and the expansion of Flagler's railway fueled waves of settlement. Population growth peaked during WWI, when the US military established an aviation training facility in Miami. Many of the thousands who came to work and train figured, 'Hey, the weather's nice,' and Miami's population shot from 1681 people in 1900 to almost 30,000 by 1920. The new Floridians wrote home and got relatives in on the act, and after the war came the first full-fledged Miami boom (1923–25), when Coconut Grove and Allapattah were annexed into what was dubbed, for the first time, Greater Miami.

Even then, Miami was built for good times. People wanted to drink and gamble; although it was illegal, liquor flowed freely here throughout the entire Prohibition period.

Depression, Deco & Another World War

Miami's growth was astronomical, and so was its eventual fall: the Great Miami Hurricane of 1926, which left about 220 people dead and up to 50,000 homeless, and the Great Depression. But it's in Miami's nature to weather every disaster with an even better resurgence, and in the interwar period Miami's phoenix rose in two stages.

The main (Downtown Miami) branch of the Miami-Dade Public Library has an extensive Florida collection that constitutes one of the best repositories of state history anywhere. The collection includes some 17,000 photos by Gleason Romer, who snapped South Florida as a photojournalist and amateur shooter from 1925 to the 1950s.

1835	1845	1861	1868
In attacks coordinated by Seminole leader Osceola, Seminoles destroy five sugar plantations on Christmas Day and soon after kill 100 US soldiers marching near Tampa, launching the Second Seminole War.	Florida is admitted to the Union as the 27th state. Since it is a slave state, its admission is balanced by that of Iowa, a free state.	Voting 62 to seven, Florida secedes from the USA, raising its fifth flag, the stars-and-bars of the Confederacy. Florida's farms and cattle provide vital Confederate supplies during the ensuing Civil War.	Florida is re-admitted to the United States, but racial tensions between Southern whites and freed blacks run high, resulting in discriminatory 'Jim Crow' legislation.

After WWII, the advent of effective bug spray and affordable air-conditioning did more for Florida tourism than anything else. With these two technological advancements, Florida's subtropical climate was finally safe for delicate Yankee skin.

First, Franklin Roosevelt's New Deal brought the Civilian Conservation Corps, jobs and a spurt of rise-from-the-ashes building projects. Then, in the early 1930s, a group of mostly Jewish developers began erecting small, stylish hotels along Collins Ave and Ocean Dr, jump-starting a miniboom that resulted in the creation and development of Miami Beach's famous art-deco district.

This led to a brief rise in anti-Semitism, as the Beach became segregated and 'Gentiles Only' signs began to appear. The election of a Jewish governor of Florida in 1933 led to improvement, as did airplane travel, which brought plenty of Jewish visitors and settlers from the north.

During WWII, Miami was a major military training ground, and afterward many of those GIs returned with their families to enjoy Florida's sandy beaches at their leisure. This marked the real beginning of tourism in Florida, and large-scale settlement of South Florida in particular.

Cuba Comes Over

During the 1950s progress seemed inexorable; in 1954 Leroy Collins became the first Southern governor to publicly declare racial segregation 'morally wrong,' while an entire 'Space Coast' was created around Cape Canaveral (between Daytona and Miami on the east coast) to support the development of the National Aeronautics & Space Administration (NASA).

Then, in 1959, Fidel Castro marched onto the 20th-century stage and forever changed the destiny of Cuba and Miami.

As communists swept into Havana, huge portions of the upper and middle classes of Cuba fled north and established a fiercely anti-Castro Cuban community, now as angry as ever about the regime to the south. At the time, counter-revolutionary politics were discussed, and a group of exiles formed the 2506th Brigade, sanctioned by the US government, which provided weapons and Central Intelligence Agency (CIA) training for the purpose of launching a US attack on Cuba.

The resulting badly executed attack is remembered today as the Bay of Pigs fiasco. The first wave of counter-revolutionaries, left on the beach without reinforcements or supplies, were all captured or killed. All prisoners were released by Cuba about three months later.

In the meantime, Castro attracted Soviet missiles to his country, but couldn't keep his people. In 1965 alone some 100,000 Cubans hopped the 'freedom flight' from Havana to Miami.

Racial Tensions

Riots and skirmishes broke out between Cubans and blacks, and blacks and whites, in Miami. In 1968 a riot broke out after it was discovered that two white police officers had arrested a 17-year-old black male, stripped him naked and hung him by his ankles from a bridge.

1905	1912	1925	1926
The first of many attempts to drain the Everglades begins. In coming decades, thousands of acres are destroyed as water is diverted from its natural flow from Lake Okeechobee.	'Flagler's Folly,' Henry Flagler's 128-mile overseas railroad connecting the Florida Keys, reaches Key West. It's hailed as the 'Eighth Wonder of the World,' but is destroyed by a 1935 hurricane.	Coral Gables, one of the first planned communities in the USA, is officially founded. The 'City Beautiful' was designed by real-estate developer George Edgar Merrick.	The Great Miami Hurricane devastates South Florida, killing 220 people, leaving up to 50,000 homeless and causing some $100 million worth of damage. The Great Depression slows recovery.

In 1970 the 'rotten meat' riot began when black locals picketed a white-owned shop they had accused of selling spoiled meat. After three days of picketing, white officers attempted to disperse the crowds and fired on them with tear gas. During the 1970s there were 13 other race-related violent confrontations.

Racial tensions exploded on May 17, 1980, when four white police officers, being tried on charges that they beat a black suspect to death while he was in custody, were acquitted by an all-white jury. When the verdict was announced, race riots broke out all over Miami and lasted for three days.

The Mariel Boatlift

In the late 1970s, Fidel suddenly declared that anyone who wanted to leave Cuba had open access to the docks at Mariel Harbor. Before the ink was dry on the proclamation, the largest flotilla ever launched for nonmilitary purposes set sail (or paddled) from Cuba in practically anything that would float the 90 miles between Cuba and the USA.

The Mariel Boatlift, as the largest of these would be called, brought 125,000 Cubans to Florida, including an estimated 25,000 prisoners and mental patients. Mariel shattered the stereotype of the wealthy Batista-exiled Cuban. The resulting strain on the economy, logistics and infrastructure of South Florida added to still-simmering racial tensions; by 1990 it was estimated that 90% of Miami's Caucasian populace was Hispanic.

The tension carried over from Hispanic-Anglo divisions to rifts between older Cubans and the new *Marielitos*. The middle- to upper-class white Cubans of the 1960s were reintroduced to that nation in the form of thousands of Afro-Cubans and *santeros,* or worshippers of Santería, Cuba's version of *vodou* (voodoo).

Miami Not So Nice

In the 1980s Miami became the major East Coast entry port for drug dealers and their product and earned the nickname 'Mi-Yay-Mi' – 'yay' being slang for cocaine. As if to keep up with the corruption, many savings and loans (S&Ls) opened in newly built Miami headquarters. While *Newsweek* magazine called Miami 'America's Casablanca,' locals dubbed it the 'City with the S&L Skyline.'

A plethora of businesses – legitimate concerns as well as drug-financed fronts – and buildings sprang up all over Miami. Downtown was completely remodeled. But it was reborn in the grip of drug smugglers: shoot-outs were common, as were gangland slayings by cocaine cowboys. At one stage, up to three people per week were being killed in cocaine-related clashes.

The police, Coast Guard, Drug Enforcement Agency (DEA), Border Patrol and the Federal Bureau of Investigation (FBI) were trying to keep

Richard Heyman, who served two terms as mayor of Key West (1983–85 and 1987–89), was perhaps the first openly gay mayor of a sizable US town (and perhaps any US town). In 2010 a documentary on his life, *The Newcomer,* was released. Heyman died of AIDS-related pneumonia in 1994.

1928	1920s–30s	1933–40	1941–45
Ernest Hemingway pens *A Farewell to Arms* in Key West, supposedly while awaiting the delivery of a car. His wife's uncle gives the Hemingways a local house in 1931.	A small spit of land located across Biscayne Bay, known as Miami Beach, becomes dotted with hotels and resorts, presaging its emergence as a tourism hot spot.	New Deal public-works projects employ 40,000 Floridians and help save Florida from the Depression. The most notable construction project is the Overseas Hwy through the Keys.	USA enters WWII. Two million men and women receive basic training in South Florida. At one point, the army commandeers 85% of Miami Beach hotels to house personnel.

track of it all. Roadblocks were set up along the Overseas Hwy to Key West (prompting the quirky and headstrong residents down there to call for a secession, which eventually sent the police on their way).

The TV series *Miami Vice* was single-handedly responsible for Miami Beach rising to international fabulousness in the mid-1980s, its slick soundtrack and music-video-style montages glamorizing the rich South Florida lifestyle. Before long, people were coming down to check it out for themselves – especially photographer Bruce Weber, who began using South Beach as a gritty and fashionable backdrop for modeling shoots in the early 1980s.

Celebrities were wintering in Miami, international photographers were shooting here, and the Art Deco Historic District, having been granted federal protection, was going through renovation and renaissance. Gay men, always on the cutting edge of trends, discovered South Beach's gritty glamour. The city was becoming a showpiece of fashion and trendiness.

The 1990s & 2000s

A combination of Hurricane Andrew and a crime wave against tourists, particularly carjackings, equaled a drop in visitors, until tourist-oriented community policing and other visible programs reversed the curse. Miami went from being the US city with the most violent crime to one with average crime statistics for a city its size. From 1992 to 1998, tourist-related crimes decreased by a whopping 80%.

In 2000 the Cuban–American population dominated headlines again during the Elián Gonzalez nightmare, an international custody fight that ended with heavily armed federal agents storming the Little Havana house where the seven-year-old was staying to have him shipped back to Cuba while anti-Castro Cubans protested in Miami streets.

On the bright side, corruption was slightly cleaned out after the removal of Mayor Xavier Suarez in 1998, whose election was overturned following the discovery of many illegal votes. Manuel 'Manny' Diaz, who had been a lawyer for the Miami-based Gonzalez family, followed Suarez as mayor and pushed for cementing ties between Miami and the Latin American world – he was fond of saying, 'When Venezuela or Argentina sneezes, Miami catches a cold.'

During the 2000s Miami proper underwent more 'Manhattanization,' with more and more skyscrapers altering the city skyline. There are currently 307 high-rise buildings in Miami, 59 of which stand taller than 400ft. At the same time, Diaz began working to use arts districts and buildings – the former represented by Wynwood and Midtown, the latter by the Adrienne Arsht Center for the Performing Arts – to revitalize blighted areas of town.

Water and a lack of it have always been nagging fears in South Florida, one of the fastest-growing population areas of the country, but the issue

1942	1947	1961	1980
From January to August, German U-boats sink more than two dozen tankers and ships off Florida's coast. By war's end, Florida holds nearly 3000 German POWs in 15 labor camps.	Everglades National Park is established, the successful culmination of a 19-year effort led by Ernest Coe and Marjory Stoneman Douglas to protect the Everglades from harm done by dredging and draining.	Brigade 2506, a 1300-strong volunteer army, invades Cuba's Bay of Pigs on April 16. President Kennedy withholds air support, leading to Brigade 2506's immediate defeat and capture by Fidel Castro.	Cuba's Castro 'opens the floodgates.' The USA's ensuing Mariel Boatlift rescues from Cuba 125,000 *Marielitos,* who face intense discrimination in Miami.

took on new urgency in the 2000s. By the late 1990s, the South Florida aquifer seemed in danger of depletion. The solution seemed to rest in the Comprehensive Everglades Restoration Plan (CERP), which was passed in 2000. Said project is aimed at restoring the flow of water to the Everglades from Lake Okeechobee, which would subsequently help replenish the South Florida aquifer and the state's most iconic wilderness space. At the time of research, the US National Research Council had determined that progress toward restoring the core of the Glades was proceeding very slowly, and quicker action was needed.

In the normally placid Keys, protests, heated town-hall meetings and various civic master plans tried to address the impact of skyrocketing costs of living on an island chain where there isn't much room to build new houses. During this period, commuter buses running from Homestead were packed full of the service industry workers, teachers and other backbone members of the community who could no longer afford a trailer or apartment in the Keys. Today there is high pressure on new housing projects in the islands to provide affordable units.

Recent History

Prior to the outbreak of the global pandemic, South Florida was thriving. It had a diverse and open-minded population, low unemployment and a strong economy. After a string of high-performing years, the state's economy reached $1.1 trillion by early 2020 — making it the fourth largest in the US. The region, however, suffered heavily during the coronavirus outbreak, with unemployment reaching above 10% in 2020, and over $50 billion in lost economic activity.

Climate change poses an even graver long-term threat to the region. Warmer ocean temperatures have led to more frequent and more destructive hurricanes striking South Florida in recent years. In September 2017, the massive category 4 Hurricane Irma made landfall in the Florida Keys and tore its way up through the state, killing 84 people. It also knocked out power to more than seven million homes, dumped record levels of rainfall — over 21in (550mm) in parts — and caused $50 billion worth of damage, making it by far the costliest hurricane in the state's history.

Florida is America's most at-risk state for sea-level rise. Chronic flooding already plagues some neighborhoods during heavy rainstorms or king tides (exceptionally high tides), and the storm damage is expected to grow worse in the years ahead. In 2020 the US Army Corps of Engineers unveiled a $4.6 billion plan to protect Miami's waterfront, given that sea levels are projected to rise 3.5ft over the next 60 years. This would include 13ft floodwalls, as well as storm surge barriers and pumps, in addition to elevating roadways, homes and businesses in vulnerable areas. Approval and funding, however, would be up to local officials and Congress — a dicey proposal given state leaders often openly disavow climate change.

Historic Homes

Merrick House
(Coral Gables)

Vizcaya Museum & Gardens
(Coconut Grove)

Biltmore Hotel
(Coral Gables)

Hemingway House
(Key West)

HISTORY THE 1990S & 2000S

1992	2000	2010	2017
On August 24, Hurricane Andrew devastates Dade County, leaving 41 people dead, more than 200,000 homeless and causing about $15.5 billion in damage.	The Comprehensive Everglades Restoration Plan (CERP) is put into action. The 30-year plan aims to restore natural water flow to the Everglades and replenish South Florida's water reservoirs.	The *Deepwater Horizon/* BP oil disaster results in 11 deaths and 4.9 million barrels of oil being spilled into the Gulf of Mexico.	Rated a category 4 hurricane at landfall, 650-mile-wide Irma blasts up the Florida coastline, killing 84 people and causing $50 billion worth of damage.

Multiculturalism & the Arts

South Florida is an intersection of Middle America, Latin America and the Caribbean, a clash of idiosyncratic types who decided miles of marshland, beach, mangroves and islets were a place where the American dream could be realized to subtropical perfection. It's also a place often misunderstood by outsiders, though the region's burgeoning arts scene – music, film, literature and the plastic arts – helps shed a light on its multilayered complexity.

Above Calle Ocho (p73)

Greater Multicultural Miami

Contemporary South Florida is certainly more than Miami, but if the local distinct regional identity has an anchor city, Miami is that town. With that said, while Miami's energy impacts the Keys and the Glades (particularly the former), these other areas are more demographically homogenous, and in the case of Key West, have their own unique histories of settlement and demographic shift.

Miami

It would still be silly not to recognize Miami as the center of South Florida's cultural gravity. Which begs the question: what makes Miami, well, Miami? Basically it's the mix: that conspicuous jumble of Cubans, Haitians, Anglos, Jews, Asians, and South and Central Americans of all stripes. Miami possesses the best and worst of its parent cultures: immigrant and migrant narratives that are embraced and rejected and spliced and diced into entirely new paradigms.

It can be difficult to meet someone from Miami who has more than two generations of connection to the city. At the negative end, this lack of connection can manifest as a detached sense of place and resentment toward other newcomers. Miami is not without tensions between its myriad communities. On the positive side are those Miamians concerned with building an identity for their town; the ones who patronize local sport and arts, and extend a helping hand toward newcomers from across America or the Gulf of Mexico. It almost goes without saying, but Miami's cultural capital, even among Asian and Anglo citizens, is largely derived from the Caribbean and Latin America.

The Everglades

Rural Florida can still evoke America's western frontier, and the Everglades, the wildest part of the state, remains very much a hinterland populated by either frontier types or people who self-conceptualize as frontier types. The Old West trope is exacerbated by the fact that there is still a settlement pattern here of colonizers and Native Americans; the Seminole and Miccosukee tribes constitute a major part of the 'Glades' population. Their neighbors in Homestead and Everglades City are largely descended from those who came here in the 19th century, after the West was won, when Florida became one of the last places where pioneers could simply plant stakes and make a life on ostensibly unclaimed land (well, unclaimed if you weren't Native American).

These pioneers became Florida's 'Crackers,' the poor rural farmers, fisherfolk, cowhands and outlaws who traded the comforts of civilization for independence on their terms. Many Crackers came from the old Southern states, and created a culture not too far removed, geographic or otherwise, from the Confederacy. In parts of Southern America, the term cracker is pejorative, but it has a specific connotation in Florida that is a badge of honor, as evidenced by the annual Cracker Storytelling Festival and *Crackers in the Glade,* a classic illustrated account of growing up in the Everglades region, among other cultural ephemera.

A bit of Southern-fried hospitality and Western independence is a feisty combination, but therein lie the roots of many Glades citizens. Even the local Native Americans share these qualities; it may surprise you to see large Confederate flags and Ford F-250 pickup trucks jamming many a Seminole nation parking lot, although many Seminole and Miccosukee also retain elements of indigenous culture. Most Everglades citizens, like rural people in much of the USA, place a high value on self-reliance and perceived freedom from government.

Finally it'd be remiss not to mention the large number of Mexicans who now call Homestead home, the majority attracted by jobs working on nearby farms. As you drive south from Miami, the shift from Cuban Spanish to Mexican Spanish is quite distinct, even to an untrained ear.

Miami Classics

....

'Bailando'
Enrique Iglesias
....
'Jaspora'
Wyclef Jean
....
'Rakata'
Wisin y Yandel
....
'Right Round'
Flo Rida
....
'Save Hialeah Park'
Los Primeros
....
'Swamp Music'
Lynyrd Skynyrd
....
'Welcome to Miami'
Pitbull

MULTICULTURALISM & THE ARTS GREATER MULTICULTURAL MIAMI

EXPERIENCING MULTICULTURAL MIAMI

The following guide may help you understand some of Miami's most prominent ethnic groups.

Cuban Miami

The most important cultural symbols of Cuban Miami are concentrated in Little Havana, particularly near 8th St/Calle Ocho. Other parts of town where you can get a strong sense of Cuban identity include Hialeah, where over 90% of the population speaks Spanish as a first language.

➡ Little Havana (p73) The old heart of Cuban Miami.

➡ Viernes Culturales (p88) A regular Latin street celebration.

➡ Versailles (p108) The most storied standby of culinary Cuban Florida.

➡ Cubaocho (p121) Meeting point of the Cuban diaspora, who come for (great) intimate concerts and art exhibitions.

➡ Máximo Gómez Park (p73) Watch old Cubans trade dominoes and jibes.

Haitian Miami

Little Haiti is by far one of the most colorful neighborhoods in the city. It can be rough after dark, so try and visit during the day, unless the Sounds of Little Haiti (p88) monthly street party is happening.

➡ Libreri Mapou (p123) A Haitian-related library.

➡ Little Haiti Cultural Complex (p73) Community center for Haitian Miami.

➡ Chef Creole (p107) Traditional Haitian food in Little Haiti.

Spanish Miami

Spaniards have been settling in Miami in large numbers for the past few decades. There is no one part of Spain that produces these new arrivals; in one part of Miami you'll find people from the Basque country who resent being called 'Spanish,' while in another you may break bread with Catalans in one restaurant and Castilians in another. Many of the best high-end grocery stores, bakeries, cheese shops and meat shops in Miami are run by Spaniards.

➡ El Carajo (p109) A semi-hidden tapas joint beloved by Spanish expats.

The Keys

The Keys constitute a fascinating combination of white Floridians, Caribbean islanders and just about anyone attracted to living an island lifestyle that's still technically in the borders of the USA. As the Keys have been settled by non–Native Americans longer than Miami, there is a distinct local culture that's a little bit country in the Outer Keys, and elegantly eccentric in Key West. Regardless of where you're from, if you're born in the Keys, you're considered a Conch – one of the members of a tribe whose bond is life amid the islands.

There's a great deal of pride in the Keys themselves and their independence from the mainland. And while many people, especially in the Outer Keys, have conservative attitudes on gun control and the environment (ie less regulation related to both), there's also a great deal of tolerance for alternative lifestyles. Maybe because just choosing to live out here is an alternative lifestyle decision.

The search for an alternative lifestyle, plus geographic isolation, led many gay people to Key West. Richard Heyman, who was mayor of the city from 1983 to '85 and 1987 to '89, was one of the first openly gay mayors of an American city. The *Key West Citizen* has even argued that, in regards to LGBTQI+ politics, Key West is essentially post-sexual identity. Anything has gone for so long that nothing (between consenting adults) is off-limits.

Jewish Miami

Jews were some of the first developers and residents of Miami Beach. They've maintained a strong presence here for decades and the Miami metro area has the nation's second-largest concentration of Jewish residents. The area around 41st St in North Miami Beach and 95th and Harding in Surfside are both streets where you'll see lots of Jewish businesses and community organizations.

➜ Jewish Museum of Florida-FIU (p59) Center for research on Jewish Florida.

➜ Temple Emanu-El (p63) One of the area's largest synagogues.

➜ Josh's Deli (p102) Delectable avant-garde (including un-kosher) Jewish fare.

➜ Roasters 'n Toasters (p102) A favorite Jewish deli.

Brazilian Miami

Miami's Brazilians are mainly found in northern Miami Beach: working, partying, eating and blending into the Miami milieu. There is also a noticeably large population of recent Brazilian expats, including designers, DJs, musicians, fashionistas, models and their respective entourages; these Brazilians tend to base themselves in South Beach with the other jet-setters.

➜ Boteco (p117) Popular Brazilian watering hole.

Colombian Miami

You'll find many Colombians with their South American brethren in northern Miami Beach, but there are also plenty of Colombians in Coral Gables (where the Colombian consulate is located).

➜ La Moon (p103) Late-night Colombian eats attract the Colombian community.

➜ San Pocho (p109) Classic Colombian restaurant in Little Havana.

Nicaraguan Miami

Central Americans make up a large percentage of the population of 'Cuban' areas such as Little Havana, with Nicaragua leading the way – currently, Nicaraguans represent nearly half of the Central American population in Miami.

➜ Yambo (p109) An enormously good-value *fritanga* (Nicaraguan diner).

The Arts in South Florida

Art, music and literature permeate South Florida's daily life. Because this region has a pretty face, many people think it has a correspondingly shallow mind. The stereotype isn't fair. Because what makes South Florida beautiful, from the bodies on the beach to the structure of the skyline, is diversity. The energies of the Western Hemisphere have been channeled into this Gateway to the Americas, and a lot of that drive is rooted in creativity and a search for self-expression.

This artistic impulse tends to derive from the immigrant experience – which this region has in spades. The pain of exile, the flush of financial success and the frustration of being shut out of the often callous American dream provide ample inspiration for the arts. Living in a country where you can't be arrested for public expression helps too. Miami's greatest quality, its inborn tolerance for eccentricity, is at the root of such public innovations as the Arab fantasy-land architecture of Opa Locka, the modernistic design of the Art Deco Historic District and the condominium-lined skyscraper corridors of Brickell.

In addition, there is always a sense of the possible coupled with the fantasy of excess. Plenty of people dismiss Coral Gables and the Vizcaya mansion as gauche and tacky, and through modern eyes they may appear as such. But they were revolutionary for their time. During the early 20th

Naked Came the Manatee (1998) is a collaborative mystery novel by a constellation of famous Florida writers: Carl Hiaasen, Dave Barry, Elmore Leonard, James Hall, Edna Buchanan and more. It's like nibbling a delectable box of cyanide-laced chocolates.

century, concepts such as a Mediterranean Revival village that served as a bulwark against sprawl, or an Italianate villa carved out of the seashore, would not have flown in the aesthetically conservative Northeast, but they found legs here.

Putting Miami on the Arts Map

Miami's citizens and their memories, realities and visions have created a burgeoning art scene that truly began to be noticed with the 2002 introduction of Art Basel Miami Beach (p26), the US outpost of an annual erudite gathering that's based in Switzerland. By its second year, the event had created a buzz throughout the national art world – and had succeeded in wooing 175 exhibitors, more than 30,000 visitors and plenty of celebs to take over the galleries, clubs and hotels of South Beach and the Design District. It has grown, in both size and strength, each year since, and its impact on the local art scene cannot be overstated; today Art Basel Miami Beach is the biggest contemporary arts festival in the Western Hemisphere.

Public Art

This city has always been way ahead of the curve when it comes to public art. Miami and Miami Beach established the Art in Public Places program back in 1973, when it voted to allocate 1.5% of city construction funds to the fostering of public art. Since then more than 700 works – sculptures, mosaics, murals, light-based installations and more – have been created in public spots.

Barbara Neijna's *Foreverglades,* in Concourse J of Miami International Airport, uses mosaic, art-installed text from *River of Grass* (by Marjory Stoneman Douglas) and waves representing the movement of water over grass to give new arrivals a sense of the flow of Florida's unique ecosystem. A series of handprints representing Miami's many immigrant communities link into a single community in *Reaching for Miami Skies,* by Connie Lloveras, which greets Metromover commuters at Brickell Station. In Miami-Dade Library, the floating text of *Words Without Thought Never to Heaven Go* by Edward Ruscha challenges readers to engage in thought processes that are inspired by, but go beyond, the books that surround them. The team of Roberto Behar and Rosario Marquardt, hailing from Argentina, have been among the most prolific public artists in town, to the degree that their work is deliberately meant to warp conceptions of what is or isn't public space; they created the giant red *M* at the Metromover Riverwalk Station for the city's centennial back in 1996. Japanese-American artist Isamu Noguchi designed Bayfront Park in 1986, which is also where you can see Noguchi's *Slide Mantra,* a Carrera marble sculpture that's both playful and meditative.

BRIGHT BRITTO

If the top public artist of a given city determines how said city sees itself, we must conclude Miami is a cartoon-like, cubist, chaotic place of bright, happy, shiny joy.

That's the aesthetic legacy Romero Britto is leaving this town. The seemingly perpetually grinning Brazilian émigré, clad in jackets leftover from a 1980s MTV video, was the hot face of public art in the 2000s, having designed the mural of the Miami Children's Museum (p71), the 'Welcome' structure at Dadeland North Station, the central sculpture at the shops at Midtown and many others. You might need sunglasses to appreciate his work, which appeals to the islander in all of us: Saturday-morning cartoon brights, sharp geometric lines and loopy curls, inner-child character studies and, underlying everything, a scent of teal oceans on a sunny day.

A good place to check out his work is at the **Britto Central** gallery at 818 Lincoln Rd.

Ball & Chain (p117)

Music

As in all things, it's the mad diversity of Miami that makes its music so appealing. The southbound path of American country and Southern rock, the northbound rhythms of the Caribbean and Latin America, and the homegrown beats of Miami's African American community get mixed into a musical crossroads of the Americas. Think about the sounds the above influences produce, and you'll hear a certain thread: bouncy and percussive with a tune you can always dance to.

These sounds, rooted in the New World, are fighting against interlopers from a far shore: Europeans and their waves of techno, house and EDM. Euro-expats have brought a strong club-music scene, best evidenced by the annual Winter Music Conference in March, which brings thousands of DJs and producers to town. The gay community has traditionally been a receptive audience for club music, and many club nights have crossover with gay parties.

Miami's heart and soul is Latin, and that goes for its music as well. Producers and artists from across Latin America come here for high-quality studio facilities, the lure of global distribution and the Billboard Latin Music Conference & Awards, held here each April. The Magic City has been the cradle of stars such as Gloria Estefan, Ricky Martin and Albita, and a scan over the local airwaves always yields far more Spanish-language stations than English, playing a mix of salsa, *son* (an Afro-Cuban-Spanish mélange of musical styles), conga and reggaeton.

Here's a quick crib sheet for your Miami nightclub explorations.

Salsa is the most commonly heard word used to reference Latin music and dance. It's a generic term developed in the mid-1960s and early '70s to pull all Latin sounds under one umbrella name for gringos who couldn't recognize the subtle differences between beats. From the Spanish word for 'sauce,' salsa has its roots in Cuban culture and has a sound that's enhanced by textures of jazz. Music that lends itself to salsa dancing has four beats per bar of music.

One specific type of Cuban salsa is *son* – a sound popularized by the release of 1999's *Buena Vista Social Club*. It has roots in African and Spanish cultures and is quite melodic, usually incorporating instruments including the *tres* (a type of guitar with three sets of closely spaced strings), standard guitars and various hand drums.

Temple Emanu-El (p63)

Merengue originates from the Dominican Republic and can be characterized by a very fast beat, with just two beats to each bar. It's typically played on the *tamboura*, *guiro* (a ridged cylindrical percussion instrument made of metal or dried gourd) and accordion.

Hailing from the Andalusian region of Spain is the folk art of flamenco, which consists of hand clapping, finger snapping, vocals, guitar and the flamboyant dance. Miami's Argentines love to tango, a Buenos Aires invention that draws off European classical dance and the immigrant experience of South America's French, Italian, African and indigenous ethnic enclaves.

The popular reggae sound, originating in Jamaica and having strong Rastafarian roots, is a total movement most popularly associated with Bob Marley. It's characterized by rhythm chops on a backbeat and, at least in its beginnings, a political-activist message. There are various styles within reggae, including roots (Marley's sound), dancehall, raga and dub.

But it's rare to just hear one of the above. Miami is a polyglot kind of town, and it loves to blend techno with *son,* give an electronic backbeat to salsa, and overlay everything with dub, hip-hop and *bomba* (African-influenced Puerto Rican dance music). This mixed marriage produces a lot of musical children, and the most recognizable modern sound derived from the above is reggaeton, a driving mash-up that plays like Spanish rap shoved through a sexy backbeat and thumpin' dancehall speakers. Pioneers of the genre include Daddy Yankee, Don Chezina, Tito El Bambino, Wisin Y Yandel, Calle 13 and producers such as Luny Tunes and Noriega, while recent artists like Luis Fonsi have garnered a worldwide following for breakaway pop-reggaeton hits like 'Despacito.' Although it largely originated in Puerto Rico, reggaeton is one of the few musical styles that can get Latinos from across the Americas – from Nicaraguans to Mexicans to Colombians – shaking it.

Miami's hip-hop has had a bit of a circular evolution, from early '90s Miami bass (dirty-dance music, exemplified by 2 Live Crew) to more aggressive, street-style rap, which has blended and morphed into today's club-oriented tracks. These modern sounds draw off the crunk beats, Southern drawls and Atlanta overproduction of the Dirty South sound. Local hip-hop heroes work hard to keep Miami on the map and strongly rep neighborhoods such as Opa Locka, Liberty City and Overtown; artists to listen for include DJ Smallz, Rick Ross, Flo Rida, Morgan Bryson, and FloKid and Nil Bambu. It'd also be remiss not to mention Pitbull, who has successfully branded his sound as a bridge between reggaeton, hip-hop and pop.

There has been a small but strong indie-rock boom over the past decade, mainly centered on Sweat Records and Churchill's in Little Haiti. Besides Churchill's, other good spots to see the cutting edge of Miami rock are Ball & Chain, Gramps and Lagniappe.

Literature

Writers need to be around good stories to keep their narrative wits sharp, and no place provides stories quite like South Florida, where farmers clash with environmentalists who fight financiers, while immigrants arrive from a hundred different countries and a hurricane hits every summer. This proximity to real-life drama means, unsurprisingly, many of Miami's best authors cut their teeth in journalism. As a result, there's a breed of Miami prose that has the terse punch of the best newspaper writing. Beginning with former *Miami Herald* crime-beat reporters Edna Buchanan and Carl Hiaasen, and leading to new names like Jeff Lindsay, the Miami crime-writing scene is alive and well.

On the other hand, local immigrant communities have lent this town's literature the poetry of exiled tongues, narratives that find a thread through the diaspora alleyways that underline Florida's identity. Look out for Carolina Garcia-Aguilera, Edwidge Danticat, Diana Abu-Jaber and Karen Russell. And finally, the subtle beauty of South Florida has produced a certain breed of nature writer that is able to capture the nuances of the region's subdued scenery while explaining the complicated science that runs through it all – Marjory Stoneman Douglas and Ted Levin spring to mind. Pulitzer Prize–finalist Karen Russell often combines sensuous nature imagery with a sprinkling of sometimes-funny, sometimes-ominous magical realism.

Film & TV

Crime sells this city – at least cinematically. Sam Katzman chose Miami for B-movies about gang wars, and several (lowbrow) classics – as well as the *Jackie Gleason Show* – in the 1960s. *Scarface,* Brian De Palma's over-the-top story of the excesses of capitalism, entered Miami into hip-hop's common lexicon; and *Miami Vice,* the 1980s TV series about a couple of pastel-clad vice-squad cops, put Miami on the international map. A pretty mediocre Hollywood film version starring Colin Farrell and Jamie Foxx, released in 2006, capitalized on the '80s nostalgia market.

There have been loads of comedies filmed here as well, including *The Birdcage,* a 1996 hit starring the late Robin Williams and Nathan Lane, who play a flamboyant couple trying to play it straight in South Beach. Deco-lined Ocean Dr (particularly the reconfigured Carlyle Hotel) played a supporting role. More recently, Amazon Prime's streaming series *The Marvelous Mrs. Maisel* filmed its third season (2019) in Miami. Iconic locales like the Fontainebleau (p93) in Mid-Beach and Key Biscayne form the backdrop to a New York housewife navigating the world of stand-up comedy in the late 1950s.

One of the best American films of recent years shined a spotlight on a community often overlooked in Miami. *Moonlight,* ostensibly a

Two of the best film festivals in Florida are the Miami International Film Festival (www.miamifilmfestival.com), which is a showcase for Latin cinema (March), and the up-and-coming Florida Film Festival (www.floridafilmfestival.com) in Orlando (April).

MULTICULTURALISM & THE ARTS THE ARTS IN SOUTH FLORIDA

CARL HIAASEN: LOVING THE LUNACY

In Carl Hiaasen's *Florida,* the politicians are corrupt, the rednecks are violent, the tourists are clueless, the women are fast and the ambience is smoky noir, brightened by a few buckets of loony pastel. Some would say the man knows his home state.

Hiaasen, who worked at the *Miami Herald* for decades and is now a Keys resident (he met his wife while reading in the Keys bar she managed), is both a writer gifted with crisp prose and a journalist blessed by a reporter's instinct for the offbeat. His success has rested in his ability to basically take the hyperbolic reality that is Florida and tell it to the world. Although his fiction is just that, in many ways it simply draws off the day-to-day eccentricities of the Sunshine State and novelizes them. In *Tourist Season* Hiaasen turns his pen on ecozealots with a story about a terrorist group that tries to dissuade tourists from coming to Florida and further wrecking the state – namely, by feeding them to a crocodile named Pavlov. In complete thematic contrast comes *Hoot,* a heart-warming tale (odd for Hiaasen) catering to young adults about a 12-year-old boy's fight against a corporation that threatens to pave over a Coconut Grove colony of burrowing owls. *Stormy Weather* takes on the corruption, bureaucracy and disaster tourism that fills the vacuum of the devastation trail left by a hurricane.

Hiaasen's work tends to career between satire and thriller, and betrays both an unceasingly critical eye and deep affection for all of Florida's quirks. Which ironically makes Hiaasen – enemy of almost every special-interest group in the Sunshine State – the state's biggest promoter. He is a man who loves Florida despite its warts and that, folks, is true romance.

coming-of-age tale, showed what it was like to grow up poor, black and gay in a Miami housing project. It's a beautifully shot film, intensely personal and full of beauty and complexity (drug dealers as father figures, close friends as betrayers). It garnered much critical praise after its 2016 release, winning three Academy Awards including the 2017 Oscar for Best Picture.

Fashion

With Miami a trendsetter in the realm of cuisine, nightlife and the arts, it makes sense that the city would gain acclaim in the world of fashion. And it has, with the annual Miami Fashion Week drawing attention from across the globe. These days the focus is on resort wear, which fits well with the city's aesthetic – since Miami is a beach-loving kind of city. The weeklong event leans heavily toward Latin American designers, representing both well-known brands and up-and-coming labels.

Miami has also gained cred among European designers (ironically ever since one of them, Gianni Versace, was killed here) and draws mavens from all over the Old World who find something inspiring in the combination of a Latin emphasis on appearance versus the American love of comfort and the dare-to-bare styles inspired by the sunny weather.

So what defines the 'Miami look'? On the one hand, you'll see a desperate desire for brand-name cred, of Louis Vuitton–endowed affirmation. But on the flip side is the understated sense of cool that comes from all that heat, exemplified by a casual dressiness the best-looking Miamians accomplish without any apparent effort. Note, for example, the older Cuban man lounging in his *guayabera,* an elegant but simple brocaded men's shirt; he's classy because he's looking good without seeming to try.

There is a distinctive South Beach style and there's no better place to buy it than at the source, but be warned: you must be bold, unabashed and bikini-waxed to pull off some of the more risqué outfits on display.

Environment

Naturalist Marjory Stoneman Douglas called Florida 'a long pointed spoon' that is as 'familiar as the map of North America itself.' On that map, the shapely Floridian peninsula represents one of the most ecologically diverse regions in the world. A confluence of porous rock and subtropical climate gave rise to a watery world of uncommon abundance and lush beauty, but this unique ecosystem could be undone by human hands in the geological blink of an eye.

The Land

Florida is many things, but elevated it is not. This state is as flat as a pancake, or as Douglas said, like a spoon of freshwater resting delicately in a bowl of saltwater – a spongy brick of limestone hugged by the Atlantic Ocean and the Gulf of Mexico. The highest point, the Panhandle's Britton Hill, has to stretch to reach 350ft, which isn't half as tall as the buildings of Downtown Miami. This makes Florida officially the nation's flattest state, despite being 22nd in total area with 58,560 sq miles.

Above: Everglades
National Park (p138)

However, more than 4000 of those square miles are water; lakes and springs pepper the map like bullet holes in a road sign. To the south is Lake Okeechobee, the 9th largest freshwater lake in North America. This sounds impressive, but the bottom of the lake is only a few feet above sea level, and it's so shallow you can practically wade across.

Every year Lake Okeechobee ever so gently floods the southern tip of the peninsula. Or it wants to; canals divert much of the flow to either irrigation fields or Florida's bracketing major bodies of water – the Gulf of Mexico and the Atlantic Ocean. But were the water to follow the natural lay of the land, it would flow down: from its center, the state of Florida inclines about 6in every 6 miles until the peninsula can't keep its head above water anymore. What was an unelevated plane peters out into the 10,000 Islands and the Florida Keys, which end with a flourish in the Gulf of Mexico. Key West, the last in the chain, is the southernmost point in the continental USA.

Incidentally, when the waters of Okeechobee do flood the South Florida plane, they interact with the local grasslands and limestone to create a wilderness unlike any other: the Everglades. They also fill up the freshwater aquifers that are required to maintain human existence in the ever-urbanizing Miami area. Today numerous plans, which seem to fall prey to private interest and public bureaucratic roadblocks, are discussed for restoring the original flow of water from Central to South Florida, an act that would revitalize the Glades and, to some degree, address the water supply needs of Greater Miami.

What really sets Florida apart, though, is that it occupies a subtropical transition zone between northern temperate and southern tropical climates. This is crucial to the coast's florid coral-reef system, the largest in North America, and the key to Florida's attention-getting collection of surreal swamps, botanical oddities and monstrous critters. The

KEEPERS OF THE EVERGLADES

Anyone who has dipped a paddle among the saw grass and hardwood hammocks of Everglades National Park wouldn't quibble with the American alligator's Florida sobriquet, 'Keepers of the Everglades.' With snout, eyeballs and pebbled back so still they hardly ripple the water's surface, alligators have watched over the Glades for more than 200 million years.

It's impossible to count Florida's wild alligators, but estimates are that 1.5 million lumber among the state's lakes, rivers and golf courses. No longer officially endangered, they remain protected because they resemble the still-endangered American crocodile. Alligator served in restaurants typically comes from licensed alligator farms, though since 1988 Florida has conducted an annual alligator harvest, open to nonresidents, that allows two alligators per person.

Alligators are alpha predators that keep the rest of the food chain in check, and their 'gator holes' become vital water cups in the dry season and during droughts, aiding the entire wetlands ecosystem. Alligators, which live for about 30 years, can grow up to 14ft long and weigh 1000lb.

A vocal courtship begins in April, and mating takes place in May and June. By late June, females begin laying nests of 30 to 45 eggs, which incubate for two months before hatching. On average, only four alligators per nest survive to adulthood.

Alligators hunt in water, often close to shore; typically, they run on land to flee, not to chase. In Florida an estimated 15 to 20 nonfatal attacks on humans occur each year, and there have been 22 fatal attacks since 1948.

Some estimate an alligator's top short-distance land speed at 30mph, but it's a myth that you must zigzag to avoid them. The best advice is to run in a straight line as fast as your little legs can go.

White pelicans and cormorants, 10,000 Islands (p146)

Everglades gets the most press, and as an International Biosphere, World Heritage Site and national park, this 'river of grass' deserves it.

But the Keys are a crucially important, vital and unique treasure as well. To explore these islands is to enter genuine jungle while still technically within the Lower 48 (admittedly, as low as you can get in that Lower 48). The teal and blue waterways that separate the Keys are as fascinating as the islands themselves; here the water gets so shallow that you can sometimes wade from key to key. Couple this shallow shelf with the rich sunlight of South Florida and you get one of the world's most productive aquatic biomes.

> The Everglades once stretched over some 11,000 square miles, but today the wetlands are less than half the size they were a century ago.

Wildlife

Get outside Miami's concrete jungle and you'd be forgiven for thinking you'd entered a real one. Alligators prowl the swamps, the USA's only crocodiles nest in the Keys, birds that resemble pteranodons flap over it all, and underneath rolls that gentle giant, the manatee.

Birds

Nearly 500 avian species have been documented in Florida, including some of the world's most magnificent migratory water birds: ibis, egrets, great blue herons, white pelicans and whooping cranes. This makes Florida a birder's paradise.

Nearly 350 species spend time in the Everglades, the prime birding spot in Florida. In fact, much of the initial attention to conservation that first popped up here was related to the illegal poaching of Everglades' wading birds; the beautiful beasts were being killed so their plumage could decorate fashionable women's hats in the early 20th century.

Songbirds and raptors fill Florida skies, too. The state has over 1000 mated pairs of bald eagles, the most in the southern USA, and peregrine falcons, who can dive up to 150mph, migrate through in spring and fall.

ENVIRONMENT WILDLIFE

Squirrel tree frog, Everglades National Park (p138)

Audubon of Florida (fl. audubon.org) is perhaps Florida's leading conservation organization. It has tons of birding and ecological information, and it publishes *Florida Naturalist* magazine.

The Everglades aren't the only place to bird-watch around here. Completed in 2006, the Great Florida Birding Trail (http://florida birdingtrail.com) runs 2000 miles across the entire state and includes nearly 500 bird-watching sites, including many South Florida stops outside the Glades. Other good spots for birding in the region:

- Oleta River State Park (p64)
- Arch Creek Park (p78)
- Haulover Beach Park (p64)
- Bill Baggs Cape Florida State Park (p77)
- Crandon Park (p77)
- Indian Key Historic State Park (p170)
- Lignumvitae Key Botanical State Park (p170)
- Curry Hammock State Park (p173)
- Crane Point Hammock (p173)
- Bahia Honda State Park (p176)

There's also the Laura Quinn Wild Bird Sanctuary (p166) in the Upper Keys, where injured birds are nursed back to health by a lovely team of volunteers. Guests are welcome to walk the paths that meander past the hurt bird life.

Land Mammals

Florida's most endangered mammal is the Florida panther. Before European contact, perhaps 1500 roamed the state. The first panther bounty ($5 a scalp) was passed in 1832, and over the next 130 years they were hunted relentlessly. Though hunting was stopped in 1958, it was too late for panthers to survive on their own. Without a captive breeding program, begun in 1991, the Florida panther would now be extinct. With only some 120 known to exist, they're not out of the swamp yet.

The biggest killers of the panthers are motor vehicles. Every year a handful – sometimes more – of panthers are killed on the road; pay particular attention to speed limits posted in areas like the Tamiami Trail, which cuts through Everglades National Park and the Big Cypress Preserve.

Endemic to the Keys are the endangered Key deer, a Honey-I-Shrunk-the-Ungulate subspecies: less than 3ft tall and lighter than a 10-year-old boy, they live mostly on Big Pine Key.

Although they are ostensibly native to the American West, the adaptable coyote has been spotted across Florida, appearing as far south as the Florida Keys.

Shy, timid and not to be messed with if encountered, there are several hundred specimens of the Florida black bear in Everglades National Park and the Big Cypress Preserve.

Reptiles & Amphibians

Boasting an estimated 184 species, Florida has the nation's largest collection of reptiles and amphibians, and unfortunately, it's growing – invasive scaly species are wreaking havoc with Florida's delicate, native ecosystem. Uninvited guests add to the total regularly, many establishing themselves after being released by pet owners. Some of the more dangerous, problematic and invasive species include Burmese pythons, black and green iguanas, and Nile monitor lizards.

The American alligator is Florida's poster species, and they are ubiquitous in Central and South Florida. They don't pose much of a threat to humans unless you do something irredeemably stupid, like feed or provoke them. With that said, you may want to keep small children and pets away from unfamiliar inland bodies of water.

South Florida is also home to the only North American population of American crocodile. Florida's crocs number around 1500; they prefer saltwater, and to distinguish them from gators, check their smile – a croc's snout is more tapered and its teeth stick out.

Turtles, frogs and snakes love Florida, and nothing is cuter than watching bright skinks, lizards and anoles skittering over porches and sidewalks. Cute doesn't always describe the state's 44 species of snakes – though Floridian promoters emphasize that only six species are poisonous, and only four of those are common. Feel better? Of the baddies, three are rattlesnakes (diamondback, pygmy, canebrake), plus copperheads, cottonmouths and coral snakes. The diamondback is the biggest (up to 7ft), most aggressive and most dangerous. But rest assured, while cottonmouths live in and around water, most Florida water snakes are not cottonmouths. Whew!

If you're not daunted by the prospect of playing with some of South Florida's scaliest citizens, head to the delightful Skunk Ape Research Headquarters (p138) in the Everglades. The zoo out back has to be one of the finest amateur reptile collections anywhere and, as a bonus, you may just spot the eponymous Skunk Ape, the American South's version of Bigfoot/Yeti.

ENVIRONMENT WILDLIFE

Green Reads

The Swamp (Michael Grunwald; 2006)

Losing It All to Sprawl (Bill Belleville; 2006)

Zoo Story (Thomas French; 2010)

Green Empire (Kathryn Ziewitz & June Wiaz; 2006)

Manatee Insanity (Craig Pittman; 2010)

Visit the Florida Native Plant Society (www.fnps.org), a nonprofit conservation organization, for updates on preservation issues and invasive species, and for a nice overview of Florida's native plants and ecosystems.

Sea Turtles

Naturalist Doug Alderson helped create the Big Bend Paddling Trail and in *Waters Less Traveled* (2005) he describes his adventures: dodging pygmy rattlesnakes, meeting Shitty Bill, discussing Kemp's ridley turtles and pondering manatee farts.

Most sea-turtle nesting in the continental USA occurs in Florida. Predominantly three species create over 80,000 nests annually, mostly on southern Atlantic Coast beaches but extending to all Gulf Coast beaches. Most are loggerhead, followed by far fewer green and leatherback, and historically hawksbill and Kemp's ridley as well; all five species are endangered or threatened. The leatherback is the largest, attaining 10ft and 2000lb.

During the May-to-October nesting season, sea turtles deposit 80 to 120 eggs in each nest. The eggs incubate for about two months, and then the hatchlings emerge all at once and make for the ocean. Contrary to myth, hatchlings don't need the moon to find their way to the sea. However, they can become hopelessly confused by artificial lights and noisy human audiences. For the best, least-disruptive experience, join a sanctioned turtle watch; for a list, visit www.myfwc.com/seaturtle, then click on 'Educational Resources' and 'Sea Turtle Viewing Opportunities.'

The Keys contains its very own Turtle Hospital (p174), a sanctuary for sick and injured gentle shelled giants. They're keen on visitors, so if you're rolling through Marathon, drop by.

Marine Mammals

Florida's coastal waters are home to 21 species of dolphins and whales. By far the most common is the bottlenose dolphin, which is highly social, extremely intelligent and frequently encountered around the entire peninsula. Bottlenose dolphins are the species most often seen in captivity.

Winter is also the season for manatees, who seek out Florida's warm-water springs and power-plant discharge canals beginning in November. These lovable, lumbering creatures are another iconic Florida species whose conservation both galvanizes and divides state residents.

FLORIDA'S MANATEES

It's hard to believe Florida's West Indian manatees were ever mistaken for mermaids, but it's easy to see their attraction: these gentle, curious, colossal mammals are as sweetly lovable as 10ft, 1000lb teddy bears. Solitary and playful, they have been known to 'surf' waves and every winter, from November to March, they migrate into the warmer waters of Florida's freshwater estuaries, rivers and springs. Like humans, manatees will die if trapped in 62°F water for 24 hours, and in winter Florida's eternally 72°F springs are balmy spas.

Florida residents for over 45 million years, these shy herbivores have absolutely no defenses except their size (they can reach 13ft and 3000lb), and they don't do much, spending most of each day resting and eating the equivalent of 10% of their body weight. Rarely moving faster than a languid saunter, manatees even reproduce slowly; females birth one calf every two to five years. The exception to their docility? Mating. Males are notorious for their aggressive sex drive.

Florida's manatees have been under some form of protection since 1893, and they were included in the first federal endangered species list in 1967. Manatees were once hunted for their meat, but today collisions with boats are a leading cause of manatee death, accounting for over 20% annually. Propeller scars are so ubiquitous among the living that they are the chief identifying tool of scientists.

Manatees also face other environmental dangers. In 2013 a bloom of red tide algae in southwest Florida, as well as illnesses, caused the death of more than 800 manatees. All the same, there has been good news in terms of the manatee population, with consistent growth in recent years. Over 6600 were counted in aerial surveys in 2017, compared to 6250 in 2016 and 6063 the year before. Owing to these encouraging figures, in 2017 the US Fish and Wildlife Service removed the manatee from the endangered list, downgrading it to 'threatened' status.

Plants

The diversity of the peninsula's flora, including more than 4000 species of plants, is unmatched in the continental USA. Florida, especially South Florida, contains the southern extent of temperate ecosystems and the northern extent of tropical ones, which blend and merge in a bewildering, fluid taxonomy of environments. Interestingly, most of the world at this latitude is a desert, which Florida most definitely is not.

In Florida even the plants bite: the Panhandle has the most species of carnivorous plants in the USA, the result of its nutrient-poor sandy soil.

ENVIRONMENT PLANTS

Wetlands & Swamps

It takes special kinds of plants to thrive in the humid, waterlogged and sometimes salty marshes, sloughs, swales, seeps, basins, marl prairies and swamps of Florida. Much of the Everglades is dominated by vast expanses of saw grass, which is actually a sedge with fine toothlike edges that can reach 10ft high. South Florida is a symphony of sedges, grasses and rushes. These hardy, water-tolerant species provide abundant seeds to feed birds and animals; they also protect fish in shallow water; and pad out wetlands for birds and alligators.

The strangest plants are the submerged and immersed species that grow in, under and out of the water. Free-floating species include bladderwort and coontail, a species that lives, flowers and is pollinated entirely underwater. Florida's swamps are abundant with rooted plants with floating leaves, such as the pretty American lotus, water lilies and spatterdock (if you love names, you'll love Florida botany). Another common immersed plant, bur marigold, can paint whole prairies yellow.

A dramatic, beautiful tree in Florida's swamps is the bald cypress, which is the most flood-tolerant tree. It can grow 150ft tall, with buttressed, wide trunks and roots with 'knees' that poke above the drenched soil.

Forests, Scrubs & Flatwoods

The forests of the mainland, such as they are, are mainly found in the Everglades, where small changes in elevation and substrate are the difference between prairie and massive 'domes' of bald cypress and towering pine trees. Cypress domes are a particular kind of swamp when a watery depression occurs in a pine flatwood.

Scrubs are found throughout Florida; they are typically old dunes with well-drained sandy soil. Scrubs often blend into sandy pine flatwoods, which typically have a sparse longleaf or slash-pine overstory, and an understory of grasses and/or saw palmetto. Saw palmetto is a vital Florida plant: its fruit is an important food for bears and deer (and a herbal medicine that's believed to help prevent cancer), it provides shelter for panthers and snakes, and its flower is an important source of honey. It's named for its sharp saw-toothed leaf stems.

Formed by the interplay of tides, coral and mangroves, the Florida Keys contain the best (and in many cases, only) examples of tropical and subtropical hardwood 'hammock,' or forest, in the continental USA. The Crane Point Hammock (p173) is an excellent starting point for learning about this extremely niche ecosystem.

Mangroves & Coastal Dunes

Where not shaved smooth by sand, South Florida's coastline is often covered with a three-day stubble of mangroves. Mangroves are not a single species; the name refers to all tropical trees and shrubs that have adapted to loose wet soil, saltwater and periodic root submergence. Mangroves also feature 'live birth,' germinating their seeds while they're still attached to the parent tree. Of the more than 50 species of mangroves worldwide, only three predominate in Florida: red, black and white.

GHOST HUNTERS

Florida has more species of orchids than any other state in the USA, and orchids are themselves the largest family of flowering plants in the world, with perhaps 25,000 species. When it comes to botanical fascination, orchids rate highly, and the Florida species that inspires the most intense devotion is the extremely rare ghost orchid.

This bizarre epiphytic flower has no leaves and usually only one bloom, which is of course deathly white with two long thin drooping petals that curl like a handlebar moustache. The ghost orchid is pollinated by the giant sphinx moth in the dead of night. This moth is the only insect with a proboscis long enough to reach down the ghost orchid's 5in-long nectar spur.

The exact locations of ghost orchids are usually kept secret for fear of poachers, who, as Susan Orlean's book *The Orchid Thief* (1998) made clear, are a real threat to their survival. But the flower's general whereabouts are common knowledge: South Florida's approximately 2000 ghost orchids are almost all in Big Cypress National Preserve and Fakahatchee Strand Preserve State Park. Of course, these parks are home to a great many other wild orchids, as is Everglades National Park.

To learn more, visit Florida's Native Orchids (www.flnativeorchids.com) and Ghost Orchid (www.ghostorchid.info).

Nature Guides

The Living Gulf Coast (Charles Sobczak; 2011)

Priceless Florida (Ellie Whitney, D Bruce Means & Anne Rudloe; 2004)

Mangroves play a vital role on the peninsula, and their destruction usually sets off a domino effect of ecological damage. Mangroves stabilize coastal land, trapping sand, silt and sediment. As this builds up, new land is created, which ironically strangles the mangroves themselves. Mangroves also mitigate the storm surge and damaging winds of hurricanes, and they anchor tidal and estuary communities, providing vital wildlife habitats.

Coastal dunes are typically home to grasses and shrubs, saw palmetto and occasionally pines and cabbage palm (or sabal palm, the Florida state tree). Sea oats, with large plumes that trap wind-blown sand, are important for stabilizing dunes, while coastal hammocks welcome the wiggly gumbo-limbo tree, whose red peeling bark has earned it the nickname of 'tourist tree' for its resemblance to sunburned visitors.

Environmental Issues

Florida's environmental problems are the inevitable result of its century-long love affair with land development, population growth and tourism, and addressing them is especially urgent given Florida's uniquely diverse natural world. These complex, intertwined environmental impacts include erosion of wetlands, depletion of the aquifer, rampant pollution (particularly of waters), invasive species, endangered species and widespread habitat destruction. There is nary an acre of Florida that escapes concern.

Since the turn of the century, Florida has enacted several conservation efforts, including the multibillion-dollar Comprehensive Everglades Restoration Plan (CERP; www.evergladesrestoration.gov). Ongoing funding however remains a contentious challenge, and residential development continues almost unabated. The Miami–Fort Lauderdale–West Palm Beach corridor (the USA's sixth-largest urban area) is, as developers say, 'built out.' Every day Miami and Homestead's urban (and in the case of Homestead, agricultural) footprint grows deeper into the west, on the edge of the Everglades. While conservation laws protect the national park itself, the runoff and by-products of such a huge urban area inevitably has its impact in the incredibly fragile Glades.

Then there's the coming apocalypse: rising seas due to global warming. Here, the low-lying Florida Keys are a 'canary in a coalmine' that's being watched worldwide for impacts. In another century, some quip, South Florida's coastline could be a modern-day Atlantis, with its most expensive real estate underwater.

Art-Deco Architecture

Art deco embodies the essence of South Beach. This distinctive style emerged in the 1930s to celebrate the onward march into the future, with bold lines and striking iconography referencing automobiles, cruise ships and futuristic rocket ships. Architects subtly blended characteristics from Miami's unique scenery: lapping waves, palm trees and curving seashells. While today this district is well protected, the whole neighborhood would have been leveled in the 1970s if not for the few preservationists who fought to keep it intact.

Deco, Design & Dreams

The early-20th-century school of design was the aesthetic backbone of old South Beach, and the driving force of its 1980s resurrection. A sustained campaign to preserve the wonderful deco hotels of Miami Beach provided what tons of tourism brochures could never create: brand. Sun, sand and surf – a lot of cities can lay claim to them, but only Miami Beach blended them with this pastel architectural heritage.

The end of WWI in 1918 ushered in an era of increased interest in the romance and glamour of travel, which lasted well into the 1930s. There was a giddy fascination with speed and cars, ocean liners, trains and planes. Not coincidentally, the US postindustrial revolution, concerned with mass production, kicked into high gear. New materials such as aluminum, polished bronze and stainless steel were utilized in new and exciting ways. Americans began looking to the future, and they wanted to be on the cutting edge.

Meanwhile in Europe, at a 1925 Paris design fair officially called the *Exposition Internationale des Arts Décoratifs et Industriels Modernes* (and eventually abbreviated to Arts Deco), decorative arts were highlighted, but the USA had nothing to contribute. Europeans were experimenting with repeating patterns in Cubism and were influenced by ancient cultures (King Tut's tomb was discovered in 1921), and Americans had to play catch-up.

Back in the USA, a mere year later, a devastating hurricane blew through Miami Beach, leaving few buildings standing. The wealthy folks who were living here before the hurricane chose to decamp. The second blow of a one-two punch for Miami's economy was delivered by the Great Depression. But in this dark time, opportunity soon came knocking. In Miami real estate, everything was up for grabs. The clean slate of the South Florida coastline was practically begging for experimentation.

Hotel rebuilding began in Miami Beach at the rate of about 100 per year during the 1930s. Many architects had 40 to 50 buildings in production at any one time until the inception of WWII. This overlapped with a surge in middle-class tourism between 1936 and 1941, when visitors started coming for a month at a time.

The post-Depression era was an optimistic period, with hopes and dreams pinned on scientific and technological revolutions. Reverence for

The Art Deco Historic District is bordered by Dade Blvd to the north, 6th St to the south, the Atlantic Ocean to the east and Lenox Ave to the west. The 1-sq-mile district feels like a small village, albeit one with freaks, geeks and the gorgeous. Which is pretty cool.

machines took on almost spiritual dimensions, and found its aesthetic expression in both symbolic and functional ways.

What does all this have to do with architecture? Everything. The principles of efficiency and streamlining translated into mass-produced, modest buildings without superfluous ornamentation – at least in the Northeast USA.

Romance, Relief & Rhythms

Miami Beach, a more romantic and glamorous resort, developed what came to be known as tropical deco architecture. It organically reflected the natural world around it. For example, glass architectural blocks let bright Florida light in but kept sweltering heat out. They also served a geometric or Cubist aesthetic. Floral reliefs, popular during the Art Nouveau period, appeared here too. Friezes on facades or etched into glass reflected native flora and fauna, such as palm trees, pelicans and flamingos. Friezes also took their cues from the uniquely American jazz movement, harmonious and lyrical. Surrounded by water, Miami Beach art deco also developed a rhythmic language, with scalloped waves and fountains.

Creating a Miami Look

Whereas Northeast art-deco buildings had industrial, socialist overtones, the clean lines of Miami Beach architecture still made room for joyful, playful, hopeful characteristics. Forward thinking and dreaming about the future took hold. Space travel was explored through design: buildings began to loosely resemble rockets, and rooflines embodied fantasies about traveling the universe. Geometric and abstract zigzag (or ziggurat) patterns not only reflected Aztec and Egyptian cultures, but also symbolized lightning bolts of electricity. Sun rays – more imagery borrowed from an ancient culture – were employed as life-affirming elements to counter the dark days of the Depression.

Since all hotels were built on the same sized lots, South Beach architects began distinguishing themselves from their next-door neighbors through decorative finials and parapets. Neon signage also helped individualize buildings. Miami Beach deco relied on 'stepped-back' facades that disrupted the harsh, flat light and contributed to the rhythmic feel. Cantilevered 'eyebrows' jutted out above windows to protect interiors from unrelenting sun. Canopy porches gave hotel patrons a cool place to sit. To reflect the heat, buildings were originally painted white, with animated accent colors highlighting smaller elements. It was only later, during the 1980s, that interior designer Leonard Horowitz created the pastel palette that became the standard.

With the effects of the Depression lingering, ornamentation was limited to the facades; interiors were stripped down. Labor was cheap and readily available. Miami Beach needed a large number of rooms, most of which ended up being built small. With no expectation that they would remain standing this long, most hotels were built with inexpensive concrete and mortar that had too much sand in it. Stucco exteriors prevailed, but locally quarried native keystone (an indigenous limestone) was also used. Except for the keystone, none of this would withstand the test of time with grace, which is one reason the district fell into such a state of disrepair and neglect. It's also why the district remains under a constant state of renovation.

Restoring the Deco District

South Beach's heart is its Art Deco Historic District (p58), one of the largest in the USA on the National Register of Historic Places. In fact the area's rejuvenation and rebirth as a major tourist destination results directly from its protection as a historic place in 1979. The National

A fun way to conduct an art-deco walking tour is to seek out certain design trends, such as Mesoamerican temple flourishes, cruise-liner-modeled buildings, space-age structures and the like. Certain Miami buildings are exemplars of one or more themes.

One of life's little ironies is this: art deco was supposed to make its contemporary viewers contemplate tomorrow. Today it puts modern viewers in mind of yesterday.

With more than 400 registered historic landmarks, you can follow the Beach boom phases through the district: in the 1930s 5th St to Mid-Beach was developed. Head toward 27th St for the late '30s to early '40s; then north into the '50s, the era of resorts, hotels and condominiums.

Register designation prevents developers from razing significant portions of what was, in the 1980s, a crime-ridden collection of crumbling eyesores populated primarily by criminals and society's dispossessed – the elderly, the mentally ill and the destitute. It's a far cry from that now. Today hotel and apartment facades are decidedly colorful, with pastel architectural details. Depending on your perspective, the bright buildings catapult you back to the Roaring Twenties or on a wacky tour of American kitsch.

The National Register listing was fought for and pushed through by the Miami Design Preservation League (MDPL), founded by Barbara Baer Capitman in 1976. She was appalled when she heard of plans by the city of Miami to bulldoze several historic buildings in what is now the Omni Center. And she acted, forcefully.

MDPL cofounder Leonard Horowitz played a pivotal role in putting South Beach back on the map, painting the then-drab art-deco buildings in shocking pink, lavender and turquoise (his color palette inspired by sunrise, sunsets, the changing hues of the sea and the play of light on the South Florida landscape). When his restoration of Friedman's Bakery made the cover of *Progressive Architecture* in 1982, the would-be Hollywood producers of *Miami Vice* saw something they liked, and the rest is history.

One of the best things about the 1000 or so buildings in the deco district is their scale: most are no taller than the palm trees. And while the architecture is by no means uniform – you'll see Streamline Moderne, Mediterranean Revival and tropical art-deco designs – it's all quite harmonious.

Interestingly, the value of these Miami Beach art-deco buildings is based more on the sheer number of structures with protected status from the National Register of Historic Places. Individually, these inexpensively constructed houses would be worth far less.

Italians were the first hired to create the terrazzo floors that are so popular in Florida. They'd pour various colors of terrazzo – crushed stones, shells, marble chips or granite, mixed with concrete – into a patterned grid and then polish it. This remarkable marriage of form and function also cools the feet.

Deco Daydreams

So what, you may ask, is the big deal about art deco? The term certainly gets thrown around enough in Miami. Given the way this architectural style is whispered about by hotel marketing types, you'd be forgiven for thinking art deco was the pièce de résistance: 'Well, the resort has a

THE CONCH CASTLES OF KEY WEST

Miami this, Miami that; yes, the flashy overstatement of the Magic City's architecture sure is beautiful. But what about Key West? Plenty of gorgeous historical buildings are packed into an easily walkable space and happen to be located on one of the prettiest islands in America. What are we waiting for?

Traditional Keys homes are known as 'Conch houses' for the conch shell that was used as a building material to supplement the traditionally low amounts of stone and wood; today the nickname also references Keys natives, known as Conchs. Conch houses are perhaps the finest example of Caribbean colonial architecture in the USA outside New Orleans. They're elegant, recognizably European homes, and while no two dwellings are identical, there are some commonalities. Shuttered windows, wraparound verandas, sloped roofs and structures built on raised piers are all elements that maximized shade and airflow in an era that preceded air-conditioning.

Many Conch houses had fallen into a state of total disrepair in the early 20th century, but as in South Beach, a community of artists, gays and lesbians established themselves here, refurbished the neighborhood and saved a bit of American heritage, all the while giving Key West the distinctive aesthetic profile that adds so much to its tourism appeal. You can see plenty of Conch houses in the Key West Historic District (the west end of the island); to see a particularly fine assortment in a small space, walk the four blocks along Eaton St from Eaton and William to Eaton and Whitehead.

lovely deco facade'; 'Our boutique properties incorporate deco porches'; 'Did you notice the deco columns in our lounge?' And so on.

But to be fair, deco has been a sort of renaissance for Miami Beach. It was art deco that made these buildings unique and that caught the eye of Hollywood, which saw something romantically American in the optimism and innovation of a style that blends Cubism, futurism, modernism and, most of all, a sense of movement. Beyond that was a nod to, and sometimes even reverence for, the elaborate embellishment of Old World decor. In art deco, we see the link between the lavish design aesthetic of the 19th century and the stripped-down efficiency of the 20th. Unlike a skyscraper, a deco hotel is modern yet accessible, even friendly, with its frescoed walls and shady window eyebrows.

But what's truly great about art-deco Miami is the example it sets. The Art Deco Historic District of South Beach, one of the hottest tourist destinations in the country, is a reminder to city officials that preserving historic neighborhoods is not just a matter of slavish loyalty to aesthetics, but sometimes the economically practical and innovative way forward. In a city built on fast real estate, it's a bit delicious that the heart of the most famous neighborhood is the child of preservation and smart planning.

Post-Deco, Miami Modern & Beyond

The tale of Miami architecture is defined by more than art deco. As in all cities, Miami's architecture reflects the tastes and attitudes of its inhabitants, who tend to adhere to the aesthetic philosophy espoused by Miami Beach's favorite architect, Morris Lapidus: 'Too much is never enough.' The earliest examples of this homegrown over-embellishment are the Mediterranean-Revival mansions of Coral Gables and the Fabergé egg fantasy of the Vizcaya. These residential wedding cakes established Miami's identity as a city of fantasies and dreams, outside the boundaries of conventional tastes, where experimentation was smiled upon as long as it was done with flashiness. They also spoke to a distinct Miami attitude that is enshrined in city tastes to this day: if you've got it, flaunt it, then shove it back in their faces for a second serving.

This penchant for imaginative, decorative flair overlaid the muscular postwar hotels and condos of the 1950s, giving birth to Miami Modernism (MiMo). MiMo drew off the sleek lines and powerful presence of International Modernism, but led by Lapidus, it also eschewed austerity for grand, theatrical staging. Lapidus himself described his most famous structure, the Fontainebleau (p93), as influenced by the most popular mass media of its time: Hollywood and cinema. The glamour Lapidus captured in his buildings would go on to define Miami's aesthetic outlook; Versace incorporated it into his clothes and Ian Schrager has decked out his hotels with this sense of fairy-tale possibility. Which makes sense: the word 'glamour' originally meant a kind of spell that causes people to see things differently from how they really are, which makes it an appropriate inspiration for the buildings of the 'Magic City.'

There are excellent art-deco renovations all along Miami Beach that manage to combine modern aesthetic tastes with classical deco details. But in a sense, the modern South Beach school of design is just the natural evolution of principles laid down by art deco in the 1930s. Conceptions of the future (a fantasy of the best the future can be), plus a deep bow to the best of historical decorative arts, still drives the design on Miami Beach. Newer hotels like Faena Hotel Miami Beach and 1 Hotel South Beach have also expanded the architectural sense of proportion, integrating art-deco features into the massive proportions of MiMo (Miami Modern) style. Whereas in the past art-deco hotels occupied a lot on a block, the megahotels of Miami Beach's future now stretch for an entire block.

The art-deco movement came about in the early 20th century, when affordable travel became a reality for many. Sea journeys represented the height of luxury, and many deco buildings are decorated with nautical porthole windows.

MICHAEL D EDWARDS/SHUTTERSTOCK ©

Art-Deco Miami

South Beach may be known for celebrity spotting, but the area's original cachet owes less to paparazzi and more to preservation. The art-deco design movement, the architectural and aesthetic backbone of SoBe, is powerfully distinctive and finds expression in soft lines, bright pastels and the integration of neon into structural facades.

Contents

Above: Betsy Hotel (p89)

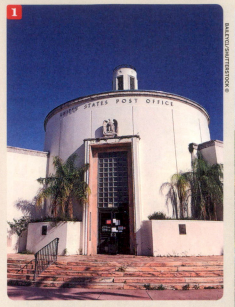

1. Post office 2. Cardozo Hotel 3. Lifeguard station,
4. Essex House Hotel

Classical Deco South Beach Structures

In the past, South Beach architects distinguished themselves through decorative finials, parapets and neon signage. Miami Beach art deco relies on 'stepped-back' facades to disrupt the harsh, flat Florida light. Cantilevered 'eyebrows' jut out above windows to protect interiors from the sun.

Cardozo Hotel

This lovely building (p63) features unusual flourishes, including keystone trim, made of dyed porous limestone. Its two hubcaplike emblems on the upper facade and its sleek curves make it reminiscent of a 1937 Studebaker. Owned by Gloria Estefan, the hotel looks more impressive than ever following a four-year, $15 million renovation completed in 2019.

Essex House Hotel

Porthole windows lend this **hotel** (Map p60; 877-532-4006; www.clevelander.com; 1001 Collins Ave; r $160-500;) the feel of a grand cruise ship, while its spire looks like a rocket ship, recalling artdeco's roots as an aesthetic complement to modernism and industrialism. Beautiful terrazzo floors also cool the lobby.

South Beach Lifeguard Stations

Besides being cubist-inspired exemplars of the classical art-deco movement, with their sharp, pleasing geometric lines, these stations (p63) are painted in dazzling colors. Found all along the beach from 1st to 17th Sts.

Post Office

This striking building (p62) has a round facade and a lighthouse-like cupola. Above the door is the characteristic art-deco stripe of glass blocks. Step inside for a glimpse of geometrically laid-out post boxes (painted gold) and a fantastical ceiling with an elaborate sunlike deco light fixture orbited by stars.

Deco Elements & Embellishments

As individualized as South Beach's buildings are, they share quirks and construction strategies. Canopy porches provide cool places to sit. To reflect heat, buildings were originally painted white (and later in pastels) with accent colors highlighting smaller elements. Some hotels resemble Mesoamerican temples; others evoke cruise liners.

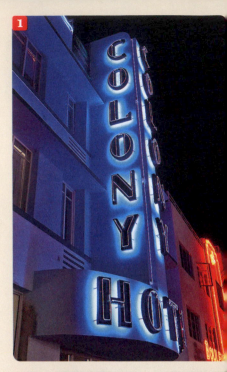

Room Mate Waldorf Towers

Art-deco pioneer L Murray Dixon designed the tower of this hotel (☏786-439-1600; https://room-matehotels.com/en/waldorf; 860 Ocean Dr; r $150-340; P✳🛜) to resemble a lighthouse, surely meant to shine the way home for drunken Ocean Dr revelers.

Colony Hotel

The oldest deco hotel (p62) in Miami Beach, Colony was the first hotel in Miami, and perhaps America, to incorporate its sign (a zigzaggy neon wonder) as part of its overall design. Inside the lobby are excellent examples of space-age interiors, including Saturn-shaped lamps and Flash Gordon elevators.

Cavalier South Beach

This hotel (p58) makes clever allusions to nautical themes. The word 'cavalier,' a kind of horseman, is a play on 'seahorse,' stylized examples of which are depicted on the facade. The tropical theme continues with figurative palm trees, whose trunks run down both sides of the facade.

Wolfsonian-FIU

The lobby of this museum (p58) contains a phenomenally theatrical example of a 'frozen fountain.' The gold-leaf fountain, formerly gracing a movie-theater lobby, shoots vertically up and flows symmetrically downward.

Crescent Resort

Besides having one of Miami Beach's most recognizable neon facades, the signage of the **Crescent** (Map p66; 1420 Ocean Dr) attracts the eye down into its lobby, rather than up to its roof.

1. Colony Hotel 2. Cavalier South Beach 3. Crescent Resort
4. Room Mate Waldorf Towers

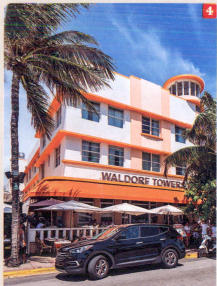

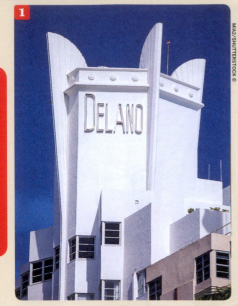

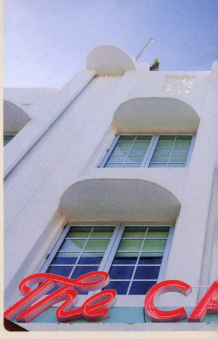

1. Delano 2. The Carlyle 3. The Betsy 4. Royal Palm

CHRISTIANTHIEL.NET/SHUTTERSTOCK ©

'New' Deco Hotels

Hoteliers such as Ian Schrager combine faith in technology with an air of fantastical glamour. Newer hotels such as the W and Gansevoort South have art-deco roots, but have expanded the architectural sense of scale, integrating deco style into Miami Modern's (enormous) proportions.

Delano

The top tower of Delano (p90) evokes old-school art-deco rocket ship fantasies, but the theater-set-on-acid interior is a flight of modern fancy. The huge backyard pool mixes jazz-era elegance with Miami muscular opulence.

The Carlyle

The 1941 Carlyle hotel (p63) was one of the last deco hotels built in Miami Beach. Here the eyebrow-like window coverings are semi-circular (rather than rectangular), and its name (borrowed from a hotel in NYC) was meant to evoke wealth and exclusivity. It also has cinematic cachet: *The Birdcage* was filmed here, as was the opening scene from *Miami Vice*.

The Betsy

One of the most unconventional landmarks of South Beach, the Betsy (p89) was designed by L Murray Dixon in 1942 and marries two wildly different styles: a deco wing facing Collins Ave, with a Florida-Georgian facade (the only one of its kind) overlooking Ocean Dr.

Royal Palm

This massive, beautifully restored hotel (p90) is an excellent place to feel a sense of seaborne movement. It has a *Titanic*-esque, ocean-liner back lobby. The mezzanine floor has modern dimensions in its enormity, mixed with classic deco styling.

Surfcomber

One of the best deco renovations on the beach, Surfcomber (p89) is offset by sleek, transit-lounge lines in the lobby and a lovely series of rounded eyebrows.

11th Street Diner

Quirky Deco Delights

Tropical deco is mainly concerned with stimulating the imagination. Painted accents lifted from archaeology sites might make a passer-by think of travel, maybe on a cruise ship. And hey, isn't it funny that the windows resemble portholes? Almost all of the preserved buildings here still inspire this childlike sense of wonder.

Avalon Hotel

The exterior of the **Avalon** (Map p60; ☎305-538-0133, 800-933-3306; www.avalonhotel. com; 700 Ocean Dr; r $185-240; ❊ ❓) is a fantastic example of classic art-deco architecture – clean lines and old-school signage lit up by tropical-green deco, all fronted by a vintage 1950s Oldsmobile.

11th Street Diner

It doesn't get much more deco than dining in a classic Pullman train car (p100). Many buildings on Miami Beach evoke planes, trains and automobiles – this diner is actually located in one.

The Bass

One of the oldest art-deco buildings in Miami, The Bass (p59) has a facade made of fossilized Paleolithic coral. Adding to this wondrous element, bas-relief friezes by the sculptor Gustav Boland depict Spanish galleons, mangroves, pelicans and flying boats.

Winter Haven Hotel

Outside the Winter Haven Hotel (Map p66; ☎305-531-5571; www.winterhavenhotelsobe. com; 1400 Ocean Dr; r $140-390; P ❊ ❓), you'll note shade-providing 'eyebrows,' and striking geometry, with an elegant zigzag of windows creating a vertical stripe down the center of the facade. Inside, check out the wild light fixtures that evoke futuristic elements (inspired perhaps by Fritz Lang's 1927 sci-fi film *Metropolis*).

Survival Guide

Directory A–Z

Accessible Travel

Most public buildings are wheelchair accessible and have appropriate restroom facilities. Transportation services are generally accessible to all, and telephone companies provide relay operators for the hearing impaired. Many banks provide ATM instructions in Braille, curb ramps are common and many busy intersections have audible crossing signals.

There are a number of organizations that specialize in the needs of disabled travelers:

Miami & the Beaches (www.miamiandbeaches.com/plan-your-trip/accessible-travel) Accessible travel information specific to the Miami area.

Mobility International USA (www.miusa.org) Advises disabled travelers on mobility issues and runs an educational exchange program.

For more information, download Lonely Planet's free Accessible Travel guide from https://shop.lonelyplanet.com/products/accessible-travel-online-resources-2019.

Customs Regulations

For a complete, up-to-date list of customs regulations, visit the website of US Customs & Border Protection (www.cbp.gov). Each visitor is allowed to bring into the USA duty-free 1L of liquor (if you're 21 years or older), 200 cigarettes (if you're 18 or older) and up to $100 in gifts and purchases.

Climate

Miami

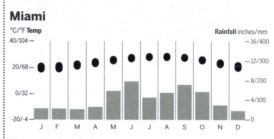

Everglades City

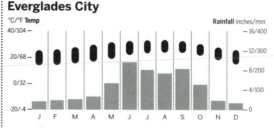

Key West

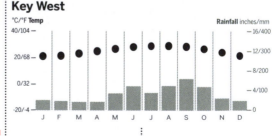

PRACTICALITIES

Newspapers South Florida's major daily newspapers include the *Miami Herald* (www.miamiherald.com). In Spanish, it's *El Nuevo Herald* (www.elnuevoherald.com). There's also the alternative weekly, the *Miami New Times* (www.miaminewtimes.com), the *Key West Citizen* (www.keysnews.com) and the *South Dade News Leader* (www.southdadenewsleader.com).

TV Florida receives all the major US TV and cable networks. Florida Smart (http://floridasmart.com/news) lists them all by region.

Radio In Miami, WLRN (www.wlrn.org) is the local National Public Radio affiliate, at 91.3FM on the dial. Elsewhere, check www.npr.org/stations to find the local National Public Radio station.

DVDs Video systems use the NTSC color TV standard, which is not compatible with the PAL system.

Weights & Measures Distances are measured in feet, yards and miles; weights are tallied in ounces, pounds and tons.

Smoking Florida bans smoking in all enclosed workplaces, including restaurants and shops, but excluding 'stand-alone' bars (that don't emphasize food) and designated hotel smoking rooms.

Electricity

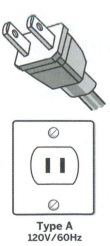

Type A
120V/60Hz

Type B
120V/60Hz

Embassies & Consulates

To find a US embassy in another country, visit the US Department of State website (www.usembassy.gov). Most foreign embassies in the USA have their main consulates in Washington, DC, but the following have representation in Miami, except Italy, which is in Coral Gables.

Brazilian Consulate (☑305-285-6200; http://miami.itamaraty.gov.br/en-us; 3150 SW 38th Ave, 1st fl; ☺visa applications 2-3:30pm Mon-Fri)

Canadian Consulate (☑844-880-6519; www.international.gc.ca; 200 S Biscayne Blvd, Suite 1600)

French Consulate (☑305-403-4150; http://miami.consulfrance.org; 1395 Brickell Ave, Suite 1050)

German Consulate (☑305-358-0290; www.germany.info; 100 N Biscayne Blvd, Suite 2200)

Italian Consulate (☑305-374-6322; www.consmiami.esteri.it/Consolato_Miami; 4000 Ponce de Leon Blvd, Suite 590, Coral Gables; ☺9am-12:30pm Mon-Wed & Fri, plus 3-5pm Wed)

Mexican Consulate (☑786-268-4900; http://consulmex.sre.gob.mx; 1399 SW 1st Ave)

Netherlands Consulate (☑786-866-0480; www.netherlandsworldwide.nl; 701 Brickell Ave, Suite 500)

UK Consulate (☑305-400-6400; http://ukinusa.fco.gov.uk/florida; 1001 Brickell Bay Dr, Suite 2800)

Food & Drink

For more on the South Florida food scene and essential advice, check out Eat & Drink Like a Local (p39) and Tipping (p240).

EATING PRICE RANGES

Price indicators in reviews apply to the typical dinner main course (in Miami and the Keys, you can raise this range by around $5 for each budget level):

$ less than $12

$$ $12–25

$$$ more than $25

Health

Florida, and the USA generally, has a high level of hygiene, so infectious diseases (apart from the odd global pandemic) are not generally a significant concern for most travelers.

➡ Vaccines are not required and tap water is safe to drink.

➡ Despite Florida's plethora of intimidating wildlife, the main concerns for travelers are sunburn and mosquito bites.

➡ Ensure you have adequate health insurance in case of accidents. If you experience a major medical emergency in the Everglades, the chances are you will end up in Miami.

➡ Most of the major islands in the Keys, including Marathon, Islamorada and Key Largo, have emergency medical facilities.

Before You Go
HEALTH INSURANCE

The USA offers a high level of health care. The problem is that it can be prohibitively expensive. If you're not a US citizen, it's essential to purchase travel-health insurance if your domestic policy doesn't cover you when you're abroad.

➡ If your health insurance does not cover you for medical expenses abroad, consider obtaining supplemental health or travel insurance.

➡ Find out in advance whether your insurance plan will make payments directly to the providers or if it will reimburse you later for any overseas health expenditures.

We have to stress: hospital bills for car accidents, falls or serious medical emergencies can run into the tens of thousands of dollars. Look for an insurance policy that provides at least $1 million of medical coverage. Policies with unlimited medical coverage are also available at a higher premium, but are usually not necessary. You may be surprised at how inexpensive good insurance can be.

MEDICATIONS

➡ Bring any medications you may need in their original containers, clearly labeled.

➡ A signed, dated letter from your physician that describes all of your medical conditions and medications (including generic names) is also a good idea.

➡ Pharmacies are abundantly supplied. However, some medications that are available over the counter in other countries require a prescription in the USA.

➡ If you don't have insurance to cover the cost of prescriptions (and sometimes even if you do), these can be shockingly expensive.

WEBSITES

There is a vast wealth of travel health advice on the internet. One of the best sources:

World Health Organization (www.who.int/ith) The superb book *International Travel and Health* is available free online.

Also, consult your government's travel-health website before departure, if one is available:

Australia (www.smartraveller. gov.au)

Canada (http://travel.gc.ca/ travelling/advisories)

UK (/www.gov.uk/browse/ abroad/travel-abroad)

USA (wwwnc.cdc.gov/travel)

AVAILABILITY & COST OF HEALTH CARE

➡ If you have a medical emergency, go to the emergency room of the nearest hospital.

➡ If you need any kind of emergency assistance, such as police, ambulance or firefighters, call 911. This is a free call from any phone.

➡ If the problem isn't urgent, call a nearby hospital and ask for a referral to a local physician; this is usually cheaper than a trip to the emergency room.

➡ Stand-alone, for-profit urgent-care centers provide good service, but can be the most expensive option.

INFECTIOUS DISEASES

In addition to more-common ailments, there are several infectious diseases to be aware of. Most are acquired by mosquito or tick bites.

Zika Miami made the news in 2016 for an outbreak of this mosquito-born illness, with more than 260 locally acquired cases in South Florida. Although the disease was considered eradicated in Miami in early 2017, epidemiologists warn that Zika could rebound with the arrival of warmer temperatures and heavier rainfall.

Zika is of gravest concern to pregnant women, as the disease can cause microcephaly (when the brain does not develop fully) and lead to serious birth defects in unborn children.

Giardiasis Also known as traveler's diarrhea. A parasitic infection of the small intestines, typically contracted by drinking feces-contaminated freshwater. Never drink untreated stream, lake or pond water. Easily treated with antibiotics.

Lyme disease Though more common in the US northeast than in Florida, Lyme disease occurs here. It is transmitted by infected deer ticks, and is signaled by a bull's-eye rash at the bite and flulike symptoms. Treat promptly with antibiotics. Removing ticks within 36 hours can avoid infection.

Rabies Though rare, the rabies virus can be contracted from the bite of any infected animal; bats are most common, and their bites are not always obvious. If bitten by any animal, consult with a doctor, since rabies is fatal if untreated.

West Nile virus Extremely rare in Florida, West Nile virus is transmitted by culex mosquitoes. Most infections are mild or asymptomatic, but serious symptoms and even death can occur. There is no treatment for West Nile virus. For the latest update on affected areas, see the CDC disease maps (www.cdc.gov/westnile/statsmaps/index.html).

ENVIRONMENTAL HAZARDS

Florida's critters can be cute, but they can also bite and sting. Here are a few to watch out for.

Alligators & snakes Neither attacks humans unless startled or threatened. If you encounter them, simply back away calmly. Florida has several venomous snakes; so always immediately seek treatment if bitten.

Jellyfish & stingrays Florida beaches can see both; avoid swimming when they're present (lifeguards often post warnings – the purple flag indicates the presence of venomous marine life). Treat stings immediately; they hurt but aren't dangerous.

Spiders Florida is home to two dangerously venomous spiders – the black widow and the brown recluse. Seek immediate treatment if bitten by any spider.

TAP WATER

Tap water is safe to drink throughout South Florida.

Insurance

It's expensive to get sick, crash a car or have things stolen from you in the USA. Make sure you have adequate coverage before arriving.

To insure yourself for items that may be stolen from your car, consult your homeowner's (or renter's) insurance policy or consider investing in travel insurance.

Worldwide travel insurance is available at www.lonelyplanet.com/travel-insurance. You can buy, extend and claim online anytime – even if you're already on the road.

Internet Access

Nearly every hotel and many restaurants, cafes and bars offer high-speed internet access. The vast majority of places provide free wi-fi, though some pricier hotels still charge a premium for wi-fi.

You can also find wi-fi in some transportation stations in city parks, and of course at a public library (many of which also have terminals, if you lack a laptop or smartphone).

If you bring a laptop/phone from outside the USA, invest in a universal AC and plug adapter.

Legal Matters

If you are stopped by the police, there is no system for paying traffic tickets or other fines on the spot. The patrol officer will explain your options to you; there is usually a 30-day period to pay fines by mail.

Medical marijuana is legal in Florida, but possession of more than 20g or any other controlled substance is a felony and can lead to your arrest. You are not allowed to smoke marijuana in public anywhere in Florida — that includes in beaches and parks.

If you're arrested, you are allowed to remain silent, though never walk away from an officer.

You are entitled to have access to an attorney. The legal system presumes you're innocent until proven guilty.

All persons who are arrested have the right to make one phone call. If you don't have a lawyer or family member to help you, call your embassy or consulate. The police will give you the number on request.

Drinking & Driving

To purchase alcohol, you need to present a photo ID to prove your age. Despite what you sometimes see, it is illegal to walk with an open alcoholic drink on the street outside of certain designated zones. More importantly, don't drive with an 'open container'; any liquor in a car must be unopened or else stored in the trunk. If you're stopped while driving with an open container, police will treat you as if you were drinking and driving. A DUI (driving under the influence) conviction is a serious offense, subject to stiff fines and even imprisonment.

LGBTQI+

Miami and Key West are out areas, where the gay scene is so integrated it can be difficult to separate it from the straight one. Popular hot spots in Miami include South Beach, North Beach, and Wynwood and the Design District. Events such as the **Winter Party** (www.winterparty.com) and **Gay8** (www.gay8festival.com) in Miami and Key West's **Fantasy Fest** (www.fantasyfest.com; ⊙late Oct) are major dates in the North American gay calendar.

Smaller towns in the Everglades region and the rest of the Keys are more culturally conservative, but gay travelers won't cause much of a stir.

Good LGBTQI+ resources:

LGBT Visitor Center (Map p66; ☏305-397-8914; www.goga ymiami.com; 1130 Washington Ave; ⏰9am-6pm Mon-Fri, 11am-4pm Sat & Sun) The best single source for all LGBTQI+ info on Miami. Check the website for Pink Flamingo–certified hotels (ie hotels that are most welcoming to the LGBTQI+ crowd). Run by the Gay & Lesbian Chamber of Commerce.

Gay Key West Business Guild (Map p180; ☏305-294-4603; www.gaykeywestfl.com; 808 Duval St; ⏰9am-5pm Mon-Sat) Serves as a welcome center for LGBTQI+ travelers. Loads of great tips on restaurants, bars, lodging and outdoor activities in Key West. Opened in 1978, this was the first LGBTQI+ chamber of commerce in the USA.

Miami Visitors Bureau (www. miamiandbeaches.com/plan-your-trip/miami-trip-ideas/gay-miami) Miami's official tourist bureau has a useful guide to gay life in the city.

Gay Cities (https://miami.gay cities.com) Everything gay about every major city in the US and beyond, including a dedicated Miami section.

Money

Exchange foreign currency at international airports and most large banks in Miami, Orlando, Tampa and other Florida cities.

There is ease and availability of ATMs. Most ATM withdrawals using out-of-state cards incur surcharges of $3 or so.

Major credit cards are widely accepted, and they are required for car rentals.

ATMs have largely negated the need for traveler's checks. However, traveler's checks in US dollars are accepted like cash at most

midrange and top-end businesses (but rarely at budget places).

Taxes & Refunds

As elsewhere in the USA, tax isn't included in the posted price. You'll have to factor in an extra 7% or 8% (which varies between municipalities) when shopping, ordering food at a restaurant, purchasing concert tickets and booking tours. Groceries are exempt from this tax.

There are higher taxes for overnight lodging, with hotels charging an extra 10% to 13%.

Tipping

Tipping is *not* optional in the US; only withhold tips in cases of outrageously bad service.

Restaurant servers Normal service 15%, good service 18%, great service 20%

Bartenders $1 per drink, $2 or more for complicated cocktails

Cafe baristas Some change in the jar

Taxis Tip 10–15%

Hairdressers Tip 10–15%

Airport & hotel porters $1 per bag

Hotel maids A few dollars after a few nights

Opening Hours

Unless otherwise noted standard business hours are as follows:

Banks 8:30am–4:30pm Monday to Thursday, to 5:30pm Friday; sometimes 9am–12:30pm Saturday

Bars In Miami, most bars 5pm–3am; in Miami Beach, most bars close at 5am; in Key West 5pm–4am, elsewhere 5pm–2am. In all places, some bars close earlier if business is slow.

Businesses 9am–7pm Monday to Friday

Eating Breakfast 7am–10:30am Monday to Friday; brunch

9am–2pm Saturday and Sunday; lunch 11:30am–2:30pm Monday to Friday; dinner 5pm–10pm, later Friday and Saturday

Post offices 9am–5pm Monday to Friday; sometimes 9am–noon Saturday

Shopping 10am–6pm Monday to Saturday, noon–5pm Sunday; shopping malls keep extended hours

Post

The US Postal Service (www. usps.com) is reliable and inexpensive. For 1st-class mail sent and delivered within the USA, postage rates are 55¢ for letters up to 1oz (15¢ to 30¢ for each additional ounce) and 35¢ for standard-size postcards. International airmail rates for postcards and letters up to 1oz are $1.20.

Public Holidays

On the following national public holidays, banks, schools and government offices (including post offices) are closed, and transportation, museums and other services operate on a Sunday schedule. Many stores, however, maintain regular business hours. Holidays falling on a weekend are usually observed the following Monday.

New Year's Day January 1

Martin Luther King Jr Day Third Monday in January

Presidents Day Third Monday in February

Memorial Day Last Monday in May

Independence Day July 4

Labor Day First Monday in September

Columbus Day Second Monday in October

Veterans Day November 11

Thanksgiving Fourth Thursday in November

Christmas Day December 25

Safe Travel

➡ Natural dangers include the strong sun (use a high-SPF sunscreen) and mosquitoes (use a spray-on repellent).

➡ Parts of Miami proper, including Liberty City, in northwest Miami; Overtown, from 14th to 20th Sts; Little Haiti; and stretches of the Miami riverfront experience high crime rates. Be careful in these areas, and avoid hanging out too much in Downtown after dark.

➡ South Beach, particularly amid the carnival-like mayhem of Ocean Dr between 8th and 11th Sts, and deserted areas below 5th St are also dangerous at night.

➡ Use caution around causeways, bridges and overpasses where homeless people have set up shantytowns.

➡ In these and other reputedly 'bad' areas you should avoid walking around late at night. It's best to take a taxi.

➡ Drunk driving is a big problem all around South Florida. Be particularly vigilant when traveling late in the evening, especially on weekends.

➡ Be mindful of swimming conditions in the ocean: rip currents and jellyfish (particularly the man o' war) can sometimes be present.

Hurricanes

Florida hurricane season extends from June through November, but the peak is September and October. Relatively speaking, very few Atlantic Ocean and Gulf of Mexico storms become hurricanes, and fewer still are accurate enough to hit Florida, but the devastation they wreak when they do can be enormous. Travelers should take all hurricane alerts, warnings and evacuation orders seriously.

Hurricanes are generally sighted well in advance, allowing time to prepare. When a hurricane threatens, listen to radio and TV news reports.

Florida Division of Emergency Management (www.florida disaster.org) Hurricane preparedness.

Florida Emergency Hotline (800-342-3557) Updated storm-warning information.

Hurricane Hotline (305-468-5400) Gives information about approaching storms, storm tracks, warnings and estimated time to touchdown – all the things you will need to know to make a decision about if and when to leave.

National Weather Service (www.weather.gov)

Telephone

➡ Always dial '1' before toll-free (800, 888 etc) and domestic long-distance numbers. Some toll-free numbers only work within the US.

➡ For local directory assistance, dial 411.

➡ To make international calls from the USA, dial 011 + country code + area code + number. For international operator assistance, dial 0.

➡ To call the USA from abroad, the international country code for the USA is 1.

➡ Pay phones are a rarity even in Miami. Local calls cost 50¢.

➡ Private prepaid phone cards are available from convenience stores, supermarkets and pharmacies.

Cell Phones

Most of the USA's cell-phone systems are incompatible with the GSM 900/1800 standard used throughout Europe and Asia. Check with your service provider about using your phone in the USA. In terms of coverage, Verizon has the most extensive network, but AT&T, Sprint and T-Mobile are decent. Cellular coverage is generally excellent, except in the Everglades and parts of rural northern Florida.

Time

South Florida is in the US eastern time zone: UTC/GMT minus five hours. Noon in Miami equals 9am in San Francisco and 5pm in London. During daylight-saving time, clocks move forward one hour in March and move back one hour in November.

Toilets

You'll find public toilets at some parks and at various posts along city beaches. Visitor centers are also reliable options. Outside of this, public toilets can be sparse. It's best to pop into a cafe, or if you're on the road, stop at a fuel station.

Tourist Information

There are plenty of chambers of commerce and visitor centers in the region itching to help you make the most of your trip and pass out veritable libraries of pamphlets and coupons. Be aware, however, that chambers of commerce typically only list chamber members, not all the town's hotels and businesses.

To order a packet of Florida information before coming, contact Visit Florida (www.visitflorida.com).

Local Tourist Offices

MIAMI

Coconut Grove Chamber of Commerce (Map p110; ☎305-444-7270; www.coconutgrove chamber.com; 3109 Grand Ave; ⊙9am-5pm Mon-Fri)

Coral Gables Chamber of Commerce (Map p118; ☎305-446-1657; www.coralgables chamber.org; 201 Alhambra Circle, Suite 100; ⊙9am-5pm Mon-Fri)

Downtown Miami Welcome Center (Map p84; ☎786-305-3015; www.downtownmiami. com; 66 W Flagler St, Suite 900; ⊙noon-5pm Mon, from 10am Tue-Sat) Provides maps, brochures and tour information for the Downtown area.

Greater Miami & the Beaches Convention & Visitors Bureau (Map p84; ☎305-539-3000; www.miamiandbeaches.com; 701 Brickell Ave, 27th fl; ⊙8:30am-6pm Mon-Fri) Located in an oddly intimidating high-rise building.

Miami Beach Chamber of Commerce (Map p66; ☎305-672-1270; www.miamibeach guest.com; 530 17th St; ⊙10am-4pm)

THE EVERGLADES

Big Cypress Swamp Welcome Center (☎239-695-4758; www. nps.gov/bicy/planyourvisit/big-cypress-swamp-welcome-center. htm; 33000 Tamiami Trail E; ⊙9am-4:30pm)

Ernest Coe Visitor Center (☎305-242-7700; www.nps. gov/ever; 40001 State Rd 9336; ⊙9am-5pm mid-Apr–mid-Dec, 8am-5pm mid-Dec–mid-Apr)

Everglades Area Chamber of Commerce (☎239-695-3941; cnr Hwys 41 & 29; ⊙9am-4pm)

Homestead Chamber of Commerce (☎305-247-2332; www.southdadechamber.org; 455 N Flagler Ave; ⊙9am-5pm Mon-Fri)

Shark Valley Visitor Center (☎305-221-8776; www.nps.gov/ ever/planyourvisit/svdirections. htm; national park entry per vehicle/bicycle/pedestrian $25/8/8; ⊙9am-5pm)

THE KEYS

Islamorada Chamber of Commerce (☎305-664-4503; www.islamoradachamber.com; Mile 87 bayside; ⊙9am-5pm Mon-Fri, to 4pm Sat, to 3pm Sun)

Key Largo Chamber of Commerce (☎305-451-1414, 800-822-1088; www.keylargo chamber.org; Mile 106 bayside; ⊙9am-6pm)

Key West Chamber of Commerce (Map p180; ☎305-294-2587; www.keywestchamber. org; 510 Greene St; ⊙9am-5:30pm)

Lower Keys Chamber of Commerce (☎305-872-2411; www.lowerkeyschamber.com; 31020 Overseas Hwy; ⊙9am-5pm Mon-Fri, 10am-4pm Sat & Sun)

Marathon Visitors Center Chamber of Commerce (☎305-743-5417; www.florida keysmarathon.com; Mile 53.5 bayside; ⊙9am-5pm)

Visas

All visitors should reconfirm entry requirements and visa guidelines before arriving. You can get visa information through www. usa.gov, but the US State Department (www.travel. state.gov) maintains the most comprehensive visa information, with lists of consulates and downloadable application forms. US Citizenship & Immigration Services (USCIS; www.uscis.gov) mainly serves immigrants, not temporary visitors.

The Visa Waiver Program allows citizens of 38 countries to enter the USA for stays of 90 days or less without first obtaining a US visa. See the ESTA website (https://esta.cbp.dhs.gov) for a current list. Under this program you must have a nonrefundable return ticket and 'e-passport' with digital chip.

Travelers entering under the Visa Waiver Program must register with the US government's ESTA program at least three days before arriving; earlier is better, since if denied, travelers must get a visa. Registration is valid for two years.

Visitors who don't qualify for the Visa Waiver Program need a visa. Basic requirements are a valid passport, recent photo, travel details and often proof of financial stability. Students and adult males also must fill out supplemental travel documents. The validity period for a US visitor visa depends on your home country. The length of time you'll be allowed to stay in the USA is determined by US officials at the port of entry.

Upon arriving in the US, foreign visitors must register with the Office of Biometric Identity Management, also known as the US-Visit program. This entails having two index fingers scanned and a digital photo taken. For information see www.dhs. gov/obim. Canadian citizens are often exempted from this requirement.

To stay longer than the date stamped on your passport, visit a local USCIS office.

Volunteering

Volunteering can be a great way to break up a long trip, and it provides memorable opportunities to interact with locals and the land in ways you never would when just passing through. Animal sanctuaries and small parks are always on the lookout for short-term volunteer help.

Florida's state parks would not function without volunteers. Each park coordinates its own volunteers, and most also have the support of an all-volunteer 'friends' organization (officially called Citizen Support Organizations). Links and contact information are on the main state park website (www.floridastateparks.org/get-involved).

Everglades National Park (www.nps.gov/ever/getinvolved/volunteer.htm) Active volunteer program recruits both individuals and groups.

Florida Keys National Marine Sanctuary (📞305-809-4700; www.floridakeys.noaa.gov/volunteer_opportunities/welcome.html) Can hook folks up with a plethora of environment-focused volunteer programs across the Keys.

Miami Habitat for Humanity (www.miamihabitat.org) Does a ton of work in Florida, building homes and helping the homeless.

Shake a Leg Miami (www.shakealegmiami.org) A community watersports complex in Coconut Grove that aims to serve economically and physically disadvantaged children.

Volunteer Florida (www.volunteerflorida.org) The primary state-run organization; coordinates volunteer centers across the state. Though it's aimed at Floridians, casual visitors can find situations that match their time and interests.

Women Travelers

Women traveling by themselves or in a group should encounter no particular problems unique to Florida besides the usual drunken loutishness in Miami and Key West.

These two national advocacy groups might be helpful:

National Organization for Women (www.now.org)

Planned Parenthood (www.plannedparenthood.org) Offers referrals to medical clinics throughout the country.

Women need to exhibit the same street smarts as any solo traveler, but they are sometimes more often the target of unwanted attention or harassment. Some women like to carry a whistle, mace or cayenne-pepper spray in case of assault. These sprays are legal to carry and use in Florida, but only in self-defense. Federal law prohibits them being carried on planes.

If you are assaulted, it may be better to call a rape-crisis hotline before calling the police (911); phone books have lists of local organizations, or contact the 24-hour National Sexual Assault Hotline on 800-656-4673 or visit www.rainn.org. Or go straight to a hospital. A rape-crisis center or hospital will advocate on behalf of survivors and can act as a link to other services, including the police, who may not be as sensitive when dealing with victims of assault.

Work

Seasonal service jobs in tourist beach towns and theme parks are common and often easy to get, if low-paying.

If you are a foreigner in the USA with a standard nonimmigrant visitors visa, you are forbidden to take paid work in the USA and will be deported if you're caught working illegally. In addition, employers are required to establish the bona fides of their employees or face fines. In particular, South Florida is notorious for large numbers of foreigners working illegally, and immigration officers are vigilant.

To work legally, foreigners need to apply for a work visa before leaving home. Student exchange visitors need a J1 visa, which the following organizations will help arrange:

American Institute for Foreign Study (www.aifs.com)

BUNAC (www.bunac.org)

Camp America (www.campamerica.com)

Council on International Educational Exchange (www.ciee.org)

InterExchange (www.interexchange.org) Camp and au-pair programs

International Exchange Programs (www.iep.org.au; www.iep.org.nz)

For nonstudent jobs, temporary or permanent, you need to be sponsored by a US employer (who will arrange an H-category visa). These aren't easy to obtain.

Transportation

GETTING THERE & AWAY

Nearly all international travelers come to South Florida by air, while most US travelers prefer air or car. Getting to South Florida by bus is a distant third option and by train an even more distant fourth. Miami is a major international airline hub, particularly for American Airlines, and it's the first port of call for many flights from Latin America and the Caribbean. Most flights come into Miami International Airport (MIA), although many are also directed to Fort Lauderdale–Hollywood International Airport (FLL). As it is located at the tip of the USA, Greater Miami is more of a termination of highways and rail lines, rather than a major land-transit interchange area.

Flights, cars and tours can be booked online at www.lonelyplanet.com/bookings.

Entering Miami & the Keys

If you're flying to the US, the first airport that you land in is where you must go through immigration and customs, even if you're flying to another destination. Upon arrival, all international visitors must register with the Department of Homeland Security's Office of Biometric Identity Management program, which entails having your fingerprints scanned and a digital photo taken.

Once you go through immigration, you collect your baggage and pass through customs. If you have nothing to declare, you'll probably clear customs without a baggage search, but don't assume this. If you're continu-ing on the same plane or connecting to another flight, your checked baggage must be rechecked. There are usually airline representatives just outside the customs area who can help you.

If you're a single parent, grandparent or guardian traveling with anyone under 18 years of age, carry proof of legal custody or a notarized letter from the non-accompanying parent(s) authorizing the trip. This isn't required, but the USA is concerned with thwarting child abduction, and not having authorizing papers could cause delays or even result in being denied admittance to the country.

Passport

Visitors from most countries only require a passport valid for their intended period of stay in the USA. However, nationals of certain countries require a passport valid for at least six months longer than their intended stay. For a country-by-country list, see the latest 'Six-Month Club Update' from US Customs and Border Protection (www.cbp.gov). If your passport does not meet current US standards, you'll be turned back at the

---

CLIMATE CHANGE & TRAVEL

Every form of transport that relies on carbon-based fuel generates CO_2, the main cause of human-induced climate change. Modern travel is dependent on planes, which might use less fuel per kilometer per person than most cars but travel much greater distances. The altitude at which aircraft emit gases (including CO_2) and particles also contributes to their climate change impact. Many websites offer 'carbon calculators' that allow people to estimate the carbon emissions generated by their journey and, for those who wish to do so, to offset the impact of the greenhouse gases emitted with contributions to portfolios of climate-friendly initiatives throughout the world. Lonely Planet offsets the carbon footprint of all staff and author travel.

border. All visitors wishing to enter the USA under the Visa Waiver Program must have an e-Passport with a digital photo and an integrated RFID chip containing biometric data.

Air

Unless you live in or near Florida, flying to the region and then renting a car is the most time-efficient option.

Airports & Airlines
Miami International Airport
(MIA; ☎305-876-7000; www. miami-airport.com; 2100 NW 42nd Ave) One of the state's busiest international airports. It serves metro Miami, the Everglades and the Keys, and is a hub for American and Delta.

Key West International Airport
(EYW; ☎305-809-5200; www. eyw.com; 3491 S Roosevelt Blvd) A much quieter airport, located off S Roosevelt Blvd on the east side of the island.

Fort Lauderdale–Hollywood International Airport (FLL; ☎866-435-9355; www.broward. org/airport; 100 Terminal Dr) A viable gateway airport to the Florida region, located 21 miles north of Downtown Miami.

Air service to Miami is frequent and direct. Flights come from all over the USA, Europe, Latin America and the Caribbean; Key West is served far less often, and often indirectly. A number of international airlines service South Florida.

Departure Tax
Departure tax is included in the price of a ticket.

Land
Bus
For bus trips, Greyhound (www.greyhound.com) is the main long-distance operator, but Megabus (https:// us.megabus.com), which can transport you to Tampa and Orlando, is an increasingly viable option. Competition between the two services has helped drop the price of bus transportation.

TRAIN ROUTES
Sample one-way fares between Miami and some major cities

TO	BASE FARE ($)	TIME (HR)
New York	170	27
Orlando	55	5¼
Tampa	50	5½

Greyhound serves Florida from most major American metropolitan areas. It also connects Miami to many major cities in Florida, but you won't be able to access smaller towns.

The main Miami **Greyhound terminal** (☎305-871-1810; 3801 NW 21st) is out by the airport. Megabus picks up from Miami International Airport.

If you are traveling very long distances (say, across several states), bargain airfares can sometimes undercut buses. On shorter routes, renting a car can sometimes be cheaper. Nonetheless, discounted (even half-price) long-distance bus trips are often available by purchasing tickets online seven to 14 days in advance. Then, once in Florida, you can rent a car to get around. Inquire about multiday passes.

Car & Motorcycle
Driving to Florida is easy; there are no international borders or entry issues. Incorporating Florida into a larger USA road trip is very common, and having a car while in Florida is often a necessity.

Sample distances and times from various points in the USA to Miami:

CITY	ROAD DISTANCE (MILES)	TIME (HR)
Atlanta	660	10½
Chicago	1380	23
Los Angeles	2750	44
New York City	1290	22
Washington, DC	1050	17

Train
If you're coming from the East Coast, Amtrak (www.amtrak.com) is a comfortable, affordable option for getting here. Amtrak's Silver Service (which includes Silver Meteor and Silver Star trains) runs between New York and Miami, with services that include major and small Florida towns in between. Unfortunately there is no longer any direct service to Florida from Los Angeles, New Orleans, Chicago or the Midwest. Trains from these destinations connect to the Silver Service route, but the transfer adds a day or so to your travel time.

Book tickets in advance. Children, seniors and military personnel receive discounts.

Sea

Apart from cruise ships, the only regular boat service in the region connects Fort Myers with Key West. The **Key West Express** (Map p180; ☎239-463-5733; www. seakeywestexpress.com; 100 Grinnell St, Key West; adult/ child/junior/senior round-trip $155/62/92/145/62, one way $95/31/68/95) departs from Fort Myers Beach five days a week (daily from January through March) at 8am for the 3½-hour cruise to Key West. Returning boats depart the seaport at 6pm. Boarding begins an hour before the boat departs. From late December to mid-February, the Express also leaves from Marco Island twice weekly.

BUS ROUTES

Sample one-way fares between Miami and major US cities

CITY	FARE ($)	TIME (HR)	DAILY
Atlanta	50-120	16-18	5-6
New Orleans	85-180	28-32	3-4
New York City	115-190	33-37	5-6
Washington, DC	90-150	31-34	5-6

Cruises

Florida is nearly completely surrounded by the ocean, and it's a major cruise-ship port. If you arrive in Miami via a cruise ship, you'll likely arrive at the Port of Miami, which receives around five million passengers each year and is known as the 'cruise capital of the world.'

Major cruise companies:

Carnival Cruise Lines (www.carnival.com)

Norwegian Cruise Line (www.ncl.com)

Royal Caribbean (www.royalcaribbean.com)

GETTING AROUND

Air

The US airline industry is reliable and safe; and serves Florida extremely well. Allow extra time for the USA's extensive airport security-screening procedures.

Airlines in South Florida

Main domestic airlines operating in South Florida:

American (www.aa.com) Has a Miami hub and service to and between major Florida cities.

Delta (www.delta.com) International carrier to main Florida cities, plus flights from Miami to Orlando and Tampa.

Frontier (www.flyfrontier.com) Services Tampa, Orlando and Fort Lauderdale from Denver, Minneapolis and the Midwest.

Southwest (www.southwest.com) One of the US's leading low-cost carriers, offering free baggage and, at times, extremely low fares.

Spirit (www.spirit.com) Florida-based ultra-discount carrier serving Florida cities from East Coast USA, the Caribbean, and Central and South America.

United (www.united.com) International flights to Orlando and Miami; domestic flights to and between key Florida cities.

Air Passes

International travelers who plan on doing a lot of flying, both in and out of the region, might consider buying an air pass. Air passes are available only to non-US citizens, and they must be purchased in conjunction with an international ticket. Conditions and cost structures can be complicated, but all include a certain number of domestic flights (from three to 10) that must be used within 60 days. Sometimes you must plan your itinerary in advance, but sometimes dates (and even destinations) can be left open. Talk with a travel agent to determine if an air pass would save you money based on your plans.

One World (www.oneworld.com) offers a Visit North America air pass, which includes the US, Canada, Mexico and the Caribbean.

Bicycle

Regional bicycle touring is very popular. Flat topography, ocean breezes on the Overseas Hwy and increasing bicycle infrastructure in Miami and Miami Beach make for great itineraries. Just be wary of your surroundings, especially if you go cycling near the north of Downtown. A few blocks north of that area it is especially tense. You may want to target winter to spring; summer is unbearably hot and humid for long-distance cycling.

Renting a bicycle is easy in South Florida. In Miami, you'll find quality rentals such as **Brickell Bikes** (☎305-373-3633; www.brickellbikes.com; 70 SW 12th St; bike hire per 4/9hr from $20/25; ⏰10am-7pm Mon-Fri, to 6pm Sat) and **Bike & Roll** (Map p60; ☎305-604-0001; www.bikemiami.com; 210 10th St; rental per 2/4hr from $15/20, per day from $25, tours $49; ⏰9am-7pm); while the **Citi Bike** (☎305-532-9494; www.citibikemiami.com; rental per 30min $4.50, 1/2/4hr $6.50/10/18, day $24) bike-share program is handy for quick jaunts. In the Keys, **Key Largo Bike and Adventure Tours** (☎305-395-1551; www.keylargobike.com; 90775 Old Hwy, Tavernier; 3hr tour $75) offer one-way rentals (with return shuttle service) for those wanting to pedal down to Key West. Bikes are ideal for getting around Key West. Many hotels rent them or provide them free to guests. You'll also find bikes for rent on the main drags of Truman Ave and Simonton St.

Some other things to keep in mind:

Helmet laws Helmets are required for anyone aged 16 and younger. Adults are not required to wear helmets, but should.

Road rules Bikes must obey road rules; ride on the right-hand side of the road, with traffic. It is legal to ride (respectfully of pedestrians) on sidewalks in Miami. Given the heavy, fast-moving traffic on many roads (ie Biscayne Blvd), you'll want to!

Transporting your bike to Florida Bikes are considered checked luggage on airplanes, but often must be boxed and fees can be high (over $200).

Theft Bring and use a sturdy lock (U-type is best). Theft is common, especially in Miami Beach.

For more information and assistance, visit these organizations:

League of American Bicyclists (www.bikeleague.org) General advice, plus lists of local bike clubs and repair shops.

International Bicycle Fund (www.ibike.org) Advice plus a comprehensive overview of bike regulations by airline.

Better World Club (www.betterworldclub.com) Offers a bicycle roadside-assistance program.

Car & Motorcycle

When you reach South Florida, traveling by car is the best way of getting around – it allows you to reach areas not otherwise served by public transportation.

While it's possible to avoid using a car on single-destination trips to Miami or Key West, relying on public transit is inconvenient for even limited regional touring. Motorcycles are also popular in Florida, given the flat roads and warm weather (summer rain excepted). In addition, motorized transport is practically a must to explore the Everglades. Greyhound buses run through the Keys, but you can't pull over and smell the roses by the side of the Overseas Hwy, which is 90% of the fun.

Roads are well kept and maintained.

Automobile Associations

The American Automobile Association (www.autoclubmo.aaa.com) has reciprocal agreements with several international auto clubs (check with AAA and bring your membership card). For members, AAA offers travel insurance, tour bookings, diagnostic centers for used-car buyers and number of regional offices.

An ecofriendly alternative is the Better World Club (www.betterworldclub.com), which donates 1% of earnings to assist environmental cleanup, offers ecologically sensitive choices for services and advocates politically for environmental causes. Better World also has a roadside assistance program for bicycles.

In both organizations, the central member benefit is 24-hour emergency roadside assistance anywhere in the USA. Both clubs offer trip planning and free maps, travel agency services, car insurance and a range of discounts (such as hotels, car rentals).

Driver's License

Foreign visitors can legally drive in the USA for up to 12 months with their home driver's license. However, getting an International Driving Permit (IDP) is recommended; this will have more credibility with US traffic police, especially if your home license doesn't have a photo or is in a foreign language. Your automobile association at home can issue an IDP, valid for one year, for a small fee. You must carry your home license together with the IDP. To drive a motorcycle, you need either a valid US state motorcycle license or an IDP specially endorsed for motorcycles.

Rental

CAR

Car rental is very competitive. Most rental companies require that you have a major credit card, that you be at least 25 years old and that you have a valid driver's license (your home license will do but an IDP is recommended). Some national companies may rent to drivers between the ages of 21 and 24 for an additional charge. Those under 21 are usually not permitted to rent at all.

Car Rental Express (www.carrentalexpress.com) rates and compares independent agencies in US cities; it's particularly useful for searching out cheaper long-term rentals.

National car-rental companies include the following:

Alamo (www.alamo.com)

Avis (www.avis.com)

Budget (www.budget.com)

Dollar (www.dollar.com)

Enterprise (www.enterprise.com)

Hertz (www.hertz.com)

National (www.nationalcar.com)

Sixt (www.sixt.com)

Thrifty (www.thrifty.com)

Rental cars are readily available at all airport locations and many downtown city locations. With advance reservations for a small car, the daily rate with unlimited mileage can start as low as $25 a day, while typical weekly rates are $200 to $400, plus myriad taxes and fees. If you rent from a non-airport location, you save the exorbitant airport fees.

An alternative in Miami is Zipcar (www.zipcar.com), a car-sharing service that charges hourly/daily rental fees with free gas, insurance and limited mileage included; prepayment is required.

MOTORCYCLE

To straddle a Harley across Florida, contact EagleRider (www.eaglerider.com), which has offices in Miami. It offers a wide range of models, which start at $160 a day, plus liability insurance. Adult riders (over 21) are not required by Florida law to wear a helmet, but you should.

MOTORHOME (RV)

Forget hotels – drive your own. Touring Florida by recreational vehicle can be as low-key or as over-the-top as you wish.

After settling on the vehicle's size, consider

the impact of gas prices, gas mileage, additional mileage costs, insurance and refundable deposits; these can add up quickly. Typically, RVs don't come with unlimited mileage, so estimate your mileage up front to calculate the true rental cost.

CruiseAmerica (www.cruise america.com) The largest national RV-rental firm has offices across South Florida.

Adventures On Wheels (www. wheels9.com) Office in Miami.

INSURANCE

➡ Insurance is legally required; if you don't have it, you risk financial ruin if there's an accident.

➡ If you already have auto insurance (even overseas), or if you buy travel insurance, make sure that the policy has adequate liability coverage for a rental car in Florida.

➡ Rental-car companies will provide liability insurance, but most charge extra. Always ask. Rental companies almost never include collision damage insurance for the vehicle. Instead, they offer optional Collision Damage Waiver (CDW) or Loss Damage Waiver (LDW), usually with an initial deductible of $100 to $500. For an extra premium, you can usually get this deductible covered as well.

➡ Most credit cards offer collision damage coverage for rental cars if you rent for 15 days or less and charge the total rental to your card. This is a good way to avoid paying extra fees to the rental company, but note that if there's an accident, you sometimes must pay the rental-car company first and then seek reimbursement from the credit card company. Check your credit card policy. Paying extra for some or all of this insurance increases the cost of a rental car by as much as $10 to $30 a day.

ROAD RULES

If you're new to Florida or US roads, here are some basics:

➡ The maximum speed limit on interstates is 70mph, but that drops to 65mph and 55mph in urban areas. Pay attention to the posted signs. City street speed limits vary between 15mph and 45mph. It's 20mph in a school zone.

➡ Florida police officers are strict with speed-limit enforcement, and speeding tickets are expensive. If caught going over the speed limit by 10mph, the fine is usually over $200.

➡ All passengers in a car must wear seat belts; the fine for not wearing a seat belt is $35. All children under three years must be in a child safety seat.

➡ As in the rest of the USA, drive on the right-hand side of the road. On highways, pass in the left-hand lane, though impatient drivers often pass wherever space allows.

➡ Unless otherwise signed, you can turn right at a red light as long as you come to a stop first. At four-way stop signs, the car that reaches the intersection first has right of way. In a tie, the car on the right has right of way.

➡ The maximum blood alcohol level while driving is 0.08%. For most people, having more than two drinks can put you in the danger zone.

Hitchhiking

Hitchhiking is never entirely safe in any country, and we don't recommend it. Travelers who hitch should understand that they are taking a small but serious risk. People who do choose to hitch will be safer if they go in pairs and let someone know where they are planning to go. Be sure to ask the driver where he or she is going rather than telling the person where you want to go.

Local Transport

Bus

Miami has a reliable bus service as well as a Metro-mover (a monorail that operates only in downtown) and trains that provide service to commuters. Getting between key neighborhoods (like Wynwood and South Beach) can be time-consuming on the limited bus routes operating. You'll find limited bus service in the Lower Keys; there's also a weekend bus service (from January until mid-April) between Homestead and one part of the Everglades.

Taxi

Outside MIA, South Beach and the Port of Miami, where there are a lot of taxis, you'll have more luck using a ride-sharing service – or calling a taxi. Try **Central Cab** (☏305-532-5555; www.centralcab.com) for a ride.

Taxis in Miami have flat and metered rates. You will not have to pay extra for luggage or for extra people in the cab, though you are expected to tip an additional 10% to 15%. Add about 10% to normal taxi fares (or a dollar, whichever is greater). If you have a bad experience, get the driver's chauffeur license number, name and license-plate number and contact the **Taxi Complaints Line** (☏786-469-2333).

In Key West, pick up a metered pink taxi from **Key West Taxis** (☏305-296-6666).

Ride Sharing

Ride sharing apps like Uber and Lyft are quite popular in Miami. Service is more limited down in the Keys.

Train

Daily Amtrak (www.amtrak. com) trains run between Jacksonville, Orlando and Miami, with one line branching off to Tampa. In addition, Amtrak Thruway motorcoach (bus) service gets passengers to Daytona Beach, St Petersburg and Fort Myers.

Behind the Scenes

SEND US YOUR FEEDBACK

We love to hear from travellers – your comments keep us on our toes and help make our books better. Our well-travelled team reads every word on what you loved or loathed about this book. Although we cannot reply individually to your submissions, we always guarantee that your feedback goes straight to the appropriate authors, in time for the next edition. Each person who sends us information is thanked in the next edition – the most useful submissions are rewarded with a selection of digital PDF chapters.

Visit **lonelyplanet.com/contact** to submit your updates and suggestions or to ask for help. Our award-winning website also features inspirational travel stories, news and discussions.

Note: We may edit, reproduce and incorporate your comments in Lonely Planet products such as guidebooks, websites and digital products, so let us know if you don't want your comments reproduced or your name acknowledged. For a copy of our privacy policy visit lonelyplanet.com/privacy.

WRITER THANKS

Regis St Louis

On the road, I'm grateful to Jeff Kesling in Key Largo, Micah and friends in Islamorada, Jen DeMaria and Bill Keogh in Big Pine Key and Analise Smith and Maura Gannon in Key West. I also thank editor Vicky Smith for inviting me on board and co-authors Adam Karlin and Anthony Ham for their hard work. I'm also indebted to Cassandra and our daughters Magdalena and Genevieve, who make homecoming the best part of travel.

Anthony Ham

Thanks to Luke Hunter, Tim Tetzlaff, Mark Lotz, Lisa and David Korte and others for their invaluable help. Thanks to the wonderful Vicky Smith and everyone at Lonely Planet for getting this book out there at an extremely difficult time. Thanks to Jan for always being the faithful follower of my journeys. And to

Marina, Carlota and Valentina: *os he echado mucho de menos y os quiero*.

Adam Karlin

Thank you: Victoria Smith, Anthony Ham, Regis St Louis, and the rest of the Florida team; Chris Romaguera, for rum, recommendations, and brotherhood; mom and dad for bringing me here; Rachel, Sanda and Isaac for being with me. *Por ti, mami*.

ACKNOWLEDGEMENTS

Climate map data adapted from Peel MC, Finlayson BL & McMahon TA (2007) 'Updated World Map of the Köppen-Geiger Climate Classification', *Hydrology and Earth System Sciences*, 11, 1633–44.

Cover photograph: Classic car, Ocean Dr, Miami Beach, Robert Harding/Alamy Stock Photo ©

THIS BOOK

This 9th edition of Lonely Planet's *Miami & the Keys* guidebook was researched and written by Regis St Louis, Anthony Ham and Adam Karlin. The previous two editions were also written by Regis and Adam.

This guidebook was produced by the following:
Senior Product Editors Dan Bolger, Vicky Smith
Cartographer Alison Lyall
Product Editor Claire Rourke
Book Designer Clara Monitto
Coordinating Editor Lorna Parkes

Assisting Editors Janet Austin, Michelle Bennett, Kate Connolly, Sandie Kestell, Rosie Nicholson
Assisting Cartographer Hunor Csutoros
Cover Researcher Brendan Dempsey-Spencer
Thanks Karen Henderson, Amy Lynch, Amy Lysen, Genna Patterson, Angela Tinson

Index

Map Legend

Sights

- Beach
- Bird Sanctuary
- Buddhist
- Castle/Palace
- Christian
- Confucian
- Hindu
- Islamic
- Jain
- Jewish
- Monument
- Museum/Gallery/Historic Building
- Ruin
- Shinto
- Sikh
- Taoist
- Winery/Vineyard
- Zoo/Wildlife Sanctuary
- Other Sight

Activities, Courses & Tours

- Bodysurfing
- Diving
- Canoeing/Kayaking
- Course/Tour
- Sento Hot Baths/Onsen
- Skiing
- Snorkeling
- Surfing
- Swimming/Pool
- Walking
- Windsurfing
- Other Activity

Sleeping

- Sleeping
- Camping
- Hut/Shelter

Eating

- Eating

Drinking & Nightlife

- Drinking & Nightlife
- Cafe

Entertainment

- Entertainment

Shopping

- Shopping

Information

- Bank
- Embassy/Consulate
- Hospital/Medical
- Internet
- Police
- Post Office
- Telephone
- Toilet
- Tourist Information
- Other Information

Geographic

- Beach
- Gate
- Hut/Shelter
- Lighthouse
- Lookout
- Mountain/Volcano
- Oasis
- Park
- Pass
- Picnic Area
- Waterfall

Population

- Capital (National)
- Capital (State/Province)
- City/Large Town
- Town/Village

Transport

- Airport
- BART station
- Border crossing
- Boston T station
- Bus
- Cable car/Funicular
- Cycling
- Ferry
- Metro/Muni station
- Monorail
- Parking
- Petrol station
- Subway/SkyTrain station
- Taxi
- Train station/Railway
- Tram
- Underground station
- Other Transport

Routes

- Tollway
- Freeway
- Primary
- Secondary
- Tertiary
- Lane
- Unsealed road
- Road under construction
- Plaza/Mall
- Steps
- Tunnel
- Pedestrian overpass
- Walking Tour
- Walking Tour detour
- Path/Walking Trail

Boundaries

- International
- State/Province
- Disputed
- Regional/Suburb
- Marine Park
- Cliff
- Wall

Hydrography

- River, Creek
- Intermittent River
- Canal
- Water
- Dry/Salt/Intermittent Lake
- Reef

Areas

- Airport/Runway
- Beach/Desert
- Cemetery (Christian)
- Cemetery (Other)
- Glacier
- Mudflat
- Park/Forest
- Sight (Building)
- Sportsground
- Swamp/Mangrove

Note: Not all symbols displayed above appear on the maps in this book

OUR STORY

A beat-up old car, a few dollars in the pocket and a sense of adventure. In 1972 that's all Tony and Maureen Wheeler needed for the trip of a lifetime – across Europe and Asia overland to Australia. It took several months, and at the end – broke but inspired – they sat at their kitchen table writing and stapling together their first travel guide, *Across Asia on the Cheap*. Within a week they'd sold 1500 copies. Lonely Planet was born. Today, Lonely Planet has offices in Tennessee, Dublin, Beijing and Delhi, with a network of over 2000 contributors in every corner of the globe. We share Tony's belief that 'a great guidebook should do three things: inform, educate and amuse'.

OUR WRITERS

Regis St John
Florida Keys & Key West

Regis grew up in a small town in the American Midwest – the kind of place that fuels big dreams of travel – and developed an early fascination with foreign dialects and world cultures. He spent his formative years learning Russian and a handful of Romance languages, which served him well on journeys across much of the globe. Regis has contributed to more than 50 Lonely Planet titles, covering destinations across six continents. His travels have taken him from the mountains of Kamchatka to remote island villages in Melanesia, and to many grand urban landscapes. When not on the road, he lives in New Orleans. Regis also wrote the Plan and Understand chapters

Anthony Ham
The Everglades & Biscayne National Parks

Anthony is a freelance writer who travels the world in search of stories. His particular passions are the wildlife, wild places and wide open spaces of the planet, from the Great Plains of the US to the Amazon, East and Southern Africa, and the Arctic. He writes for magazines and newspapers around the world, and his narrative nonfiction book on Africa's lions was published in 2020. An Australian, he divides his time between Melbourne and Madrid (where he lived for 10 years).

Adam Karlin
Miami

Adam has contributed to dozens of Lonely Planet guidebooks, covering an alphabetical spread that ranges from the Andaman Islands to the Zimbabwe Border. As a journalist, he has written on travel, crime, politics, archeology, and the Sri Lankan Civil War, among other topics. He has sent dispatches from every continent barring Antarctica (one day!) and his essays and articles have featured in the BBC, NPR, and multiple nonfiction anthologies.

Adam is based out of New Orleans, which helps explain his love of wetlands, food and good music. http://walkonfine.com; Instagram @adamwalkonfine.

Published by Lonely Planet Global Limited
CRN 554153
9th edition – Jun 2021
ISBN 978 1 78701 717 7
© Lonely Planet 2021 Photographs © as indicated 2021
10 9 8 7 6 5 4 3 2 1
Printed in Singapore

🚲 Bicycle

Citi Bike (www.citibike miami.com) is a bike-share program where you can borrow a bike from scores of kiosks spread around Miami and Miami Beach. Miami is flat, but traffic can be horrendous (abundant and fast-moving), and there isn't much of a biking culture (or respect for bikers) just yet. Free paper maps of the bike network are available at some kiosks, or you can find one online.

The Citi Bike Miami app shows you where the nearest stations are.

Note that a variety of scooters are also available to rent via third-party apps throughout Miami Beach, Downtown and Wynwood.

🚗 Car & Motorcycle

Driving is the most convenient way of getting around Miami.

You have to pay for street parking almost everywhere in Miami and Miami Beach; rates vary by neighborhood and it's easiest to pay by the PayByPhone app in Miami or ParkMobile app in Miami Beach.

Miami Beach is linked to the mainland by four causeways built over Biscayne Bay. They are, from south to north: MacArthur (the extension of US Hwy 41 and Hwy A1A); Venetian ($3 toll); Julia Tuttle and John F Kennedy. There's also a $3 toll over the Rickenbacker Causeway to Key Biscayne. The tolls are automated, so ask about hiring a SunPass if you're renting a vehicle (which reduces the toll to $2.25).

---

lonely planet

✈️ JUST LANDED
• MIAMI •
Easy steps from airport to city

Miami International Airport

TEAR OUT, FOLD UP & KEEP WITH YOUR PASSPORT

📶 Get Connected

Free airport wi-fi The free MIA-WiFi Network can be accessed throughout all of the airport's indoor areas.

Charging stations There are free charging stations throughout the airport. All outlets are standard North American/Japanese.

SIM card You can usually buy a SIM card at the currency-exchange counters, but they will be cheaper if you get them in town.

💵 Money

Around $70 to $140 per person should cover transportation and meals for a few days.

Credit cards Credit cards are accepted throughout the airport. All charge fees for use.

ATMs ATMs can be found in all terminals and operate 24 hours.

Currency exchange There are currency-exchange kiosks in all terminals, typically open from 7am to 8pm. You'll probably get better rates at banks in the city.

BEST TRANSPORTATION FROM MIAMI AIRPORT TO DOWNTOWN MIAMI

 Metro

30mins from $5

The regional Tri-Rail double-decker commuter train can be accessed at Miami Airport Station (connected by electric rail to the airport). It's not useful for actually going into the city of Miami, but it does connect north through Dade, Broward and Palm Beach counties.

Buy tickets at kiosks in Miami Airport Station. Fares are calculated on a zone basis – the shortest distance costs $5 round trip and the most you'll pay is for the ride between MIA and West Palm Beach ($17.50 round trip).

For a list of stations, visit the Tri-Rail website (www.tri-rail.com).

Local Bus **CHEAPEST**

40–60mins $2.25

Metro buses leave from Miami Airport Station (connected by electric rail to the airport) and run throughout the city; the fare is $2.25.

The Miami Beach Airport Express (bus 150) also costs $2.25 and makes stops all along Miami Beach, from 41st St to the southern tip; it runs from 6am to 11:40pm. The buses have luggage racks.

Buy a ticket from the EASY Card vending machines in Miami Airport Station.

Taxi **FASTEST**

25mins from $22

Taxis charge a flat rate, which varies depending on where you're heading.

It's $22 to Downtown, Coconut Grove or Coral Gables; $35 to South Beach; and $44 to Key Biscayne. Count on 40 minutes to South Beach in average traffic and about 25 minutes to Downtown.

Taxis line up curbside just outside of the baggage claim areas.

MIA Mover

The rental car center needs to be accessed via the free MIA Mover train, which departs from the 3rd floor between the Dolphin and Flamingo garages.